American Evangelicals
and the U.S. Military
1942–1993

American Evangelicals and the U.S. Military 1942–1993

ANNE C. LOVELAND

Louisiana State University Press
Baton Rouge and London

Copyright © 1996 by Louisiana State University Press
All rights reserved
Manufactured in the United States of America
First printing
05 04 03 02 01 00 99 98 97 96   5 4 3 2 1
Designer: Michele Myatt
Typeface: Janson
Typesetter: Impressions Book and Journal Services, Inc.
Printer and binder: Thomson-Shore, Inc.

Library of Congress Cataloging-in-Publication Data

Loveland, Anne C., 1938–
    American Evangelicals and the U.S. military, 1942–1993 / Anne C.
  Loveland
        p.   cm.
    Includes index.
    ISBN 0-8071-2091-X (alk. paper)
      1. Evangelicalism—United States—History—20th century.
  2. United States—Armed Forces—Religious life.   3. United States—
  Military policy.   4. United States—Church history—20th century.
  5. United States—Politics and government—20th century.   I. Title.
  BR1644.5.U6L68   1996
  277.3'0825'088355—dc20   96-26309
                                                                            CIP

The paper in this book meets the guidelines for permanence and durability of
the Committee on Production Guidelines for Book Longevity of the Council
on Library Resources. ♾

To Otis B. Wheeler

Contents

Contents

Preface

This book traces the history of American evangelicals' mission to the armed forces of the United States beginning in the early 1940s and continuing into the present. It describes how they succeeded in winning thousands of military men and women to evangelical religion and, through the influence they gained among the military leadership, exerted a significant impact on the armed forces as an institution.

The evangelicals who undertook this spiritual offensive included civilians as well as military personnel. Various evangelical groups organized and led the campaign. Foremost among them was the National Association of Evangelicals (NAE), which from its founding in 1942 advertised itself as a "united evangelical voice" serving "all the segments of evangelical Protestantism."[1] The NAE's allies included the Associated Gospel Churches, the more recently established Chaplaincy Full Gospel Churches, and denominations such as the Assemblies of God, the Church of God (Cleveland, Tennessee), the Christian and Missionary Alliance, and the Southern Baptist Convention. Parachurch groups such as the Navigators, Officers' Christian Fellowship, and the Full Gospel Business Men's Fellowship International also played a major role in evangelizing the armed forces, as did hundreds of evangelical chaplains, commanders, and enlisted people in the various services.[2]

I use the term *evangelical* to describe a wide range of conservative Christians and their religious and ideological assumptions. The spec-

---

1. See, for example, "NAE Launches Anti-Communist Program," *UEA*, June, 1960, p. 10.
2. On the parachurch groups within the evangelical community, see Stephen Board, "The Great Evangelical Power Shift," *Eternity*, June, 1979, pp. 17–21.

trum includes fundamentalists of the 1950s and 1960s such as Carl Mc-
Intire and John Rice, as well as evangelists of the New Christian Right
of the 1980s such as Jerry Falwell and Pat Robertson. It encompasses
the so-called new evangelicals of the 1950s such as Billy Graham, Harold
John Ockenga, and Carl F. H. Henry and the mainstream evangelicals
of the 1960s, 1970s, 1980s, and 1990s, represented by the National Association of Evangelicals and *Christianity Today*. The term also extends
to pentecostals, a growing presence within the evangelical community
by the 1970s and 1980s, and to conservative Christians belonging to
mainline denominations such as the Presbyterians, Methodists, and
Episcopalians. All of these groups and individuals make up the 42 percent of the American population who currently describe themselves as
born-again or evangelical Christians.[3]

Notwithstanding certain doctrinal differences, all of these members
of the evangelical community affirm three principal religious beliefs. All
regard the Bible as the inerrant authority on faith and life. All agree that
one achieves salvation only through faith, by undergoing a conversion
experience in which one gives up one's life to Jesus Christ as Lord and
Savior. And, finally, all are devoted to carrying out the Great Commission handed down by Jesus in Matthew 28:19 to "go . . . and teach all
nations, baptizing them in the name of the Father, and of the Son, and
of the Holy Ghost." Their evangelizing compulsion was, of course, the
vital impulse behind evangelicals' spiritual offensive within the armed
forces, just as in the civilian sector.

3. "Born-Again or Evangelical—1993," in *Religion in America 1992–1993: 1994
Supplement* (Princeton, 1994), 5. For a good definition of evangelicals and evangelical-
ism, see George Marsden, "The Evangelical Denomination," in *Evangelicalism and Mod-
ern America*, ed. Marsden (Grand Rapids, 1984), vii–xvi; Robert K. Johnston, "American
Evangelicalism: An Extended Family," in *The Variety of American Evangelicalism*, ed.
Donald W. Dayton and Robert K. Johnston (Knoxville, 1991), 252–72. For a brief
discussion of the development of various segments of the evangelical community, see
George M. Marsden, "Preachers of Paradox: The Religious New Right in Historical
Perspective," in *Religion and America: Spiritual Life in a Secular Age*, ed. Mary Douglas
and Steven Tipton (Boston, 1982), 150–68. On Southern Baptists as evangelicals, see
George M. Marsden, "Unity and Diversity in the Evangelical Resurgence," in *Altered
Landscapes: Christianity in America, 1935–1985*, ed. David W. Lotz (Grand Rapids, 1989),
71; James Leo Garrett, Jr., E. Glenn Hinson, and James E. Tull, *Are Southern Baptists
"Evangelicals"?* (Macon, Ga., 1983). On conservative Christians within the mainline
denominations, see Martin E. Marty, ed., *Where the Spirit Leads: American Denominations
Today* (Atlanta, 1980), passim.

Paralleling, sometimes overlapping, their mission to the military, evangelicals waged another, equally important campaign—to secure a prominent role in American public affairs and thereby influence national policy. This effort was an outgrowth of evangelicals' gradual shift away from the political disengagement of the early twentieth century toward political and social involvement. In the course of their mission to gain national influence, evangelicals articulated positions on a variety of defense-related issues—universal military training and selective service, the Cold War, the Vietnam War, the nuclear arms race, and, most recently, the status of homosexuals in the armed forces. During the second half of the twentieth century, evangelicals generally maintained a pro-defense, pro-military stance that had obvious implications for national security policy. Such views reveal a broader political agenda on the part of evangelicals than has generally been recognized.

Not surprisingly, evangelicals' mission to the military and the campaign to influence national policy exacerbated their conflicts with liberal, mainline Protestants. Not only did evangelicals regard such groups as rivals in a competition for chaplains and converts within the armed forces; they also conducted a running battle with mainline Protestantism on theological and political issues. Throughout the period covered by this book, even after their own ideological consensus had begun to disintegrate and the liberal denominations were declining numerically (within civilian society as well as the military), evangelicals challenged them on the defense-related issues mentioned above.[4]

In part as a result of their evangelization of the armed forces, but also as a consequence of their pro-defense, pro-military orientation, evangelicals' position in the armed forces underwent a dramatic change. Once a distinct minority occupying a marginal position in the military, they became highly visible and well-respected—indeed, the "dominant" religious element in the armed forces, according to Richard G. Hutcheson, Jr., former navy chaplain and author of *The Churches and the Chap-*

---

4. For a good definition of mainline religious groups, see Richard G. Hutcheson, Jr., *Mainline Churches and the Evangelicals* (Atlanta, 1981), Chap. 3; Jackson Carroll and Wade Clark Roof, eds., *Beyond Establishment: Protestant Identity in a Post-Protestant Age* (Louisville, 1993), 11–12. For a brief discussion of the recent historical development of mainline Protestantism, see Wade Clark Roof, "America's Voluntary Establishment: Mainline Religion in Transition," in *Religion and America*, ed. Douglas and Tipton, 130–49.

laincy.[5] Their adversarial relationship with the military leadership gave way to a more harmonious one, although tensions remained that had the potential of provoking a serious confrontation. Moreover, an increasing number of high-ranking military leaders not only evinced respect for evangelicals and evangelical religion but publicly identified themselves as fellow Christians. The careers of Generals Harold K. Johnson, Ralph E. Haines, and John A. Wickham demonstrate the influence religious conviction exerted not only on their leadership but on the military policies and programs they implemented.

The Vietnam era was the pivotal period in the history of American evangelicals and the United States military. When evangelicals began their mission to the armed forces in the 1940s and 1950s, they were on the defensive and working against considerable odds. The turning point in their campaign came during the 1960s and early 1970s, when, largely as a result of their support for the Vietnam War, they earned the appreciation and gratitude of the military leadership. Once regarded with indifference, disdain, or suspicion, by the mid-1970s evangelicals had attained not only membership and visibility but also respect and influence within the United States armed forces.

The success of evangelicals' campaign within the armed forces matched their growing presence and political influence in American society as a whole. Nevertheless, despite the increasing attention the media and historians have paid to evangelicals in recent years, their relationship with the United States military and their views on national security policy have been neglected. I hope this book will remedy that neglect and contribute to a fuller understanding of the history of American evangelicals during the latter half of the twentieth century.

5. Richard G. Hutcheson, Jr., to author, June 23, 1995.

Acknowledgments

During the course of researching and writing this book, I benefited from the assistance of many people. Among the several librarians and archivists who helped me, I especially thank Glenn Gohr, David Keough, Janyce H. Nasgowitz, Diana Ruby Sanderson, John Slonaker, and Richard J. Sommers and all the members of the Louisiana State University Middleton Library Interlibrary Loan Department.

I also wish to express my appreciation to the following individuals who provided information, guidance, and encouragement: Richard F. Abel, E. H. Jim Ammerman, Don Baker, George W. Baugham, John W. Brinsfield, Jr., Robert P. Dugan, Jr., James A. Edgren, Mike Hamilton, Jerry Hansen, William J. Hourihan, D. James Kennedy, Don L. Lair, Billy W. Libby, Robert L. Maginnes, Don Martin, Jr., James M. Meredith, David L. Meschke, Robert Pickus, David B. Plummer, Floyd Robertson, Ted Shadid, Ron Soderquist, Robert W. Spoede, David Stedman, Vinson Synan, John E. Taylor, Jr., Grant Wacker, Clifford T. Weathers, James W. White, and Robert K. Wright, Jr.

Three of my colleagues at LSU, Gary A. Crump, Gaines M. Foster, and Karen E. Fritz, read the final manuscript and offered helpful criticism and suggestions. Their advice and friendship have meant a great deal to me. And I am especially grateful to Richard G. Hutcheson, Jr., for reading the manuscript and giving me the benefit of his expertise.

I also thank Laura C. Meaux for her efficient, painstaking work at the computer preparing numerous drafts of the manuscript.

I received financial assistance in the form of grants from the U.S. Army Military History Institute, Carlisle Barracks, Pennsylvania, and the Institute for the Study of American Evangelicals, Wheaton, Illinois, and a sabbatical and a Manship Endowment Summer Faculty Research Fellowship from LSU.

This book is dedicated with love and gratitude to my husband.

Abbreviations Used in Notes

CT	*Christianity Today*
MCR	*Military Chaplains' Review*
NYT	*New York Times*
PE	*Pentecostal Evangel*
UEA	*United Evangelical Action*

American Evangelicals
and the U.S. Military
1942–1993

1

Focusing on the Armed Forces

The conviction that military personnel desperately needed the saving influence of the Gospel impelled the spiritual offensive evangelicals waged in the armed forces of the United States following World War II. Like other Americans in the immediate postwar period, they regarded the military environment as a particularly corrupting influence. Even before World War II, profanity, drunkenness, and gambling were legendary in the armed services. During the war Americans on the home front worried about rumors of soaring rates of promiscuity and venereal disease among draftees. Demobilization revealed the full story. In November, 1946, the Veterans of Foreign Wars (VFW) criticized the military for failing to provide wholesome recreation and entertainment for servicemen, especially at overseas installations. "Many of our young veterans have returned physical, mental, moral and social wrecks, having been infected with venereal diseases, in the treatment of which they have been coddled by a complacent service attitude which encourages promiscuity and even condones prostitution," the VFW charged. The baneful effects of military life also made headlines when United States newspapers began exposing the failure of General Dwight D. Eisenhower's "nonfraternization" policy in occupied Germany and the sanctioning of prostitution by army and navy officials in Japan. In the fall of 1947, when a group of American clergymen, including three evangelical leaders, visited United States occupation forces in Europe, they returned home deploring the extent of venereal disease, drunkenness, vulgarity, and black marketeering among American troops.[1]

1. *NYT*, November 18, 1946, p. 5, June 15, 1947, p. 9, October 5, 1947, p. 2,

The Cold War military buildup of the late 1940s, which increased the services to some three and a half million men and women by the 1950s, also helped to focus evangelicals' attention on the armed forces. When President Harry S. Truman began the buildup in 1945, he proposed a program of universal military training (UMT), requiring a year of compulsory military service for all males beginning at age eighteen or upon completion of high school, whichever was later, followed by six years in a general reserve. Although Truman stressed certain nonmilitary benefits of UMT—such as fostering the moral and spiritual welfare of American youth and instilling ideals of American citizenship—almost every major religious organization in the United States opposed it. Except for the fundamentalist American Council of Christian Churches (ACCC), which favored UMT, evangelicals joined with liberal, mainline religious groups in denouncing what a 1952 National Association of Evangelicals convention resolution called "the militarization of the nation in peacetime." That same year an editorial in the NAE magazine, *United Evangelical Action,* declared that UMT "has raised grave doubts in the minds of many loyal Americans. It seems that the Pentagon crowd is capitalizing on the anxieties of the present world crisis to introduce a system of militarism strangely like those inflicted upon the people in the Old World." Citing a statement by "one of our military leaders . . . that no man makes a good soldier or sailor unless he drinks, curses, runs with women," the magazine editors said that when "Christian people" heard that, they "were shocked, and we began to wonder what might happen to our youth removed from home and church influences and subjected to the temptations for which military training camps are notorious."[2]

November 16, 1947, p. 21; John Costello, *Virtue Under Fire: How World War II Changed Our Social and Sexual Attitudes* (Boston, 1985), 251–53; Rodger R. Venzke, *Confidence in Battle, Inspiration in Peace: The United States Army Chaplaincy, 1945–1975* (Washington, D.C., 1977), 26–27; Jacob Simpson Payton, "The Story of a Letter," *Chaplain,* III (March, 1946), 41–43; "Chaplain Condemns Army Entertainment," *UEA,* March 15, 1946, p. 16. The three evangelical leaders were Harold John Ockenga, pastor of Boston's Park Street Church, Alfred Carpenter, director of the Southern Baptist Convention Chaplains Commission, and W. O. H. Garman, director of Civil Affairs, American Council of Christian Churches.

2. Lawrence S. Wittner, *Cold War America: From Hiroshima to Watergate* (New York, 1974), 79; Harry S. Truman, "Address Before a Joint Session of the Congress on Universal Military Training," October 23, 1945, in *Public Papers of the Presidents of the United*

Despite concerted efforts on the part of the Truman administration and military leaders such as Omar Bradley, J. Lawton Collins, and Dwight D. Eisenhower, Congress refused to enact UMT. In 1948, however, two events increased Cold War tensions and fear of war: the communist *coup d'état* in Czechoslovakia and the Berlin Blockade. As a result, Truman persuaded the Congress to resurrect the selective service system on June 24, 1948. The Korean War prevented the draft from expiring in 1950, and Congress regularly renewed it thereafter. In 1955 Senator Richard Russell of Georgia, the chairman of the Armed Services Committee, described the regular draft as "the keystone of our national defense."[3]

Although evangelicals had joined with liberal and mainline groups in opposing UMT, they parted company on the resumption of selective service. The great majority of evangelicals endorsed it immediately and without qualification. In a November, 1950, editorial, *United Evangelical Action* declared that "national defense is essential. The action of the American government in drafting army, navy and air forces sufficient to cope with the enemies of the American way of life is commendable. The necessities of the hour demand emergency action." Liberal Protestants were more skeptical and remained so throughout the 1950s. In August, 1948, more than a hundred ministers, including Harry Emerson Fosdick and leaders of the Episcopal, Methodist, Presbyterian, and Congregational churches, protested against the recently passed Selective Service

States. *Harry S. Truman. Containing the Public Messages, Speeches, and Statements of the President, April 12 to December 31, 1945* (Washington, D.C., 1961), 407–409; Harry S. Truman, "Commencement Address at Princeton University, June 17, 1947, in *Public Papers of the Presidents of the United States. Harry S. Truman. Containing the Public Messages, Speeches, and Statements of the President, January 1 to December 31, 1947* (Washington, D.C., 1963), 284; "NAE Convention Resolutions," *UEA*, July 1, 1952, p. 8; "Military Training," *UEA*, January 15, 1955, p. 11; "What of UMT?" *UEA*, February 15, 1952, p. 7. For a list of religious and other groups opposed to UMT, see *Universal Military Training: Hearings Before the Committee on Armed Services, United States Senate, Eightieth Congress, Second Session, on Universal Military Training, March 17, 18, 22, 23, 24, 25, 29, 30, 31, April 1, 2, and 3, 1948* (Washington, D.C., 1948), 254–55. For the development, modification, and attempted passage of the Truman administration's UMT plan, see Richard F. Haynes, *The Awesome Power: Harry S. Truman as Commander in Chief* (Baton Rouge, 1973), 79–87.

3. George Q. Flynn, *The Draft, 1940–1973* (Lawrence, Kan., 1993), 108; John Whiteclay Chambers, II, ed., *Draftees or Volunteers: A Documentary History of the Debate Over Military Conscription in the United States, 1787–1973* (New York, 1975), 365–68.

Act. In a statement issued through the National Council Against Conscription they urged American youths to refuse to register for the draft and called upon the churches and people of the United States to observe a day of "mourning and repentance" to show opposition to that "dangerous and iniquitous measure." In response, a group of evangelical clergymen denounced the protesting ministers for taking a position that was "unbiblical, unpatriotic, un-American, [and] contrary to the historic Christian faith." It "would leave America helpless before Communist expansion and encourage Russia to overrun other lands." The protesters were using the church "as a fifth column," the evangelicals charged, and should be investigated by the House Committee on Un-American Activities. In addition, they merited "the opposition of all who love America."[4]

Overriding fear of and antipathy toward communism and the Soviet Union—what the NAE magazine editorial referred to as "the enemies of the American way of life"—impelled evangelicals to support the military buildup and the draft in the 1950s. Their thinking was summarized in a guidebook published by the Nazarene Service Men's Commission in 1953 for young men about to enter or already serving in the armed forces. Explaining the reason for the draft, the guidebook began by pointing out that "the world is divided into two distinct camps—the Communist dictatorships and the Christian democracies." As a member of the United Nations, the United States was pledged to go to the aid of any nation overrun by an aggressor. "The stricken nations are looking to the free world for material, money, and man power to help them. We are our 'brother's keeper.'" The draft, the guidebook concluded, was necessary to maintain "the freedom of the nations, our own included."[5]

Although they had opposed UMT, evangelicals could accept peacetime conscription. Fear of communist aggression eclipsed the worries about militarism they had expressed in the UMT debate. Also, though they generally respected the right of their pacifist brethren to refuse to bear arms, the majority of evangelicals had no problem with war or military service. Gordon H. Clark, professor of philosophy at Butler University, concluded in an article published in *United Evangelical Action*

4. "Drafted to What?" *UEA*, November 1, 1950, p. 9; *NYT*, August 9, 1948, pp. 1, 17, August 11, 1948, p. 14.

5. Chaplain Claude Chilton, *The Nazarene Serviceman* (Kansas City, Mo., 1953), 14.

that "the New Testament, as well as the Old, authorizes . . . the waging of war."[6] He and other evangelicals generally agreed that there was no contradiction between being a Christian and serving in the armed forces. They insisted that killing the enemy in combat was not murder and therefore did not violate the Sixth Commandment. They believed that the use of force by government was sanctioned by God as a means of protecting the rights of individuals and maintaining order. It followed that in using force, members of the armed forces, like the police, were carrying out one of the legitimate and divinely ordained functions of government.

The Cold War military buildup of the 1950s prompted evangelicals more than ever to look upon the armed forces as "a primary missionary target." An article published in *United Evangelical Action* in the mid-1950s pointed out that since 1941, 22 million young men had served in the armed forces, and another estimated that the military buildup would continue "until possibly forty-five million young Americans [will] have seen duty in the Armed Services." Evangelical leaders recognized that a growing number of the men serving in the armed forces were or would be evangelicals. The need was clear: "Evangelicals must provide evangelical chaplains for evangelical youth." But the mission field embraced more than evangelical youth. An article in the NAE magazine declared, "It is an established fact that 50% of all who pass through the military service have no religious background or church connection." The other 50 percent were two-thirds Protestant and one-third Catholic and Jewish. "Of the two-thirds Protestant, 80% are Protestant because their parents claimed that affiliation or because they were christened in the church," the article continued. "They have no practical Christian experience. This is the ripe harvest field in which our chaplains are working."[7]

Evangelicals were not the only ones to look upon the military as a mission field. In the postwar period, many of the liberal Protestant denominations and religious groups began to expand their efforts among the armed forces. The National (formerly the Federal) Council of

6. Gordon H. Clark, "Is Pacifism Christian?" *UEA*, August 1, 1955, p. 23.

7. "NAE Chaplains in Active Service," *UEA*, April, 1959, p. 12; James DeForest Murch, "Responsibility in Leadership and Service," *UEA*, May 15, 1955, p. 21; James DeForest Murch, "Forward March! God Wills It!" *UEA*, June 1, 1954, p. 21; "Commission on Chaplains Host to Chaplaincy Heads," *UEA*, November 15, 1955, p. 13.

Churches (NCC), a federation embracing many of the liberal denominations, seemed to be in the forefront of the effort. Through its magazine, the *Outlook*, it exhorted member churches to recognize "our Christian responsibility for youth in the armed forces," including supplying chaplains. In December, 1951, the NCC and its chaplain-endorsing agency, the General Commission on Chaplains, made plans to sponsor annual tri-faith "preaching missions" by civilian clergymen to military bases in the United States. In 1952, the first year they went into effect, eighty-three week-long missions were held at army and navy installations in the United States, and 166 civilian ministers participated. The missions featured Sunday services, evening and noonday devotions during the week, and personal counseling, all focused on the theme "Christ Is the Answer." The General Commission on Chaplains also helped establish two organizations to promote religion in the armed forces. One was the United Fellowship of Protestants in the Armed Services, an organization for Protestant servicemen and women. The other was the United Fellowship of Protestant Churches, designed to facilitate interdenominational cooperation in ministering to the military and to foster closer relations between local churches and military chaplains. In addition to supporting the work of the national organization, many of the denominations affiliated with the NCC devised their own programs targeting members serving in the armed forces.[8]

Evangelicals viewed their ministry to the military as crucial in countering the evangelizing efforts of the National Council and liberal mainline churches. Many believed the NCC used its virtual monopoly on American Protestantism not only to promote liberal religion but to restrict the influence of nonmember denominations—for example, by

---

8. "Our Christian Responsibility for Youth in the Armed Forces," *National Council Outlook*, June, 1953, pp. 17–18; Stewart M. Robinson, "The Armed Forces Preaching Missions," *Chaplain*, IX (May–June, 1952), 12–13; *NYT*, December 11, 1951, p. 7, January 13, 1952, p. 30, January 27, 1952, p. 14; "Churchmen Visit G.I.'s," *National Council Outlook*, February, 1953, p. 25; "Armed Forces Missions," *National Council Outlook*, January, 1954, p. 7. On the United Fellowship of Protestants in the Armed Forces and the United Fellowship of Protestant Churches, see *NYT*, February 18, 1951, p. 28, May 29, 1951, p. 23, February 2, 1952, p. 9; Luther Wesley Smith, "A Christian Fellowship for Protestant Youth in the Armed Services," *Chaplain*, VIII (January–February, 1951), 12–14; "United Fellowship of Protestants," *Chaplain*, VIII (May–June, 1951), 1; "Progress of U.F.P.," *Chaplain*, VIII (November–December, 1951), 17; Fred C. Reynolds, "Program of Fellowship," *Chaplain*, VIII (September–October, 1951), 7–9.

keeping evangelicals from serving in the military chaplaincies.[9] In 1944, to offset the influence of the NCC and the General Commission on Chaplains, the National Association of Evangelicals created its own chaplain-endorsing agency, the Commission on Army and Navy Chaplaincies (later called the Commission on Chaplains), and many evangelicals counted on it to challenge the dominance of liberal, mainline religion within the armed forces.

Besides worrying about competition from liberal Protestant chaplains in the military, evangelicals expressed concern about the predominance of Catholic chaplains. When the Cold War buildup prompted the military to issue a call for additional chaplains, the executive director of the NAE urged evangelical ministers to volunteer their services. The army alone would need at least 450 new chaplains in 1952, he pointed out. "On some of our Naval Bases the only chaplains to be found are Catholics," he warned. "Evangelicals must not fail the proportionately large number of men in the armed forces who are anxious that the New Testament Gospel be preached, and a real evangelistic work be carried on by our chaplains." The continuing rivalry evangelicals felt toward Catholics may also be seen in their reaction to Billy Graham's 1953 Korean Mission. "Evangelist Billy Graham's mission in Korea gained an average of nearly 400 converts to Christianity nightly at open-air services in hastily improvised sites here [Pusan] and in other Korean cities," *United Evangelical Action* boasted. "Graham reached many thousands more than the much-publicized Archbishop Spellman." According to the magazine, the State Department had initially withheld permission for Graham to visit Korea, "but when Spellman was granted visas Protestant pressure became so great that State finally succumbed."[10]

Yet another irritant was Catholic influence with the federal government, similar to that evangelicals believed the NCC and the General Commission on Chaplains enjoyed. Evangelicals thought it explained why Catholics seemed to be favored for top chaplaincy posts. When President Eisenhower appointed Chaplain (Brigadier General) Frank A. Tobey, an American Baptist, as the new chief of army chaplains, evan-

9. See, for example, James DeForest Murch, "Why Evangelicals Cannot Co-Operate in the FCCCA," *UEA*, September 15, 1946, p. 7.

10. Rutherford L. Decker, "The Holy Spirit Works Through the NAE," *UEA*, May 15, 1952, p. 6; "Graham's Korean Mission Wins Thousands to Christ," *UEA*, February 1, 1953, p. 23.

gelicals breathed a sigh of relief. For a brief period during 1958, before Tobey took office, all three chaplaincies were headed by Roman Catholics, *United Evangelical Action* pointed out. "In at least one or two instances," it added, "the order of rotations at the top level was traced to Catholic pressure, according to sources in Washington." In 1959 the Full Gospel Business Men's Fellowship *Voice* sounded another alarm regarding Catholic influence in the armed forces. It reported an effort initiated at Fort Benning, Georgia, to dedicate the United States Infantry to Saint Maurice. Fort Leonard Wood in Missouri had already adopted Saint Maurice as the United States Infantry patron saint. The gymnasium and officers' club had been named after him, and "wooden scrolls were placed in the barracks bearing this inscription: 'We live, fight and die for God, Country and Saint Maurice.'" When evangelicals protested to Chief of Chaplains Tobey, his office investigated and recommended terminating the dedication. Nevertheless, the movement continued to expand, *Voice* noted. There were reports from Korea that a United States Army artillery battalion had been named Saint Barbara's Own Battalion and of plans "to dedicate the United States Army Engineers to Saint Patrick, the United States Air Force Paratroopers to Saint Michael, and the entire United States Military Service to Saint Sebastian."[11]

Although they supported resumption of selective service, evangelicals continued to express misgivings about the corrupting influence of the military environment. In the November, 1950, editorial in which *United Evangelical Action* conceded that national defense was essential, the magazine noted that the "moral laxity" of many officers and enlisted personnel had "become so outrageous that draftees face almost certain moral deterioration." The government itself, the magazine charged, was "aiding and abetting" the destruction of draftees' "moral and spiritual heritage." As evidence, it pointed to consumption of liquor by troops in Korea: "In some sort of hazy liaison with the manufacturers and distributors of intoxicating beverages the government is permitting the sousing of our armed forces in Korea in beer," it declared. "Thousands of men who never touched the stuff before they were drafted will come out of the service confirmed alcoholics because Uncle Sam encouraged

11. "Evangelical Chief of Army Chaplains," *UEA*, July 15, 1958, p. 10; "Catholic Chaplain Shortage," *UEA*, February, 1959, p. 16; "United States Infantry Dedicated to St. Maurice," *Voice*, January, 1959, p. 15.

them." The magazine also cited reports of "moral laxity among American occupation troops" in Germany. "There is looseness in dealing with social diseases. We are told that it is no sin to commit adultery. The only offense is failure to report a bad case of syphilis or ghonorrhea [*sic*]. Drunkenness is so common that American discipline has become a byword. Are our young men to be drafted into this maze of immorality?"[12]

Of all the types of "armed forces immorality" evangelicals decried, liquor consumption became the principal preoccupation in the 1950s. The NAE, along with various other groups, including the Woman's Christian Temperance Union (WCTU) and the National Temperance League, protested government or military policies that they believed encouraged liquor consumption and urged the passage of regulations or restrictions that would eliminate it. For example, in 1953, when the military liberalized restrictions on the sale of liquor on army and air force bases, *United Evangelical Action* published a two-page editorial in which it quoted the president of the WCTU charging that the United States Army was "rapidly becoming a school for alcoholism for uniformed youngsters." To the magazine's editors, the 1953 action signaled the continuation of a policy evangelicals had long considered abhorrent. It reached back at least as far as "the debacle at Pearl Harbor, which was largely due to the fact that both officers and men charged with the defense of the harbor were on a week-end liquor binge," the magazine observed. Speaking for evangelicals, it declared, "We are willing to make sacrifices for national defense even unto death, but we do not want a repetition of Pearl Harbor." Pointing to the new, more liberal regulations governing the sale of liquor on military bases, the magazine commented: "The stuff that devastates morality and makes men muddle-headed is to be dispensed right in the officers' mess and since it is being freely sold to and by the NCO's it will be an unusual post where the enlisted men cannot find ways and means to obtain all the fire water they want. What sort of national defense will this give us when the Reds are over America with their H-bombs?" That evangelicals felt frustrated and insulted by the government's apparent dismissal of their protests is clear in the conclusion of the editorial: "These military and political leaders evidently have so lost their sense of right and wrong that they cannot conceive of Christian men and women having such a strong basic

12. "Drafted to What?" *UEA*, November 1, 1950, p. 9.

moral and ethical conviction on the use of intoxicating liquors that they would oppose it regardless of times, places, persons or circumstances involved." [13]

In response to the criticisms leveled against universal military training and selective service by religious groups—which included mainline, liberal Protestant denominations as well as evangelicals—the Truman administration and military leaders began implementing an unprecedented religious and moral welfare program in the armed forces. It mandated compulsory moral (or character) education for all military personnel, provided increased opportunities for religious activities, and greatly enhanced the role chaplains played in military training.

The moral education program had had a trial run in 1947 at Fort Knox, Kentucky, in an experimental unit organized to showcase universal military training. The lectures on morality and citizenship, prepared by an instructor at the U.S. Army Chaplain School and delivered by the unit's three chaplains, proved so successful that Secretary of War Robert Patterson ordered field commanders to institute the program of "Character Guidance," as it was called, throughout the army. In 1951 Secretary of Defense George C. Marshall mandated moral training programs throughout the armed forces. In a memorandum to the secretaries of the army, navy and air force, the chief of naval operations, and the chiefs of staff of the army and air force, Marshall declared that it was "in the national interest that personnel serving in the armed forces be protected in the realization and development of moral, spiritual, and religious values consistent with the religious beliefs of the individual concerned." He directed commanding officers to make "increased efforts" to promote the morals and spiritual welfare of personnel under their command. By the early 1950s programs similar to the army's Character Guidance were under way in the navy and the air force. [14]

13. "Liquor and Our National Defense," *UEA*, October 15, 1953, p. 10. See also *NYT*, September 15, 1950, p. 19, September 23, 1956, p. 44, February 15, 1957, p. 11; "Immorality in Army Is Revealed by WCTU," *UEA*, July 1, 1952, p. 8; "Ask Liquor Be Barred to Young UM Trainees," *UEA*, February 15, 1952, p. 9; "'Armed Forces Immorality Not Exaggerated'—Yaeger," *UEA*, April 15, 1955, p. 20.

14. The Chaplain School, Carlisle Barracks, Pennyslvania, *The Army Character Guidance Program* (ST 16-151, March 1, 1950), 3; G. C. Marshall to Secretary of the Army, Secretary of the Navy, Secretary of the Air Force, Chief of Staff, U.S. Army, Chief of Naval Operations, Chief of Staff, U.S. Air Force, May 26, 1951 (Xerox 2607/ SD 000.3), Box 607, in Marshall Papers, George C. Marshall Research Library, Lex-

According to a 1958 army regulation governing the Character Guidance program, its purpose was "to assist the commander in promoting healthy moral, social, mental, and spiritual attitudes in the personnel under his command" and to "insure the continuance of the wholesome influences of home, family, and community." Character Guidance was a command responsibility, but chaplains were assigned the task of providing instruction in the program.[15]

When Character Guidance was introduced at Fort Dix, the *New York Times* reported that chaplains were giving lectures on morality and citizenship "based on . . . nonsectarian religious principles." Although the army claimed that Character Guidance was separate and distinct from religious programs offered in the armed forces and that chaplains taught morality, not religion, many of the lectures included a strong element of what Richard Hutcheson calls "common denominator religion" and Rodger Venzke refers to as Bible-based morality. The religious basis was explicitly stated in a 1950 Army Chaplain School publication, *The Army Character Guidance Program*, and in the 1961 *Character Guidance Manual*, which pointed out that the principles taught in Character Guidance classes originated in the "Natural Law" and the "Moral Law," both of which came from the same source, God, and were universal, unchanging, and eternal.[16]

A look at the titles and content of some of the lectures reveals the strong religious element. "Man Is a Moral Being" concluded with the declaration that "our chief responsibility as moral beings is toward God." One of the stated objectives of "Worship in Life" was to persuade men "that the worship of God is a requirement of moral living," and "Religion in Our Way of Life" reminded men that religion was not only "the source of our way of life" but "that service to the nation is

---

ington, Va. For brief surveys of the development of moral training programs in the army, navy, and air force, see Venzke, *Confidence in Battle, Inspiration in Peace*, 39–46; Richard G. Hutcheson, Jr., *The Churches and the Chaplaincy* (Atlanta, 1975), Chap. 7; Daniel B. Jorgensen, *Air Force Chaplains, 1947–1968* (Washington, D.C., [1961?]), Chap. 12.

15. Headquarters, Department of the Army, *Personnel-General: Character Guidance Program* (Army Regulation 600-30, October 15, 1958), 1, 2.

16. *NYT*, July 28, 1947, p. 14; Hutcheson, *Churches and the Chaplaincy*, 154, 155, 159; Venzke, *Confidence in Battle, Inspiration in Peace*, 44; Chaplain School, *The Army Character Guidance Program*, 10–11; Headquarters, Department of the Army, *Character Guidance Manual* (FM-16-100, 1961), 11–12.

most effective only when religion becomes part of individual life." Similarly, "The Nation We Serve" described the United States as a "covenant nation" which "recognizes its dependence upon God and its responsibility toward God." In such a nation, the lecture continued, "public institutions and official thinking reflect a faith in the existence and the importance of divine providence." Character Guidance lectures often appealed to God, "the final source of authority," or his laws, or the Ten Commandments, the Bible, or the Golden Rule to enforce good conduct. A lecture on marriage advised the instructor to point out, among other things, that "it is God's law . . . that men and women who marry stay married to each other."[17]

In publicizing its new religious and moral welfare programs, the military emphasized the expanded role of the chaplain. An article in the *Chaplain* about training new recruits at the Great Lakes Naval Training Center portrayed the chaplain as a nearly omnipresent figure. Beginning with his first day at the receiving center, the recruit discovered the "assuring presence" of the chaplain. Some time in the first week of basic training, he and the other members of his company had a two-hour session called the "chaplain's interview," in which they talked individually with chaplains of their own faith. "If a man has not been baptized, or has not affiliated with a church, the interviewing chaplain encourages him to consider enrolling in a church instruction class of his own denominational choice," the article pointed out. Recruits also attended six character education lectures delivered by the chaplain, which offered "an excellent opportunity . . . to reinforce the moral and spiritual strength of Navy men during the most impressionable period of their Naval career." According to the article, religious instruction classes had a wide appeal and had resulted in 2,226 baptisms and 2,560 men being received into church membership during a one-year period. Twenty-

17. Departments of the Army and the Air Force, *Character Guidance Discussion Topics: Duty, Honor, Country. Series VI* (Department of the Army Pamphlet 16-10, 1952), 8; Departments of the Army and the Air Force, *Character Guidance Discussion Topics: Duty, Honor, Country. Series I* (Department of the Army Pamphlet 16-5, 1951), 68, 46–47, 88; Departments of the Army and Air Force, *Character Guidance Discussion Topics: Duty, Honor, Country. Series V* (Department of the Army Pamphlet 16-9, 1952), 67, 79; Departments of the Army and Air Force, *Character Guidance Discussion Topics: Duty, Honor, Country. Series III* (Department of the Army Pamphlet 16-7, 1951), 3, 88; Headquarters, Department of the Army, *Character Guidance Discussion Topics: Duty, Honor, Country* (Department of the Army Pamphlet 16-8, 1962), 52.

eight Sunday worship services also attracted congregations with attendance as high as 1,700. The article concluded that the chaplains' "thor-
ough, dynamic program of evangelism" offered large numbers of young
men moral guidance "and the presentation of a vital religion that may
never have been available to them in civilian life." [18]

The effort to "stimulate spiritual welfare" and encourage "high standards of morality" became one of the most publicized features of the
"New Army" of the late 1940s and 1950s. In an article written for
the News Bureau of the National Lutheran Council and reprinted in
the *Chaplain*, Erwin Endress declared that "the most significant change"
wrought by the New Army was "the new emphasis on the spiritual
health of the American soldier." A key assumption of the army's training
program was that "faith is an integral part of being a good soldier,"
Endress observed. *Coronet* magazine aided the army's publicity campaign by printing an article entitled "Good News for Parents of Today's
Soldiers," featuring Fort Dix, one of four major induction centers in
the United States, as "an outstanding example of the 'New Army' in
action." Along with reassurances that "the new soldier sleeps under
olive-drab blankets spread on a springy mattress" and was "outfitted in
a variety of summer and winter uniforms in his exact size," the author
declared: "Never before have chaplains played such a vital role in caring
for the spiritual needs of America's recruits. Every rookie at Dix may
chat informally with a chaplain of his own faith; more than 90 per cent
consult one of the 15 chaplains there at least once during their stay." [19]

The military's religious and moral guidance programs appear to have
paid off. Throughout the 1950s civilian as well as military observers
commented on the improved moral behavior of American troops, their
remarkable interest in religion, their high rates of attendance at religious
services at military installations, and the continuing concern of the Defense Department and commanding officers for the moral and spiritual

18. "Great Lakes Recruit Command: The Chaplains' Program," *Chaplain*, IX
(March–April, 1952), 34–35.
19. General Jacob L. Devers, "Training the Army of Today," *Army Information
Digest*, IV (April, 1949), 7; Erwin Endress, "Christianity in Uniform," *Chaplain*, VI
(May, 1949), 20, 22; Ralph H. Major, Jr., "Good News for Parents of Today's Soldiers,"
Coronet, November, 1950, pp. 53–55. See also, for statements by Secretary of the Army
Frank Pace, Jr., General Matthew Ridgway, and General Maxwell Taylor praising the
army's concern for the spiritual and moral strength of its troops, *NYT*, October 19,
1952, p. 49, June 6, 1955, p. 25, July 2, 1956, p. 23.

well-being of young men and women in uniform. In 1956, following a tour of army bases in the Far East and Alaska, Army Chief of Chaplains Patrick J. Ryan reported that the army's religious program was in a stronger position than at any time in his twenty-eight years of service. Army men were attending worship services in greater numbers than ever before, and religious retreats, for which soldiers received three-day leaves, were "extremely popular." Ryan dismissed reports of immorality among GIs by saying: "Unquestionably our soldiers are exposed to more temptations in a pagan country like Japan or Korea. But, by and large, they are withstanding those temptations quite well." The implication, of course, was that the army's religious and moral program was helping them resist. The GI of the mid-1950s was a "high-type" soldier, Ryan declared, who "represents the spiritual heritage of America."[20]

Given their long-standing concern about the corrupting influence of the military environment, it is not surprising that evangelicals welcomed the armed forces programs that expanded religious opportunities and provided moral training for service personnel. Nevertheless, reports appeared now and again in *United Evangelical Action* testifying that the military had not wholly eradicated "immorality." And despite their praise for the military's religious and moral training programs, evangelicals remained distressed by the "nonsectarian" approach. In their view, moral behavior depended on a surrender to Christ and "new birth," not just obedience to law. Nor did they share the programs' liberal, perfectionist assumptions. In an article entitled "Morals in Training," published in December, 1955, the NAE magazine quoted the first statement in the recommendations of the National Security Training Commission concerning a six-month training program being instituted by the Department of Defense: "'The average young American will do the right thing if he is not unduly tempted by the wrong.'" The "doctrinal" and "moral implications" of the statement "have caused some concern on the part of Evangelicals," the article noted. Evangelicals believed that to approach moral training "from the viewpoint that the average American is inherently a saint and not a sinner is to accept an insupportable premise."[21]

---

20. *NYT*, October 7, 1956, p. 75. See also *NYT*, September 16, 1950, p. 12, March 23, 1953, p. 3, March 4, 1956, p. 82, October 7, 1956, p. 75; "GIs Go to Church," *National Council Outlook*, January, 1954, p. 14.

21. "Morals in Training," *UEA*, December 15, 1955, p. 8. For *UEA* reports of

In 1955 Douglas G. Scott, executive director of the NAE Commission on Chaplains, reflected on the benefits and limitations of the military's religious and moral guidance programs and evangelicals' obligation to service personnel. In an article published by *United Evangelical Action*, he extolled "the great effort the military is making to provide wholesome surroundings for our boys." The hobby and woodworking shops, photo labs, reading rooms and libraries, and high school and university extension courses he had seen while visiting United States bases in the Far East and Europe all demonstrated the "extensive effort of the Military to provide good clean recreation for the serviceman." Scott also complimented the armed forces for the "most important and greatly needed ministry that is provided for our boys, through the Chaplains' Program." But having praised the military, he went on to admit that he was "appalled" at "how poorly equipped spiritually the boys in the military as a whole are." The military was providing "wholesome recreation." But, Scott warned, that was not enough, for "unless the home and the church provide spiritual aid too, many a boy will be lost forever to the church, and to God and heaven." A few months later, reporting to the 1955 NAE convention, Scott reiterated his praise for the military's concern for the "moral and spiritual upbuilding of the men in service." But he also repeated his warning. Leaving such matters entirely in the hands of the military would be a mistake. "Bowling alleys, hobby shops, photo-labs and even the educational facilities that are at their disposal will not and do not take the place of the spiritual," he insisted. The USO (United Service Organizations), he observed, "will never take the place of the church." Evangelicals "should be equally concerned."[22] In fact, evangelicals in the NAE and other groups were ready and willing to take up Scott's challenge.

"immorality," see "Drafted to What?" *UEA*, November 1, 1950, p. 9; "Immorality in Army Is Revealed by WCTU," *UEA*, July 1, 1952, p. 8; "'Armed Forces Immorality Not Exaggerated'—Yaeger," *UEA*, April 15, 1955, p. 20; "Immorality Hits 90 Percent of Servicemen in Korea," *UEA*, November, 1963, pp. 23–24.

22. Douglas G. Scott, "Our Sons and Daughters in This Military Era," *UEA*, March 1, 1955, pp. 9–10; James DeForest Murch, "Responsibility in Leadership and Service," *UEA*, May 15, 1955, p. 21.

2

Missionaries to the Military

The National Association of Evangelicals stood foremost among the associations, denominations, and parachurch groups engaged in evangelizing the armed forces after World War II. By the late 1940s its chaplain-endorsing agency, the Commission on Chaplains, had placed nearly 100 chaplains from various evangelical and fundamentalist denominations. By 1955 the number had risen to 154. The commission also acted as a liaison between NAE member denominations and churches on the one hand and the armed forces on the other. From its inception, it made a concerted effort to win recognition for evangelicals in the military. As early as 1950 the chairman of the Commission on Chaplains reported to the Eighth Annual NAE Convention that the commission was equally recognized with the other commissions representing chaplains in the armed forces. Some twenty years later, Clyde W. Taylor reported that the commission had "an excellent reputation" and "enjoyed the best rapport with the military in general and the Chiefs of Chaplains in particular."[1]

Beginning in the late 1950s the NAE sponsored spiritual life retreats

1. Joel Allan Carpenter, "The Renewal of American Fundamentalism, 1930–1945" (Ph.D. dissertation, Johns Hopkins University, 1984), 217; "NAE Agencies Rendering a Wide-spread Service," *UEA*, April 1, 1955, p. 24; James DeForest Murch, *Cooperation Without Compromise* (Grand Rapids, 1956), 136, 141, 206; Richard V. Pierard, "Cacophony on Capitol Hill: Evangelical Voices in Politics," in *The Political Role of Religion in the United States*, ed. Stephen D. Johnson and Joseph B. Tamney (Boulder, Colo., 1986), 79–80; "Spirit of Revival Marks NAE at Indianapolis," *UEA*, May 1, 1950, p. 16; Clyde W. Taylor, "Remembering . . . We Press Forward," *UEA*, Winter, 1974, p. 15; Clyde W. Taylor, "NAE Celebrates 30 Years of Service," *UEA*, Spring, 1972, p. 12.

for United States military forces in Japan and Korea and at Berchtesgaden, West Germany. From 1960 through the late 1970s the NAE also sponsored the Christian Servicemen's Fellowship under the leadership of retired naval officer Floyd Robertson, who also served as executive secretary of the Commission on Chaplains.[2]

Supplementing the work of the NAE in the postwar period, evangelical denominations continued and in many cases enlarged the ministries established among the military during World War II. The Assemblies of God (AOG), for example, had a Servicemen's Division working exclusively with members of the armed forces, and during the 1950s and 1960s it steadily expanded its services. These included sending letters as well as tracts, booklets, and pamphlets to servicemen on its mailing list, which increased from some eight thousand names in 1951 to fifteen thousand at the end of 1969. It also published and distributed millions of copies of *Reveille*, a devotional bulletin. In addition, the division maintained contact with and supplied various publications, tracts, and other resources to AOG chaplains as well as to hundreds of those serving other denominations who requested such materials. The division also supplemented the work of the AOG chaplains by supplying civilian "contact pastors" to serve at military installations.[3]

Beginning in 1957 the AOG began holding annual servicemen's retreats at the General Walker Hotel in Berchtesgaden. Sponsored by and for AOG military personnel and their dependents and coordinated by senior chaplains of the denomination, the camp-meeting-style gatherings attracted not only AOG members but chaplains and personnel belonging to many other denominations. By the mid-1960s, the retreats drew nearly four hundred participants annually, and by the mid-1970s, attendance reached over six hundred. Beginning in the late 1960s, the AOG inaugurated a similar program of annual retreats in Asia. The first

2. "Far East Servicemen's Retreats," *UEA*, September, 1959, p. 8; "Chaplaincy Retreats," *UEA*, July, 1960, p. 17; "Servicemen's Retreat," *UEA*, October, 1960, p. 34; "N.A.E. at Work," *UEA*, December, 1966, p. 29.

3. Leon G. Kircher, Jr., "The History of the Organizational Development and Ministry to the Military by the Assemblies of God, December 1941–December 1979" (Photocopied typescript of research paper, Assemblies of God Graduate School, Springfield, Mo., December 13, 1979), 17; Edith L. Blumhofer, *The Assemblies of God: A Chapter in the Story of American Pentecostalism* (2 vols.; Springfield, Mo., 1989), II, 141–42; Ernest Kalapathy, "There IS a Servicemen's Division," *PE*, November 4, 1951, p. 10; "Publications for Servicemen," *PE*, November 4, 1951, p. 11.

year, 1968, Far East retreats were held at Tokyo and Misawa in Japan, on Okinawa, and in Thailand, the Philippines, and Taiwan.[4]

Supplementing the work of the denomination and its chaplains, AOG missionaries operated servicemen's homes and centers near military posts in the United States, Europe, and Asia. Besides providing food, lodging, and recreational activities, such places scheduled Bible studies, prayer meetings, worship services, and evangelism training. According to a 1975 report by Helen Braxton, at the Berea House Servicemen's Center in Eschborn near Frankfort, West Germany: "Many members of the American Armed Forces have found a home away from home. . . . Almost every week, one or two are born again and several are baptized in the Holy Spirit. Others find strength in Christian fellowship and sharing among their peers."[5]

In 1964 the AOG appointed missionary Richard C. Fulmer as its first full-time servicemen's representative for Europe. During twenty years of service, Fulmer coordinated a military ministry employing an ever-increasing number of AOG chaplains, missionaries, civilian pastors and evangelists, and military lay leaders. Besides serving as a liaison between AOG groups and the military and helping to direct the Berchtesgaden retreats, Fulmer also inaugurated a program of "holiday rallies." These pentecostal convention-type meetings for servicemen and dependents on Labor Day, Memorial Day, and other American holidays featured

4. Ruby Enyart, "Continued Victory in Retreat," *PE*, June 26, 1988, pp. 16, 19; "Hundreds Attend 1964 Retreat at Berchtesgaden," *PE*, July 5, 1964, p. 7; "Revival Fires Linger Following 13th Annual Servicemen's Retreat," *PE*, January 18, 1970, p. 28; "30 Saved, 40 Filled with Holy Spirit During 15th Annual Servicemen's Retreat," *PE*, January 16, 1972, p. 28; "Servicemen's Work in Europe at a Glance," *PE*, August 24, 1974, p. 16; "Five Retreats Planned for U.S. Servicemen in the Far East," *PE*, November 10, 1968, p. 29.

5. Helen Braxton, "All Over Europe the Spirit Is Moving!" *PE*, August 24, 1975, pp. 16–17. See also "The 'Contact Pastor' Program," *PE*, November 4, 1951, p. 11; "Twin Weapons Against Our Boys in Japan," *PE*, October 4, 1953, p. 6; Maynard L. Ketcham, "A Pentecostal Home for Servicemen in the Far East," *PE*, May 31, 1959, p. 27; Paul Pipkin, "Servicemen in Taiwan . . . a Challenge and a Blessing," *PE*, November 22, 1964, p. 22; Helen Braxton, "Serving Our Servicemen in Europe," *PE*, June 26, 1966, p. 16; "CBC Students Provide Coffeehouse Ministry for Military Base," *PE*, June 29, 1980, pp. 12–13; "Servicemen's Home in Korea Reaches Varied Audience," *PE*, June 29, 1980, p. 29; Jim Smith, "Making Disciples in the Armed Forces," *PE*, February 27, 1983, pp. 18–19; Kristine Bryant, "Twenty Years of Military Ministry," *PE*, March 4, 1984, p. 11.

Bible classes for children, teenagers, and adults; religious, counseling, and personal growth sessions; musical entertainment; and special speakers. Perhaps the most important aspect of Fulmer's work was his organization of full gospel fellowship groups, first in Germany and then throughout Europe. By 1966, forty-six such groups operated in Germany, France, England, Italy, and Spain. Although they were aimed at AOG service personnel, they attracted men and women from numerous other denominations. As described in a 1964 issue of the *Pentecostal Evangel*, such groups featured weekly services "of truly Pentecostal caliber," which were generally held in the base chapel and "usually led by a Spirit-filled line officer or some other serviceman whose life and testimony has thrust him into a place of leadership." The magazine noted that "people are saved and baptized in the Holy Spirit in nearly all these meetings."[6]

In the mid-1970s, the Servicemen's Division changed its name to Ministries to Military Personnel, but its programs continued. In 1985, for example, 233 contact pastors appointed by the AOG ministered at all major military installations in the United States. By 1987, *At Ease*, which had replaced *Reveille*, was being distributed to seventeen thousand military men and women. In addition, each year in July the Ministries to Military Personnel coordinated Military Personnel Day, designed to give AOG churches throughout the United States an occasion to pray for and honor military personnel and chaplains and acquaint their congregations with its ministry to servicemen and servicewomen.[7]

As one of the largest and fastest growing of the evangelical denominations, the AOG was bound to make a significant impact within the armed forces. Another even larger, burgeoning denomination, the

6. Bert Webb, "Ministering to Servicemen in Europe," *PE*, July 5, 1964, p. 6. See also "Captain Recalls Blessings of Rallies in Europe," *PE*, April 4, 1965, p. 11; Robert R. Way, "Our Mission to the Military," *PE*, September 26, 1965, p. 7; Braxton, "Serving Our Servicemen in Europe," 16–17; "American Servicemen in Europe Find Pentecostal Fellowship," *PE*, March 4, 1979, p. 12; Bryant, "Twenty Years of Military Ministry," 10–11.

7. Lemuel D. McElyea, "The Mission of the Chaplaincy," *PE*, August 4, 1985, p. S24; Blumhofer, *Assemblies of God*, II, 142; T. E. Gannon, "'Under Orders,'" *PE*, June 24, 1979, p. 11. For other articles on Ministries to Military Personnel, see T. E. Gannon, "Ministering to the Military," *PE*, June 25, 1978, pp. 6–7; T. E. Gannon, "Everywhere Preaching . . . in the Military," *PE*, June 29, 1980, p. 13; Robert C. Cunningham, "Thank God, We're Free—But Freedom Isn't," *PE*, June 28, 1981, p. 30; Ruby M. Enyart, "Meeting the Spiritual Needs of the Military," *PE*, June 26, 1983, pp. 11–12.

Southern Baptist Convention (SBC), also operated a wide-ranging ministry to hundreds of thousands of military personnel during the 1960s and 1970s. In those two decades, the Southern Baptist Chaplains' Commission, through its Military Personnel Ministries, took the lead in developing the denomination's ministry to military men and women. Its efforts were supplemented by the Women's Missionary Union and the Brotherhood Commission, which cooperated on projects relating to military personnel. A special department of the Sunday School, Young People Away, also operated a program for maintaining servicemen's ties with the church during their enlistment.[8]

Besides endorsing chaplains, most of the efforts of the SBC Chaplains' Commission aimed at encouraging churches to maintain or establish contact with men and women on active duty. In the late 1960s a random survey of Southern Baptist churches showed that some 30 percent provided an organized ministry to preinduction youth, and almost 70 percent kept an up-to-date roster of military members to whom they sent church bulletins, newsletters and pastoral letters, and religious reading material. The pastors and members of the congregation also wrote personal letters to the men in service. Some churches, such as the Roswell Street Baptist Church in Marietta, Georgia, designated a special evening prayer meeting focusing on all military personnel, especially those serving overseas, and their family members. The SBC Chaplains' Commission encouraged churches located near military bases to devise a variety of programs to attract service personnel and their dependents, such as community orientation for newcomers, a onetime or regular military fellowship, child care or baby-sitting services, a coffeehouse, special meals, visits in homes, a transportation service, an in-town sleeping facility, and crisis intervention.[9]

The Church of God (Cleveland, Tennessee) is an example of how the smaller evangelical denominations were able to develop an extensive and effective ministry to military personnel. With a membership about one-fourth that of the AOG, the Church of God organized a worldwide

8. Wayne Dehoney, *Disciples in Uniform* (Nashville, 1967), 117, 119.

9. Barbara Joiner, "Current Missions Groups: Missions and National Issues, Session III," *Royal Service*, LXVII (March, 1973), 46; Mrs. John T. Rogers, "Disciples unto the Uttermost," *Royal Service*, LXIV (July, 1969), 24; Willis A. Brown, "Interest Mounting in Ministry to GIs," *Home Missions*, XXXVII (July, 1966), 26–27; Gladys Bryant, "Homes Away from Home," *Contempo*, V (February, 1975), 31; Kenneth Day, "Military Families—Disciples," *Royal Service*, LXIII (July, 1969), 6–7.

network of fellowships, servicemen's centers, and churches focusing on the needs and spiritual nurture of military men and women. In addition to a Chaplains Commission, established in 1978, the denomination also supported a Ministry to the Military Department, which sponsored a wide-ranging "Save Our Servicepersons" (SOS) program. By the late 1980s it coordinated activities of over 120 "Military Contact Churches" located near military bases in the United States and featuring programs designed especially for military personnel and their families. Like the AOG, the Church of God held annual retreats at Berchtesgaden and other locations in Europe and the Far East. It also sponsored sixty Christian Servicemen's Centers, as well as innumerable pentecostal fellowships within military chapels throughout the world. Most local Church of God congregations in the United States observed Ministry to the Military Day annually. Many were part of a program begun in 1987 to organize a fellowship group bringing together veterans, servicemen, military families, and their friends in what was described as "a practical comprehensive program covering the full spectrum of individual needs from the time of induction until discharge and reestablishment in the civilian church in the community." In 1990 the Fellowship of Cornelius, as it was called, numbered about eight hundred persons.[10]

Even the historically noncombatant Seventh-day Adventists recognized and sought to meet the challenge presented by the armed forces. During World War II, the Seventh-day Adventist church had warned its ministers against accepting commissions as military chaplains, but in November, 1950, it reversed its position. As a result, in the early 1950s, Seventh-day Adventist military chaplains, working in coordination with the denomination's National Service Organization, began establishing a variety of programs for military personnel. In West Germany, one of the denomination's nine army chaplains, William Howard Bergherm, teamed up with Harold Enoch Kurtz, the first Seventh-day Adventist

10. "Service Ministries in the Church: The Church of God Chaplains Commission" (Typescript provided by John E. Taylor, Jr., Program Coordinator, Church of God Chaplains Commission) [1990?]; Richard Y. Bershon, *With the Cross of Jesus: A History of Church of God Chaplaincy and Ministry to the Military* (Cleveland, Tenn., 1991), 143; Robert Moore, "SOS: (Save Our Servicepersons) Effective Outreach for Military Ministry," *Church of God Evangel*, LXXVIII (May 23, 1988), 16; Robert Moore, "The Fellowship of Cornelius," *Church of God Evangel*, LXXVIII (May 23, 1988), 16; John E. Taylor, Jr., Program Coordinator, Church of God Chaplains Commission, to the author, June 28, 1990.

civilian chaplain to the American military community in Europe, to organize Bible conferences, religious retreats, chapel groups, Sabbath schools, and churches for Seventh-day Adventist servicemen. An Adventist Servicemen's Center was established in Frankfurt, and the denomination began publishing a quarterly newsletter for servicemen, *Overseas Loyalty News* (later known as *For God and Country*). Between 1953 and 1960 the number of Adventist Sabbath schools and churches in Europe varied between eight and eighteen, attended by an estimated three thousand Seventh-day Adventist servicemen and their dependents. In Japan and Korea, beginning in the 1950s, Adventists organized programs for American servicemen similar to those in Europe. In later years other Adventist servicemen's centers like the one in Frankfurt were established in such places as San Antonio, Texas, and Washington, D.C., and Adventist civilian chaplains to the military, based in those two cities as well as San Diego, California, and Columbia, South Carolina, and at military installations such as Fort Ord and Fort Hood, continued to augment the work of their military counterparts.[11]

All of the associations and denominations engaging in evangelical missions to the military recognized the crucial role their chaplains played in evangelizing the armed forces. In the mid-1960s, the number of such chaplains began to increase dramatically. The military allotted chaplaincy slots to various denominations and faith groups using a quota system to ensure that the distribution of chaplains in the armed forces was roughly equivalent to the proportional distribution of different denominations and faith groups in American society as a whole (based on church membership statistics reported annually in the *Yearbook of American Churches*). By the mid-1950s, Southern Baptists, the NAE Chaplains Commission, and the Assemblies of God had acquired a considerable number of chaplains under the quota system. In the 1960s, even smaller, less well-known evangelical groups were filling more—and a larger proportion of—chaplaincy slots. In 1965 the Army Office of the Chief of Chaplains remarked that it was "noteworthy" that some denominations or endorsing agencies with a fixed quota of five or fewer chaplains had exceeded their quotas, some by a considerable margin. They included the Seventh-day Adventists, with six against a quota of four; the Church

---

11. Robert L. Mole, *God Also Loves Military People: A Brief Story of the Seventh-Day Adventist Church and the American Military Chaplaincy, 1860–1976* (N.p., 1977), 62–64, 66–70, 77, 109–10, 318–19, 328, 332, 333, 337, 342, 344, 352, 356–60, 362.

of the Nazarene, eleven against four; the Salvation Army, four against three; the Church of God (Anderson, Indiana), six against two; the Independent Fundamental Churches of America, eight against one; and the Christian and Missionary Alliance, four against one. During the 1969–70 fiscal year, the Army Office of the Chief of Chaplains noted, only small, conservative denominations showed an increase in the number of chaplains.[12]

A combination of factors contributed to the increasing number and proportion of evangelical chaplains. First, the growth of evangelical religion in American society meant that, under the armed forces' quota system, evangelical denominations merited ever-larger quotas. Then, too, in the mid- and late 1960s, many of the mainline churches and faith groups either failed to meet their quotas (as in the case of the Roman Catholic Church, Jewish groups, the Eastern Orthodox Communion, the African Methodist Episcopal Church, the African Methodist Episcopal Zion Church, and certain black Baptist churches) or endorsed fewer chaplains than in previous years. During the 1969–70 fiscal year, for example, when conservative bodies increased their number of chaplains, many mainline churches registered a decline in the number of chaplains serving in the military. Evangelicals leaped at the opportunity to take up the slack, and the military, seeking to meet the demand for chaplains caused by increased draft calls and recruiting drives during the Vietnam War, encouraged them to do so. In 1966, of an estimated forty evangelical churches listed with the Armed Forces Chaplains Board (of which nineteen were represented by the NAE Chaplains Commission), nearly all were meeting or exceeding their quotas.[13]

12. Office of the Chief of Chaplains, "Historical Review, 1 July 1964 to 30 June 1965" [1965] (Typescript at Washington National Records Center, Suitland, Md.), 139–40; U.S. Army Office of the Chief of Chaplains, *Historical Review, 1 July 1969 to 30 June 1970* (1971), 129.

13. Office of the Chief of Chaplains, "Historical Review, 1 July 1964 to 30 June 1965," 136–37; U.S. Army Office of the Chief of Chaplains, *Historical Review, 1 January 1967 to 30 June 1968* (1969), 126–27, and *Historical Review, 1 July 1969 to 30 June 1970,* 126–27; Phil Landrum, "Missionary to the Military," *UEA,* July, 1966, pp. 7–8. On the growth of evangelical denominations and the decline of mainline groups, see Richard Hutcheson, *God in the White House: How Religion Has Changed the Modern Presidency* (New York, 1988), 67–69. According to Hutcheson, the Assemblies of God had increased by 242 percent in the last twenty years, making it larger than several of the major mainline denominations. The Church of the Nazarene grew by 41 percent and the Seventh-day Adventists by 61 percent, the smaller Christian and Missionary Alliance

Another factor was that in the 1960s evangelicals demonstrated even greater interest in the chaplaincies than before. Writing in 1966, Phil Landrum noted "an unprecedented enthusiasm over the prospects of the chaplaincy as an evangelistic ministry." Evangelical pastors had long been skeptical of the military chaplaincy, he observed, because they regarded it as a bastion of religious liberalism in which evangelical chaplains would probably not have "true freedom." But now, he wrote, "Pastors are taking a new look at their military counterparts and a significant number are leaving the civilian pastorate for service as a chaplain in the army, navy, air force or coast guard."[14] Moreover, during the Vietnam War, when the liberal, mainline denominations' opposition to the war and the military often translated into hostility to or at least disinterest in the chaplaincy, the vast majority of evangelical denominations were untrammeled by such concerns.

Evangelicals worked hard at establishing endorsing agencies able to place the greatest number of chaplains possible in the armed forces. Some denominations, such as the Assemblies of God and the Church of God (Cleveland, Tennessee), terminated their affiliation with the NAE Chaplains Commission and set up their own agencies to endorse and represent chaplains on the assumption (which generally proved correct) that individual representation by a denominational chaplains commission rather than collective representation through the NAE would enable them to increase their number of chaplaincy slots. Other, smaller denominations formed umbrella endorsing agencies similar to the NAE's Chaplains Commission so as to improve their access to the chaplaincies. An early example of such a group was the Independent Fundamental Churches of America (IFCA); it withdrew from the American Council of Christian Churches (which had been endorsing IFCA chaplains for the military) in 1953 and established its own Committee on Military Chaplains. According to the historian of the IFCA, an impor-

---

by 61 percent, and the Church of God (Cleveland, Tennessee) by 107 percent. The U.S. Army Office of the Chief of Chaplains, *Historical Review, 1 July 1969 to 30 June 1970*, 128–29, showed the declines in the number of mainline chaplains during the Vietnam War: Southern Baptist Convention, from 302 to 273; United Methodist, from 264 to 245; Jewish, from 42 to 28; Disciples of Christ, from 70 to 56; Lutheran (all branches), from 169 to 157; American Baptist Convention, from 81 to 71; United Presbyterian Church in the U.S.A., from 97 to 88; Presbyterian Church in the U.S., from 39 to 33; Protestant Episcopal, from 57 to 51; United Church of Christ, from 52 to 47.

14. Landrum, "Missionary to the Military," 7–8.

tant reason for withdrawing from the ACCC was its "contentious" attitude toward the armed forces chiefs of chaplains, which hindered its ability to place chaplains. The IFCA soon established a much more cordial relationship with the chiefs and as a result made considerable headway in placing its chaplains. From twelve chaplains on active duty in the armed forces in 1954, the IFCA increased the number to thirty-nine by 1990. In recent years one of the fastest growing umbrella endorsing agencies has been the Chaplaincy Full Gospel Churches (CFGC), approved by the Armed Forces Chaplains Board in 1984 to endorse pentecostal chaplains. Representing 2.6 million members belonging to 25,000 churches and 41 independent fellowships and associations, the CFGC had 107 Full Gospel men and women officially endorsed as military and civilian chaplains in 1989. By 1993 the membership had risen to just over 5 million, and the CFGC had 147 chaplains in the armed forces.[15]

A final factor contributing to the increase in the number of evangelical chaplains in the 1960s was a new concern on the part of the military leadership to make room for chaplains from evangelical denominations or groups that before the 1960s had had a very small representation or none at all. This new concern grew out of the aggressive lobbying by evangelical endorsing agencies and denominations and the recognition that an increasing number of military personnel, especially in the enlisted ranks, belonged to fundamentalist, evangelical, or pentecostal denominations. One result, beginning in the 1960s, was the "quota juggling act," whereby evangelical denominations were allowed to increase

15. Kircher, "History of the Organizational Development and Ministry to the Military by the Assemblies of God," 21, 30–33; Bershon, *With the Cross of Jesus*, 117–18; James O. Henry, *For Such a Time as This: A History of the Independent Fundamental Churches of America* (Westchester, Ill., 1983), 258, 263; "Annual Report of the Independent Fundamental Churches of America: Reports and Minutes of the 61st Annual Convention Held at Grace Community Church, Sun Valley, California, June 23–28, 1990" (Photocopy enclosed in letter of Richard I. Gregory, National Executive Director, IFCA, to author, August 15, 1991), 21; R. Alan Plishker, Captain, CHC, USN, Executive Director, Armed Forces Chaplains Board, to Reverend E. H. Jim Ammerman, Director, Chaplaincy Full Gospel Churches, Inc., July 27, 1984 (Photocopy supplied by Ammerman in letter to author, July 16, 1990); "Full Gospel Chaplaincy Vision Bearing Record Fruit," CFGC news release (1989?), supplied by Ammerman in letter to author, July 16, 1990; "Chaplaincy of Full Gospel Churches Tops Five Million," CFGC news release, March 24, 1993, supplied by David B. Plummer, Associate Director, Chaplaincy Full Gospel Churches, Inc., in letter to author, March 24, 1993.

their number of chaplains beyond their allotment when other denominations failed to meet their quotas. Also, in the late 1980s, as the concern for religious representation persisted, the military agreed to allow the NAE Chaplains Commission to act as an endorsing agent for any church body it represented, meaning not just for denominations but for individual local churches as well. The military also made it easier for individual churches not identified with any denomination to place chaplains, without being required to have a certain number of constituents. And finally, the military moved away from allotting quotas to denominations on the basis of the nation's religious demographics and began endorsing chaplains based on such considerations as the religious demographics of the armed services or the qualifications of individual candidates. That, too, helped increase the number of evangelical chaplains.[16]

Statistics provide the most graphic evidence of the increase of evangelical chaplains in the military beginning in the 1960s. In 1969, the NAE represented 18 denominations and had 122 chaplains. In 1987 it represented 26 denominations and had 163 chaplains. By 1963 active-duty AOG chaplains numbered 25 (11 in the army), and by 1970, during the Vietnam War, AOG chaplaincy strength almost doubled to 42. In the 1970s and 1980s the number continued to increase, partly as a result of the denomination's unprecedented growth during those decades but also as a consequence of the more favorable accession policy adopted by the army. By 1979 a total of 51 AOG chaplains served in the armed forces (31 in the army); almost ten years later the number had risen to 88. In 1978 the Church of God (Cleveland, Tennessee) had only 11 full-time endorsed chaplains; by the late 1980s it counted 34 active-duty military chaplains and 10 reserve military chaplains. In 1983 the Christian and Missionary Alliance (C&MA) reported that although technically it was entitled to only 2 chaplains, it actually had 13 on active duty and 10 more in process as endorsed candidates. By 1988 it had 36 chaplains serving in the armed forces, with 21 on active duty, the largest number since World War II. In 1965 the Southern Baptist Convention listed the total number of chaplains in the armed forces as 489. Of those,

16. Landrum, "Missionary to the Military," 7–8; Clifford T. Weathers, Coordinator, National Conference on Ministry to the Armed Forces, to the author, July 22, 1992; Bradley J. Lewis, "Commission Aids Evangelical Chaplains," *UEA,* January–February, 1987, p. 11; John E. Groh, "Lively Experiment: A Summary History of the Air Force Chaplaincy," *MCR,* Winter, 1990, p. 80; John E. Groh, *Facilitators of the Free Exercise of Religion: Air Force Chaplains, 1981–1990* (Washington, D.C., 1991), 11.

195 served in the army, 128 in the navy, and 166 in the air force. By 1978 the SBC counted 414 active-duty and 321 reserve chaplains in the military, a grand total of 735.[17]

Besides the NAE, the various evangelical denominations, and their chaplains, numerous evangelical parachurch groups also played an important role in the mission to the military. Six such groups were the Navigators, the Officers' Christian Fellowship (OCF), the Overseas Christian Servicemen's Centers (OCSC), the Christian Military Fellowship (CMF), Campus Crusade for Christ, and the Full Gospel Business Men's Fellowship International (FGBMFI). Although there are differences among them, all six groups shared a similar approach and objective—personal evangelism aimed at converting military men and women to evangelical Christianity and training them to become "disciplemakers" themselves who would win and train still other converts.

The oldest of these parachurch groups, the Navigators, was founded during World War II by Dawson Trotman. In the immediate postwar period, the Navigators concentrated most of their efforts on navy and air force enlisted personnel. In the 1960s they began working with cadets at the U.S. Military Academy, the Air Force Academy, and the Citadel and with midshipmen at the Naval Academy. Starting with two or three contacts, they quickly multiplied. For example, the Navigator staff member assigned to Annapolis began with only two midshipmen. By 1975, 26 men served on the ministry training team and 250 midshipmen participated in Bible studies. Almost a decade later the head of the Navigators' Naval Academy ministry reported that more than 300 midshipmen were taking part in regular Bible studies and between 100 and 130 were attending monthly rallies.[18]

17. William Willoughby, "Chaplains' Role Under New Scrutiny," *CT*, April 25, 1969, p. 32; Bradley J. Lewis, "Commission Aids Evangelical Chaplains," *UEA*, January–February, 1987, p. 11; "Twenty-five Assemblies Chaplains Now Serving," *PE*, July 7, 1963, p. 10; "A/G Chaplains Number 42 with New Appointments," *PE*, February 15, 1970, p. 29; McElyea, "The Mission of the Chaplaincy," S24; "Assemblies of God Chaplains Now on Active Military Duty," *PE*, June 24, 1979, p. 11; "Faithful," *PE*, June 28, 1987, p. 9; "Service Ministries in the Church"; Warren Bird, "Inside the Alliance Military Chaplaincy," *Alliance Witness*, June 22, 1983, pp. 9–10; "Situation Report: Department of Chaplaincy Ministries" (Typescript, dated July, 1988, received from Office of Chaplaincy Ministries, Christian and Missionary Alliance, Nyack, N.Y., in letter to author, August 1, 1988); Morris Ashcraft, "Office of the Chaplain," *Spire*, February, 1965, p. 1; "Today's Army Gets Old-Time Religion," *Home Missions*, XLIV (December, 1978), 15.

18. Monte C. Unger, "The Man Who Lives for Others," *Navigators Log*, October,

In the late 1970s Navigator work among the armed forces lagged behind community and collegiate evangelizing, but in the early 1980s the organization began to reemphasize its military ministry. By 1984 the number of Navigator staff whose primary ministry was to military personnel had doubled to over seventy since 1977. Participation in Navigator-led Bible studies registered a corresponding increase, particularly in Europe, where Navigators operated on United States bases in England, Spain, Italy, Turkey, and West Germany. In the last named country, the number of men attending weekly Bible studies increased from 150 in 1981 to over 750 in 1985.[19]

The Officers' Christian Union (OCU), founded in 1943 and renamed the Officers' Christian Fellowship in 1972, developed out of a Bible study group that met in Washington, D.C., during World War II. The group included General Hayes Kroner, who became the first president of the new organization. After the war, when demobilization began thinning the ranks of likely members of senior rank, the OCU decided to focus its evangelizing efforts on the midshipmen and cadets of the service academies. By 1947, after a year of ministry at West Point and Annapolis, the OCU had persuaded forty-one cadets and midshipmen to join.[20]

By the early 1950s the OCU had acquired a nucleus of dedicated members who took seriously the objectives of the organization: "to exalt the Lord Jesus Christ in the Armed Forces, to promote Christian fellowship among all born-again members of the Armed Forces, and to lead in positive action and witnessing for Jesus Christ in the Armed Forces."[21] With the members rather than a professional staff assuming

---

1971, pp. 4–6; Bernard Thompson, "From the Air Force Academy to the World," *Navlog,* July, 1977, p. 4; Monte C. Unger, "There Is Something Different About a Citadel Man," *Navigators Log,* January, 1973, p. 5; Seto Wing Luk, "Midshipmen Who Combine Naval Tradition and Christian Discipleship," *Navlog,* July, 1975, pp. 3–4; "Navigator Military Ministries: Serving the Servicemen," *Navlog,* December–January, 1982–83, p. 15.

19. Richard S. Greene, "San Diego Military World Sparked by Navigators," *Navlog,* April–May, 1984, p. 12; Richard Greene, "Facing the Frontline in Europe," *Navlog,* April–May, 1985, pp. 10–11.

20. Robert W. Spoede, *More Than Conquerors: A History of the Officers' Christian Fellowship of the U.S.A., 1943–1983* (Englewood, Colo., 1993), 19–21, 94.

21. *Ibid.,* 33.

most of the responsibilities of ministry and outreach, the organization grew steadily throughout the decade.

By the late 1950s OCU membership had expanded to nearly two thousand, from less than a hundred in the late 1940s. Several chapters operated in the Far East and Europe, in addition to some thirty in the United States. By the end of 1962 the OCU counted almost 150 Bible study groups at home and abroad. During the Vietnam era the OCU continued its program of evangelization through outreach at the academies, Bible study groups, *Command* magazine, and "man-to-man" witnessing.[22]

In the early 1970s the OCU had a new name, Officers' Christian Fellowship, and about 2,000 regular members and 250 prayer partners, with approximately 250 local Bible study groups meeting regularly. In 1978, when the OCF celebrated its thirty-fifth anniversary, it had grown to around 3,800 members, with over 400 local Bible study groups operating at military bases and aboard ships at sea. By the mid-1980s the membership had passed 5,600 regular members and boasted over 650 local Bible study groups meeting regularly on military installations of all the services. In January, 1991, the OCF numbered 6,839 regular members and 2,231 associate members, with 42 percent coming from the army, 27 percent from the air force, 18 percent from the navy, and 4.5 percent from the Marine Corps.[23]

The Overseas Christian Servicemen's Centers originated in the early 1950s. The main purposes of the association, as stated in its constitution, were "to preach the Gospel of the Lord Jesus Christ to members of the armed forces, both those of the United States of America and of other countries" and "to establish and operate homes and centers accessible to military personnel where they may gather for fellowship and to receive instruction in spiritual matters." Some of the homes functioned like private residences where servicemen could find home-cooked meals and sleeping quarters, whereas others operated as centers providing scheduled recreational and religious activities. The focal point of both types of establishments was Bible study conducted in small groups. Other religious activities included worship services, field trips to mis-

22. *Ibid.*, 33, 41, 42, 50, 51, 69, and Chap. 6, *passim*.
23. Don Martin and Karen Martin, "Celebrating 40 Years of God's Faithfulness," *Command*, Fall, 1983, pp. 10, 21; Robert J. Phillips, "The Officer's Christian Fellowship: An Inquiry and Evaluation," *MCR*, Fall, 1991, p. 116 and n.

sionaries in the area, individual counseling, week-long Bible conferences, and evangelistic programs. By 1964 the OCSC had three homes
in the Philippines, two in Panama, one on Okinawa, and another on
Taiwan. By 1970 its military ministry had expanded to twelve centers
operating in the Canal Zone and the Far East, including one in Vietnam.
Some twenty years later the organization sponsored fifteen centers in
England and Europe, eight in Asia, one in Panama, and twelve
stateside.[24]

The Christian Military Fellowship describes itself as "a nondenominational fellowship of believers who are committed to Jesus Christ
and to carrying out the Great Commission (Matthew 28:18–20) within
the military society." It was founded in 1958 when retired lieutenant
commander Floyd Robertson, the West Coast representative of the
OCU, persuaded that organization to work with a committee of non-
commissioned officers in establishing a group called the Enlisted Men's
Christian Union. When Robertson became director of the NAE Chaplains Commission in 1960, the name was changed to the Christian Servicemen's Fellowship, operating under the auspices of the NAE. In 1977,
the group reverted to independent status and adopted its present name.
Since its founding in the late 1950s it has maintained a close relationship
with the OCF and, although its main thrust has been to the enlisted
ranks, largely patterned its ministry after that of the OCF. In the late
1980s Craig Conrad, CMF executive director, defined the organization's mission in terms similar to those used by the OCF and the Navigators: "TO WIN—TO DISCIPLE—TO EQUIP—TO WIN the members of our
population who are tasked with making the sacrifices necessary to protect the freedom we all enjoy." In addition to sponsoring Bible study
and fellowship meetings, the CMF offers its membership a worldwide
prayer network, monthly newsletters, prayer reminders and other educational and devotional literature, local and regional retreats and conferences, and a referral service linking members when they travel or
transfer.[25]

24. Wilson Gene Parks, "The History and Development of Overseas Christian
Servicemen's Centers" (Master's thesis, Fuller Theological Seminary, 1965), 7–14, 22–
25, 28, 32, 33, 40; Allan Robert Latty, "The Ministry of Overseas Christian Servicemen's Centers: A Survey and Evaluation" (M. Theology thesis, Dallas Theological
Seminary, 1970), 6, 19–23, 28, 67; *OCSC Directory of Worldwide Ministries* ([Englewood,
Colo.], 1990).
25. *"Founding Faith . . . Forging the Future"* (CMF tenth anniversary bulletin, n.p.,

Campus Crusade for Christ, founded in 1951 by Bill Bright, began evangelization of the armed forces in 1965, when it established a Military Ministry under the leadership of retired air force colonel John M. Fain. Like the Navigators, OCF, and CMF, Campus Crusade used personal evangelism and Bible study as the primary means of "discipling" individuals who in turn became "committed multipliers" winning others to Christ. Military personnel who became disciples joined a worldwide network called the Military Affiliate, whose headquarters supplied various resources to enable members to cultivate their own personal spiritual growth, as well as evangelize others, while pursuing a military career. Such resources included a referral network to help individuals keep in touch with other active Christians in the military, a book and tape service providing growth and ministry materials at discount prices, a prayer network enabling military personnel to join in prayer for the specific needs of the military around the world, and training conferences in military evangelism.[26]

Full Gospel Business Men's Fellowship International spearheaded the growth of pentecostal religion among the armed forces. Founded in the early 1950s by Armenian-American dairyman Demos Shakarian and promoted by a rising young evangelist named Oral Roberts, the organization was "fully pentecostal" in doctrine and unabashedly encouraged pentecostal practices such as baptism in the Holy Spirit, speaking in tongues, and faith healing. Initially, FGBMFI drew most of its members from pentecostal denominations such as the Assemblies of God, the Pentecostal Holiness Church, the Church of God (Cleveland, Tennessee), the International Church of the Foursquare Gospel, and the Pentecostal Church of God. But in the 1960s the Fellowship began tapping the neopentecostal or charismatic movement sweeping through the Roman Catholic and mainline Protestant churches. The result was a period of astronomical growth. By the early 1970s membership had reached three hundred thousand persons, meeting in nine hundred

[1987]); Martin and Martin, "Celebrating 40 Years of God's Faithfulness," 18–19, 22. I am indebted to Floyd Robertson, CMF founder, and Ernest E. Miller, executive director emeritus, for information on the organization.

26. Bill Bright, *Come Help Change Our World* (San Bernardino, Calif., 1979), 97; Richard Quebedeaux, *I Found It! The Story of Bill Bright and Campus Crusade* (San Francisco, 1979), 56–57, 142; *Here's Life World: Taking the Message to the Military* (San Diego, n.d.).

chapters around the world, seven hundred of them in the United States. The Fellowship's monthly periodical, *Voice*, boasted a subscription list almost double the size of the membership, and some five hundred thousand persons were being converted annually in FGBMFI-sponsored ministries.[27]

Many of the converts were military men. Like the larger membership, some of the servicemen came from pentecostal churches, while others were recruited from mainline groups. As Vinson Synan has noted, the Spirit-filled business- and professional men who constituted the Fellowship routinely appealed to members of the armed forces. Chapter meetings, banquets, and special convention dinners often highlighted the American military, as did special military issues of *Voice* magazine and military breakfasts featuring the testimonies of enlisted men as well as high-ranking officers. During the Vietnam War, the Fellowship sponsored a Far Eastern airlift which sent thirty-two FGBMFI members to South Vietnam to witness to American servicemen in Saigon and at various military bases. It also supported a Christian Center for armed forces personnel in Vung Tau. In the early 1970s FGBMFI counted a number of upper-echelon Defense Department and military men as members, including James E. Johnson, assistant secretary of the navy, and General Ralph E. Haines, commanding general of the U.S. Continental Army Command, both of whom became well-known as speakers at Full Gospel rallies and dinners.[28]

Notwithstanding their different origins and emphases, all of these associations, denominations, and parachurch groups shared a common orientation. As born-again Christians, their members regarded the Bible as "the supreme and all-sufficient authority in faith and life" and felt compelled to carry out the Great Commission given by Jesus Christ.[29] It was these evangelicals, both civilian and military, who became the missionaries to the armed forces during the half-century following World War II.

27. Vinson Synan, *Under His Banner* (Costa Mesa, Calif., 1992), 11, 53–54, 81, 87, 103–105, 119.

28. *Ibid.*, 79–80, 132–33; "A Vision for Viet Nam," *Voice*, July–August, 1968, p. 25.

29. "Article III. Statement of Doctrines [from OCU Constitution]," *Command*, 25th Anniversary Issue [1968], p. 10.

3

Securing a Beachhead
in the Federal Government

In the 1940s and 1950s, when evangelicals began their quest for a role in shaping American public policy, they concentrated on winning recognition from and access to the federal government. One of the purposes behind the formation of the NAE in 1942 was to lessen the federal government's reliance on the theologically liberal Federal Council of Churches, particularly, as we saw in Chapter 1, its chaplain-endorsing agency, the General Commission on Chaplains. Thus William Ward Ayer, in an address to the NAE organizing conference, complained that the federal government seemed to "recognize only three great divisions in religion—Catholic, Jew, Protestant" and that whenever it sought to work with them, the Federal Council "steps forth and claims to be the official representative of all Protestant churches" and the government "gladly does business" with it. Even though the Federal Council served as the official spokesman for twenty-two denominations, it certainly did not represent "the great body of evangelical Christians in faith and doctrine," Ayer insisted. The NAE was set up to do that—to act as evangelicals' representative to the government and express their collective view on public policy. The two NAE agencies established to carry out that assignment were the Chaplains Commission, which negotiated with the government in matters relating to the moral and religious welfare of the armed forces, and the Office of Public Affairs, which monitored and lobbied the government on national issues of interest to conservative Christians.[1]

1. Joel Allan Carpenter, "The Renewal of American Fundamentalism, 1930–1945" (Ph.D. dissertation, Johns Hopkins University, 1984), 184, 186, 190, 207, 209; William Ward Ayer, "Evangelical Christianity Endangered by Its Fragmentized Condition," in

The Truman administration was not particularly receptive to evangelicals, but the 1952 election placed in the presidency a man whom evangelicals came to identify as one of their own and who advanced their cause by lending it not only personal support but the prestige of his office.

Billy Graham played a crucial role in forging the link between evangelicals and Dwight Eisenhower. Following Eisenhower's election, he told his "Hour of Decision" radio audience: "It has been my privilege during the past year to talk with Mr. Eisenhower on two occasions. I have been deeply impressed by his sincerity, humility, and tremendous grasp of world affairs. I also sense a dependence on God. He told me on both occasions that the hope of building a better America lay in a spiritual revival." Also encouraging, Graham added, "is that he is taking advice from some genuine, born-again Christians." Chief among them was Graham himself. Though he had not formally endorsed Eisenhower, he had encouraged the general to run for the presidency, and during the campaign he had advised him about joining a church and reinforced his decision to offer a prayer at the inauguration. The Sunday following the ceremony, Graham declared, "The overwhelming majority of the American people felt a little more secure realizing that we have a man who believes in prayer at the helm of our government at this crucial hour." Throughout Eisenhower's eight years in office, Graham continued to portray him as sympathetic to evangelical religion and praise him for the "spiritual revival" he supposedly helped bring about during his administration.[2]

Another prominent clergyman who encouraged evangelicals to believe that Eisenhower was one of their own was his pastor at the National Presbyterian Church, the Reverend Edward L. R. Elson.

Evangelical Action! A Report of the Organization of the National Association of Evangelicals for United Action, comp. and ed. National Association of Evangelicals Executive Committee (Boston, 1942), 42–43.

2. William G. McLoughlin, Jr., *Billy Graham: Revivalist in a Secular Age* (New York, 1960), 96, 117, 118; Mark Silk, *Spiritual Politics: Religion and America Since World War II* (New York, 1988), 68; Marshall Frady, *Billy Graham: A Parable of American Righteousness* (Boston, 1979), 255–57; Richard V. Pierard, "Billy Graham and the U.S. Presidency," *Journal of Church and State*, XXII (Winter, 1980), 115–16; "Graham Visits President," *UEA*, February, 1961, p. 28. See also William Martin, *A Prophet with Honor: The Billy Graham Story* (New York, 1991), 147–49, 151, 207–10; *NYT*, November 4, 1953, p. 23, March 7, 1958, p. 15.

Although the former army chaplain was a member of a mainline denomination (the United Presbyterian Church, U.S.A.) and the National Council of Churches, he was also a founder and contributing editor of the newly established evangelical magazine *Christianity Today*. In the best-seller *America's Spiritual Recovery* (1954), he appealed to and identified himself with "evangelical Christians" and declared that Americans "must return in a very real and earnest way to the basic principles of American life as expressed in evangelical Christianity." As "the President's Pastor" he continually praised Eisenhower's "masculine Christian testimony," his doctrinal fidelity, and his "disciplined habits of worship." For Elson, the president served as both the symbol and exemplar of a new "religious spirit in Washington" as well as the religious awakening sweeping the country as a whole. The dedication of *America's Spiritual Recovery* lauded Eisenhower as a man "who by personal example and public utterance is giving testimony to the reality of America's spiritual foundations." The president, Elson declared in the book, had "brought a new moral tone and spiritual virility into American life" and thus had become "the focal point of a moral resurgence and spiritual awakening of national proportions."[3]

To be sure, Eisenhower had not been particularly religious during his military career, and some evangelicals may have been put off by the nonsectarian character of the religion he exhibited as a candidate and, later, as president. He espoused a "religion in general" that embraced all of the major American faith groups, and he became famous for his statement, "Our Government has no sense unless it is founded in a deeply felt religious faith and I don't care what it is." No wonder *United Evangelical Action* noted that the prayer Eisenhower offered at his inauguration was "weak in the formalities of diction and orthodoxy." Nevertheless, the magazine went on to stress how impressed it was with the new president: with his "godly sincerity," his decision to open cabinet meetings with prayer, and that during the inauguration, he had placed his hands on two Bibles as he took the oath of office. Significantly, the magazine reported, one of the Bibles had been opened to evangelicals' favorite Scripture passage, 2 Chronicles 7:14: "If my people

3. *Current Biography Yearbook, 1967* (New York, 1967, 1968), 107–10; Edward L. R. Elson, *Wide Was His Parish* (Wheaton, Ill., 1986), 128; Edward L. R. Elson, *America's Spiritual Recovery* (Westwood, N.J., 1954), 53, 56–57, 90, 111, 186; *NYT*, June 24, 1957, p. 17, March 12, 1956, p. 24, May 23, 1955, p. 12.

which are called by my name, shall humble themselves and pray, and seek my face, and turn from their wicked ways; then will I hear from heaven and will forgive their sin and will heal their land." The magazine also quoted a statement Eisenhower made to members of the Washington Ministerial Union and Ministerial Alliance when they paid a courtesy call to the White House. Turning to a group of chaplains accompanying the clergymen, the president said: "I occasionally have had quarrels with chaplains. It was always because they were too diffident in their preaching. I think they should have been a little more belligerent in what they had to say." Didn't his endorsement of "militant preachers and chaplains" sound like a recommendation of the very kind of preaching evangelicals believed necessary to bring about the spiritual and moral renewal of America?[4]

Eisenhower's penchant for invoking religious and moral notions similar to those uttered by their own religious leaders also helped him win evangelicals' approval and reinforced their image of him as a fellow believer. An example is Eisenhower's definition of the Cold War as a moral and spiritual struggle and his call for a religious awakening as the principal means of winning it. In a speech to the directors of the Freedoms Foundation in December, 1952, he declared: "The great struggle of our times is one of spirit. It is a struggle for the hearts and souls of men—not merely for property, or even merely for power. It is a contest for the beliefs, the convictions, the very innermost soul of the human being." He insisted that "if we are to be strong we must be strong first in our spiritual convictions. . . . If we are going to win this fight we have got to go back to the very fundamentals of all things." Shortly after taking office as president, Eisenhower asserted his "unshakable belief that it is only through religion that we can lick this thing called communism." Statements like these echoed the views Billy Graham, Harold John Ockenga, and other evangelicals trumpeted in their sermons and revival campaigns—that the American-Soviet struggle was above all a

---

4. *NYT*, December 23, 1952, p. 16; "Good Beginning," *UEA*, February 15, 1953, p. 15; "Eisenhower Calls for 'Militant' Preachers," *UEA*, July 1, 1953, p. 8. Stephen Ambrose and other historians characterize Eisenhower's faith as nondenominational civil religion. See Stephen E. Ambrose, *Eisenhower: The President* (New York, 1984), 38; Richard V. Pierard and Robert D. Linder, *Civil Religion and the Presidency* (Grand Rapids, 1988), 192–205. But for the opposing view, along with an explanation of Eisenhower's appropriation of civil religion, see Elson, *Wide Was His Parish*, 132–33.

spiritual struggle "for the minds of men" and that only a "genuine spiritual revival" would ensure victory over atheistic communism.[5]

Other pronouncements by Eisenhower reminded evangelicals of their notion of the United States as a nation in covenant with God—a "nation under God," as the phrase added to the Pledge of Allegiance in 1954 stated. *United Evangelical Action* quoted him as saying that "all free government is soundly based on religious faith." Such a declaration sounded very much like those evangelicals heard from Billy Graham: "If you would be a true patriot, then become a Christian. If you would be a loyal American, then become a loyal Christian." It also echoed articles they read in *United Evangelical Action.* In a 1957 editorial the magazine observed that Americans "look upon the USA as a Covenant nation. From its beginnings to the present hour its leaders have recognized their dependence upon God and their respect to God. They believe He is the source of all human freedoms. . . . As a Covenant nation we recognize the necessity of putting God and His purposes first and we believe that the highest role our nation can play is to reflect His righteous will in national and international policy."[6]

Admittedly, Eisenhower's rhetoric about the struggle against communism and America's covenant with God was a staple of what Mark Silk calls the "spiritual politics" of the postwar era.[7] Many of his views reflected those of a majority of the American people, not just evangelicals. So did his support of "religion in general" in the midst of the religious awakening of the 1950s. But it is also true that besides expressing views many evangelicals shared, Eisenhower allowed himself to be enlisted in specifically evangelical enterprises. This, added to the image promoted by men such as Graham and Elson, not only provided further encouragement to conservative Christians who claimed him as an evangelical; it also conferred the blessing of the president of the United States on evangelical religion.

One of these evangelical enterprises was the 1953 March of Freedom. The brainchild of the NAE, the march was originally proposed by Carl F. H. Henry. Nevertheless, NAE leaders shrewdly publicized it as a

5. *NYT,* December 23, 1952, p. 16, April 10, 1953, p. 12; McLoughlin, *Billy Graham,* 143; Harold John Ockenga, "The World Challenge to the Churches," *UEA,* July 15, 1954, p. 22.

6. "Eisenhower Calls for 'Militant' Preachers," 8; Winthrop S. Hudson, *Religion in America* (3rd ed.; New York, 1981), 387; "Covenant Nation," *UEA,* July 1, 1957, p. 7.

7. Silk, *Spiritual Politics.*

response to a plea by none other than the president of the United States. Writing in the April, 1953, *Reader's Digest,* Stanley High declared, "What President Eisenhower wants for America is a revival of religious faith that will produce a rededication to religious values and conduct." NAE officials seized upon the article and portrayed the March of Freedom, a year-long campaign to proclaim the Gospel to the American people, as the fulfillment of that wish.[8]

The NAE also persuaded the president to participate in the ceremony launching the March of Freedom. Senator Frank Carlson of Kansas and Congressman Walter H. Judd of Minnesota, both good friends of Eisenhower, invited him on behalf of the organization. In the ceremony held on July 2, in Washington, D.C., Eisenhower signed a "Declaration of Seven Divine Freedoms" (also referred to as a "Declaration of Dependence upon God"), which affirmed that "the heritage of freedom which we cherish as Americans is from God" and listed seven "divine freedoms" derived from the Twenty-third Psalm: freedom from want, hunger, thirst, sin, fear, and enemies and freedom to live abundantly.[9]

NAE leaders did not hide the self-serving motives behind the March of Freedom. It provided an occasion for them to display their representation in the federal government. "Many of our outstanding government

8. Stanley High, "What the President Wants," *Reader's Digest,* April, 1953, p. 2; "'March of Freedom' Growing Movement," *UEA,* July 1, 1953, p. 7; R. L. Decker, "The March of Freedom," *UEA,* July 1, 1953, pp. 3, 4.

9. James DeForest Murch, "NAE's 'March of Freedom' Launched in Washington," *UEA,* August 1, 1953, p. 3; "A Declaration of Seven Divine Freedoms," *UEA,* August 1, 1953, p. 3. In addition to the president of the United States, the NAE enlisted the support of other prominent politicians and business leaders who made up a Citizens' Sponsoring Committee, headed by Senator Frank Carlson of Kansas. They included Governor Sigurd Anderson of South Dakota; H. A. Bullis, chairman of the board, General Mills Corporation, Minneapolis; Senator Paul Douglas of Illinois; Senator Ralph E. Flanders of Vermont; Paul Harvey of the American Broadcasting Company; Congressman Walter H. Judd of Minnesota; Charles E. Kellogg, publisher of the *Norwalk Hour,* Norwalk, Connecticut; Governor Arthur B. Langlie of Washington; V. J. Lee, chairman of the board, Convac Corporation, Cleveland, Ohio; Herbert J. Lorber, president, Rollins, Burdick, Hunter Company, Chicago; F. O. Masten, cotton grower, Sudan, Texas; Bradshaw Mintener, vice-president, Pillsbury Mills, Minneapolis; Governor Theodore McKeldin of Maryland; J. L. McCaffrey, president, International Harvester Corporation; Fred Poor, chairman of the board, Poor and Company, Chicago; Congressman Percy Priest of Tennessee; Senator Charles Tobey of New Hampshire; Luther Youngdahl, U.S. judge of the District of Columbia; and William A. Petterson, president of United Airlines, Chicago. See Murch, "NAE's 'March of Freedom,'" 5.

officials from, and including, the President on down, are earnest, evangelical Christians," Executive Director R. L. Decker asserted, noting that the march would give them an opportunity "to express their individual faith and convictions." Eisenhower did not disappoint the NAE leaders in this regard. *United Evangelical Action* editor James DeForest Murch, who attended the opening March of Freedom ceremony, commented: "Although the President of the United States must represent citizens of all religious faiths and those of no faith equally under the Constitution, nevertheless Mr. Eisenhower gave a clear-cut Christian testimony to our delegation. . . . We have a Chief Executive who is sincerely seeking to be God's man in government in this crucial hour in the history of the world." Echoing Billy Graham's postinaugural declaration, Murch added, "And that should make every American citizen thank God and take courage!"[10]

Evangelicals also anticipated that the march would publicize and win respect for evangelical religion nationally. Decker urged fellow Christians to use the march as a "pulpit" from which to proclaim "to the whole land" that "it is not just faith for faith's sake, but the evangelical faith in the sufficient Saviour Jesus Christ . . . which lies at the foundation of our freedom." Such proclamations, Murch agreed, uttered at the multitude of March of Freedom breakfasts, dinners, days of prayer, and mass meetings scheduled for the coming year and printed in the hundreds of thousands of publications to be distributed nationwide, would publicize "the evangelical Christian philosophy of government" on an unprecedented scale. "In this and countless other ways the Nation will be made conscious, as never before, of the evangelical viewpoint." Given their objective, it is no wonder that evangelical leaders crowed about the publicity the march received as a result of Eisenhower's participation. "The AP, UP, INS and other agencies covered the President's act and the NAE's program in a truly marvelous way," Murch wrote. Newspapers gave it "double-column spreads," television and radio networks provided "spot coverage," and stations in Washington, D.C., broadcast special programs that included interviews with NAE leaders.[11]

10. Decker, "The March of Freedom," 4; "God and Government," *UEA*, August 1, 1953, p. 11.

11. Decker, "The March of Freedom," 4; Murch, "NAE's 'March of Freedom,'" 4, 5. See also "'March of Freedom' Growing Movement," 7. The *New York Times* was

Another evangelical enterprise to which Eisenhower gave his blessing was International Christian Leadership (ICL), which also figured in evangelicals' strategy to gain influence in the federal government. Founded by Abraham Vereide, a Norwegian immigrant, ICL sponsored prayer breakfasts for civic and business leaders throughout the United States. In the early 1940s it established headquarters in Washington, D.C., and organized the Congressional Prayer Breakfast and two breakfast groups made up of members of the Senate and House of Representatives who met weekly for Bible study, discussion, and prayer. During the late 1940s and early 1950s, ICL continued to focus its ministry on government officials and workers, not only in the legislative but the other branches of the government. Through one-on-one evangelizing, breakfast, luncheon, and fireside groups, a speakers' bureau, and annual conferences on topics such as "Living Christianity Versus Militant Materialism," ICL developed an effective network of evangelical Christians, both civilian and military, in the federal government. Lieutenant General Willard S. Paul served as president of ICL in the 1950s; others involved in ICL during that decade included Chief Justice Earl Warren, Deputy Secretary of Defense Robert Anderson, and Senators Stuart Symington, Walter H. Judd, and Frank Carlson.[12]

In February, 1953, Senator Carlson invited Eisenhower to participate in a meeting of the Senate Breakfast Group. According to Drew Pearson, who broke the story in the *Washington Post*, the president, being "a great believer in prayer," accepted, and Carlson then got in touch with Conrad Hilton, who offered the Mayflower Hotel for the occasion. What would have been a small group of ten to fifteen senators and Eisenhower turned into the first presidential prayer breakfast (later

---

more restrained than the newspapers Murch referred to; it printed a story on the signing ceremony in a small box on page 4. See *NYT*, July 3, 1953, p. 4. The story in the *Washington Post*, July 3, 1954, p. 11, was slightly longer and featured a larger headline.

12. On ICL activities in Washington, D.C., see Norman Grubb, *Modern Viking: The Story of Abraham Vereide, Pioneer in Christian Leadership* (Grand Rapids, 1961), 109–36; J. Edwin Orr, *Good News in Bad Times: Signs of Revival* (Grand Rapids, 1953), 88–90; "God at the Nation's Capital," *UEA*, March 15, 1946, pp. 8–9; "NRB Joins ICL in 'Spiritual Offensive,'" *UEA*, January 15, 1955, pp. 16–17; Elson, *America's Spiritual Recovery*, 165; A. Roy Eckardt, *The Surge of Piety in America: An Appraisal* (New York, 1958), 46; Richard V. Pierard, "Cacophony on Capitol Hill: Evangelical Voices in Politics," in *The Political Role of Religion in the United States*, ed. Stephen D. Johnson and Joseph B. Tamney (Boulder, Colo., 1986), 78–79.

called the national prayer breakfast), attended by some five hundred persons. The crowd included cabinet members, Supreme Court justices, members of Congress, and representatives of foreign nations, as well as delegates to the annual conference of ICL, which was meeting on the same day. Billy Graham cut short a vacation in Miami to attend.[13]

Of course, Eisenhower's attendance at the breakfast guaranteed a large crowd. The president spoke only briefly and, unlike other speakers on the program, in a nonsectarian vein, neatly condensing his oft-expressed notions about the religious basis of "free government." Still, the mere fact of his participation and the blessing it implied generated publicity that evangelicals welcomed for their cause. As ICL historian Norman Grubb observed a few years later, it not only "put prayer . . . on the front page of the newspapers" but focused national attention on the ICL and its work.[14]

The 1950s proved to be a crucial decade for evangelicals. The activities sponsored by the March of Freedom and ICL in Washington, D.C., demonstrate the headway evangelicals made in establishing a presence in the nation's capital and gaining access to the federal government. In turn, the official, public recognition they received from President Eisenhower as well as other government leaders helped them win the attention of the media and the American people as a whole.

In the military, too, evangelicals scored similar success. As the next two chapters will show, General William K. Harrison in the U.S. Army and John C. Broger in the Defense Department played major roles in helping them gain prominence and influence for their faith in the armed forces.

13. Drew Pearson, "Ike to Attend Breakfast Prayer," *Washington Post*, February 3, 1953, p. 33; *Washington Post*, February 6, 1953, p. 1; *NYT*, February 6, 1953, p. 6.

14. *Congressional Record*, XCIX (83rd Cong., 1st Sess.), A573; Grubb, *Modern Viking*, 128.

4

William K. Harrison, "The Bible-Reading General"

In the late 1940s and early 1950s, when evangelicals began their mission to the armed forces, they counted very few high-ranking military leaders as nationally known spokesmen. One was William K. Harrison, Jr., an army general who publicly identified himself as a Bible-believing Christian and who became what his biographer D. Bruce Lockerbie calls evangelicals' "first highly visible 'born-again' celebrity."[1] Harrison won the admiration, even adulation, of conservative Christians as much for his high military rank and national prominence as for his endorsement of evangelical religion.

Evangelicals first discovered Harrison in occupied Japan, where he was serving under General Douglas MacArthur. As supreme commander for the Allied Powers, MacArthur aggressively promoted Christianity in occupied Japan by facilitating extensive missionary work on the part of American religious groups and encouraging the distribution of millions of Bibles and Testaments by such organizations as the American Bible Society and the Pocket Testament League. Harrison was in full accord with MacArthur's encouragement of Christian evangelism in Japan. "No question about it," he said later, "General MacArthur reopened Japan to Christianity." Harrison and his wife became acquainted with many of the Christian missionaries who came to Japan, entertained them in their Tokyo home, and introduced them to chaplains and others in the military who could help them in their work. The

1. D. Bruce Lockerbie, *A Man Under Orders: Lieutenant General William K. Harrison, Jr.* (San Francisco, 1979), 178.

missionaries appreciated the support Harrison provided for their evangelistic crusades in and around Tokyo.[2]

In September, 1950, Harrison became commanding general of the 9th Infantry Training Division at Fort Dix. Back in the United States, he found himself, according to Lockerbie, "becoming something of a religious celebrity." The American missionaries who had worked with him in Japan "had brought back accounts of meeting a high-ranking officer who was also a confessing Christian." Harrison received numerous invitations to appear at youth rallies and to speak on national broadcasts and at Bible conferences and revival campaigns. After one radio appearance, on which he gave his personal testimony, the American Tract Society asked him about publishing it. Harrison agreed, and the resulting tract, *The General Speaks*, received wider circulation than any previously published by the society. More than a million copies were distributed during the first year, and it was translated into several foreign languages and reprinted in newspapers and magazines.[3]

Harrison gained national attention in May, 1952, when he succeeded Vice-Admiral Charles Turner Joy as head of the Allied delegation negotiating with the communists for an armistice in Korea. The story made the front page of the *New York Times*, which described the fifty-six-year-old major general as "deeply religious" and added that he "does not swear, drink or smoke." According to the story, Harrison's "penchant for solitary Bible-reading" was well-known. *Time* magazine described him as "a Baptist who occasionally preaches at G.I. services" and "a man given to solitary prayer and meditation." Headlines in other American newspapers identified Harrison as "a Lay Minister" or "Two-Star Evangelist." Some reporters called him "deeply religious," while others labeled him "the Bible-reading General," noting his abstinence from liquor, tobacco, and barracks humor. That he preached at an Easter sunrise service was also duly noted.[4]

The publicity Harrison received as senior delegate at the Panmunjom

2. Harrison was executive for economic affairs and, later, chief of the Reparations Section, Allied Powers' General Headquarters, under MacArthur. See Lawrence S. Wittner, "MacArthur and the Missionaries: God and Man in Occupied Japan," *Pacific Historical Review*, XL (February, 1971), 77–98; Lockerbie, *A Man Under Orders*, 130, 134, 135.

3. Lockerbie, *A Man Under Orders*, 136, 138, 139.

4. *NYT*, May 20, 1952, pp. 1, 3; "War in Korea," *Time*, June 2, 1952, p. 24; Lockerbie, *A Man Under Orders*, 5, 154, 155.

talks, along with his promotions in rank (in 1952, to lieutenant general and deputy commanding general of the United States Army Forces, Far East, and finally, in the spring of 1954, to commander-in-chief of the Caribbean), made him even more attractive to evangelicals as a spokesman for their cause. In the midst of the Cold War, at a time when many Americans perceived themselves engaged in a spiritual struggle between Christianity and atheism, the fact that Harrison was both a military man and a Christian seemed especially appropriate. Moreover, as Lockerbie points out, in the 1950s, in contrast to later decades, there were no nationally known entertainers, politicians, or sports figures who were identified as evangelicals. No wonder "the evangelical community seemed eager to bask in his fame."[5]

Harrison's religious faith had developed during early childhood. In an article entitled "My Life as a Christian in the United States Army," he noted that he was "born in a Christian family" and was brought up in the "nurture and admonition of the Lord." His father, a navy commander and a devout Christian, served as a deacon in the First Baptist Church in Washington, D.C., while working in the Navy Department and often taught Bible classes on his ships. His mother was an Episcopalian, and Harrison was christened and later attended confirmation classes at St. Margaret's Episcopal Church. He remained a communicant in the Episcopal Church until the late 1920s. When he and his wife went to Fort Riley, Kansas, in 1927, there were no chapel services on the base, so they decided to attend the nearby Episcopal church. But the rector "had nothing to offer as a pastor," Harrison said. The Harrisons looked for and began attending a Baptist church, and eventually the whole family was baptized and joined the First Baptist Church of Junction City, Kansas, where they continued to worship for the next five years. Harrison did a preaching stint there during a six-month period when the church lacked a pastor, and he also taught Bible study on Wednesday evenings.[6]

5. Lockerbie, *A Man Under Orders*, 164, 177–78.

6. William K. Harrison, Jr., "My Life as a Christian in the United States Army," 8 (originally published in the *Sunday School Times*, 1950), in Appendix E: Articles on Christianity in the Military by Lieutenant General William K. Harrison, Jr., USA, Retired, in U.S. Army Military History Institute, "Senior Officers Oral History Program: Project 81-B, William K. Harrison, Jr., USA, Retired, Interviewed by Robert N. Mathis, Colonel, ADA, 1981" (3 vols.; typescript in William K. Harrison, Jr., Papers, U.S. Army Military History Institute, Carlisle Barracks, Pa., hereafter cited as Harrison Oral His-

Harrison was one of those evangelicals, increasingly rare by the
1960s, who did not specifically identify the moment of his conversion.
"Although many persons can recall the exact moment when they were
converted, I cannot remember any time when I did not believe in Jesus
Christ," he wrote in "My Life as a Christian in the U.S. Army." "I must
have made a decision when I was very young," he told a writer for *Moody
Monthly*, "but I do not remember any special incident."[7]

He took his evangelical faith with him to West Point, where he was
a member of the class of 1917. Brigadier General Harold Jackson, remembering their days at the academy, recalled that Harrison "read his
Bible every day." He does not seem to have felt particularly uncomfortable in the worldly environment of the academy, although he remembered that he and a few other cadets who were reputed to pray or
read the Bible or who identified themselves as believers "were known,
slangily, but in a friendly sense, as 'hell dodgers.'" Chapel attendance
was required, but Harrison later said that he did not remember gaining
"any particular spiritual blessing" from it. West Point was, after all, a
"secular institution" and thus spiritually lacking from his point of view.
There were no formal organizations for cadets who wished to engage
in prayer or Bible study. Harrison, however, taught a Bible class in one
of the barracks rooms and became a member of a group of cadets who
visited the home of Susan Warner, who taught them the Bible and
served them tea.[8]

Besides the Bible, Harrison's other favorite book at West Point, according to General Jackson, was G. F. R. Henderson's *Stonewall Jackson
and the American Civil War*. The life of the Confederate general whose
religious zeal and aggressive fighting spirit evoked comparisons with
Oliver Cromwell ("another Cromwell without Cromwell's ambition,"
Henderson wrote) clearly had a great influence on the pious cadet. Significantly, the Stonewall Jackson portrayed in the Henderson biography
was not the legendary zealot who led religious meetings among his
troops, distributed tracts, and took over the pulpits of his chaplains.
Jackson's "devout habits"—prayer and Bible reading and attendance at

tory); Lockerbie, *A Man Under Orders*, 19, 46–47; Tom Watson, "Three-Star General
Under Higher Orders," *Moody Monthly*, November, 1969, p. 34.

7. Harrison, "My Life," 8; Watson, "Three-Star General," 34. See also Harrison
Oral History, I, 93.

8. Lockerbie, *A Man Under Orders*, 29, 30; Harrison, "My Life," 8, 9.

worship services—were well-known in camp, Henderson pointed out, but he was not a proselytizer. However accurate Henderson's portrayal may have been, it was the Jackson he described whom Harrison emulated during his military career. He must have been especially influenced by the way, according to Henderson, "Jackson's religion entered into every action of his life," and by his avowed dependence upon God. Jackson's favorite maxim, Henderson pointed out, was "Duty is ours, consequences are God's." Harrison, who in later years would publish articles delineating the character of the Christian soldier, took as his own exemplar a general described as "the very model of a Christian gentleman."[9]

Although Harrison was not able to date precisely his conversion experience, he did describe two occasions when he agonized over the compatibility of his Christian faith and a military career. The first time was in 1926, during a tour of duty in the Philippines. The details of the story varied as he told and retold it, but the outline remained the same. He remembered it vividly fifty-five years later during an interview for the U.S. Army Military History Institute's Senior Officers Oral History Program:

> Out in the Philippines in 1926, I guess it was, I was studying the Bible one time and all of a sudden I was overwhelmed by the conviction that I was to leave the Army and become a missionary out there. Christ said to me to be His witness, you know. Well, that was a shock to me. All I had was my pay and a wife and two little kids. I didn't know anything at all about being a missionary. It never entered my mind, anything but soldiering. Well, I was so overwhelmed that I got down on my knees and I told the Lord, I said, "This is my problem. I don't know anything about it and this is all I've got, but I can depend on You. If You want me to go, I'll go." And while I was still on my knees—I knew I was to look at the Bible. So I just flipped it open like that, I wasn't looking for anything I just glanced at the page. And I only saw one thing; First Corinthians 12:29 and it says: "They are not all Apostles, are they; they are not all Prophets, are they; or teachers." And as I read that, I knew I was to stay in the Army and be a soldier.[10]

9. Lockerbie, *A Man Under Orders*, 29; Lieutenant Colonel G. F. R. Henderson, C.B., *Stonewall Jackson and the American Civil War* (2 vols.; New York, 1903), II, 494, 495, I, 444, 442n, 61, 72.

10. Harrison Oral History, I, 96–97. See also Harrison, "My Life," 10; Lockerbie, *A Man Under Orders*, 45–46; Watson, "Three-Star General," 36.

The second ordeal occurred around 1930, during his first year on the faculty at Fort Leavenworth. "Pacifism was rampant, particularly in certain denominations," Harrison remembered, and he felt "bombarded by pacifist tracts and pamphlets by various church-related organizations." He could not avoid dealing with the issues the pacifists raised about war and his chosen vocation. In his Officers' Christian Union tract *May a Christian Serve in the Military?*, written many years later, he alluded to his ordeal and the quest it prompted. "As it must to every Christian soldier, this question presented itself to me. It was something that could not be ignored, but had to be solved." Turning to the Bible for answers, he found instances where "war was commanded by God to the Israelites" and "men of God" were soldiers (Abraham, Joshua, and David in the Old Testament and the four centurions in the New Testament). All of his investigations convinced him of the compatibility of his Christian faith and service in the armed forces: "After considerable study of the Scriptures . . . I became convinced that while I as a Christian should love my enemy and pray for him, turning the other cheek as necessary, yet the use of force by communities and government is ordained of God to protect the rights of individuals and also society in a world where dishonesty, cruelty, and hate are so prevalent."[11] The question never troubled him again; indeed, in later life, Harrison wrote several articles defending warfare and military service in addition to the tract published by the OCU.

Harrison believed that just as God had shown him the way out of each of the two ordeals by guiding him to passages in the Bible that answered his questions about the compatibility of soldiering and Christianity, so he guided and protected him throughout the remainder of his military career. During World War II, he served as assistant division commander of the 30th Infantry Division, also known as the "Old Hickory" Division, which spearheaded the Allied breakout from Normandy at St.-Lô in July, 1944, and continued on through the Low Countries and across the Rhine. His men called him the most fearless man they had ever known. "I just trusted God," he explained in the Military His-

11. William K. Harrison and W. Robert Smith, "Christian Perspectives on War," 4, in Harrison Oral History, III, Appendix E; Harrison Oral History, I, 101; Harrison, "My Life," 10; William K. Harrison, Jr., *May a Christian Serve in the Military?* (Englewood, Colo., N.d.), 1, 2, 3. See also William K. Harrison, Jr., "May a Christian Be a Soldier?" [*Command*, 25th Anniversary Issue, 1968], p. 25, in Harrison Oral History, III, Appendix E.

tory Institute interview, echoing Stonewall Jackson: "God has a time and a place for me and I knew that until he wanted to take me it couldn't happen. . . . I didn't have anything to worry about, I was in His hands. If He wanted to take me because it was my time He'd take me and that was it, and I knew that if I went, where I was going. I was going to be with God because Christ died for my sins and I believed and I trusted Him." [12]

Harrison also entrusted his military career to God. He wrote in 1977 that after "God had settled the matter once and for all" in 1926, "I knew without question I was to stay a soldier, serving God in that capacity." "Because my career was purposed by God, I never asked for assignments except when required to state a preference. The Lord put me where He wanted me." During World War II and later, during the Korean War, he wanted to lead a major unit (such as a division or a corps) in wartime, but the assignment never came his way. The appointment to serve on and ultimately head the armistice delegation foiled his chance of getting a field command during the Korean War. "That ended my military career . . . because I was getting pretty old for my rank," he said many years later in the Military History Institute interview; "that was my last chance ever to get a third star." He decided God had another purpose in mind. Harrison believed, as he told Tom Watson of *Moody Monthly*, that God used the assignment to the armistice team to focus national attention on him and thereby "give my testimony as a Christian much wider attention than it would have had otherwise." [13]

Just as Harrison believed God used him to spread the Gospel, he also believed that it was his duty, as a Christian believer to whom God had given "definite guidance to remain in the Army," to serve in the military as a "servant of God, an ambassador for Christ." Before he became a celebrity-evangelical in the early 1950s, Harrison pursued his calling by witnessing to the officers and men around him. He attended chapel regularly and encouraged the ministry of chaplains, especially the relatively few "born-again," "Bible-believing" chaplains serving in the armed forces at that time. Occasionally he conducted Bible studies; he

12. Harrison Oral History, I, 83–84, and see also pp. 95–96; Lockerbie, *A Man Under Orders*, 83, 84; Harrison, "My Life," 12–13, 16.
13. Untitled article, *Command*, Spring, 1977, p. 1, in Harrison Oral History, III, Appendix E; Harrison Oral History, I, 96, 98, 99, 100; Watson, "Three-Star General," 36. See also Lockerbie, *A Man Under Orders*, 55, 135.

also preached in chapel a few times. In 1942 he contributed a brief statement for an inspirational pamphlet entitled *Fourteen Officers and Service Men Look at Life.* Harrison recalled that in the 1940s, during visits to small units and unit headquarters, while talking about the war with his men, he would use such occasions "to mention the Gospel. In such an atmosphere I believe I was able to avoid the impression of preaching at them, yet giving a testimony of what the Lord Jesus Christ means to me." He also seized opportunities to witness to individuals such as cab drivers and fellow plane passengers and, of course, to fellow soldiers. One of the veterans of the 30th Infantry Division recalled visiting Harrison in the Pentagon. "Just as I was leaving him, he asked me if I'd ever been saved. I thought back to those days at Mortain and replied, 'Yes, General Harrison, I've been saved.' His question, of course, had a deeper spiritual meaning. As I left, he handed me a small book which he had personally inscribed. He asked me to carry it with me in life and to always seek salvation." [14]

In the late 1940s, while working at the Pentagon, Harrison became involved with the Officers' Christian Union. In 1949 he joined a newly formed Pentagon Christian Fellowship Group, which was affiliated with the OCU. Later that same year he testified on Jack Wyrtzen's "Word of Life" radio program, which was broadcast from the annual OCU Army-Navy game banquet. In 1951 he spoke again at the OCU banquet, on "Service of Christ and Country." In 1954, he became president of the OCU and served in that capacity until 1972. [15]

By the time he became OCU president, Harrison had become something of a celebrity whose testimony extended beyond the confines of the army to the evangelical community. In January, 1956, his name became linked with an event that galvanized the American evangelical community, the Auca massacre in Ecuador. Five American missionaries working among the Aucas, a tribe known for its hostility to outsiders, lost contact with their home base during an expedition to one of the Auca settlements and were later discovered to have been ambushed and slaughtered. Harrison was commander in chief of the Caribbean at the

14. William K. Harrison, Jr., "Some Lessons from Experience," *Command,* September, 1957, pp. 5, 1; Wm. K. Harrison, Jr., "Leadership Session," *Command,* April, 1961, pp. 8, 16; "My Life," 11, all in Harrison Oral History, III, Appendix E; Lockerbie, *A Man Under Orders,* 123–24, 132.

15. Robert W. Spoede, *More Than Conquerors: A History of the Officers' Christian Fellowship of the U.S.A., 1943 to 1983* (Englewood, Colo., 1993), 34.

time. He was away from his headquarters in Panama, having gone to Washington for a medical examination, when the missionaries were reported missing. Upon receiving word of the incident, he authorized his chief of staff, Colonel Robert May, to coordinate a search and rescue effort using personnel from both the United States and Ecuadorian air forces. Of course, the Caribbean Command, like any other United States military command, was ready to help any Americans in difficulty within its jurisdiction. But the fact that Harrison was, as James and Marti Hefley noted, "an evangelical believer" must have seemed providential to evangelicals.[16]

Even after his retirement from the army in 1957, Harrison remained an evangelical celebrity. Besides serving as president of the OCU, he accepted appointment as executive director of the Evangelical Welfare Agency, an affiliate of the National Association of Evangelicals, which arranged adoption or foster care in Christian homes for orphaned or deserted children. He was in even more demand than before retirement as a speaker at churches, colleges, schools, and seminaries, as well as annual OCU banquets. He conducted Bible studies for military men and women at such places as Fort Leavenworth, Elmendorf Air Force Base, and the Citadel. At OCU summer camp in Colorado he taught a two-week course in the New Testament. He also served on the governing boards of evangelical schools such as the Stony Brook School and Dallas Theological Seminary.[17]

But Harrison was more than simply an evangelical celebrity valued for his high military rank and eloquent Christian testimony. During the 1950s and 1960s he became the first of a long line of "military experts" to whom evangelicals looked for information and advice on national defense policy and international relations. Conservative Christians regarded him as a man who spoke from experience and with authority about the communists and matters of war and peace and, equally important, from an evangelical perspective. In addresses to such groups as

16. Lockerbie, *A Man Under Orders*, 181; James Hefley and Marti Hefley, *Unstilled Voices* (Chappaqua, N.Y., 1981), 33. I wish to thank Mike Hamilton for calling to my attention this incident and Harrison's part in it and for supplying me with information and bibliographical leads. Besides the Hefleys and Lockerbie, see also Abe Van Der Puy, "Mission to the Aucas," *HIS*, April, 1956, pp. 5–8, 18, 23–24; and Elisabeth Elliot, *Through Gates of Splendor* (New York, 1957), 197.

17. "Gen. Harrison to Head Evangelical Welfare," *UEA*, March 1, 1957, p. 8; Lockerbie, *A Man Under Orders*, 189, 31.

the Christian Businessmen's Committee International and NAE, and in evangelical journals such as *Christianity Today* and *Eternity*, Harrison delivered essentially the same message. It was impossible to prevent war, he declared, given the sinful nature of human beings. "The real cause of war is in the sinful heart of man," he wrote. He expressed skepticism about various ways being proposed to prevent war and obtain peace: "the efforts of philosophy, the proclamation of the 'Christian ethic,' redistribution of wealth, disarmament, international organization, or published laws." Even maintaining "a powerful military force constantly ready to retaliate [against the Soviet Union] with deadly effect" he dismissed as a "faint and not very dependable hope." He explained, "An armament race causes psychological and financial tensions which cannot endure indefinitely. Eventually explosion occurs. Were the strength of nuclear armaments to give hope for victory, such a victory would be of doubtful value." The only way peace would be obtained was through God, not men, Harrison insisted. "The full and final answer to the problem of war will come with the return of Jesus Christ. With that event, peace becomes historically inevitable." In the meantime, Christians and the Christian church should work for peace and against aggression, but they must also be ready and willing to fight if necessary.[18]

During the Vietnam War, Harrison mustered similar arguments against opposition to United States intervention in Southeast Asia and criticism of the conduct of the war. In 1966, writing in *Christianity Today*, he justified American bombing of North Vietnam as strategically and morally sound. In concluding the article he returned to the theme he had been sounding since the late 1950s: "The whole problem of the war in Viet Nam is complicated by the sincere but erroneous idea that mankind can in some way bring peace to the world. . . . Wars will continue until man's rebellion runs its full course, terminating in the wars of the great tribulation at the end of this age. Only the second coming of the Lord Jesus Christ, as so often foretold in the Bible, will end the rebellion and bring an age of peace and prosperity (Matt. 24; Isa. 2:1–5)."[19]

18. Harrison, "May a Christian Be a Soldier?" 30; William K. Harrison, "Christianity and Peace in Our Day," *CT*, October, 1956, pp. 14, 15, 16; William K. Harrison, "The Search for Peace on Earth," *CT*, April 13, 1959, p. 8; James DeForest Murch, "Responsibility in Leadership and Service," *UEA*, May 15, 1955, p. 6; William K. Harrison, Jr., "Pacifism Is Not the Answer," *Eternity*, November, 1961, pp. 21–22, 50; "Gen. Harrison Replies," *Eternity*, April, 1962, p. 3.

19. William K. Harrison, "Is the United States Right in Bombing North Viet Nam?" *CT*, January 7, 1966, pp. 25–26.

As Harrison's reference to "the wars of the great tribulation at the end of this age" suggests, his perspective on war and peace included a strong element of premillennialism. Like the great majority of evangelicals in the 1950s and 1960s, he subscribed to an eschatology based on biblical prophecy which holds that the "end time" or "last days" of the present age will be a period of terrible "tribulation" culminating in the Battle of Armageddon, where the reign of Antichrist will be destroyed by the triumphant return of Christ. Premillennialists believe that Christ will then establish his millennial kingdom, which will last for a thousand years and end with the resurrection of the dead, the judgment, and the creation of a new heaven and earth. Harrison himself spent many years studying biblical prophecy and even wrote a book on the subject. In the 1950s, when he became president of the OCU, it was strongly premillennialist. The statement of doctrine which all officials were required to affirm "without mental reservation" included a belief in "the personal and imminent return of our Lord and Saviour, Jesus Christ."[20]

So it is not surprising that in the 1950s and 1960s, Harrison's premillennialist views surfaced in his addresses and articles regarding war and peace. In 1955, for example, speaking on "Christianity and War in Our Times" at the NAE convention, Harrison pointed to Bible prophecies declaring that the "period immediately preceding the end of this age and the second advent of Christ will include great wars with the

---

20. Timothy P. Weber, *Living in the Shadow of the Second Coming: American Premillennialism, 1875–1982* (Chicago, 1987), 10–11, and see Chap. 8 on premillennialism in the post–World War II period; Lockerbie, *A Man Under Orders*, 41; Spoede, *More Than Conquerors*, 26–27, 38, 190. The premillennial doctrine was part of a nine-point statement of doctrine the 1953 OCU constitution required the general secretary, all council members and elected officers, and all supervisory personnel of OCU to subscribe to. Spoede points out (p. 27) that the premillennial doctrine was phrased in such a way as to include both fundamentalist and evangelical positions but, by using the word *imminent*, to exclude adherents of modernist or liberal religion. The OCU membership was not required to subscribe to the nine-point statement; instead, it was required to subscribe to an "affirmation of faith" declaring, "Inasmuch as I am a sinner and deserve the wrath of God, and since Jesus Christ died for my sins, was buried and has been bodily resurrected, according to the Scriptures, I have accepted Him as my own personal Saviour and am saved by His grace alone" (Appendix 2: 1953 Constitution of the Officers' Christian Union, May 1, 1953, in Spoede, *More Than Conquerors*, 190). In the new constitution adopted by the OCU in 1962, the word *imminent* had been deleted from the premillennial doctrine (Spoede, *More Than Conquerors*, 51).

terrible sufferings that accompany war, famines, pestilences and death."
He stated his conviction that "the course of civilization is toward self-
destruction—only God can prevent its totality."[21]

By the late 1950s he had become even more convinced that international developments were tracking "biblical prophecies concerning
the end of the age and the second advent of Christ." Like many other
evangelicals, he endorsed the centuries-old notion that the Bible predicted a Russian attack on Israel in the "last days." It was a scenario that,
as Paul Boyer has shown, gained particular credence in the context of
the Cold War. Thus, in an article in *Christianity Today* entitled "Reminiscences and a Prophecy," Harrison reviewed the developments of the
post–World War II period that portended a breakdown of the balance
of power between the Soviet Union and the free world. (Such a breakdown was inevitable, of course, for the hope that peace would endure
was "illusory," given the sinful nature of men.) "The war that might
result when the balance becomes unequal might well be a great world
war of a destructive nature never before known to man," he wrote. "A
prize sought by that war would probably be the Near and Middle East,
one of the critical economic and strategic areas of the world today and
in the foreseeable future. Right in the vortex of the conflict would be
the land of Israel and the Jewish nation." Such statements by the man
evangelicals considered their military expert on international affairs
surely reinforced their anticipation, well documented by Boyer, of "a
global cataclysm of horrendous proportions" brought on by Soviet aggression. "For prophecy believers," Boyer observes, "the Cold War
posed not merely military, diplomatic, and ideological challenges—it
was quite literally a struggle with a power singled out by God for a
demonic end-time role."[22]

Besides offering information and advice on national defense policy
and international affairs, Harrison wrote numerous articles on the character and role of the Christian officer in the military. Though they were
often addressed specifically to members of the OCU, they surely pro-

---

21. Murch, "Responsibility in Leadership and Service," 5.
22. William K. Harrison, "Reminiscences and a Prophecy," *CT*, March 4, 1957, p.
14; Paul Boyer, *When Time Shall Be No More: Prophecy Belief in Modern American Culture*
(Cambridge, Mass., 1992), 152. See also Chap. 5; Harrison Oral History, I, 94–95, II,
286–95.

voked reflection on the part of other evangelical military persons, whether in the officer corps or enlisted ranks, who read them.

Harrison did not just contend that there was no contradiction between being a Christian and serving in the armed forces. Addressing members of the officer corps, he insisted that the principles and methods of military leadership not only were compatible with but enjoined by Christian beliefs. In a frequently reprinted article entitled "Professional Excellence for the Christian Officer," he declared that a "true believer in Christ" should not find it difficult to be a good military leader. "Such things as loyalty, diligence, self-preparation, integrity, dependableness are all necessary to Christian conduct," he pointed out. "Firmness and insistence on high standards are essential to the best achievements and fully Christian; our faith is not something for weaklings. The Golden Rule is as important and applicable for the work of the Christian military leader as in other careers."[23]

Describing the role of the Christian officer in the military, Harrison wrote,

> [He] has a dual citizenship, the first in the kingdom of God, the other in our country. As to the first we are in this world as ambassadors for Christist, bearing witness to men of the salvation which He offers to them. As to the second we are responsible for the administrative and combat efficiency of the unit which we command. These responsibilities are not mutually contradictory. A Christian soldier should serve his country faithfully, in a manner to glorify God.[24]

Harrison urged Christian officers to fulfill their duty as ambassadors for Christ through both testimony and conduct, but he emphasized conduct over testimony. "Men will scorn our Christian testimony unless our lives exhibit true Christian character," he warned in "Professional Excellence." The Christian officer must first "define what a Christian is" by exemplifying Christian virtues and practicing his religious faith,

23. William K. Harrison, Jr., "Professional Excellence for the Christian Officer," 8, in Harrison Oral History, III, Appendix E. See also William K. Harrison, Jr., "Professional Excellence" (first published in *Command*, Spring, 1965), in Harrison Oral History, III, Appendix E. The OCF also published a booklet, *Professional Excellence*, based on these articles.

24. William K. Harrison, Jr., "The Christian Officer: His Moral and Spiritual Leadership," *Command*, Spring, 1967, p. 54, in Harrison Oral History, III, Appendix E.

all the while exhibiting "the joy, inner peace and assurance" he had received through God's grace. Only then would others see "a difference between themselves and one who has genuinely committed his life to Christ and is experiencing the grace of Christ in his everyday living." Only then, he emphasized, would "what we say about Christ, about sin, and about salvation . . . mean something to unsaved men."[25]

Drawing on his own experience in advising would-be Christian disciplers, Harrison wrote, "I found it helpful not to announce aggressively that I was a Christian and by implication better than others." Perhaps he was thinking not only of his own career as a Christian officer but of his hero, Stonewall Jackson, when he warned:

> Don't try to convert. Your job is to testify only to what the Lord has done for you. Do not be concerned if you do not have opportunity to explain the entire Gospel early in your relationship with your fellow men. The time will come when the Lord will give opportunity to explain the Gospel to those who are open to it. You can safely assume that the word will get around that you have strong religious convictions, that you are a person who honors and reads the Bible. This reputation will bring men to you when they are in a time of difficulty or under conviction of the Holy Spirit.[26]

Harrison exerted an even greater and more lasting influence among military evangelicals than he did among civilians. As president of the OCU for almost twenty years and even after his retirement in 1972, he had a profound effect on the development of that organization and on the lives of many of its members. Especially in the 1950s and 1960s, at a time when few high-ranking officers publicly identified themselves as evangelicals, Harrison stood out as an exemplar of the Christian officer in the armed forces, a man who from his early days at West Point through his entire military career prayed, read the Bible, and witnessed to others and had nevertheless risen to the rank of lieutenant general and played a key role in the Korean armistice negotiations.

25. William K. Harrison, Jr., "Professional Excellence," *Command*, n.d., 47, in Harrison Oral History, III, Appendix E; Harrison, "Leadership Session," 8, 16; Harrison, "Some Lessons from Experience," 7.
26. Harrison, "Leadership Session," 8.

5

John C. Broger, Christian Cold Warrior

John C. Broger never achieved the national prominence General Harrison did, but he proved much more aggressive and influential in advancing the evangelical cause within the armed forces. For nearly thirty years he occupied a strategic position in the Pentagon, serving as deputy director (1956–1961), then director (1961–1984) of Armed Forces Information and Education (AFIE).[1] As the head of Troop Information in the late 1950s and 1960s, he played a central role in the ideological indoctrination of armed forces personnel.

Born in Nashville, Tennessee, in 1913, educated at Georgia Institute of Technology, Southern California Bible College, and Texas A&M, John Christian Broger had served as a warrant officer on board the aircraft carrier *Bon Homme Richard* in the Pacific during World War II. In 1945 he and two friends, both radio evangelists, formed the Far East Broadcasting Company (FEBC), a nonprofit, interdenominational corporation of which Broger became president. Its stated purpose was to disseminate the Gospel throughout Asia, proclaiming "the power of Christ to redeem men from sin." Using funds supplied by conservative Protestant denominations, the FEBC set up its first transmitter in Manila and went on the air in 1948. By the early 1960s the FEBC operated

1. *Military Cold War Education and Speech Review Policies: Hearings Before the Special Preparedness Subcommittee of the Committee on Armed Services, United States Senate, Eighty-Seventh Congress, Second Session* (1962), 994. The directorate for AFIE was located in the Office of the Deputy Assistant Secretary of Defense (Education and Manpower Resources). In 1968 AFIE changed its name to Armed Forces Information Service, in 1971 to Office of Information for the Armed Forces, and in 1977 back to Armed Forces Information Service.

fifteen medium and shortwave transmitters in the Philippines, Taiwan, Okinawa, and California, broadcasting to Asia, Russia, Africa, the Middle East, and Latin America in nearly forty languages and dialects.[2]

Broger came to the Defense Department with the recommendation of Admiral Arthur W. Radford, chairman of the Joint Chiefs of Staff. The two men had met in the early 1950s. Broger had impressed the admiral, himself a deeply religious man and a mainstay of the National Presbyterian Church, with his "missionary zeal for spreading Christian and American principles in the Far East." Radford also discovered in Broger someone who might be able to provide the "spiritual stiffening" soldiers, sailors, and airmen needed in the struggle against communism. That was why he hired Broger in 1954 as a consultant in the area of troop indoctrination.[3] Other military leaders shared Radford's concern, especially in the wake of the popular furor over the American prisoners of war in Korea.

When Americans learned that North Korean and Chinese communists had "brainwashed" and indoctrinated American POWs during the Korean War, that twenty-one of them had refused repatriation, and that many others had collaborated with enemy propagandists or committed serious offenses against their fellow prisoners, they concluded that the POWs had succumbed because they were not sufficiently patriotic or committed to American ideals. The two best-known advocates of this indictment of American prisoners, which was widely promulgated by the mass media, were Eugene Kinkead and Lieutenant Colonel William E. Mayer. Kinkead wrote the best-selling *In Every War But One*, and Mayer, a psychiatrist who helped interview repatriated POWs, afterward made a career of speechmaking and testifying before government hearings regarding POW behavior.[4]

2. Stephen D. Wesbrook, "Historical Notes," in *The Political Education of Soldiers*, ed. Morris Janowitz and Stephen D. Wesbrook (Beverly Hills, 1983), 266; *Military Cold War Education Hearings*, 989, 990; William Harlan Hale, "Militant Liberty and the Pentagon," *Reporter*, February 9, 1956, p. 31; Gleason H. Ledyard, *Sky Waves: The Incredible Far East Broadcasting Company Story* (Chicago, 1963), 16, 17, 18, 29–30, 39; "Far East Broadcasting Company, Inc.," in *The Encyclopedia of Modern Christian Missions* (Camden, N.J., 1967), 280; Thomas Alfred Palmer, "'Why We Fight,' A Study of Indoctrination Activities in the Armed Forces" (Ph.D. dissertation, University of South Carolina, 1971), 46–47.

3. Hale, "Militant Liberty," 31; see also Ledyard, *Sky Waves*, 178.

4. H. H. Wubben, "American Prisoners of War in Korea: A Second Look at the 'Something New in History' Theme," *American Quarterly*, XXII (Spring, 1970), 5–6;

Although the military never accepted total responsibility, as soon as the POW issue surfaced, it began revamping AFIE. In November, 1953, Assistant Secretary of Defense John A. Hannah announced a new direction for the information and education program. To ensure that American servicemen were taught simply and directly what it meant to be an American, AFIE had decided to go back to "fundamentals," with the accent on the contrast between democracy and communism. In 1955, a Defense Advisory Committee appointed by Secretary of Defense Charles Wilson recommended further enhancement of moral and citizenship training in the armed forces. In explaining the need for such action, the committee pointed to the "handicap" under which American POWs in Korea had operated. "Many of the POWs knew too little about the United States and its ideals and traditions. So the Chinese indoctrinators had the advantage," the committee observed. To the committee, "It seemed that these POWs . . . had lost their battle before they entered the Service. Good citizens—loyal Americans—the responsibility for their building lies with the home, the school, the church, the community. When men enter the Armed Forces, the Military Services must carry on with this development." Thus the committee emphasized the responsibility of both the armed services and the civilian community to erect "spiritual and educational bulwarks against enemy political indoctrination."[5]

In effect, the Defense Advisory Committee concluded that mere patriotism would no longer serve as a sufficient weapon in "the worldwide war for the minds of men." An ideology strong enough to defeat that of the communists was needed. By the mid-1950s numerous government and military leaders shared that view. As Thomas Palmer has pointed out, "There were officials who felt that one of the great advantages of the communists in the Cold War was the possession of a clearly enunciated ideology. One of the major reasons for Soviet and Red Chinese 'victories,' so this reasoning went, was that the communists had

---

Wesbrook, "Historical Notes," 264; Morris Janowitz, "Civic Consciousness and Military Performance," in *The Political Education of Soldiers*, ed. Janowitz and Wesbrook, 65. Albert D. Biderman, *March to Calumny: The Story of American POW's in the Korean War* (New York, 1963), concluded that lack of political indoctrination was not a major cause of American POW misconduct.

5. *NYT*, November 8, 1953, p. 6; "Report of the Defense Advisory Committee on Prisoners of War," in *The U.S. Fighting Man's Code* ([Washington, D.C.], 1955), 12–13. See also *NYT* (editorial), November 5, 1953, Sec. 4, p. 10.

ready, even though spurious, ideological answers for every question while members of democratic societies were often unable to explain 'what they stood for.'" [6]

In such a context, it is not difficult to understand why United States military leaders and Defense Department officials responded so positively to John Broger and his views. In a speech to an Asiatic Seminar sponsored by FEBC in the fall of 1951, Broger declared communism "not only a political party, not only a concept of life or a theory of economy," but "akin to extreme religious fanaticism, for how else could Communism gain in its converts such tenacity of purpose and such complete mastery over every realm of mental, political, moral, economic and spiritual life?" Therefore, Broger insisted, the fight against it could not be waged "wholly on the basis of military manpower or production potential, gun for gun, ship for ship, propaganda for propaganda." Only "godly precepts and principles" would provide an understanding of communism, and any plan to fight it "must find its source of strength and inspiration in godly righteousness." To Admiral Radford and other military men Broger presented a solution to the problem of instilling in armed forces personnel the ideals and beliefs crucial to winning the war against communism. While working as a consultant in Radford's office, Broger had developed the concept of "militant liberty," which he offered as an ideology to be used by the armed forces for troop indoctrination. Communism, he explained in a brochure entitled *Militant Liberty*, was "a dynamic ideology" that could be defeated only by "a stronger *dynamic* ideology." Communists knew what they believed, whereas Americans and others in the so-called free world sometimes were unable to explain or defend their beliefs. Broger contended that his concept of militant liberty explained the "ideals of liberty" in such as way as to motivate individuals to be vigilant and aggressive ("militant") in upholding and spreading them. He promised that if Americans worked with other peoples of the free world, armed with the ideology of militant liberty, they would eventually become stronger than "the Communist bloc." [7]

6. "Report of the Defense Advisory Committee on Prisoners of War," 31; Thomas A. Palmer, "Why We Fight: A Study of Indoctrination Activities in the Armed Forces," in *The Military in America: From the Colonial Era to the Present*, ed. Peter Karsten (New York, 1980), 385.

7. Ledyard, *Sky Waves*, 74, 75; U.S. Department of Defense, *Militant Liberty: A Program of Evaluation and Assessment of Freedom* (1955), 1–2, 16.

Broger's concept of militant liberty, as several commentators have pointed out, was a mishmash of pseudo-scientific jargon and high-sounding clichés, contrasting the "sensitive individual conscience" of the free world with the "annihilated conscience" of the so-called communist world, for example, and using charts and graphs to measure various nations' trends toward such things as "evolution for freedom" and "revolution of aggression." Nevertheless, Radford, chairman of the Joint Chiefs of Staff, approved it, and so did Charles Wilson, secretary of defense. In 1955 the Defense Department promulgated a program called "Militant Liberty" to provide "unified and purposeful guiding precepts for all members of the Armed Forces."[8]

Always eager to publicize the good works of fellow evangelicals, *United Evangelical Action* applauded the Militant Liberty program as a "moral and ethical . . . base on which to build toward spiritual truth" and congratulated Broger (identified as FEBC president) on the positive reaction to it. International Christian Leadership also endorsed Militant Liberty. In October, 1956, the Pentagon reported that ICL had adopted it as a "major strategy." Besides issuing a pamphlet and other material in accord with the program, ICL had made a "color movie in Washington, D.C. with Mr. Broger making the presentation to a panel consisting of Generals Willard Paul and Thomas A. Lane, Senator Frank Carlson, Congressman Charles Bennett, Dr. Meliquiades J. Gamboa, and Mr. Abraham Vereide." (Unlike the secular version of Militant Liberty promulgated by the Defense Department, the ICL film apparently had a religious emphasis. Broger later described the film as "a motion picture for training in the principles which underlie a Christian society in contrast to the Communist threat which challenges the free way of life.") In April, 1957, Senator Frank Carlson reported that ICL had introduced Militant Liberty to "churches, schools, Service Clubs, J.C.'s, and Civitans."[9]

The Defense Department also worked hard disseminating Militant

8. U.S. Department of Defense, *Militant Liberty*, i; Palmer, "Why We Fight," 385; Morris Janowitz, *The Professional Soldier: A Social and Political Portrait* (New York, 1960), 406–407. For criticism of Broger's concept of militant liberty see, for example, Hale, "Militant Liberty," 30–31, and, perhaps the most scathing, Samuel P. Huntington, *The Soldier and the State: The Theory and Politics of Civil-Military Relations* (Cambridge, Mass., 1957), 397.

9. "Militant Liberty," *UEA*, January 15, 1956, p. 6; Palmer, "'Why We Fight,' A Study of Indoctrination Activities," 56, 55; *Military Cold War Education Hearings*, 1035.

Liberty. Broger himself conducted scores of briefings throughout the country, appearing before both military and civilian groups, but none of the services agreed to use Militant Liberty in troop indoctrination. Still, the rejection of the program by the armed forces did not impede the Defense Department career of its author. In 1956, he became deputy director and, in 1961, director of AFIE. Although the services refused to use his program, Broger continued to believe in it and promote it among the military leadership and before various civilian audiences. In testimony before a Senate committee in 1962 he recalled lecturing on the subject "on a number of occasions at the various war colleges and service schools," including the Air University, where he delivered an "average of four or five" lectures a year. He also had been invited to speak to public school authorities and teachers in various states; on one occasion he had promoted Militant Liberty at a conference of seven thousand teachers in Texas.[10]

Once installed in AFIE, in the late 1950s and 1960s, Broger developed a troop information program based on the same strident, emotional, anticommunist ideology that informed Militant Liberty. Before the mid-1950s anticommunist troop indoctrination focused mainly on "international communism" as a threat to Europe and Asia. During Broger's administration AFIE materials laid special emphasis on the threat of communist subversion or takeover of the United States. For example, programs broadcast over Armed Forces Radio and films entitled *Freedom and You* and *Red Nightmare* used a common formula, in which an American citizen suddenly finds his town taken over by communists. Another recurring theme drew on the notion that the armed forces are a special target of the communists. According to Thomas Palmer, AFIE films and other materials generally presented "a stark, bipolar view of international relations in which neutrality [was] discouraged and anti-communist movements encouraged. . . . Within Troop Information materials Communist countries, automatically viewed as totalitarian with all the concept's pejorative connotations, emerge not simply as the inevitable enemy but also the embodiment of evil and of a heresy to be isolated."[11]

10. Palmer, "'Why We Fight,' A Study of Indoctrination Activities," 49, 50, 52–60; *Military Cold War Education Hearings*, 1047, 1034, 1035.

11. Palmer, "'Why We Fight,' A Study of Indoctrination Activities," 74, and see also 64, 70–78, 103–104; Wesbrook, "Historical Notes," 266–67; John M. Swomley, Jr., *The Military Establishment* (Boston, 1964), 189.

Two widely used films produced by sources outside the military provide another good indication of the slant of AFIE troop indoctrination. *Operation Abolition*, produced by the House Committee on Un-American Activities (HUAC), portrayed the 1960 anti-HUAC student demonstrations in San Francisco as commmunist-led and inspired. *Communism on the Map* was produced by the National Education Program (NEP), a right-wing patriotic organization founded by George S. Benson, president of Harding College, a small, fundamentalist (Church of Christ) institution located in Searcy, Arkansas. The hour-long film portrayed the United States in the final phase of communist encirclement— as a result of the insidious growth of communism throughout the world—and in mortal danger from communist agents who had infiltrated the government, labor unions, the schools, press, and other American institutions. According to Irwin Suall, "whole sections of the film are virtually identical, word for word," with passages in the John Birch Society Blue Book, which is not surprising because Glen A. Green, an NEP officer and "coordinator" for the Birch Society, wrote the script. During the Military Cold War Education Hearings by the Special Preparedness Subcommittee of the Senate Armed Services Committee, Broger admitted under questioning that although he thought *Communism on the Map* had "a lot of good information," it was "probably" inappropriate for troop indoctrination because it conflicted with national policy. Pressed to elaborate, he said, "Well, there were strong indications in the film that Canada was pretty pink, that some of our allies in NATO are overly pink. These are nations that we have alliance with, and I presume even in the interest of good taste, you would not do such a thing in a troop I. & E. program."[12]

As the use of films produced by HUAC and the National Education Program demonstrates, during Broger's administration AFIE developed ties to a number of nonmilitary groups involved in the ideological indoctrination of the American people. Besides NEP and HUAC, they included two conservative patriotic organizations, the Freedoms Foundation and the American Heritage Foundation. Thomas Palmer con-

12. *NYT*, July 16, 1961, p. 42; Palmer, "'Why We Fight,' A Study of Indoctrination Activities," 65; Irwin Suall, *The American Ultras: The Extreme Right and the Military-Industrial Complex* (New York, 1962), 16–17, 44–45; *Military Cold War Education Hearings*, 1050. In response to controversies over each of the two films, the services ultimately stopped using them.

cluded that AFIE's relationship with them "helped shape the content of at least part of the indoctrination material used for presentation to members of the Armed Forces." Both groups presented awards to AFIE and Broger for promoting patriotism, and beginning in 1963 Broger served as chairman of the Board of Visitors of the Freedoms Foundation. Nor was he the only military representative among the foundation's officers. They included his mentor, Admiral Radford, several other retired military men, and Dwight Eisenhower, who served as an honorary officer.[13]

Although AFIE materials exhibited the strong anticommunist line espoused by evangelicals and fundamentalists (as well as other Americans) in the 1950s and 1960s, they did not promulgate a specifically sectarian view. Discussions of religion in the materials were generally framed in accord with the civil religion of the period. A good illustration is the chapter on religion in *Ideas in Conflict: Liberty and Communism*, a book published by AFIE in 1962 to serve as a guide and source of materials for commanders, information officers, and others involved in Troop Information. It quoted the 1952 Supreme Court decision *Zorach v. Clauson*, stating that "we are a religious people whose institutions presuppose a Supreme Being," noted that "modern democracies not only guarantee religious freedom but also encourage the practice of religious faith," and declared that "America led the world, in the 1700's, toward religious freedom." The bulk of the chapter concentrated on showing the antireligious bias of Marxian ideology (by, for example, quoting—actually misquoting—"Marx's aphorism, 'Religion is the opium of the people'") and describing "the Soviet regime's long battle against organized religion."[14]

If Broger did not officially promote evangelical religion through AFIE materials, neither did he stop being an evangelist when he began working for the Defense Department. As president of the Far East Broadcasting Company he had expanded the gospel message to include a strong dose of anticommunist propaganda. He used his position as

13. Palmer, "'Why We Fight,' A Study of Indoctrination Activities," 173, 174–77; *Military Cold War Education Hearings*, 1006, 1035; "John C. Broger, Director, Armed Forces Information and Education (AFIE), Department of Defense, Washington, D.C." (Typescript in Collection 165-6-26, Archives of the Billy Graham Center, Wheaton College, Wheaton, Ill.); Suall, *American Ultras*, 36–37.

14. Armed Forces Information and Education, Department of Defense, *Ideas in Conflict: Liberty and Communism* (1962), 96, 98, 100, 101.

director of AFIE and the connections it provided, among civilians as well as the military and inside as well as outside the government, to promulgate a message that combined evangelical Christianity and anti-communism. During his career in the Pentagon the peripatetic evangelist lectured at the National War College, the Industrial College of the Armed Forces, the Army War College, the Air War College, the Marine Corps Senior School, the Armed Forces Staff College, the Air Command and Staff College, the Military Assistance Institute, the Harvard Business School, and various other civic, educational, and private organizations. From 1956 to 1961, he served as vice-chairman of the Armed Services Committee of the President's People-to-People program, which provided another opportunity for speaking engagements throughout the United States. In the mid-1960s he was a featured speaker at the Pentagon Protestant Pulpit, weekday noon-hour services arranged by armed forces chaplains in the Concourse of the Pentagon. His address "The Challenge of Freedom" rehearsed familiar Cold War themes and added a plug for the Defense Department's troop information program: "There should be no question as to why the Department of Defense is concerned today about the convictions, ideals, motivations, loyalties or any other of those intangible qualities which appear to be a major contest area in this latter part of the twentieth century. . . . What the citizen-soldier of today believes, the depths of his loyalty, the knowledge of his enemy, the toughness of his character—all these things and more may well determine the effectiveness of our national will to resist." Elaborating on the notion of a nation under God, Broger described the U.S. Constitution as "hewn and shaped to the spiritual concepts of biblical truths," containing "all the guarantees of Christian freedoms." The will to resist communism depended on American faithfulness not only to the Constitution per se but to the biblical concepts on which it was based. The Constitution, Broger declared, "is our shield and armor so long as its provisions prevail and so long as the majority of our peoples sustain a belief in, and an adherence to, the great truths from which this document has drawn its strength and significance."[15]

While serving as AFIE director, Broger continued working with vari-

15. "John C. Broger, Director"; Harmon D. Moore *et al.*, *And Our Defense Is Sure: Sermons and Addresses from the Pentagon Protestant Pulpit* (New York, 1964), 157, 158, 162, and, for the purpose and operations of the Pentagon Protestant Pulpit, 7–8.

ous evangelical groups. He remained president of the FEBC until 1959 and served on the executive committee of the National Religious Broadcasters. In 1958 he was elected one of three vice-presidents of International Christian Leadership. He devoted much of his energy to the NAE, speaking at rallies and conventions and working with its Office of Public Affairs and the director, Clyde W. Taylor. Broger helped start the Office of Public Affairs annual seminars, initially held for college students and later for pastors and laymen. That Broger sometimes involved AFIE personnel in these seminars is suggested by a letter Taylor wrote in 1968, thanking him for "the excellent cooperation of your agency in helping to make possible our seminars for clergy and laymen" and for "the very willing service given by your assistants."[16]

Broger's indefatigable efforts earned him a reputation as "one of the outstanding evangelical leaders in Washington," to quote Clyde Taylor. In 1965 Wheaton College awarded him an honorary Doctor of Laws degree. By then evangelicals had come to regard him as an authority not only on anticommunism but on what he called the Christian view of government. He had treated both topics in his Pentagon Pulpit address. In an article published in *United Evangelical Action* in 1967 he focused on evangelicals' notion of America as a nation in covenant with God and the responsibility that entailed. The founding fathers based the government of the United States on biblical principles and concepts, he argued. As proof, he cited scriptural passages he claimed sanctioned trial by jury, free enterprise, equal justice for all, and freedom of religion, speech, press, and assembly. Christians today must accept "the full responsibility of citizenship," he declared. This included voting "for candidates of character and conviction who look upon their lives and their offices as being under the constant scrutiny of God." He also urged Christians to see to it that "the biblical values which were so important to the founding fathers and so essential to the development of the nation. . . . be restored to a vigorous place in our citizen-government relationship." And not only there. "If government is to be ordained of

16. *Military Cold War Education Hearings*, 989; "NRB Joins ICL in 'Spiritual Offensive,'" *UEA*, January 15, 1955, p. 16; "International Christian Leadership Holds Meet," *UEA*, March 15, 1958, p. 7; "A Vital Church," *UEA*, Spring, 1969, p. 9; "Moving Toward Revival," *UEA*, Summer, 1971, p. 16; Clyde W. Taylor to Evangelical Action Commission, January 17, 1968, in Collection 165-6-26, Archives of the Billy Graham Center; Clyde W. Taylor to John C. Broger, May 16, 1968, in Collection 165-6-29, Archives of the Billy Graham Center.

God," Broger observed, "then spiritual and moral concepts must undergird and relate all political, economic, educational and cultural areas of national life." The 1968 Public Affairs Office seminar, which Broger and some of his assistants helped with, also considered the topic "Christian Responsibility to Government."[17]

By 1968, when the NAE named Broger Layman of the Year, he had become an evangelical celebrity. Significantly, even though he occupied a civilian position as AFIE director, evangelicals clearly regarded him as a military man. "The 1968 Layman of the Year has been involved in some variety of military service for 26 years," the citation read. And when Clyde Taylor proposed Broger for the award, he described the position of AFIE director as "equivalent to a two-star general."[18] Thus Broger joined President and Commander in Chief Eisenhower and General William K. Harrison in the pantheon of evangelical military heroes. Although he was less widely known than those two men, in the eyes of many of his fellow Christians he seemed equally worthy of veneration.

17. Clyde W. Taylor to Evangelical Action Commission, January 17, 1968; "1968 Layman of the Year" (Typescript in Collection 165-6-26, Archives of the Billy Graham Center); John C. Broger, "Government," *UEA*, April, 1967, pp. 24–26; John A. [*sic*] Broger, "Renewal and Social Concern," *UEA*, April, 1965, pp. 16–18; Clyde W. Taylor, "Report of the Commission on Evangelical Action, April 22, 1968" (Typescript in Collection 165-6-26, Archives of the Billy Graham Center), 2.

18. "1968 Layman of the Year"; Clyde W. Taylor to Evangelical Action Commission, January 17, 1968.

6

Disciple-Making in the Armed Forces

As we saw in Chapter 1, the religious and moral guidance programs developed by the military in the late 1940s and 1950s assuaged some, but not all, of the fears evangelicals had about the corrupting influence of military service on American youth. That concern persisted into later decades. Evangelicals continued to view the military environment as apathetic, even hostile, toward Christianity.

According to evangelical thinking, the great majority of service personnel, young men and women in their "formative years," were ill prepared to cope with the debilitating influence of the military environment. Part of the reason was that they had grown up in an increasingly secular, relativistic, permissive culture. In May, 1963, *Christianity Today* published a series of essays discussing the spiritual condition of military men and women. The problem most often cited was "their lack of a sense of ultimate values and fixed standards." Base Chaplain Bruce C. Herrstrom of the 126th Air Refueling Wing, Illinois Air National Guard, described young airmen as "teen-agers who have little or no concept of discipline and responsibility. They come into military life with no respect for authority and seem to thrive on a philosophy of relativism. For them there are no absolutes." [1]

The spiritual and moral deficiency of American servicemen and servicewomen rendered them vulnerable to all the temptations presented in the military environment. Chaplains and commanders quoted in the

---

1. "Mission Field in the Military," *Christian Life*, September, 1958, p. 52; "The Image of America's Serviceman," *CT*, May 24, 1963, p. 5. See also Charles Hall, "Proposed Program for a Servicemens Center" (Paper presented to the faculty of the Department of Christian Education, Dallas Theological Seminary, May, 1973), 11.

Christianity Today series sketched a disheartening portrait of the typical soldier, sailor, marine, or airman. Lonely, far from home and "the close scrutiny of family and . . . community," subject to both peer pressure and the corrupting influence of older servicemen, he succumbed to a myriad of vices: profanity, excessive drinking, frequenting houses of prostitution, chasing women, indulging in spendthrift habits.[2]

What *Christianity Today* called "spiritual vitality" was another casualty of military life. Several articles in the series cited low rates of chapel attendance—only 5 percent on one naval vessel, for example. The magazine also described chaplains as "continually astonished over the spiritual apathy of draftees who regard themselves as 'Protestant.' A distressing number cannot repeat the Ten Commandments or the Lord's Prayer, nor identify Abraham, Moses, or Paul." Such "spiritual illiteracy" seemed to go hand in hand with religious vacuousness. *Christianity Today* quoted a chaplain's observation that the serviceman "prefers a vague philosophy to a personal commitment to God" and a marine lieutenant's statement that "the Protestant's information about Christ and His Gospel is tragically fuzzy; he generally believes in a sort of salvation by good works, and a 'hope for the best when it's all over' philosophy, if he is concerned about spiritual matters at all."[3]

Throughout the 1960s, 1970s and 1980s, evangelicals continued to worry that military life rendered armed forces personnel vulnerable to temptation. Assignment abroad, whether in Asia or Europe, seemed especially fraught with danger. Commenting on the situation of American servicemen based in Europe, a Navigators writer described them as "a distinct breed" whose overseas assignment entailed "a radical upheaval" in their lives, leaving them feeling "cut off and alone," separated from their families and intimidated by foreign culture. Similarly, a writer for an OCSC bulletin referred to servicemen in both Europe and Asia as "strangers in a strange land" tempted by "all that the world uses to allure and deceive." Vulnerable servicemen and women capitulated to sin out of "loneliness, pressure from the crowd, lack of righteous courage, a forgotten sense of values, possibility of premature death, alcoholic

2. "The Image of America's Serviceman," 4; "Sin and Virtue in Military Life," *CT*, May 24, 1963, pp. 7–9.
3. "The Image of America's Serviceman," 5, 6; "Sin and Virtue in Military Life," 10; "Reaching Servicemen for Christ," *CT*, May 24, 1963, p. 11.

drinks abundantly available, and legalized prostitution and gambling."[4]

Although evangelicals described spiritual conditions in the military in generally negative terms, they insisted—somewhat paradoxically—that the armed forces constituted "one of the most open harvest fields in our society today." In the 1963 *Christianity Today* special issue, chaplains and commanders theorized that the vicissitudes of military life made service personnel peculiarly receptive to the evangelical message. Some pointed to the effect of boot camp training on the new inductee: "He is homesick, lonesome, and in real need of a good solid friend. What better friend could he find than the Lord Jesus Christ?" Others cited a change in assignment, professional, or marital status or a "time of trouble—be it serious illness, marital difficulty, loss of a loved one, or landing in the brig"—which seemed to induce "special openness to spiritual ministration." Even "succumbing to gross sin" could have that effect. Lieutenant Commander Eric A. Nelson, Jr., executive officer of the USS *Darter*, observed that youthful sinners sometimes developed "an inward sense of shame," which provided "an open opportunity to present the claims of Jesus Christ, and his power to save, keep, and satisfy, even in the service." And, finally, facing the possibility of death, whether in war or peacetime, seemed to make servicemen receptive to the evangelical message. A retired naval officer, recounting an incident on an LST during a hurricane, said that when some of the men took out their Bibles, he seized the opportunity to "talk of things eternal." *Christianity Today* pointed out the lesson to be learned: "Surrounded by the live possibilities of fatal explosions, collisions, and other accidents, the serviceman always lives on the edge of eternity; it is quite proper to remind him then to be ready for death and the life beyond."[5]

For evangelicals, the military mission field embraced two groups of armed forces personnel. One was made up of young persons who had been brought up in the evangelical faith and who entered the services as members of one or another of the evangelical denominations. The other, much larger group was made up of personnel who either had had

4. Richard Greene, "Facing the Frontline in Europe," *Navlog*, April–May, 1985, p. 10; Allen Robert Latty, "The Ministry of Overseas Christian Servicemen's Centers: A Survey and Evaluation" (Master of Theology thesis, Dallas Theological Seminary, 1970), 8.

5. Greene, "Facing the Frontline in Europe," 10; "Reaching Servicemen for Christ," 11, 12. See also Phil Landrum, "Missionary to the Military," *UEA*, July, 1966, p. 7.

no religious training or who had been brought up in a nonevangelical denomination or faith group. During the 1960s, 1970s, and 1980s, evangelicals adopted different approaches to each of the two groups.

In the case of the first group, evangelicals sought to help fellow believers maintain a "Christian witness" while serving in the armed forces. During the Vietnam War, for example, when thousands of young men were drafted into the armed forces, several denominations published books on the subject, and magazines such as *Pentecostal Evangel, Ambassador Life*, and *HIS* printed articles with such catchy titles as "Service with a Smile" or "Don't Hide from Your Hitch," often written by young enlistees who could speak from personal experience and in the language of their contemporaries. These publications presented the would-be Christian serviceman with a detailed checklist designed to instill godly behavior: he should review the doctrines of his church so as to prevent being shaken by the other faiths and philosophies he would encounter in the armed forces; avoid temptations such as liquor, profanity, gambling, and sexual immorality and the ungodly, profane men who engaged in such activities; select Christian friends instead; keep in touch with his family and home church; worship regularly in a "Bible-believing" church or, failing that, the military chapel; maintain personal devotions (Bible study, prayer); and get to know his chaplain and become active in the chapel program. "Some 'wise guys' may poke fun at you. They will probably call you 'deacon,' 'holy Joe,' or what have you," Stanford Linzey warned. He and other writers admitted that sustaining a Christian witness was difficult. Van Smith quoted a fellow marine who said, "If you're a Christian when going into the service, expect bad persecution. It's acceptable to be a Christian at home, but while in the service the persecution is worse than you would ever imagine. It's especially bad in basic. The military will make or break you. You can't be a 'Sunday-go-to-meeting' type of Christian. It has to be a personal faith in Christ. Your parents' religion won't carry you through; it has to be yours." Still, Linzey, Smith, and other writers expressed hope and confidence that despite such pressures—and with all the support civilian and other military evangelicals could provide—the Christian serviceman's faith would not be shaken, that the experience of serving in the armed forces would make him "a stronger and better Christian."[6]

6. Stanford E. Linzey, Jr., *Filling Your Boots* (Springfield, Mo., n.d.), n.p.; Van Smith, "Don't Hide from Your Hitch," *Moody Monthly*, September, 1970, p. 84. See also David

When addressing the second group of servicemen and women, evangelicals exhorted their fellow Christians in the military to take up the Great Commission, discipling them by one-to-one witnessing or starting fellowship, Bible study, or prayer groups. "You can be a missionary to your friends in the armed forces," Linzey declared. "Many of your friends may not have heard the simple gospel! Some may have rarely attended church. Here is the chance for you to let your life and your language speak for God." A Southern Baptist Convention booklet entitled *Your Life and Military Service* prescribed procedures and quoted Scriptures the soldier-evangelist might employ in "tell[ing] a buddy how to be a Christian."[7]

Evangelicals also urged military chaplains to extend their ministry beyond the members of their own denomination. The Church of God Chaplains Commission, for example, counseled its chaplains "to evangelize the lost." And the Christian and Missionary Alliance (C&MA), in its "Military Chaplains Manual," advised its chaplains not only to concern themselves with the spiritual welfare of C&MA personnel or converts but also to "seek opportunities to minister to the unchurched, encouraging them to make a Christian commitment and endeavoring to relate them to civilian congregations as well as military fellowships of Christians."[8]

By their own accounts, evangelical chaplains found numerous opportunities to engage in evangelization and exploited them to the fullest. Some used personal conferences and consultations to advantage. Chap-

W. Plank, *Called to Serve* (Springfield, Mo., 1967); *Your Life and Military Service* (Atlanta, [1966]); Lawrence Fitzgerald, "What Can Our Churches Do for the Men in Vietnam?" *Eternity*, May, 1967, pp. 30–31; Warren F. McPherson, "To Join or Not to Join?" *PE*, July 1, 1962, pp. 6–7; Evertt Hullum and Robert D. O'Brien, "Service with a Smile," *Ambassador Life*, XXI (November, 1966), 1–2; Jay Chance, "A Silent Service," *Ambassador Life*, XXI (November, 1966), 2; Ralph G. Bowles, "No More Wasted Years for Me," *PE*, June 25, 1967, p. 11; David Self with John Schwarz, "Your First Two Months in the Army," *HIS*, June, 1971, pp. 8–10.

7. Linzey, *Filling Your Boots*, n.p.; *Your Life and Military Service*, 16-V. See also Plank, *Called to Serve*, Chap. 8.

8. "Service Ministries in the Church: The Church of God Chaplains Commission" (Typescript provided by John E. Taylor, Jr., Program Coordinator, Church of God Chaplains Commission [1990?]); Christian and Missionary Alliance, "Military Chaplains Manual" (Photocopied typescript, dated March 16, 1983), 5, 7. See also Robert L. Mole, *God Also Loves Military People: A Brief Story of the Seventh-Day Adventist Church and the American Military Chaplaincy, 1860–1976* (N.p., 1977), 62–64, 66–70, 77.

lain Raymond Pritz, who had served six years as a civilian pastor before becoming an air force chaplain, averaged about 130 personal problem interviews a month. "These are all potential opportunities to personally witness to a man about his need of Christ. What pastor would have that many beat a trail to his door?" he observed. Chaplains were able to reach many more men just by visiting and talking with them. They had what Christian and Missionary Alliance chaplain James A. Edgren termed "a 'tailor-made' mission field for the proclamation of the gospel." As he explained, "The chaplain can talk to any soldier on the job at virtually any time and in any place." Another C&MA chaplain, serving with marines, spent several hours twice weekly walking through each squadron's work area and "casually conversing" with the men. "Many times these conversations lead to setting up appointments for further, more formal counseling," he noted. Recreational facilities on or off the post provided another arena where chaplains could extend their ministrations far beyond the members of their own denomination or even those involved in the base chapel program.[9]

The so-called incoming interview with a chaplain required on many military posts presented another opportunity for evangelization. Every man reporting to a new station, whether officer or enlisted man, recruit or old-timer, saw the chaplain shortly after arriving on base. "What an opportunity," commented one chaplain. "What if every Protestant in your community were asked to report to your pastor?" An air force chaplain noted that because the interview was required, "honest care must be exercised lest the individual's religious freedom be violated. However, the needs that are often revealed, the confidences that are offered, and the confessions that are made offer the discerning chaplain many golden oppportunities for personal ministry." Sometimes, he observed, men made the chaplain's office "a place of repentance for past sin and a starting place for a new or renewed life in Christ. . . . If men do not accept the Saviour here, at least they are reminded that *God is* and that He has a claim to the worship of all His creatures."[10]

The moral education sessions of the 1950s and 1960s, also required,

9. "Mission Field in the Military," 54–55; George W. Cummins, "Missionaries in Uniform," *Baptist Program*, February, 1969, pp. 5–6; Warren Bird, "Serving God and Country," *Alliance Witness*, CXVIII (June 22, 1983), 7–8.

10. Landrum, "Missionary to the Military," 8; Chaplain (Capt.) Orville McCormack, "Can a Man Serve God in the Military?" *PE*, July 1, 1962, pp. 24–25.

could be used to advantage. "The sessions deal with morality, rather than religion," Chaplain Pritz pointed out. "But," he noted, "the chaplain then automatically gets before all the men once a month." He quoted an instructor who advised student army chaplains: "You tell the men what kind of lives to live. Then you say, 'This isn't easy, is it? Would you like to know *how* you can live this way? Come out on Sunday and I'll tell you!' "[11]

Revivals and retreats sponsored by the NAE and various evangelical denominations enabled chaplains to go beyond consultation and counseling and engage in evangelistic preaching. Individual chaplains also organized retreats and revivals on the military installations they served. In the late 1960s Chaplain Talmadge F. McNabb reported that while on assignment with the Combat Support Training Brigade at Fort Dix, he approached his commanding officer, "a devout Lutheran Christian," and received permission to set up an all-day retreat for the troops on a quarterly basis. The program had been going on for almost a year and a half when McNabb wrote an article about it for the *Pentecostal Evangel*. Usually from four hundred to five hundred men applied to attend, but only two hundred could be accepted because of limited chapel accommodations and to ensure that the men would have a chance to become acquainted with the retreat speakers and the chaplain during the day. The retreats featured outside speakers (for example, Donald Wilkerson, director of Teen Challenge in Brooklyn, New York), Christian films, question-and-answer periods, coffee breaks, testimonies, and hymn singing, interspersed with periods of meditation and quiet prayer. According to McNabb, "Toward the end of the retreats one of the speakers presents the claims of Jesus Christ as all-sufficient Saviour. Then an invitation is given for those desiring to accept Him personally. The response has been most encouraging. It is a solemn and inspiring scene when these young men come forward and kneel at the altar, confessing their need of Christ and asking His forgiveness for sins."[12]

Some chaplains found Bible study classes to be a good vehicle for evangelization. Because they were voluntary, like the revivals and re-

11. "Mission Field in the Military," 54–55.
12. Chaplain (Lt. Col.) Talmadge F. McNabb, "GI's Find Christ at Fort Dix Retreats," *PE*, June 30, 1968, pp. 12–13. See also McCormack, "Can a Man Serve God in the Military?" 24–25; Dan Martin, "Today's Army Gets Old-Time Religion," *Home Missions*, XLIX (December, 1978), 15.

treats, they offered the chaplain an opportunity to present distinctive sectarian doctrines. If he succeeded in awakening a participant's interest, he might eventually persuade him or her to join his denomination.[13]

Many chaplains added an evangelistic element to the General Protestant Service, the interdenominational Sunday morning worship service open to Protestants of all denominations. Air force chaplain Orville McCormack, of the Assemblies of God, writing in the *Pentecostal Evangel* in 1962, observed that contrary to what many people thought, "no curbs are placed on chaplains to hinder evangelistic preaching." Although he noted that "the 'sawdust trail' type of evangelism" was seldom seen in the General Protestant Service, he and other evangelicals were able to preach "full salvation" and seek "decisions for Christ." Other chaplains also reported giving the "altar call" or "invitation" on a regular basis. A navy chaplain who claimed to have won over three thousand men and women to Jesus Christ wrote a letter to the editor of *Christianity Today* declaring that he had "given opportunity for decisions again and again in public services" and had "never been called in question by the command about my methods and principles." Chaplain George Swanson said he issued an invitation at both the Sunday morning and evening services.[14]

Chaplains reported considerable success as a result of their evangelizing efforts. Individual soul-winning, Bible studies, indoctrination classes, spiritual growth and prayer groups, retreats, and revivals netted an increasing number of decisions for Christ. By the mid-1950s Assemblies of God chaplains were reporting in excess of a thousand such decisions annually. In 1962, the denomination's chaplains reported 2,006 "definite decisions for Christ among the servicemen they serve." Larger denominations, with more chaplains in service, made even more impressive gains, especially in the 1960s and 1970s. The Southern Baptist

13. See Barry C. Black, "The Seventh-Day Adventist Military Chaplain: A Study of Beliefs and Functions in Tension with Military Life" (Doctor of Ministry dissertation, Eastern Baptist Theological Seminary, 1982), 17, 122; W. Herbert Scott, "Ministry in the Military," *World Vision*, XX (November, 1976), 21.

14. McCormack, "Can a Man Serve God in the Military?" 24; Commander Stanford E. Linzey, Jr., Chaplain Corps, United States Navy, to the editor, *CT*, February 4, 1966, p. 44; George Swanson, "There's a Challenge in the Chaplaincy," *UEA*, August, 1960, p. 11. See also Leonard E. Hill, "Ministers Uniformed," *Baptist Program*, November, 1971, p. 11; Billy M. Goodwin, "Like a Mighty Army," *PE*, June 25, 1978, p. 7.

Convention claimed that over the ten-year period from 1963 to 1973, its chaplains "led from ten to fourteen thousand each year to profess Christ as Saviour." By 1978 records of the denomination's Chaplaincy Division showed about fourteen thousand professions of faith reported by its active-duty and reserve chaplains with the military.[15]

Besides chaplains, lay evangelists served as missionaries to the military. Some worked independently, witnessing to others whenever they saw an opportunity, or through Bible studies, Sunday schools, or fellowship groups. Others were enlisted by their denominations. An AOG armed forces center on Guam, for example, sponsored a Disciples in Action program that offered training sessions four times a week where military personnel were taught Bible, prayer, intercession, and soul winning. The goal, as described by the pastor of the church that operated the center, was to ensure that "when these Christian military personnel leave us, they will become disciple makers wherever they find themselves."[16] Many other lay evangelists were affiliated with parachurch groups that regarded disciple-making as the duty of every member.

Later chapters will discuss the independent lay evangelists and those associated with chapel or denominational programs. Here the focus is on the members of parachurch groups like the Navigators and Officers' Christian Union. Lorne Sanny, president of the Navigators, used the term *spiritual reproduction* to describe his organization's method of evangelism, which was similar to that used by other parachurch groups. Working singly or in small "bands of men," Navigators would begin their efforts on an aircraft carrier or Polaris submarine or army base by witnessing among other personnel and organizing prayer meetings. Then they would follow up initial contacts with intensive, "man-to-man" evangelizing. Once a few converts were recruited, they would meet in small groups where the Navigators would train the new Christians to practice regular prayer habits, memorize Scripture, study and

15. Leon G. Kircher, Jr., "The History of the Organizational Development and Ministry to the Military by the Assemblies of God December 1941–December 1979" (Research paper, Assemblies of God Graduate School, Springfield, Mo., December 13, 1979), 29; "Twenty-five Assemblies Chaplains Now Serving," *PE*, July 7, 1963, p. 10; Barbara Joiner, "Current Missions Groups: Missions and National Issues, Session III," *Royal Service*, LXVII (March, 1973), 44; Martin, "Today's Army Gets Old-Time Religion," 15.

16. Jim Smith, "Making Disciples in the Armed Forces," *PE*, February 27, 1983, p. 19.

apply the teachings of the Bible, and, most important, witness to and evangelize others. As soon as a group had grown to eight or more, it would split in two and divide the territory to be evangelized, each new group taking responsibility for a particular area. By remaining small, Sanny noted, groups retained the "camaraderie of close fellowship" that enabled them to maintain their own spirituality and evangelize others. These "multiplying bands of dedicated men," engaging in barracks visitation, Bible study, chapel activities, and personal witnessing, provided the key to the Navigators' success in "reaching men for Christ."[17]

A sampling of the recruiting efforts of the Officers' Christian Union during the 1950s and 1960s provides additional insight into the evangelism employed by parachurch groups in the military. In those decades OCU members, rather than a professional staff, assumed most of the responsibilities of ministry and outreach. For example, they would invite a fellow officer to lunch or dinner or to a Bible study class as a means of persuading him to "accept Christ" and join the OCU. Or they would see to it that copies of *Command* were placed in officers' club reading rooms, day rooms, and libraries. A membership committee sought out other evangelicals in the military by writing to Christian institutions such as Wheaton or Gordon College or Bob Jones University to obtain the names of former students serving as officers. During the 1952 Billy Graham Crusade in Washington, D.C., the OCU contacted officers who had made decisions for Christ to acquaint them with the organization and persuade them to join it. The OCU also worked closely with other evangelical parachurch groups such as Inter-Varsity Christian Fellowship, the Navigators, the Christian Business Men's Fellowship, and Campus Crusade for Christ. And finally, the OCU sponsored "Spring Leave" conferences for cadets and midshipmen from the military academies, as well as area conferences at various locations throughout the United States and in the Far East.[18]

Probably because of its affiliation with a large civilian-based evan-

17. Lorne Sanny, "A Band of Fighting Men," *Eternity*, December, 1963, pp. 12, 30, 33, 34.

18. Robert W. Spoede, *More Than Conquerors: A History of the Officers' Christian Fellowship of the U.S.A., 1943–1983* (Englewood, Colo., 1993), 39, 40–41, 45–46, 69–71. For good descriptions of discipling by OCU members, see Lieutenant Colonel Philip C. Shafer, "Reflections—An Air Force Officer Looks Back to OCF Beginnings," *Command*, Spring, 1993, pp. 8–9; and Lieutenant Colonel Ward C. Graham, "The Remarkable Chain," *Command*, Spring, 1993, pp. 10–11.

gelical group, Campus Crusade Military Ministry was able to go beyond the individual and small-group evangelism used by the other parachurch groups and by Campus Crusade's own Military Affiliate to sponsor programs of mass evangelism. "Evangelistic mass outreaches" Bill Bright called them, designed "to expose hundreds of men and women to the gospel at one time." These included the annual Operation Pro Bowl, a four-day program sponsored jointly with Athletes in Action (the Campus Crusade sports ministry) and featuring National Football League players witnessing to soldiers, sailors, and airmen at various military posts. Campus Crusade also promoted a variety of other performers or events for use on military installations, including speakers such as Josh McDowell for banquets and retreats, special events like Andrew Kole's "World of Illusion," concerts, and other forms of entertainment, as well as films, tapes, and multimedia shows.[19]

In the highly regimented, bureaucratically administered armed forces, where personnel experienced a high degree of mobility and depersonalization, evangelical religion exercised a special appeal. It prescribed and enabled adherents to live what Joel Carpenter, writing about the fundamentalists of the 1920s, terms the "separated life." Among the fundamentalists, leading the separated life involved maintaining certain standards of morality and piety as well as engaging in regular Bible study, frequent prayer and attendance at worship services, and active witnessing and evangelizing. To protect their beliefs and practices from secular corrosion, fundamentalists formed religious communities in which they cultivated the friendship of persons who thought and acted as they did. According to Carpenter, these local church fellowships provided members with constant instruction, a sense of calling, and lasting friendships. As the heirs, to a greater or lesser extent, of early twentieth-century fundamentalism, evangelical groups in the military functioned in a similar fashion, providing their members with a sense of worth and identity, a source of absolute authority, and a discipline or way of life that supported them amid the vicissitudes of military experience. This was true of denominational groups, whether in the form of evangelical church fellowships on or off military posts, prayer groups, spiritual

19. Bill Bright, *Come Help Change Our World* (San Bernardino, Calif., 1979), 85–87, 99; Colonel Glenn Jones, Director, Military Ministry, "The Military Ministry" (Typewritten brochure, n.d.); *Here's Life World: Taking the Message to the Military* (San Diego, n.d.), n.p.

growth meetings, or Bible study classes, as well as parachurch groups. All of them served, in the words of an OCSC writer, as "spiritual oases" in the armed forces.[20]

Evangelical groups in the military advertised their separated life by means of aggressive witnessing and evangelizing. If some observers dismissed them as "Jesus freaks" and fanatics, others were intrigued by their distinctive lifestyle. A staff sergeant who dropped in on a Navigators football game one Saturday afternoon at Dover Air Force Base noticed the contrast between them and his friends back in California. "I was used to guys cussing at football games. These guys didn't," he said. Afterward, the Navigators invited him to go out for a pizza. "Going to the pizza parlor," the sergeant said, "they carried Bibles, and I recalled how I laughed at 'Jesus freaks' like them." But when his newfound friends showed him "how Jesus died for him, that he could receive eternal forgiveness, and that he could have a personal relationship with God through Jesus Christ," he paid attention. "Since those guys showed an honest interest in me, I listened. . . . I prayed right there and yielded my life to Christ."[21]

Two Citadel men explained what attracted them to the Navigators. One said, simply, "I saw that these guys had a happiness and a sureness." Another man claimed to recognize something different in the life of the Navigator who befriended him. "He had a confidence about him. It seemed that there wasn't anything that could faze him." Didn't non-Christian leaders exhibit confidence? "Yes, but a lot of times you can see them shaking." The Navigator "didn't act like the other leaders. Other leaders would get up and put on a big show of bravado for their confidence. Or some would be harsh and strict. But Walt was getting his confidence from somewhere besides himself. I could just tell there was something in his life that I had never seen in anybody else. . . . I guess I was seeing Christ." Another military man who eventually decided to work with the Navigators explained his decision by saying, "There is a unique *quality of life* I observed in the Navigators I met."[22]

20. Joel Carpenter, "The Renewal of American Fundamentalism, 1930–1945" (Ph.D. dissertation, Johns Hopkins University, 1984), 38–45, 70–72, 75–84; Wilson Gene Parks, "The History and Development of Overseas Christian Servicemen's Centers (Master's thesis, Fuller Theological Seminary, 1965), 32.

21. Greene, "Facing the Frontline in Europe," 12–13.

22. Monte C. Unger, "There Is Something Different About a Citadel Man," *Navigators Log*, January, 1973, pp. 6–7; Monte C. Unger, "The Man Who Lives for Others," *Navigators Log*, October, 1971, p. 6.

Servicemen suffering from "emptiness" or a "spiritual vacuum," even those who considered themselves religious but in a nebulous way, were attracted by the interest the disciple-makers showed in them. The staff sergeant was impressed when the Navigators "showed an honest interest" in him. Similarly, one of the Citadel students, speaking of Walter Teger, his initial contact with the Navigators, recalled, "There was love from Walt. He cared about me the way I was. I followed him." When he attended a Navigator Bible study with Walt, he discovered "the rest of the guys were just like Walt. They had this quality that was lacking in other people. It really made me feel warm. I felt they could help me and make me happy." Later, at a retreat, he said the Navigators' "love toward me radiated God's love for me. It just radiated through them. It really attracted me. They cared about me in the way I was and they were not caught up with their own problems and worries."[23]

The men or women who responded to such discipling and surrendered their lives to Christ acquired a new identity as "Christians" that set them apart from so-called nonbelievers. And in taking up the separated life, they embraced beliefs that were traditionally associated with evangelical Christianity but seemed especially meaningful or relevant in the military.

One example was the belief in the Bible as the inerrant, inspired Word of God and "the supreme and all-sufficient authority in faith and life." In the midst of a rapidly changing world characterized by increasing secularization and moral relativism, such a belief provided stability and certainty to military men, just as it did for civilians. During the post-Vietnam era, this belief had a special appeal for military men disturbed by the ethical disintegration of the armed forces. In an article in *Command* in the fall of 1983, Lieutenant Commander Bradley Y. Winsted, USN, issued "a cry for moral action": "We are called on to stand firm in a time of global retreat from responsibilities," he wrote. "Our Western culture is finding it increasingly more difficult to define right from wrong. . . . As military officers, we are required to be moral examples in a time of situational ethics." Writing as "a Christian officer," Winsted offered his fellow officers "a perfect leadership manual that is thousands of years old"—the Bible. "This manual clearly demonstrates what is to be expected of men in authority and how they must

23. Unger, "There Is Something Different," 7.

conduct themselves morally. . . . It gives man the absolutes for which he craves, absolutes by which he may measure himself."[24]

"As Christians, we have access to power, God's power, and a source of strength that unbelievers don't have," a Navigator observed. In particular, the doctrine of divine sovereignty seemed to help evangelicals cope with the vicissitudes of military life. Thus some cadets and midshipmen claimed that faith in the sovereignty of God enabled them to handle the regimentation, stress, discipline, and competition they encountered at the military academies. Similarly, a Navigator draftee explained how he had gotten through basic training at Fort Knox in the early 1970s. "Much of the anxiety of military life results from the unknown," he observed, but a Christian who believes in the sovereignty of God need not " 'faint in the day of adversity' . . . worry over the next move or . . . complain when the next assignment takes us further from home."[25]

Belief in divine sovereignty proved especially meaningful and relevant to men anticipating or involved in combat. During the Vietnam War, a serviceman wrote to *Eternity* magazine's "Your Questions Answered" department. Expecting to be sent to Vietnam, he said, "I know I am a Christian, but the thought of death terrifies me. What can I do?" The fear of death is "a normal fear," the author of the column responded. "It will help you to realize that no harm can come to you unless the Lord allows it. Further, He will not allow it unless it is for the ultimate good of all concerned—yourself included—and for His glory. . . . If death should come to you, what is it but an entrance into a far more beautiful existence with Jesus Christ. . . . Trust the Lord to be with you. He is!" Chaplain David L. Meschke offered similar counsel to a group of servicemen in Faribault, Minnesota, in January, 1967: "If I live, wonderful! Praise God for that! If I get shot, well, praise God for

24. "Article III: Statement of Doctrines [from OCU Constitution]," *Command*, 25th anniversary issue, 1968, p. 10; Spoede, *More Than Conquerors*, 68, 81–82, 98–99; Lieutenant Commander Bradley Y. Winsted, USN, "A Cry for Moral Action," *Command*, Fall, 1983, pp. 3, 4, 29.

25. Bernard Thompson, "From the Air Force Academy to the World . . . *a Unique Disciplemaking Ministry*," *Navlog*, July, 1977, pp. 3–4; Richard S. Greene, "The Annapolis Aura," *Navlog*, December–January, 1984–85, p. 10; Mark Fackler, "How to Live the Christian Life During Military Basic Training," *Navigators Log*, July, 1972, p. 6. See also Carlos Kizzee, "A New Definition of Excellence," *Navlog*, December–January, 1984–85, p. 12.

that! Maybe there is somebody down in a hospital that he wants me to witness to, somebody in the next bed. If I go home to Glory, well, that's better yet. Whether we live or die, to know Christ is what is important, and the moment I leave this life I am with Christ, which is far better, our Scripture says."[26]

In the midst of combat in Southeast Asia, few evangelical chaplains seem to have rhapsodized about dying and "going to Glory," as Chaplain Meschke had back in the United States, but they did present the doctrines of divine sovereignty and eternal life to their men. And evangelical magazines printed the testimony of servicemen like Van Smith, a marine who recounted a month-long operation in Quang Nam province, Vietnam. His company had suffered more than 50 percent casualties, including his company commander, the executive officer, and two platoon commanders. "Jesus said, 'I am with you always.' He said it and He meant it," Smith declared. "The God I had worshiped around stained glass windows and organ music was with me all through February, 1969." Some years later a marine who survived the October, 1983, suicide bomb attack on the marine compound at the Beirut, Lebanon, airport recalled: "Never in my whole life, until Beirut, had I learned to trust God daily. His sovereignty took on a new meaning because every morning you woke up in Lebanon, you understood that God loved you and was taking care of you."[27]

Just as their belief in the inerrancy of Scripture and divine sovereignty sustained evangelicals amid the vicissitudes of military life, so did spiritual discipline help them resist temptation. Through Bible study, prayer, and meditation they sought to strengthen their "walk with God." They also drew support from fellowship with other Christians. Major General Clay T. Buckingham testified that "the OCF has been the principal 'means of grace' in my life as a Christian. The OCF family, over the years, provided the impetus to continue on to know the Lord, to demonstrate His love and holiness, and to live openly as a Christian before my contemporaries." Similarly, Lieutenant Colonel Al (Alexan-

26. "Your Questions Answered," *Eternity*, October, 1966, p. 39; David L. Meschke, "What the Chaplain Said," *Decision*, May, 1967, p. 2. "Officers, Staff and Council of the Officers' Christian Union of the U.S.A.," *Command*, Spring, 1967, p. 55, lists Meschke as a member of the OCU Council.

27. James M. Hutchens, *Beyond Combat* (Chicago, 1968), 25, 37–38, 41, 60, 68, 87, 124–25; Smith, "Don't Hide from Your Hitch," 84; Richard S. Greene, "God's Sovereignty While Under Artillery Fire," *Navlog*, June–July, 1984, p. 12.

der P.) Shine recalled that fellowship with Christian cadets at West Point enabled him to "love the Word of God" and encouraged him "to submit my beliefs and my actions to the authority of the Scriptures as the only reliable source of Christian belief and practice." The "vital Christian fellowship" he first encountered as a plebe in the West Point OCF continued to sustain him during his twenty years of commissioned service. For Shine and his wife, OCF became their "primary Christian home."[28]

Notwithstanding the support they received from their religious faith and the fellowship of other Christians, living the separated life was not easy for evangelicals in the armed forces. They sometimes felt scorned or ridiculed. During the 1940s and 1950s, and into the 1960s, they constituted a marginal group within the military. Moreover, as the next chapter will show, their sectarian views thrust them into a series of confrontations with the military leadership.

28. Latty, "Ministry of Overseas Christian Servicemen's Centers," 20, 23; "The Objectives of the Officers' Christian Fellowship," *Command*, War and Peace Issue, Spring, 1975, p. 47; Fackler, "How to Live the Christian Life," 6; Spoede, *More Than Conquerors*, 55–56, 108; Lieutenant Colonel Al Shine, USA, "An 'OCF Christian,'" *Command*, Winter, 1983–84, pp. 27–28.

7

Engaging the Military Leadership

Evangelicals won access to the federal government and public recognition nationwide in the 1950s and 1960s. Their relationship with the military leadership was characterized by tension and conflict, however—in part because before the late 1960s the great majority of military leaders belonged to mainline Protestant denominations. According to Morris Janowitz, in 1950, 63 percent of army leaders came from "traditional" denominations such as Episcopalian (which accounted for fully 40 percent), Presbyterian, Congregationalist, and Lutheran, as opposed to only 18 percent from "pietistic" groups such as Baptists, Methodists, and Disciples of Christ. Denominations Janowitz termed "revivalist," including fundamentalists, were wholly unrepresented among the military elite. Given their mainline orientation, military leaders, not surprisingly, viewed evangelicals as alien, even suspect, because of their beliefs. Brigadier General Robert H. Buker, president of the Officers' Christian Fellowship in the mid-1980s, remembered that in the 1950s and 1960s "we were looked upon as freaks." The Navigators earned the nicknames "God's Gestapo" and "Green Berets of the Christian community" because of their aggressive evangelizing, and Campus Crusade gained a reputation for being uncooperative and uncomplimentary toward both chaplains and churches. Although the OCU urged its members to be active in military chapel programs and supportive of Protestant chaplains, Lieutenant General William K. Harrison admitted that "cooperation with Chaplains who reject the Bible as the plenary, verbal inspired Word of God may be difficult or impossible." As a result, on a few occasions in the late 1950s and early 1960s, the OCU clashed with religiously liberal chaplains.[1]

1. Morris Janowitz, *The Professional Soldier: A Social and Political Portrait* (Glencoe,

At both West Point and Annapolis, administrators tended to be suspicious of the OCU, and evangelical cadets and midshipmen ran into difficulties establishing chapters there. In September, 1953, the superintendent of West Point proposed that OCU activities among cadets be reviewed, relenting only when General Harrison questioned interference with the right of Christian officers and cadets to free religious expression and association and reassured him and other authorities at the academy regarding the OCU and its goals. In 1959 the OCU's standing once again appeared to be in jeopardy as a result of a dispute between its staff representative and one of the West Point chaplains over the interpretation of Matthew 25; the crisis eventually passed. At the Naval Academy, the same year, the head chaplain and a midshipman named Ross Campbell became involved in a confrontation over Bible study classes and prayer meetings Campbell was conducting. He claimed that the chaplain influenced the superintendent to issue an order restricting religious meetings at Annapolis to those sponsored by the chapel. Again, General Harrison reminded academy authorities that midshipmen, as citizens of the United States, had the right to freedom of religious expression and association. In addition, Commander Robert L. Baughan, Jr., an OCU council member serving in the office of the chief of naval operations, warned the assistant chief of naval personnel, who was responsible for Naval Academy affairs, that the National Association of Evangelicals or some other conservative Christian organization might raise objections. As a result, Annapolis officials, including the chaplain, retracted the order prohibiting religious activities outside the chapel.[2]

As the disputes with administrators and chaplains at the academies indicate, in the 1950s and early 1960s evangelicals were just as suspicious of the military leadership as it was of them. They resented its mainline orientation. In particular, they worried that military leaders were promoting ecumenism, which evangelicals associated with such organiza-

Ill., 1960), 98–99; Robert W. Spoede, *More Than Conquerors: A History of the Officers' Christian Fellowship of the U.S.A., 1943–1983* (Englewood, Colo., 1993), 39, 58–59; Robert J. Phillips, "The Navigators: An Inquiry and Evaluation," *MCR*, Spring, 1984, p. 77; John Dolaghan, "Evangelicals Around Your Base," *Chaplain*, XXXI (Fall, 1974), 65, 67.

2. Spoede, *More Than Conquerors*, 23, 25, 43–45; Ross Campbell with Randall Gray, *How to Keep Going When the Storms Keep Coming* (Wheaton, Ill., 1986), 28–51.

tions as the National Council of Churches and, especially, the World Council of Churches (WCC). Since the beginning of the ecumenical movement, evangelicals had declaimed against its evils. Efforts to promote church union, for example, conjured up images of a "World Superchurch" that, in the words of an Assemblies of God resolution, "would probably culminate in the Scarlet Woman or Religious Babylon of Revelation." The ecumenical movement embraced the Orthodox churches (including the Roman Catholic Church), which, Clyde Taylor of the NAE pointed out, "ignore the new birth as God's method of salvation," also causing unease, as did the movement's "doctrinal deviations"—relativism, universalism, and humanism, among others.[3]

In the 1950s, evangelicals' suspicion of the mainline orientation and ecumenism of the military leadership provoked complaints about the General Protestant Service, mainstay of the military chapel program. Devised to meet the challenge of providing worship services for armed forces personnel who came from more than one hundred religious denominations, the General Protestant Service was a regular Sunday service conducted by a Protestant chaplain in accordance with liturgical forms chosen by him and usually adapted to the needs of worshipers from a variety of denominational backgrounds. Writing in the *Military Chaplain* in 1958, Chaplain Roy J. Honeywell emphasized the chaplain's obligation to the men attending the service. They were, he pointed out, accustomed to various forms of religious expression, from the liturgical to the evangelical, and their views ranged from liberal to conservative. To offer them a sectarian service would confuse or even repel them. Although Honeywell recognized the chaplain's debt to members of his denomination and encouraged chaplains to provide the distinctive rites or sectarian doctrines to those who desired them, he insisted that the chaplain's "debt to the few must not outweigh his obligation to the many." In preaching to the latter, he should seek to offer "a living message which relates helpfully to the problems of great numbers of men."[4]

3. Edith L. Blumhofer, *Assemblies of God: A Chapter in the Story of American Pentecostalism* (2 vols.; Springfield, Mo., 1989), II, 97; Clyde W. Taylor, "Evangelicals Examine Ecumenicity," *UEA*, April, 1963, p. 20. See also Carl F. H. Henry, "A Door Swings Open," *UEA*, July, 1965, p. 10. For a discussion of the ecumenical movement in the post–World War II period, see H. George Anderson, "Ecumenical Movements," in *Altered Landscapes: Christianity in America, 1935–1985*, ed. David W. Lotz, Donald W. Shriver, Jr., and John F. Wilson (Grand Rapids, 1989), 98–105.

4. Roy J. Honeywell, "The New Religion," *Military Chaplain*, 31 (April, 1958),

Most evangelicals regarded the General Protestant Service as "more or less ecumenical," to quote the chairman of the Assemblies of God Commission on Chaplains, and they were suspicious of it for that reason.[5] Their complaints against the General Protestant Service dissipated, however, as the number of evangelical chaplains in the armed forces increased and—more important—when they discovered or created opportunities for preaching their own sectarian views.

Another, longer-running controversy between evangelicals and the military leadership involved the Unified Protestant Sunday School Curriculum used in the armed forces Sunday schools. Before that curriculum was adopted, chaplains had been free to choose whatever literature they wished to use in Sunday schools under their supervision. The Unified Protestant Sunday School Curriculum, which began operation in 1954, was developed to ensure continuity of religious instruction for children of servicemen attending chaplain-organized Protestant Sunday schools. A committee made up of one chaplain from each of the three service branches, along with the executive secretary of the Armed Forces Chaplains Board, selected the literature to be used from materials submitted by church-owned publishing houses. Because the curriculum was intended to represent a cross section of the Protestant denominations, the committee of chaplains selected materials designed for interdenominational use and excluded specifically denominational or sectarian materials.[6] Most evangelicals thought the curriculum had an ecumenical, theologically liberal orientation. Like the General Protestant Service, it was objectionable on that score if on no other.

No sooner had the unified curriculum become operative than the National Sunday School Association asked the NAE to investigate it. The association had discovered that chaplains were canceling orders for

---

7. See also Richard G. Hutcheson, Jr., *The Churches and the Chaplaincy* (Atlanta, 1975), 120.

5. T. E. Gannon, "Ministering to the Military," *PE*, June 25, 1978, p. 6. See also Warren Bird, "Inside the Alliance Military Chaplaincy," *Alliance Witness*, CXVIII (June 22, 1983), 9.

6. "NAE Charges Basic Rights Are Violated," *UEA*, October, 1962, p. 20; Grover G. DeVault, "The Dilemma of Evangelical Chaplains," *UEA*, February, 1962, p. 14. For background information on the development of the unified curriculum (as well as Catholic and Jewish curricula) and related matters, see Rodger R. Venzke, *Confidence in Battle, Inspiration in Peace: The United States Army Chaplaincy, 1945–1975* (Washington, D.C., 1977), 109–10.

Sunday school materials published by independent evangelical publishers in deference to the new, standardized curriculum. (The committee that drew up the curriculum chose materials only from church-owned publishing houses, which ruled out independent interdenominational literature such as that published by David C. Cook, Scripture Press, Gospel Light Press, or other evangelical outlets.) In response to its inquiries, NAE received word that use of the unified curriculum was not mandatory. The army contended that the decision whether to use the curriculum rested with the local installation, the navy insisted that it only "encouraged" but did not require chaplains to use the curriculum, and the air force declared that there was no directive making the curriculum mandatory. Despite such assurances, the NAE remained skeptical. As an article in *United Evangelical Action* pointed out, in the military a recommendation that chaplains use the curriculum "is almost equal to an order to use it." Moreover, on most bases, the chaplains committee that would oversee the Sunday school curriculum would likely include "liberal men," which would "insure that no independent evangelical literature will be used." The author added, "We know of no remedy for this."[7]

The stalemate between evangelicals and the military leadership over the unified curriculum continued into the early 1960s, when evangelicals revived the issue. The NAE led the way. In early 1962, the Chaplains Commission protested against the air force's requirement that chaplains use the unified curriculum. Speaking for the commission, the Reverend Bert Webb, assistant general superintendent of the Assemblies of God, charged that the requirement was "inconsistent with basic American liberty when a chaplain is required to use materials with which he cannot conscientiously agree." Noting the liberal orientation of the curriculum, Webb declared it to be "theologically and doctrinally inconsistent with the Bible."[8]

In August, 1962, and again in February, 1963, the president of the NAE wrote to the Armed Forces Chaplains Board protesting compulsory use of the unified curriculum. In the spring of 1963, the NAE took up the matter at its annual convention and released a statement charging that the constitutional liberties of chaplains were being violated. The

7. "NSSA Probe of USAS Sunday School Lessons," *UEA*, February 15, 1955, p. 16.

8. "Chaplains Group Hits Curriculum," *UEA*, June, 1962, p. 20.

chairman of a special NAE committee formed to study the issue told the convention that his committee would take its case directly to Secretary of Defense Robert McNamara if it were not resolved at a lower level.[9]

The Officers' Christian Union joined the controversy in October, 1962, when its governing board agreed on the following resolution: "Whereas: It has come to the attention of the Officers' Christian Union that restrictions have been placed upon the material normally made available to military chaplains for use in religious education, and whereas the OCU views such restriction with alarm as being a curtailment of basic freedom, be it therefore resolved that: military chaplains at all levels be permitted freedom in the selection of material for use in the Christian education program." The OCU sent copies of the resolution to the chiefs of the three service chaplaincies and to the denominational heads who sent representatives to the conferences that selected unified curriculum materials; it also disseminated it among all OCU members. The following year OCU president General Harrison wrote to the army chief of chaplains expressing the OCU's "grave concern" regarding "what appears to be the effort of the chiefs of military chaplains to exercise ecclesiastical authority over all chaplains of the different Protestant denominations in matters essentially theological" by means of "regulations making mandatory in Sunday schools at military chapels the use of . . . materials chosen by the chiefs." Harrison argued that such regulations constituted "a definite violation of the Constitution and of the freedom of religion of certain Protestant chaplains and Sunday school teachers" and were "nothing other than the age-old effort of sectarian groups to force their particular brand of theological beliefs and church polity on others of different beliefs." He was not above threatening a broader campaign against the unified curriculum if the army chief of chaplains failed to respond appropriately. If necessary, he indicated, complaints would be made "to other high military and government authorities." The matter might even be taken to the courts, "which would result in bad publicity to the military department," Harrison warned. "In view of past court decisions," he added, "it would appear unlikely that the regulation would be sustained, a result which

9. "Military Sunday Schools," *UEA*, April, 1967, p. 6; "Chaplains' Liberties Championed," *UEA*, June, 1963, p. 16.

would not increase the popularities of the chief of chaplains with the military or other authorities."[10]

The appeals to the Armed Forces Chaplains Board, the chiefs of the chaplaincies, and the military leadership proved unavailing, and in December, 1963, the air force issued a directive to chaplains declaring that the unified curriculum "is not only suggested; it is the Air Force Program, and Command Chaplains are expected to give it their leadership and support." The directive did allow for the substitution of alternate materials but only upon written appeal to the office of the air force chief of chaplains.[11]

The more unresponsive the military leadership appeared, the more evangelicals increased the volume of their criticism. In June, 1964, using language calculated to make national headlines, the NAE charged that chaplains were being required to use Sunday school materials containing "heresy." Both *Christianity Today* and *United Evangelical Action* followed up on the NAE attack. An editorial in *Christianity Today* criticized the "official promotion" of the unified curriculum in the army and navy, and its "mandatory use" in the air force as a violation of the First Amendment of the Constitution. The magazine admitted that curriculum materials (as opposed to the curriculum itself) were "not technically required in the Armed Forces," but it insisted that the materials "are so firmly backed by senior officers of the respective chaplaincies as to tip the scale heavily in favor of their use by chaplains." And in the air force, it noted, substitute materials could be used only by special permission.[12]

The *United Evangelical Action* article, written by a retired army chaplain, Michael E. Reynolds, carried the inflammatory title "Can the Military Sunday School Survive Socialism?" Reynolds contended that the stated purpose of the unified curriculum, which was to provide continuity of instruction, masked another, dangerous objective. Focusing on its "modernist thrust," he charged that the "Unified literature has had

10. Spoede, *More Than Conquerors*, 59; Office of the Chief of Chaplains, "Historical Review, 1 July 1962 to 30 June 1963" [1963] (Typescript at the Washington National Records Center, Suitland, Md.), 81–82. See also Venzke, *Confidence in Battle*, 112.

11. "Religious Liberty and the Armed Forces Sunday Schools," *CT*, July 17, 1964, p. 21.

12. *NYT*, June 16, 1964, p. 47; "Religious Liberty and the Armed Forces Sunday Schools," 21. The NAE's charge also was reported in the *Chicago Tribune;* see Office of the Chief of Chaplains, "Historical Review, 1 July 1963–30 June 1964" (1964) (Typescript at the Washington National Records Center, Suitland, Md.), 77.

a greater emphasis for ecumenism than for solving the continuity problem of military Sunday schools. It has kept a steady stream of social
gospel materials pouring into the Sunday schools of our armed forces
and blocked the use of evangelical literature on most installations." Pro-
ponents of the unified curriculum intended to "perpetuate religious liberalism in the armed forces" by requiring chaplains to use it, Reynolds
claimed. He recalled a meeting he and other chaplains, along with a post
commanding general, had had in September, 1963, with Army Chief of
Chaplains Major General Charles E. Brown, Jr. "There was nothing
unclear about his warning to chaplains who rejected the Unified materials that he controlled their next assignments," Reynolds remembered.
"Those who have been in the military understand such orders can mean
professional banishment," he explained. "The general was threatening
these men and could just as well have said, 'Outer Slobbovia needs a
chaplain of your caliber and it is my duty to see that they get a conscientious clergyman.' Many chaplains have found themselves in this type
of military pressure chamber where they are deprived of their traditional
freedom to reject literature they cannot in conscience support." In
Reynolds' view, the religious freedom of chaplains was being abrogated
by a Washington-based "military hierarchy" that commanded chaplains
to "co-sponsor the government's brand of religion."[13]

Evangelicals challenged the Unified Protestant Sunday School Curriculum by appealing to the free exercise clause of the First Amendment
to the United States Constitution. Thus they claimed that in prescribing
the curriculum, the armed forces (and therefore the federal government)
violated the constitutional right of free exercise of religion on the part
of chaplains, lay teachers, and pupils involved in armed forces Sunday
schools. They also invoked the no-establishment clause of the First
Amendment and even cited the Supreme Court's school prayer (*Engel
v. Vitale*) and Bible reading and Lord's Prayer (*Abington School District
v. Schempp*) decisions—generally regarded as anathema by evangelicals—in arguing their case against the unified curriculum. Those decisions, the editors of *Christianity Today* noted, said "that for government
to prescribe religious and devotional materials is unconstitutional. But
in the Armed Forces this very thing is being done extensively and against
continued protest." Evangelicals maintained that prescription of the

13. Michael E. Reynolds, "Can the Military Sunday School Survive Socialism?"
UEA, August, 1964, pp. 12, 19.

unified curriculum constituted an establishment of religion, not only in the air force, where it was mandatory, but also in the army and navy, where it was only strongly recommended. In their view, as the editors of *Christianity Today* argued, "official promotion" violated the First Amendment just as much as "mandatory use." Evangelicals also complained that "various pressures, other than written regulations," were employed to persuade chaplains to use the unified curriculum.[14]

In addition to the constitutional argument they leveled against the unified curriculum, evangelicals also mustered what might be called a sectarian argument. They focused on what they regarded as pervasive elements of theological liberalism and ecumenism. The importance of this argument should not be underestimated. Indeed, it seems to have informed most of the protest letters evangelicals sent to the chief of chaplains of the army. In its annual *Historical Review*, the Army Office of the Chief of Chaplains summarized the content of letters received in the early 1960s. Some had to do with the cost of curriculum materials and distribution problems, especially in Europe, but most focused on the theological orientation of the curriculum. "Some critics described it as Church-centered and morals-centered rather than Christ-centered. . . . The objection was voiced that the Unified Curriculum does not provide a knowledge of basic Bible stories and teachings and that it does not deal directly enough with the Sacred Scriptures or explain and apply them adequately. It was criticized for not sufficiently including the 'conservative Evangelical' aspect of the Christian faith, for lacking 'evangelical appeal,' for being inadequately coordinated with important periods of the Christian Year such as Christmas and Easter, and for being too much environment-centered and experience-centered." A few of the letters even raised ideological objections to the curriculum, claiming that the materials inculcated pacifism, opposed universal military training, and sanctioned conscientious objection—issues that were becoming controversial in the midst of the Vietnam War.[15]

14. "Religious Liberty and the Armed Forces Sunday Schools," 21, 22; Don Gill, "Capital Commentary," *UEA*, November, 1961, p. 4. See also "The Pentagon and the Chapel Program," *UEA*, May, 1964, p. 2, which cites "compulsory use of the present 'Unified Curriculum' by various types of coercion."

15. Department of the Army, Office of the Chief of Chaplains, *Summary of Major Events and Problems, 1 July 1960 to 30 June 1961* (n.d.), 77–79. The Army Office of the Chief of Chaplains responded to evangelical protests against the unified curriculum by declaring that though it encouraged implementation of the unified curriculum, no chap-

The NAE not only led the way in protesting the unified curriculum; it also supported and encouraged individual complaints against it. Articles published in *United Evangelical Action* gave the impression of a groundswell of evangelical protest against and resistance to it during the 1960s. According to the magazine, there was "wide dissatisfaction among evangelical chaplains" regarding the curriculum. It also cited a Southern Baptist chaplain's estimate that 85 percent of the chaplains from his denomination opposed it. In 1962, *United Evangelical Action* reported that a chaplain at a navy base had suspended use of the unified curriculum when nearly all of his teachers protested that it was not sufficiently Bible-centered and that Sunday school teachers at several army installations had resigned because they felt they could not teach materials used in the curriculum. That same year a chaplain reportedly resigned rather than teach the curriculum. In 1965, the magazine printed a letter written by a senior air force officer, who was superintendent of a chapel Sunday school, to the air force chief of chaplains objecting to the compulsory use of the unified curriculum. Some of the material was "so denominationally slanted it cannot be used without extensive rework on the teachers' part," he wrote. "If one of the purposes of compulsory use of the Unified Curriculum is to discourage and drive away the best qualified teachers, it is succeeding very well." In 1967 *United Evangelical Action* reported that a group of evangelicals at Fort Knox had started a separate Sunday school and were using their own literature instead of the prescribed materials. "Every possible effort was made by the evangelical group to cooperate with those responsible for the overall religious program at Fort Knox," the magazine noted. "The Army Chief of Chaplains was informed about the situation and we sent a letter urging him to condone the arrangements for a separate evangelical Sunday school in the same way he approves separate denominational worship services when there is sufficient interest to support them. However, effort is still being made to force the maverick evangelicals back into the mold at Fort Knox where they will again have to use the Unified Curriculum." The same year as the Fort Knox protest,

---

lain was compelled to use it, that no chaplain or Sunday school teacher need fear punishment for refusing to do so, and that no serviceman or dependent was forced to attend the Sunday schools that used the unified curriculum. It also noted that nothing prohibited the establishment of denominational Sunday schools where the need existed. See Venzke, *Confidence in Battle*, 112.

United Evangelical Action reported that Sunday school teachers at an air force base near Washington, D.C., had asked the superintendent "to call a meeting to get something done about the Unified Curriculum literature they received for use beginning April, 1967."[16]

OCU members also joined the campaign against the unified curriculum. The organization's historian, Robert W. Spoede, describes how OCU members and other conservative Christians serving as Sunday school teachers on military installations "complained about the liberal Unified Curriculum and forced chapels to provide Bible-based materials." In other cases, OCU members involved in base chapel programs were sufficiently vocal and numerous to see to it that children in the Sunday schools had access to "biblical teaching." In addition to the NAE, the OCU, *Christianity Today*, and *United Evangelical Action*, representatives of various Protestant denominations and even a few members of Congress who received complaints from their constituents—including Congressmen Mendel Rivers and Clarence D. Long and Senator Richard B. Russell—became involved in the fight by the mid-1960s.[17]

Even though the unified curriculum continued as a subject of controversy, in the late 1960s the tension between evangelicals and the military leadership abated and a new, more positive relationship began to develop.[18] Several factors worked together to make this happen.

16. "NAE Charges Basic Rights Are Violated," 20; DeVault, "The Dilemma of Evangelical Chaplains," 14; "Unified Curriculum," *UEA*, March, 1965, p. 6; "Capital Commentary," *UEA*, April, 1967, p. 6; "Military Sunday Schools," *UEA*, April, 1967, p. 6. For complaints addressed to the Army Office of the Chief of Chaplains, see U.S. Army Office of the Chief of Chaplains, *Historical Review, 1 July 1965 to 31 December 1966* (1969), 159–60; U.S. Army Office of the Chief of Chaplains, *Historical Review, 1 January 1967 to 30 June 1968* (1969), 99–100.

17. Spoede, *More Than Conquerors*, 59, 41; Office of the Chief of Chaplains, "Historical Review, 1 July 1963–30 June 1964," 77–78; Office of the Chief of Chaplains, "Historical Review, 1 July 1964 to 30 June 1965" [1965] (Typescript at the Washington National Records Center, Suitland, Md.), 98, 99.

18. Evangelical protests against the Unified Protestant Sunday School Curriculum continued into the 1970s and 1980s. According to James A. Edgren, director of the NAE Chaplains Commission, evangelicals won "a major battle" when the Department of Defense agreed to cease "mandating" the use of the unified curriculum. But, Edgren noted, "The individual services never fully complied. By the mid-to-late 70's both the Air Force and Navy were mandating its use and the Army was actually doing the same, though not saying so in writing." In the early 1980s, Edgren, then a chaplain, helped to rewrite the army regulations regarding the unified curriculum. "We eliminated the

One reason for the improved relationship was that evangelicals became more willing to tolerate ecumenical programs such as the General Protestant Service when they discovered, as we saw in Chapter 6, that they had ample opportunity to evangelize service personnel through counseling, moral education sessions, Bible study classes, revivals, and retreats. Many incorporated evangelistic preaching and the altar call or invitation into the General Protestant Service. The controversy over the unified curriculum proved more difficult to resolve, but even it became less vexing. In 1967, the intransigence of the military leadership provoked Clyde Taylor of the NAE Public Affairs Office to declare that "it is impossible for the church to exercise any administrative and policy control over what goes on in the chaplaincy" and Floyd Robertson, director of the NAE Chaplains Commission, to describe the military chaplaincy as "a religious establishment that is completely controlled by the government." Still, evangelicals made some headway in circumventing the required unified curriculum, as William Willoughby noted in an article in *Christianity Today* published in April, 1969. After pointing to the NAE's "running controversy with the military for years over directives that Protestant chaplains teach from standardized Sunday-school material which the NAE feels may be theologically heretical," he observed that "even though such regulations have been issued in the past, chaplains exercise the option to present the suggested materials from their own theological stance."[19]

Second, evangelicals promoted the new, more harmonious relation-

---

language that virtually mandated use of the Unified Curriculum and inserted regulatory language that enabled local chaplains to purchase whatever curriculum they chose. Later, in 1985–86, we revised the regulations to provide appropriated funds for purchase of materials other than the Unified Curriculum," he remembered. Those regulations (formulated in AR 165-1 1989) were in force in the army in 1991, when Edgren reported on them. The air force and the navy, by contrast, did "not have the same regulatory guidance," Edgren noted, "and the Unified Curriculum enjoys a most favored position in those services" (James A. Edgren, Chaplain [Colonel] U.S. Army, Retired, Director, NAE Chaplains Commission, to the author, October 30, 1991). On the unified curriculum in the air force in the 1970s and 1980s, see John E. Groh, "Lively Experiment: A Summary History of the Air Force Chaplaincy," *MCR*, Winter, 1990, p. 97; John E. Groh, *Facilitators of the Free Exercise of Religion: Air Force Chaplains, 1981–1990* (Washington, D.C., 1991), 176.

19. "Muzzled Ministry," *UEA*, January, 1967, p. 2; "Official Advisory Commission on Military Chaplains Recommended," *UEA*, January, 1967, p. 26; William Willoughby, "Chaplains' Role Under New Scrutiny," *CT*, April 25, 1969, p. 32.

ship with the military leadership by adopting a more positive approach to chaplains and chapel programs. Both denominational and parachurch groups made a concerted effort to improve relations with chaplains. For example, in a 1969 policy statement regarding servicemen's work, the Assemblies of God advised that such work should be carried out in "close cooperation" with chaplains and base chapel programs. The statement urged workers to establish pentecostal fellowships in military chapels wherever feasible, but it emphasized that AOG servicemen should be active in chapel programs, too. In the mid-1960s the OCU council set up various committees and staff positions to ensure good relations with chaplains. The organization designated members as liaisons to the chiefs of chaplains of each of the services, established a committee to work with chaplains, and for a brief time hired a retired army chaplain as a staff member to further cooperation between the OCU and active-duty chaplains. Similarly, in its Military Ministry issue for 1969, the *Navigators Log* ran an article urging Navigators to develop a "gung ho" attitude toward their chaplains. Unfortunately, the author noted, Navigators had not always cooperated with chaplains in the past. But that was changing. He offered a list of seven ways Navigators could "uphold the chaplains" and concluded with the admonition, "Think of what can lighten the chaplain's load . . . then pitch in and help."[20]

Richard G. Hutcheson, Jr., author of *The Churches and the Chaplaincy* and for many years a chaplain in the U.S. Navy, agrees that the new, more harmonious relationship between evangelicals and the military leadership was "very real and very important." In his view, it reflected a change occurring within evangelicalism generally during the postwar period—the increasing prominence of "new evangelicals" as compared with separatist fundamentalists. In the armed forces during the 1940s, 1950s, and early 1960s, he observed, it was the fundamentalists who "adopted a confrontational stance" toward the mainline military and chaplaincy leadership. By the late 1960s, however, the new evangelicals in the armed forces, like their counterparts in the civilian sector, were taking "a more accommodationist stance," which resulted in greater

20. "Policy Statement, Servicemen's Work of the Assemblies of God Overseas" (Mimeographed copy dated January 9, 1969, from AOG Archives), n.p.; Spoede, *More Than Conquerors*, 87; Paul Drake, "How You Can Be 'Gung Ho,'" *Navigators Log*, December, 1969, p. 16.

cooperation with military and chaplaincy leaders.[21] Also important was the changing situation of evangelicals in the military. As they gained numbers and recognition in the armed forces, they felt less marginal (and less marginalized) and consequently more willing to adapt to the religiously pluralistic context in which they functioned.

Although evangelicals adopted an adversarial stance on the General Protestant Service and the unified curriculum, they took quite a different position in another controversy that also developed in the 1960s over the military chaplaincy. In the early years of that decade mainline religious groups became increasingly uneasy about the chaplain's dual role as a military officer and a clergyman. These critics of the chaplaincy contended that chaplains experienced a tension or conflict between the two roles and generally resolved it, consciously or unconsciously, in favor of the military role. By the mid-1960s, growing opposition to the Vietnam War reinforced such concern. As the war escalated, religious groups that questioned the morality of United States intervention and the conduct of the war also indicted the chaplaincy—on one hand for supporting and participating in it and on the other for failing to speak out against it.[22]

Interestingly, some of the mainline critics of the chaplaincy charged the military leadership with violating the religious freedom of chaplains, just as evangelicals had in protesting the General Protestant Service and the unified curriculum. For example, the United Church of Christ Task Force on Ministries to Military Personnel criticized the army regulation defining chaplains' duties on the grounds that it subordinated the mission of the church to the mission of the military. But the viewpoint of the task force differed significantly from that of most evangelicals. The task force sought to protect what it described in its report as "the chaplain's complete freedom of conscience in exercising his or her duties as a minister and a representative of the church" to promote the prophetic role of the chaplain, which was "to be a Christian sign of contradiction

---

21. Richard G. Hutcheson, Jr., to the author, June 23, 1995.

22. See, for example, Martin Siegel, "Revamping the Military Chaplaincy," *Christian Century,* LXXIX (August 8, 1962), 959–60; Norman MacFarlane, "Navy Chaplaincy: Muzzled Ministry," *Christian Century,* LXXXIII (November 2, 1966), 1338–39; William Robert Miller, "Chaplaincy vs. Mission in a Secular Age," *Christian Century,* LXXXIII (November 2, 1966), 1335–37; Gordon C. Zahn, "The Scandal of the Military Chaplaincy," *Judaism,* XVIII (Summer, 1969), 313–19; Harvey G. Cox, ed., *Military Chaplains: From a Religious Military to a Military Religion* (New York, 1971).

within the military and the State, fulfilling the prophetic calling of discerning God's judgment on the policies and practices of the nation" and "serving as counselor and critic to the commander and his staff on all matters of religion, morality, and ethics in the life and work of the military." Evangelicals, by contrast, raised the issue of the religious freedom of chaplains to promote their pastoral role—evangelizing and instructing service personnel in accord with the tenets of their endorsing denomination. And because evangelicals generally supported the war in Vietnam, they were not particularly concerned about the right of chaplains to speak against it, and they certainly did not censure chaplains for complicity in an immoral war. Indeed, their criticism of the unified curriculum notwithstanding, chaplains as well as laymen writing in evangelical magazines during the late 1960s and early 1970s generally emphasized the freedom chaplains enjoyed in preaching the gospel in accord with the doctrines and beliefs of their own denominations. Thus when the *Christian Century* published an article by a former navy chaplain labeling the military chaplaincy a "muzzled ministry," *United Evangelical Action* responded by quoting a statement by the navy chief of chaplains which dismissed such opinions as "a distorted caricature of a deeply committed and highly effective ministry." Similarly, an air force chaplain writing in the *Baptist Program* insisted that "one of the greatest luxuries in the chaplaincy is that of latitude. From the pulpit to the flight line there is a great horizon that is limited only by time and imagination. No commander or senior chaplain has ever suggested that I restrict my preaching to any degree in subject or contents." Answering the charge by mainline critics that chaplains were warmongers, evangelicals celebrated chaplains first and foremost as "missionaries in uniform," "serving God and country."[23]

Thus despite their continuing complaints about the Unified Protestant Sunday School Curriculum, evangelicals took a generally positive view of the military chaplaincy as an institution. In 1969 *United Evan-*

23. United Church of Christ, Task Force on Ministries to Military Personnel, *Ministries to Military Personnel: Report of a United Church of Christ Task Force to the Ninth General Synod, St. Louis, Missouri, June 22–26, 1973* (Philadelphia, 1973), 81, 82; Clyde W. Taylor, "Capital Commentary," *UEA*, January, 1967, p. 2; Preston C. Brown, "I Am in the Ministry!" *Baptist Program*, February, 1969, p. 14; George W. Cummins, "Missionaries in Uniform," *Baptist Program*, February, 1969, pp. 5–6. See also Earl W. Minor, "Not Every Minister Can Wait at the Bus Station," *Baptist Program*, February, 1969, p. 212.

gelical Action observed that although the NAE remained concerned about "enforced use" of the unified curriculum, on the matter of the chaplaincy it believed that "until a more feasible way is found to meet the complex spiritual needs in the military, the present system should continue."[24] Such a position, articulated in the midst of growing controversy over the chaplaincy, could not fail to garner support for evangelicals even from theologically liberal chaplains.

Another factor that contributed to a more harmonious relationship between evangelicals and the military leadership was that although some leaders continued to regard evangelical religion as theologically alien, they recognized that ideologically it was sympathetic to and supportive of the military. George Marsden has pointed out that evangelicalism "benefited from the upheavals of the 1960s." In particular, he observes, it gained from the reaction against a "counterculture" identified with permissiveness, lawlessness, and secularism. Evangelicals' opposition to such impulses, along with the "fierce patriotism" they exhibited during the Vietnam era, when attacks on the nation and authority reached a crescendo, synchronized with the growth of political conservatism within American society. "Evangelicals benefited also from the uncertainties of the Vietnam era and its aftermath by offering decisive answers," Marsden points out. "Confronted with a crisis in authority in a changing and pluralistic society, evangelicals could point to the sure certainty of the word of God. . . . Evangelicals generally could draw on the immense residual prestige of the Bible in America as a firm rock in a time of change."[25] In much the same way, evangelicalism gained stature among military leaders who felt increasingly beleaguered by antimilitary and antiwar sentiment. In the crucible of the Vietnam War, as we shall see in Chapters 9, 10, and 11, evangelicals demonstrated their support for the military in ways the leadership could not fail to appreciate.

A final factor that helped reduce tension between evangelicals and the military leadership was that as membership in the mainline religions

24. Clyde W. Taylor, "Capital Commentary," *UEA*, Fall, 1968, p. 49. See also Porter Routh, "Personally," *Baptist Program*, February, 1969, p. 22, and for an even more emphatic defense of the constitutionality of the chaplaincy, Cummins, "Missionaries in Uniform," 5–6.
25. George M. Marsden, "Preachers of Paradox: The Religious New Right in Historical Perspective," in *Religion and America: Spiritual Life in a Secular Age*, ed. Mary Douglas and Steven Tipton (Boston, 1982), 156–57.

declined and that of evangelical denominations increased, the number of men entering the military from conservative Protestant churches also increased.[26] The dramatic increase in the number of evangelical chaplains that began during the mid-1960s was noted in Chapter 2. Evangelical religion also grew among enlisted personnel. Perhaps most important, among the officer corps, traditionally mainline in religious persuasion, the number of evangelicals increased significantly. Thus the mid- to late 1960s constitute a watershed in the spread of evangelical religion in the armed forces. Evangelical religion became increasingly visible, respectable, even influential. Evangelicals evolved from a small minority scorned by much of the military leadership to a respected and growing element of the armed forces. Of the military leaders in the 1960s who helped this process along, none was more significant than Army Chief of Staff General Harold K. Johnson.

26. For a summary of the decline of membership in the mainline denominations and increase in that of evangelical denominations, see Richard G. Hutcheson, Jr., *God in the White House: How Religion Has Changed the Modern Presidency* (New York, 1988), 67–69.

8

Harold K. Johnson,
a Christian Commander

In December, 1960, Henry G. Perry, executive secretary of the American Tract Society, wrote to then major general Harold K. Johnson, commandant of the Army Command and General Staff College at Fort Leavenworth, Kansas. Some time ago, Perry pointed out, Lieutenant General William K. Harrison had written a testimony for the society, but he had retired and it was now seeking one from a general officer on active duty. "Would you be good enough to pray about this and give it your consideration?" Perry asked. Johnson responded two weeks later, sending Perry a proposed statement entitled "Let Your Light So Shine." "Anyone who has heard the whine of a bullet fired in anger is deeply aware of the presence of a Supreme Being," Johnson began. Later in the testimony he described his own relationship with God: "I like to think of God as an all-enveloping, all-encompassing God, completely surrounding me with His love. My God is understanding, tender, compassionate and loving. He stands ready to guide me whenever I turn to Him for advice, that I might advance His work on earth." He concluded by quoting Matthew 5:16, which he described as "a guiding light in my life": "Let your light so shine before men, that they may see your good works, and glorify your Father, which is in heaven."[1]

On close scrutiny Johnson's testimony may not have measured up to fundamentalist or new evangelicals' doctrinal standards in the early

1. Henry G. Perry to Harold K. Johnson, December 22, 1960, and [Harold K. Johnson], "Let Your Light So Shine" (Typescript, n.d., in Johnson to Perry, January 7, 1961, both in Harold Keith Johnson Papers, U.S. Army Military History Institute, Carlisle Barracks, Pa.).

1960s. Indeed, some fundamentalists and evangelicals might have detected an element of modernism in Johnson's description of an "all-enveloping, all-encompassing God." But if Johnson's choice of words was less than satisfying, his willingness to write a testimony for the American Tract Society and to stand forth as a public supporter of evangelical religion could not but please conservative Christians within and outside the military. During the 1960s he helped evangelical religion achieve greater respect and visibility than ever before within the armed forces and civilian society. In this regard, he continued the work of General William K. Harrison. But Johnson was in a position to do more than Harrison had been able to do. As chief of staff of the army, Johnson not only proclaimed his evangelical beliefs and made them an element of his leadership, he also implemented them as military policy.

Born in North Dakota in 1912, Johnson was brought up in a strict, religious home. He was baptized an Episcopalian but not confirmed; when the family lived in a place where there was no Episcopal church, they attended the Methodist church, and he joined it. As a member of the class of 1933 at West Point, however, Johnson decided that the Methodist denomination was too active in the pacifist movement. During summer vacation between his second and third years at the academy, he later remembered, "I removed my certificate of church membership from its frame on the wall of my room at home and carried it back to my pastor. And I've not rejoined the church since."[2] Johnson felt much more comfortable with the religious program at the academy, where the chaplain was an Episcopalian, and with the interdenominational chapel programs operating on the various army posts where he served after graduation.

But neither the West Point nor the post chapel programs formed Johnson's intense religious faith. That was forged in the crucible of imprisonment and combat during World War II and in Korea. Johnson's account of his religious experience may be found in the prayer breakfast speeches he delivered in the 1960s and in a 1972 interview at the U.S. Army Military History Institute. Serving with the 57th Infantry

2. "Senior Officers Debriefing Program: Interview with Harold Keith Johnson by Colonel Richard W. Jensen, 6 February 1972" (Typescript, Carlisle Barracks, n.d., in Johnson Papers). See also "Address by General Harold K. Johnson, Chief of Staff, United States Army, Second Annual Governor's Prayer Breakfast, Curundu, Canal Zone, Tuesday, February 8, 1966" (Typescript in Johnson Papers), 2; Martin Blumenson, "A Most Remarkable Man," *Army*, XVIII (August, 1968), 21.

in the Philippines when World War II broke out, he was captured by the Japanese in April, 1942, when Bataan fell. He survived the Death March, only to be imprisoned at Camp O'Donnell, Camp Cabanatuan, and Bilibid Prison. "There were a lot of times when you just wondered whether God up there in the sky was going to pull you through," Johnson remembered. "God was close and very real in those hours." In December, 1944, as he and other Americans were being transferred to Japan, the prison ship came under attack by U.S. bombers. "I sat huddled at the bottom of a ladder that led into a baggage hold with 487 other Americans," Johnson recalled. The Japanese ship put up a desperate defense; shells whistled around the hatch leading into the baggage hold, sometimes striking the men. "I bowed my head and prayed," Johnson said, "and in the course of my prayer said 'Lord, I am ready if you want me,' and I knew a great peace." In 1950, Johnson's faith was renewed in the midst of combat in Korea. In December of that year, he and the men of the 8th Cavalry were fighting just southeast of Pyongyang, the North Korean capital. As battalion commander, Johnson said he felt "deeply troubled by the threat to the men that he was charged with safeguarding. Could he do the job that was his to do and still give his men a fighting chance to survive? Out of the still of the night, as if from a great distance, came God's voice, saying, 'Be strong. Have no fear. I am with you.'"[3]

Thus when Johnson wrote that "anyone who has heard the whine of a bullet fired in anger is deeply aware of the presence of a Supreme Being," he drew on his own wartime experiences. Religion was a part of the fabric of his life as a soldier. No doubt that is why he saw nothing strange or improper about making it an element of his military leadership.

During the late 1950s, while serving as chief of staff at 7th Army Headquarters in Stuttgart-Vachingen, Johnson became active in the Protestant Men of the Chapel (PMOC), a religious organization that originated in the chapels of the U.S. Army in Europe (USAREUR) in the early 1950s. An interdenominational laymen's group with local

3. "Senior Officers Debriefing Program," 50; "Remarks by General Harold K. Johnson, Chief of Staff, United States Army, at the Presidential Prayer Breakfast, Shoreham Hotel, Washington, D.C., Thursday, February 4, 1965—8:00 A.M. (EST)" (Typescript in Johnson Papers), 1, 2. See also Blumenson, "A Most Remarkable Man," 21–22.

chapters serving units or military posts throughout Europe, the PMOC functioned like a vestry, session, or board of deacons in civilian churches, aiding the chaplain in developing and maintaining his chapel program. PMOC chapters also held monthly meetings for the members which featured a worship service and one or more inspirational talks by a member or an invited guest. Johnson served as president of the PMOC USAREUR Council during 1957–58. In an interview with Margaret Frakes of the *Christian Century*, he described the organization as "God's recruiting service." Its purpose was not to evangelize those unaffiliated with a church but to renew and maintain the faith of members who had been active church members before entering the armed forces. "Our sole reason for being is to bring men into purposeful lay activities, to open the hearts and minds of our associates so they become reacquainted with God," he explained to Frakes. "All of us were told about God as children—I know I was—but at some point along the way a door closed. Our job is to open that door, grasp a hand and lead men through to meet God face to face."[4]

As PMOC president Johnson believed that the way to "attract men to God" was by example. The PMOC theme during the year he headed the organization was based on Matthew 5:16 ("Let your light so shine"), the same verse that he later invoked in the testimony he sent to the American Tract Society. In a speech he delivered at Goeppingen in October, 1957, Johnson explained the relevance of the verse and that it was being used as the PMOC theme "because it so closely parallels the manner in which Jesus spread his teachings. It is the one assured way of making Christianity a living, lasting religion." As he observed at the conclusion of his speech, preaching was only one way of spreading God's word. Teaching was another, and, in Johnson's view, one of the best teaching devices was "demonstration." Repeating the verse he had used as the text of his speech, Johnson urged his listeners to conduct themselves so that others would see their good works and glorify God.[5]

In July, 1964, Johnson became army chief of staff. At the swearing-in ceremony, when asked if he would like to say a few words, Johnson

4. Margaret Frakes, "PMOC of USAREUR," *Christian Century*, LXXVI (April 1, 1959), 393–94. See also Daniel B. Jorgensen, *Air Force Chaplains, 1947–1960* (Washington, D.C., [1961?]), 242–43; James S. Griffes, "We Need the 'Men of the Chapel,'" *Chaplain*, XIV (August, 1957), 3–6.

5. Harold K. Johnson, "Delivered at Goeppingen on Laymen's Sunday—20 October 1957" (Typescript in Johnson Papers), 1, 7.

took the opportunity to ask for divine guidance in coping with the high responsibilities of the office. That action provided a graphic illustration of one of the themes he stressed throughout his career—that military men need faith in God. He had first learned that lesson in World War II and Korea, where such faith provided him with a sense of divine protection. By the 1950s the theme had become part of his general philosophy of soldiering. He believed that religious faith not only afforded the soldier a sense of divine protection but also provided a necessary basis for moral obligation. In his 1960 testimony for the American Tract Society, he declared that "Christianity is the very foundation of military leadership." The year before he became army chief of staff, he reiterated his conviction about the importance of faith in a testimony he wrote for a special "Ministering to the Military" issue of *Christianity Today*. He argued that "spiritual strength" supplied soldiers with the determination and will to win that they needed to ensure victory against the enemy.[6]

Shortly after he became army chief of staff, the International Christian Leadership invited Johnson to speak at the 1965 presidential prayer breakfast in Washington, D.C. Why the ICL chose him is not clear. Johnson himself claimed not to know the reason. Surely the invitation had something to do with Johnson's having become part of the evangelical network as a result of agreeing to write the American Tract Society testimony and, more recently, the one for *Christianity Today*. The ICL invitation thrust Johnson into the evangelical circuit. He never became quite the celebrity General Harrison did during his retirement years, but for several years following the 1965 gathering, Johnson was the featured speaker at various prayer breakfasts conducted under ICL auspices, including governors' prayer breakfasts in Kansas, Colorado, Massachusetts, and the Panama Canal Zone and mayors' prayer breakfasts in Augusta, Georgia, Chicago, Illinois, and Martinsville, Indiana. He received many more invitations than he could honor. Apparently he combined his appearances with the performance of military duties, using military transportation and refusing honoraria.[7]

6. Blumenson, "A Most Remarkable Man," 25; [Johnson], "Let Your Light So Shine"; Harold K. Johnson, "Consulting the 'Master Gunner,'" *CT*, May 24, 1963, p. 13. See also [Harold K. Johnson], "Address to Regular Army Lieutenants of the 8th Infantry Division, Given in Late June and Early July, [1960]" (Typescript in Johnson Papers).

7. For correspondence regarding invitations to and acceptances of prayer breakfast

At these prayer breakfasts, Johnson delivered essentially the same address, mostly made up of quotes from the Bible, including his favorite, Matthew 5:16. He elaborated two basic themes, sometimes emphasizing one, sometimes the other, depending on the audience and the context in which he spoke. In the 1965 presidential prayer breakfast address, aware of and wanting to emphasize that he was the first military man to address the annual gathering, he focused on the soldier's need for religious faith. It was in that address that he rehearsed the story of his POW and wartime experience and the peace he found in relying on God. "In the years that have since passed by," he went on, "I continued to turn to God, both in my infrequent hours of accomplishment or achievement to thank Him, and in my more frequent hours of tribulation, to seek His help." The following year, speaking at the governor's prayer breakfast in the Canal Zone, Johnson reminded listeners of his "great privilege" the year before in being the lay speaker at the president's breakfast. He said he had received a great deal of mail from all over the United States "expressing surprise, and even bewilderment, that a man in uniform could express publicly his own belief in Almighty God." He said he found such remarks perplexing and puzzling because, he asserted, "God is the soldier's refuge. God is the soldier's strength. God must be the soldier's constant companion."[8]

Because he addressed a mostly civilian audience at these prayer breakfasts, Johnson broadened his message to include civilians as well as soldiers. Thus his other theme was the need for all individuals to have faith in God. In the Canal Zone address, he declared: "Not only must God be the soldier's companion; God must be a companion to all men. There can be no doubt in any man's mind nor in any man's heart that God is our sustenance and our strength. Each of us must believe wholeheartedly and fiercely in the power and the glory and the strength of God. . . .

---

speaking engagements, see Johnson Papers. Besides the prayer breakfasts, Johnson was invited to speak at other evangelical gatherings. In November, 1966, for example, he appeared as the featured speaker at the evening banquet of the NAE's Midwest Regional Annual Convention. (Another speaker on the program was John Broger, director of Armed Forces Information and Education.) See "N.A.E. at Work," *UEA*, November, 1966, p. 32. On Johnson's combining prayer breakfasts and military duties, see, for example, Johnson to Rev. John G. Sjoblom, December 7, 1966, in Johnson Papers.

8. "Remarks by Johnson at Presidential Prayer Breakfast," 2; "Address by Johnson, Second Annual Governor's Prayer Breakfast, Curundu, Canal Zone," 1.

Each man must seek the companionship of God; God awaits each one of us."[9]

In his most publicized address, delivered at the sixteenth annual presidential prayer breakfast in Washington, D.C., in February, 1968, Johnson rephrased the message slightly to urge not only that individuals seek God but that Americans as a nation do so. Probably he decided that the nature of the gathering and the critical situation of the United States in 1968 dictated such a change. This, after all, was the *national* prayer breakfast. He addressed the leaders of the nation and, beyond them, the nation as a whole. The more than 1,450 persons attending the breakfast included the president and vice-president, several cabinet members, a Supreme Court justice, and seven state governors, as well as members of Congress and high-ranking military officers. "Our Nation today is troubled and uneasy," he observed, citing drug use among young people, a general questioning of the "laws of our land," and public controversy over the Vietnam War and aid to the underprivileged. The answer, Johnson declared, was to "turn to God": "There is a solution to the problems of this world—turn to God. There is a solution to the conflicts between nations—turn to God. There is a solution to the problems of our cities and of our streets—turn to God. . . . There is a solution to the problem of our young—together with them, turn to God."[10]

U.S. News and World Report published an excerpt from the address under the title "Turn to God." The editor, David Lawrence, termed it a "stirring address." It did win considerable praise in the form of letters from those who attended the breakfast and others who read it in *U.S. News.* Most lauded the man who, as one writer put it, "dare[d] to be a Daniel, and in the face of possible sneering, tell a group of a thousand people that the solution to our problems is to turn to God!" Many of the letters revealed a religious, if not a specifically evangelical, viewpoint; several included the phrase "God bless you." Not all the letters were favorable, however. A few individuals seized upon his address as an opportunity to criticize United States policy in Vietnam. One writer

9. "Address by Johnson, Second Annual Governor's Prayer Breakfast, Curundu, Canal Zone," 2.

10. Harold K. Johnson, "'Turn to God,'" *U.S. News and World Report,* February 12, 1968, p. 92. See also, "Leaders Gather with President Johnson for Prayer Breakfast," *UEA,* March, 1968, p. 24.

charged Johnson with hypocrisy for quoting the words of Jesus while the military was wreaking destruction in Vietnam. Johnson did not reply to such letters. He indicated to his clerical staff that such an effort would be pointless because he and his critics viewed the war in Vietnam from different perspectives. Johnson, after all, held to the typical Cold War view. He defended the Vietnam War as an episode in the long-standing conflict between the so-called free world and communism, as a fight between a nation that believed in God and sought to preserve what he called its "God-given rights to freedom and personal dignity" and a regime that recognized no Supreme Being and was committed to an "ideology seeking to enslave men."[11] He had little respect for the anti–Vietnam War movement or those who voiced its opinions.

Perhaps, as Johnson mentioned in one of his prayer breakfast addresses, civilians *were* surprised to hear a four-star general of the army speaking unselfconsciously about his need for and reliance on God. In the military, however, Johnson had already earned a reputation for being a man of intense religious faith. To those who knew and worked with him, he seemed "anchored in spiritual values," as a Defense Department employee put it. A subordinate once remarked that any unit Johnson was assigned to would not need a chaplain. So military people, including evangelicals, probably expected that when he became chief of staff his religious convictions would continue to inform his leadership as they had in the past, that he would continue to emphasize high moral standards and support the army's religious and moral welfare programs.[12]

11. Johnson, " 'Turn to God,' " 92; Corda Leman to Johnson, July 25, 1968, and Alex B. Graven to Johnson, February 8, 1968, both in Johnson Papers; Harold K. Johnson, "Candles of Faith," *Command*, War and Peace issue, 1967, pp. 1, 2. For other letters regarding the 1968 prayer breakfast address see Boxes 57 and 106, Johnson Papers.

12. Lawrence J. Korb, *The Joint Chiefs of Staff: The First Twenty-five Years* (Bloomington, 1976), 43. On Johnson's moral legacy, see Chapter 19 of this book; his support for the army's religious and moral welfare programs is indicated by two policies that expanded the role of the army chaplaincy. One significantly increased the number of worship opportunities available to soldiers (from just under 260,000 in 1965 to over 300,000 in 1967), while the other provided that chaplains would spend 50 percent of their duty time each week with the troops, in addition to offering consultation in their offices at least one evening per week ("Challenge" [Typescript (1968?)] in Johnson Papers). See also Department of the Army, Office of the Chief of Chaplains, Monthly Newsletter (Typed, photocopy, file 701-01 Chaplain's Administrative Files [68], Record Group No. 247, Acc. No. 71-A-3095, Washington National Records Center, Suitland, Md.), July 1, 1968, p. 1.

Military people, including evangelicals, probably did not anticipate, however, that Johnson would go out of his way to show his respect and support for the Officers' Christian Union, which he did early in his term as chief of staff. In December, 1964, *Command* published a Christmas letter from Johnson addressed to the OCU membership. In it he reiterated his long-standing conviction regarding the soldier's need for religious faith but in strikingly sectarian language: "There is a special need for the soldier to understand the strength and purpose that can be provided by a deep and abiding faith in our Father through His son Jesus," he wrote. "Only a conscious awareness of the limitless reservoir of strength available through faith in Jesus Christ can provide that inner strength that is essential to meet the wide variety of conditions encountered in the environment of the warrior." Citing the teachings and example of Jesus as a touchstone for the military, Johnson declared, "He established a standard of conduct, a standard of morality, a standard of compassion, and a standard of understanding that we can emulate to the advantage of mankind."[13]

It was a significant gesture that certainly demonstrated support for the OCU, not to mention the teachings of Jesus. The letter gained added significance because Johnson was not a member of the OCU. He explained why in a letter written in 1967 to Major General Sir Robert Ewbank, a member of the British Officers' Christian Union who had been visiting OCU chapters in the United States. "I have stayed at arm's length from OCU because of my fundamental belief that Christianity is not reserved for officers," Johnson wrote, referring to the organization's restriction of membership to officers. He hastened to point out that his not being a member did not indicate opposition to the OCU: "Certainly I do not oppose OCU because I favor any group that is committed to spreading God's Word and the teachings of Jesus Christ." And he expressed satisfaction at the expansion of OCU groups at army installations, especially West Point. But he thought that his position as army chief of staff dictated a more neutral position on religion than the one the OCU represented: "[I] find that I cannot favor Protestant over Roman Catholic, neither can I disparage the Jew."[14] (Apparently he did

13. Harold K. Johnson, "What Christmas Means to Me," *Command*, Christmas, 1964, p. 3.

14. Johnson to Major General Sir Robert Ewbank, October 17, 1967, in Johnson Papers.

not consider his appearances at the ICL prayer breakfasts, which were markedly Christian, if not Protestant, in orientation, as a case of favoritism.)

Writing the Christmas letter to the OCU hardly qualified as keeping the organization "at arm's length." It is difficult to determine why Johnson wrote it. One can only speculate that he wanted to send a signal that he sympathized with the organization and, as he indicated privately to Ewbank, supported its purpose of "spreading God's Word and the teachings of Jesus Christ." Certainly OCU members interpreted the letter in this light and were understandably gratified by his gesture of sympathy and support. They were probably correct in interpreting it as an indication that their organization—and evangelical religion in general—had become more "acceptable" in the military than before.[15]

A few months later, OCU members—indeed all evangelicals in the military—had even more reason to be pleased with the religious and moral stance adopted by the new army chief of staff. In March, 1965, Johnson circulated an order entitled "The Image of the Army" prohibiting "offensive language and off-color stories" in army service schools and as a part of military training. In the order he explained what had provoked such action. On a recent visit to an army post, he had seen a skit performed as part of a training demonstration. "During the course of this skit," Johnson observed, "the soldier-actors employed language that I can only describe as offensive to the average person. . . . I am fully conscious of the fact that we cannot regulate sin," he continued. "However, I do not believe that we need blink at or condone those instances where the impropriety of the actions of our leaders and instructors can be interpreted clearly as offensive to many of the individuals who are subordinate to them."[16]

When the OCU council learned of the order, it quickly endorsed it. *United Evangelical Action* published excerpts, without editorial comment, apparently assuming that readers would interpret it the way Robert Spoede says the OCU did, as a welcome change in the moral climate of the military. When a young OCU member by the name of James Meredith read the word *sin* in Johnson's order, he said, "it blew me

15. Robert W. Spoede, *More Than Conquerors: A History of the Officers' Christian Fellowship of the U.S.A., 1943–1983* (Englewood, Colo., 1993), 69.

16. Harold K. Johnson, "Image of the Army" (Typescript, March 2, 1965, in Johnson Papers). See also *NYT*, May 11, 1965, p. 11.

away." Talking about the incident many years later, he claimed it was the first time he had heard a high-ranking military man use that word in a military context. To him, it sent a signal that Johnson was a truly religious man.[17] For other evangelicals, Johnson's order probably reinforced the notion, already planted by the Christmas letter in *Command*, that Johnson was not only a religious man—even an evangelical Christian—but was determined to translate his religious convictions into military policy whenever possible, particularly in the area of morality.

They were correct. To be sure, Johnson himself presented the order as an outgrowth of concern for the army's image. But it seems likely that his own religious and moral convictions, as well as a concern for the convictions of other military personnel, were the more important influence. The demurrer, "we cannot regulate sin," seemed designed to disarm critics, but the word *sin* betrayed Johnson's conviction (which he apparently believed other military personnel shared) that offensive language and off-color stories were more than offenses against good taste, that they constituted offenses against God, which is to say sin. He believed that soldiers, especially, dared not offend God by using such language. In a speech Johnson made to the PMOC executive council in the late 1950s, he talked about the everyday problems of military life that cropped up in the barracks or the mess or the officers' club. "How many times do you hear people take the name of the Lord in vain?" he asked. "What do you do about it?" It was particularly a problem, he observed, in a combat theater where the men were "away from the normal restraints." He recalled his experience with the problem in Korea:

> I used to talk to my people in Korea, after we'd had some what you might term worse-than-usual engagements or periods of time. . . . And I'd say, "Who do you suppose had His hand on the elbow of that Chinese or North Korean gunner and jiggled it at just the right time?" Or for any of us, who drive a car, "Who do you suppose triggers the reflexes that move our foot from the accelerator to the brake to avoid an accident?" And you people who jump [paratroopers] I think have more reason than anyone else to stop and think every once in a while. Our lives are in God's hands all day, all night, every day and every night. And this we should

17. Spoede, *More Than Conquerors*, 69; "Image of the Army," *UEA*, May, 1965, p. 2; Colonel (Ret.) James Meredith, conversation with author, Washington, D.C., May 26, 1989.

remember, and I would keep telling this to people—"You don't take His name in vain; you don't talk about the fellow that can drop you like that if He wants to, the way that you do." And strangely enough, you didn't hear it any more. Occasionally somebody would forget, but he shamefacedly would very quickly remember it.[18]

For Johnson, then, offensive language constituted an offense against a sovereign God to whom soldiers looked for protection—a God who could, if He wished, also punish them by dropping them into hell. Johnson undoubtedly had a concern for the image of the army, but the principal impetus behind his order was surely religious.

Another policy matter that shows the religious perspective Johnson brought to the office of chief of staff involved the army's Character Guidance program. In December, 1962, a controversy developed over the program as a result of a protest letter Lawrence Speiser, director of the Washington office of the American Civil Liberties Union (ACLU), sent to Secretary of the Army Cyrus Vance. In it Speiser complained that trainees at Fort Devens, Massachusetts, were being subjected to "religious indoctrination" during Character Guidance lectures and programs. Initially, the Office of the Army Chief of Chaplains, to which the complaint was referred, responded by defending the religious orientation of the program. It insisted that it was upholding the moral and spiritual principles, including a belief in God, on which America was founded. Although it conceded that the Character Guidance program was "theistically oriented," it declared that it was "not a religious program" and was not devised to support any religious doctrine or institution. The discussions offered instruction, not in "religious principles" but in "ethical, moral and psychological principles" underlying "traditional American concepts of personal integrity and responsible social conduct."[19]

At the same time, the Office of the Chief of Chaplains took steps to revise the program so as to shield it from further complaints. For ex-

18. Harold K. Johnson, untitled speech to Executive Committee of the PMOC USAREUR Council (Typescript, [1957?] in Johnson Papers), 5–6.

19. Office of the Chief of Chaplains, "Historical Review, 1 July 1962 to 30 June 1963" [1963] (Typescript at Washington National Records Center, Suitland, Md.), 70–71; Department of the Army Office of the Chief of Chaplains, *Summary of Major Events and Problems, 1 July 1960 to 30 June 1961* (N.d.), 58–59; Office of the Chief of Chaplains, "Historical Review, 1 July 1963–30 June 1964" (1964) (Typescript at Washington National Records Center, Suitland, Md.), 69–70.

ample, in June, 1963, to ensure the "nonreligious nature" of Character Guidance training and to prevent its being confused with religious instruction, the office specifically prohibited chaplains from using classes "to deliver a sermon, to announce religious services, to upbraid troops for nonparticipation in chapel programs, to show religious films or to expound their own theological views." Only the scheduled topic was to be discussed, and only approved Department of the Army training materials were to be used. Then, in May, 1966, the chief of chaplains directed that the topic "One Nation Under God" no longer be used in the Character Guidance program for basic trainees. Explaining the action, the chief pointed to two concerns: first, that "an inadequately instructed chaplain" might present the topic "in such a way as to provide at least a superficial basis for criticizing the Character Guidance program as trespassing on the sphere of religion"; and second, that the topic violated the First Amendment. A look at the lesson plan for "One Nation Under God" suggests that the office had good reason for both concerns. The first of four lectures presented to soldiers during basic training in the 1950s and 1960s, "One Nation Under God" provides a graphic illustration of the overlapping of religion, morality, and patriotism so characteristic of the Character Guidance program as a whole. The lesson plan listed two objectives of the session: "To help the individual to understand the effect that faith in a Supreme Being has had on the origin and development of our country" and "To lead the individual to a recognition of the importance of the spiritual element in his training."[20]

Notwithstanding these and other changes the chief of chaplains made, in April, 1968, the ACLU revived the issue of religion in the Character Guidance program. Director Lawrence Speiser sent a letter to the undersecretary of the army stating the ACLU's view that the "religious flavor" of the program violated the First Amendment of the Constitution.[21]

20. Office of the Chief of Chaplains, "Historical Review, 1 July 1962 to 30 June 1963," 74–75; U.S. Army Office of the Chief of Chaplains, *Historical Review, 1 July 1965 to 31 December 1966* (1969), 145; U.S. Army Office of the Chief of Chaplains, *Historical Review, 1 January 1967 to 30 June 1968* (1969), 85; Department of the Army, *Character Guidance Discussion Topics: Duty, Honor, Country* (1957), 1; Headquarters, Department of the Army, *Character Guidance Discussion Topics: Duty, Honor, Country* (1966), vii.

21. U.S. Army Office of the Chief of Chaplains, *Historical Review, 1 January 1967 to 30 June 1968*, 89.

As army chief of staff, Johnson took the lead in holding deliberations over the proper response to make to the ACLU complaint. On April 20, having received a memorandum from the general counsel of the army regarding Spieser's latest letter, Johnson assigned the issue to the deputy chief of staff for personnel, with the judge advocate general and the chief of military personnel policies as the principal action officers. For some reason, he did not notify the chief of chaplains of his decision. Then on April 25, he called a conference (at which the Office of the Chief of Chaplains was not represented) to discuss the general counsel's memorandum. During the conference he expressed a desire to adopt a strong stand in favor of the Character Guidance program. He also said that he saw nothing wrong with using the Bible in support of the program and that he wanted to challenge the ACLU complaint "to the extent that this was legally possible." When the acting judge advocate general reminded Johnson of the 1963 directive that chaplains were not to "preach" when they presented Character Guidance topics, Johnson directed that a new reminder to that effect be published. He also issued a directive ordering certain Character Guidance pamphlets and other materials to be revised and reprinted so as to eliminate elements that appeared to inculcate religious principles.[22]

Although the Office of the Chief of Chaplains resented being left out of the initial deliberations, it considered Johnson an ally in the controversy over Character Guidance. The office declared itself "strongly opposed to any inclusion of religion or religious dogma" in the subject matter taught in the Character Guidance classes because that would violate the rights of the soldiers required to attend them. It was equally opposed to "any attempt totally to prohibit the use of religious references, illustrations, or materials." The general counsel of the army and the judge advocate general, however, insisted that the program could be successfully defended only if all religious matter were deleted from the training materials.[23]

Johnson seemed to want to establish a policy that would enable religious material to be retained in the Character Guidance program in

22. *Ibid.*, 89, 91.
23. U.S. Army Office of the Chief of Chaplains, *Historical Review, 1 July 1968 to 30 June 1969* (1970), 75, 77; U.S. Army Office of the Chief of Chaplains, *Historical Review, 1 January 1967 to 30 June 1968*, 90; and see also U.S. Army Office of the Chief of Chaplains, *Historical Review, 1 July 1968 to 30 June 1969*, 74.

the form of references or illustrations while at the same time avoiding the inculcation of religious principles. He did not succeed. The controversy came to a climax after he had stepped down as chief of staff and was finally resolved in a way that Johnson probably would not have approved.[24] In 1970, the army dropped the program and replaced it with a wholly secular program, Our Moral Heritage.

Still, that Johnson took the position he did is significant. His effort to retain the religious orientation of Character Guidance provides a further demonstration of the role religious and moral convictions played in his leadership. His own experience in combat and as a POW had convinced him of the sustaining power of religious faith in the life of a soldier. During the 1950s and 1960s, he continued to believe that military men, especially, needed religion. It is hardly surprising, then, that he thought military training should have a religious and moral component, particularly in the 1960s, when he became increasingly concerned about the threat posed by rampant materialism, widespread moral deterioration, and the general questioning of authority in the United States.[25] Moreover, Johnson probably believed, as the discarded Character Guidance topic "One Nation Under God" taught, that the United States was a nation in covenant with God. How could there be anything wrong in teaching that to men and women who had pledged their lives to the service of God and country?

24. In March, 1969, when the army directed the chief of chaplains to implement a policy eliminating certain religious material from the Character Guidance program, protest erupted from the Congress, the media, and other public opinion leaders. Secretary of Defense Melvin Laird, a Presbyterian elder and a member of a conservative evangelical organization called Presbyterians United for Biblical Concerns, became the hero of the moment for supposedly restoring God to the program. See *Congressional Record*, CXV (91st Cong., 1st Sess.), 7343–44; Lawrence L. Knutson, "Lectures Revised: Army Bans 'God' in Talks," *Washington Evening Star*, March 28, 1969, p. A-18; *NYT*, March 29, 1969, pp. 1, 4; William R. MacKaye, "Row Over God in Army Talks Intensified," *Washington Post*, April 5, 1969, p. B-4; William Willoughby, "Chaplains' Role Under New Scrutiny," *CT*, April 25, 1969, p. 32; *Washington Post*, April 4, 1969, p. A4; "God Back in Army Lectures," *UEA*, Summer, 1969, p. 33. On Laird and the Presbyterians United for Biblical Concerns, see *NYT*, May 24, 1970, p. 70; Richard Quebedeaux, *The Worldly Evangelicals* (San Francisco, 1978), 47.

25. See, for example, Johnson, "Address to Regular Army Lieutenants of the 8th Infantry Division"; Harold K. Johnson, "I Believe," *Military Chaplain*, XLII (May–June, 1969), 30, 32; "Senior Officers Debriefing Program: Interview with Harold Keith Johnson by Lieutenant Colonel Rupert F. Glover, 22 January, 1973" (Typescript, Carlisle Barracks, n.d., in Johnson Papers), 23–24.

The position Johnson took aligned him with evangelicals and against many mainline denominations and groups. As early as the mid-1960s the tri-faith National Study Conference on Church and State and the United Presbyterian Church, U.S.A., criticized the religious orientation of mandatory character education instruction in the armed forces. And in 1969, when an army directive prohibiting religious references in Character Guidance materials was made public, a number of mainline religious leaders supported it as conforming to the American tradition of separation of church and state. They included representatives of the National Council of Christians and Jews, the United Church of Christ, the General Commission on Chaplains, and the Massachusetts Council of Churches. Evangelicals, in contrast, bruised by the recent Supreme Court decisions prohibiting prayer and Bible reading in the public schools, regarded efforts to remove religion from the Character Guidance program as yet another attempt to "remove God from our national life." In 1965, at its twenty-third annual convention, the NAE had called upon Congress to pass legislation to "allow reference to, or invoking the aid of, God in any governmental or public document, proceeding, activity, ceremony or situation." Evangelicals shared Johnson's belief in religion as a necessary basis of morality. They did not see any way to inculcate moral responsibility in men without reference to God and religion. They also shared Johnson's notion of America as a nation in covenant with God, the source of human beings' inalienable rights. They believed, as he did, that the founders of the nation had established a political system based on religious convictions and that that religious heritage should be taught to succeeding generations of Americans.[26]

Like William K. Harrison, Johnson played a crucial role in the spread of evangelical religion in the military. Evangelicals within and outside

---

26. "National Study Conference on Church and State," *Chaplain*, XXI (June, 1964), 41–42; "United Presbyterian Report on the Military Chaplaincy [1965]," in *Church, State and Chaplaincy: Essays and Statements on the American Chaplaincy System*, ed. A. Ray Applequist (Washington, D.C., 1969), 37, 44; *NYT*, March 29, 1969, p. 4; "Chaplains Affected as Army Prohibits Religious References in Character Guidance," *Religious News Service, Domestic Service*, March 28, 1969, pp. 28–29; "Discharging God from the Army," *CT*, April 25, 1969, p. 23; "How Can Evangelicals Meet the Spiritual Demands of a World in Crisis?" *UEA*, June, 1965, p. 9. See also Robert D. Linder and Richard V. Pierard, *Twilight of the Saints: Biblical Christianity and Civil Religion in America* (Downers Grove, Ill., 1978), 102.

the military recognized him as a fellow believer.[27] Even though he did not refer to it as such, his religious testimony about his experience in combat and as a POW had the familiar ring of a born-again experience. His addresses on the prayer breakfast circuit identified him with one of the key evangelical organizations of the 1960s. Above all, his public espousal of his religious convictions and his effort to implement them as military policy convinced military evangelicals that the chief of staff of the army was one of their own.

When Johnson retired as chief of staff, the Office of the Chief of Chaplains praised him for "the spiritual and religious dedication which he brought to every assignment" and noted that "wherever he went and whenever he spoke, he conveyed an image of the devout religious man at his best." Johnson, the office pointed out, "is known throughout the Army as a man of great integrity as well as of outstanding ability." The respect he won for his own religious beliefs and practice could not help but redound to the benefit of evangelical religion. He helped to remove some of the stigma of being an evangelical. Martin Blumenson noted that although some in the military found him "rather rigid and somewhat narrow in his moral outlook," they could not but be impressed by the high standard of personal behavior he followed and inspired in others. He certainly dispelled the notion that an evangelical military man was some kind of freak. And no one doubted the authenticity of his faith. As a newspaper reporter once observed, "He can say a prayer without sounding phony."[28]

In certain respects Johnson may have done more than Harrison to aid the spread of evangelical religion in the military. Not only did he reach a wider civilian audience through his prayer breakfast addresses (and the notice he received in *U.S. News and World Report*), but he had a broader appeal within the military than Harrison did. Harrison became identified with the relatively small percentage of evangelicals who belonged to the Officers' Christian Union. Although Johnson publicly supported the OCU, he never allowed himself to become exclusively identified with such a narrow constituency. Then, too, Johnson exhibi-

27. See, for example, Wesley G. Pippert, "The Four-Star General Who Calls Men to the Lord," *Moody Monthly*, November, 1972, p. 24.

28. Department of the Army, Office of the Chief of Chaplains, Monthly Newsletter (Typed photocopy, file 701-01 Chaplain's Administrative Files [68], Record Group No. 247, Acc. No. 71-A-3095, Washington National Records Center, Suitland, Md.), July 1, 1968, p. 1; Blumenson, "A Most Remarkable Man," 20, 19.

ted a more ecumenical, less sectarian outlook than Harrison. This is not to say that Johnson could not and did not speak in sectarian terms. Addressing evangelical groups such as the OCU or the prayer breakfast audiences, he readily invoked the example and teachings of Jesus Christ. But speaking to more religiously diverse audiences, he exhibited a tolerance for and acceptance of different religious viewpoints that Harrison never did. In the testimony he sent to the American Tract Society, for example, he declared that "each individual's relationship with God is peculiarly his own," and in the Christmas letter published in *Command*, he reiterated that notion, saying, "I hold the view that each man's relationship with his God is purely his own." In the same paragraph that invoked Jesus' life and teaching as a standard for all men to follow, he noted that "our individual views of Jesus may very well differ." And finally, whereas Harrison often occupied an adversarial position vis-à-vis the military leadership, Johnson *was* the military leadership, which enabled him to implement his evangelical convictions as military policy.

Johnson served as army chief of staff at a time when evangelicals in the military were making the transition from being regarded with scorn to being viewed with respect. As we have seen, Johnson himself aided the transition in significant ways. Another equally important factor that facilitated the transition was the position evangelicals took on the Vietnam War, the subject of the next three chapters.

9

Debating the Vietnam War

In 1960, during its eighteenth annual meeting, the National Association of Evangelicals launched an "Emergency Christian Mobilization" aimed at stopping the spread of communism at home and abroad. The crusade, which grew out of a resolution urging "all Christian Americans" to join the NAE in "an aggressive and unrelenting campaign against this enemy of righteousness and freedom," set the tone for the rest of the decade. As in the 1950s, evangelical spokesmen continued to fulminate against a movement they defined as "militant atheism" and believed was bent on "world revolution and world conquest."[1]

When the NAE began the Emergency Christian Mobilization, the United States had already committed close to seven hundred American military advisers as well as significant amounts of equipment and financial aid to South Vietnam. During the next three years the number of advisers increased substantially, as did the flow of money and matériel. But it was not until 1965, when President Lyndon B. Johnson commenced air strikes against North Vietnam and sent the first American combat troops to South Vietnam, that a significant religiously based antiwar movement developed.[2]

---

1. "NAE Launches Anti-Communist Program," *UEA*, June, 1960, p. 10; Dave Breese, "Fight Communism?" *UEA*, April, 1962, p. 17; Harold John Ockenga, "The Communist Issue Today," *CT*, May 22, 1961, p. 10. See also "Text of Resolutions," *UEA*, June, 1962, p. 20.

2. On the U.S. military commitment in South Vietnam, see Stanley Karnow, *Vietnam: A History* (New York, 1983), 250, 255, 414–18, 679.

It arose among the leadership, lay as well as clerical, of the mainline churches. James Smylie names the American Lutheran Church, the American Baptist Convention, the Methodist Episcopal Church, the United Church of Christ, and the United Presbyterian Church as the most "activist" in opposing the war. The religious antiwar movement also gained support from prominent mainline spokesmen such as Bishop Fulton Sheen, the Berrigan brothers, William Sloan Coffin, Jr., John C. Bennett (president of New York's Union Theological Seminary), Eugene Carson Blake (general secretary–elect of the World Council of Churches), Robert McAfee Brown, Reinhold Niebuhr, Peter Berger, and Martin Luther King, Jr. Periodicals such as the *National Catholic Reporter, Christianity and Crisis,* and *Christian Century* published articles and editorials criticizing the war, and ad hoc organizations such as Clergy and Laymen Concerned About Vietnam and the Clergymen's Emergency Committee passed resolutions and held protest meetings. Both the National Council of Churches and the World Council of Churches regularly issued statements urging cessation of the bombing of North Vietnam, negotiations under United Nations supervision, and gradual withdrawal of United States troops.[3]

The spokesmen for mainline antiwar groups in the United States (voluntary interfaith organizations as well as religious denominations) advanced a moral argument against the war, generally based on traditional just war doctrine, which questioned not only United States intervention in Vietnam but also the conduct of the war. A typical statement read, "Our nation is embroiled in a conflict in Vietnam which we find it impossible to justify, in the light of either the message of the prophets or the gospel of Jesus of Nazareth." Antiwar spokesmen were especially concerned about "the immorality of the warfare in Vietnam," as evidenced by the high level of civilian casualties, the commonplace use of napalm and white phosphorous, the forced evacuation of towns

3. James H. Smylie, "American Religious Bodies, Just War, and Vietnam," *Journal of Church and State,* XI (Autumn, 1969), 389–402. See also Richard John Neuhaus, "The War, the Churches, and Civil Religion," *Annals of the American Academy of Political and Social Science,* CCCLXXXVII (January, 1970), 128–33; A. James Reichley, *Religion in American Public Life* (Washington, D.C., 1985), 250–53; James L. Adams, *The Growing Church Lobby in Washington* (Grand Rapids, 1970) 213–22, 231–44. For a brief discussion of the evolution of the liberal Protestant position on the war, see Dale Suderman, "A Failure of Liberalism," *Post-American,* October–November, 1975, pp. 22–23.

and villages, the defoliation of crops, and the torture of prisoners to secure information.[4]

"What special wisdom do clergymen have on the military and international intricacies of the United States government's involvement in Viet Nam?" *Christianity Today* asked in a February, 1965, issue. Its answer: "None." The mainline churches might "speak piously about our difficulties in Viet Nam, but a vocal and uninformed piety is worse than silence," declared the editor, Carl F. H. Henry. Their long-standing rivalry with mainline denominations and especially the NCC almost guaranteed that once those bodies had taken a stand against the war, evangelicals would feel compelled to enter the controversy on the opposite side. Throughout the long and bitter debate over the war, *Christianity Today* continued to question the "presumptuousness" of "social activists of the Protestant establishment" who "profess to speak for Christian conscience as such, or for their church constituencies."[5]

But even if the mainline groups had not protested, the anticommunist rhetoric the Johnson administration used to justify its policies would

4. Robert McAfee Brown, Abraham J. Heschel, and Michael Novak, *Vietnam: Crisis of Conscience* (New York, 1967), 7, 67, 68.

5. "Ignorance Often Has a Loud Voice," *CT*, February 12, 1965, p. 511; "Putting First Things Second," *CT*, March 1, 1968, p. 551. See also "Clergymen on Viet Nam," *CT*, January 29, 1965, p. 469; "Who Speaks for the Church?" *CT*, June 9, 1967, pp. 26–27; William Martin, *A Prophet with Honor: The Billy Graham Story* (New York, 1991), 343–44. Historical treatment of the religious response to the Vietnam War is surprisingly limited. Thomas Powers, *Vietnam, the War at Home: Vietnam and the American People, 1964–1968* (Boston, 1984), pays almost no attention to it. Smylie and Neuhaus, cited previously, focus on the mainline response. See also Mitchell K. Hall, *Because of Their Faith: CALCAV and Religious Opposition to the Vietnam War* (New York, 1990). For the evangelical response I found two treatments especially helpful, even though I do not entirely agree with their interpretations: Andrew LeRoy Pratt, "Religious Faith and Civil Religion: Evangelical Responses to the Vietnam War, 1964–1973" (Ph.D. dissertation, Southern Baptist Theological Seminary, 1988), and Richard V. Pierard, "Billy Graham and Vietnam: From Cold Warrior to Peacemaker," *Christian Scholar's Review*, X (1980), 37–51. See also Robert Booth Fowler, *A New Engagement: Evangelical Political Thought, 1966–1976* (Grand Rapids, 1982), 221–24. Kent B. Blevins, "Southern Baptist Attitudes Toward the Vietnam War in the Years 1965–1970," *Foundations*, XXIII (1980), 231–44, describes much the same response to the war on the part of Southern Baptists as Pratt attributes to evangelicals generally. Both Blevins and William L. Marshall, "Changing Attitudes Toward War: A Study of Southern Baptist Attitudes Toward War" (Master of Theology thesis, Midwestern Baptist Theological Seminary, 1970), 49–51, reveal something less than unconditional support for the Vietnam War on the part of Southern Baptists.

surely have persuaded the evangelical community. When President
Johnson declared in an address on Vietnam in April, 1965, that the war
presented "the new face of an old enemy" and was "part of a wider
pattern of aggressive purposes," he tapped evangelicals' deep-seated fear
of and hostility toward international communism.[6] Like Johnson, in the
mid-1960s evangelicals justified American intervention in Southeast
Asia as a means of halting the spread of communism and upholding the
freedom and liberties of a people unable to protect themselves against it.

Fundamentalists, represented by *Sword of the Lord* editor John Rice,
Carl McIntire and the American Council of Christian Churches, and
Billy James Hargis and Christian Crusade, took the most extreme position in supporting the war in Vietnam. They regarded it as a struggle
"to prevent godless communism with its murder and torture and persecution from taking over other lands which ask our help," as Rice declared in *War in Vietnam: Should Christians Fight?* To fundamentalists,
as Andrew LeRoy Pratt points out, communism was more than just a
competing political ideology. "It was the manifestation of the supreme
demonic threat to Christianity and Western civilization." Thus the conflict with communism "took on dimensions of the unseen, yet ever present, spiritual struggle between good and evil, Christ and anti-Christ,
God and Satan." Fundamentalists believed the threat posed by communism justified a religious crusade, a holy war. Rice wrote in *War in
Vietnam:* "Nothing can be clearer than that God sometimes approves
of people going to war for principles and that He is with them, and
when they call on Him and trust Him, He will give them victory and
deliverance." In Vietnam, American troops "would be carrying out the
command of God." Carl McIntire declared, "It is the message of the
infallible Bible that gives men the right to participate in such conflicts,
and to do it with all the realization that God is for them, that God will
help them, and that if they believe in the Son of God, the Lord Jesus
Christ, and die in the field of battle, they will be received into the highest
Heaven."[7]

6. "Text of the President's Address on U.S. Policies in Vietnam," *NYT*, April 8,
1965, p. 16.

7. Robert G. Clouse, "The Vietnam War in Christian Perspective," in *Protest and
Politics: Christianity and Contemporary Affairs*, ed. Robert G. Clouse, Robert D. Linder,
and Richard V. Pierard (Greenwood, S.C., 1968), 256; Pratt, "Religious Faith and Civil
Religion," 102–104, 160, 162, 162n, and see also 163, 163 n. 17, and 163 n. 18. George
M. Marsden, "Fundamentalism and American Evangelicalism," in *The Variety of Ameri-*

Just as in the 1950s fundamentalists had targeted alleged communist infiltration of the mainline churches and the NCC and WCC, in the 1960s they cited the mainline groups' opposition to the Vietnam War as further evidence of their procommunist orientation. Rice and McIntire characterized conscientious objectors and antiwar protesters as friends of communism (the "voice of Hanoi" in McIntire's phrasing) who hindered the war effort and promoted disobedience and rebellion among American citizens.[8]

Fundamentalists never wavered in their support for United States intervention in Southeast Asia to halt communist aggression. As far as the conduct of the war was concerned, they insisted on nothing less than military victory. In October, 1970, a group describing itself as "fundamental Christian ministers" delivered a statement on the Vietnam War to Secretary of Defense Melvin Laird, saying that "we want our fighting men in Vietnam to be permitted to win." Contending that their stand was based on "the Word of God," they asserted, "The war in Vietnam is both morally just and absolutely necessary to wage to victory, for the freedom and the security of those who love liberty are at stake." At a March for Victory rally in December, 1971, Carl McIntire also invoked Scripture in denouncing demands for American withdrawal from Vietnam as "abject surrender to the enemy." A year earlier, protesting "our immoral conduct of the war in Vietnam," he declared: "For a people who believe in God to cringe and retreat in the presence of a growing power which repudiates God is an offense. Our 'no-win' policy is a sin against righteousness, the heritage of our nation, the mothers and wives of boys who have sacrificed for political expediency." Fundamentalists also enlisted retired military men to support their position on the war.

---

can Evangelicalism, ed. Donald W. Dayton and Robert K. Johnston (Knoxville, 1991), 22, cites Rice as perhaps the prototypical fundamentalist leader and credits him with playing a significant role in shaping a fundamentalist consensus through his weekly newspaper, which had a circulation of some 250,000, as well as more than a hundred books. Martin, *Prophet*, 219, says that by mid-century Rice's was "the most popular and influential journal in the Fundamentalist orbit."

8. Carl McIntire, "Manifesto of Peace," *Christian Beacon*, January 6, 1972, p. 4; Pratt, "Religious Faith and Civil Religion," 168, 168n, 169, 169n. On fundamentalist charges against mainline churches and organizations in the 1950s, see Ralph Lord Roy, *Apostles of Discord: A Study of Organized Bigotry and Disruption on the Fringe of Protestantism* (Boston, 1953); Erling Jorstad, *The Politics of Doomsday: Fundamentalists of the Far Right* (Nashville, 1970).

Christian Crusade and *Christian Beacon* featured articles and speeches by retired army generals Edwin A. Walker, Charles A. Willoughby, and Thomas A. Lane and retired admiral U. S. Grant Sharp, all of whom argued against gradual escalation, limited war, Vietnamization, negotiation, and withdrawal. The United States military, they insisted, should be allowed to use its full power (including "'mass destruction' weapons to offset the inexhaustible manpower of Asia," according to Willoughby) to obtain total victory in Vietnam.[9]

Like the fundamentalists, mainstream evangelicals, represented by the NAE, Billy Graham, Carl F. H. Henry, Harold John Ockenga, and periodicals such as *Christianity Today, Eternity, United Evangelical Action, Moody Monthly, Christian Life,* and *Decision,* remained as anticommunist in the 1960s as they had been in the 1950s. To be sure, in comparison to fundamentalists, they tended to use less inflammatory, less visceral language in denouncing communism. But evangelicals did not accept the demythologized view of communism prevalent among mainline groups in the 1960s. They continued to view communism as a monolith bent on nothing less than world domination and a threat to both Christianity and the political and economic system of the West. In 1965, in an address to the North Carolina Press Association, Billy Graham warned against "Communist tyranny" and urged Americans not to listen "to the siren song which would have us believe that the tide has turned or that communism has changed its goal for world revolution."[10]

9. "Fundamental Christian Ministers Carry Statement on War to Pentagon," *Christian Beacon,* October 8, 1970, p. 2; "Manifesto of Peace," *Christian Beacon,* January 6, 1972, p. 4; Carl McIntire, "Victory Under God," *Christian Beacon,* October 8, 1970, p. 7; Pratt, "Religious Faith and Civil Religion," 164–66, 219, 174–75; Charles A. Willoughby, "The American Dilemma from Laos to S. Viet Nam," *Christian Crusade,* February–March, 1964, pp. 28–31; U. S. Grant Sharp, "We Could Have Won in Vietnam Long Ago," *Christian Beacon,* June 19, 1969, pp. 3, 7; Thomas A. Lane, "Strategy for Victory," *Christian Beacon,* October 8, 1970, p. 7; Charles A. Willoughby, "Vietnam and Cambodia in Light of MacArthur's Views," *Christian Crusade Weekly,* November 29, 1970, pp. 1, 3.

10. Martin, *Prophet,* 311. For differing perceptions of evangelicals' attitudes toward communism, see Fowler, *New Engagement,* 214–15; George M. Marsden, "Preachers of Paradox: The Religious New Right in Historical Perspective," in *Religion and America: Spiritual Life in a Secular Age,* ed. Mary Douglas and Steven Tipton (Boston, 1982), 155; George Marsden, *Reforming Fundamentalism: Fuller Seminary and the New Evangelicalism* (Grand Rapids, 1987), 154–61; Pratt, "Religious Faith and Civil Religion," 129–30; Dennis P. Hollinger, *Individualism and Social Ethics: An Evangelical Syncretism* (New York, 1983), 187.

In justifying U.S. intervention in Southeast Asia, Graham and other evangelicals appealed to the domino theory and the principle of containment. In 1965, after combat troops had been dispatched to Vietnam, the evangelist declared at a press conference: "We are dealing with naked aggression. . . . Communism has to be stopped somewhere, whether it is in Hawaii or on the West Coast. The President believes it should be stopped in Vietnam." The conflict in Vietnam was not a civil war, Robert J. St. Clair insisted in *Eternity* magazine. It was "part and parcel of the whole pattern of Communist aggression," and not to help South Vietnam would mean "the complete abandonment of Asia to aggression." Similarly, David W. Breese, writing in *United Evangelical Action*, appealed to "the policy of the West to contain communism and expand the frontiers of freedom," and Carl Henry, in an editorial in *Christianity Today*, justified intervention on the basis of "our long-held policy to contain world Communism."[11]

Like the fundamentalists, evangelicals had long regarded the liberal Protestant denominations and federations as soft on communism. When *United Evangelical Action* reported the launching of the Emergency Christian Mobilization, it noted that the NAE had taken "a characteristically vigorous stand against the Red menace," in sharp contrast to "the silence or apologetic attitude of some religious organizations toward Communism." A year later, addressing the 1961 NAE convention, Harold John Ockenga declared unequivocally that the faith necessary to fight communism "may only be found in evangelical Christianity. Liberalism, through its embrace of naturalism, has softened resistance to the intellectual aspects of communism." In the midst of the debate over Vietnam, such thinking led evangelicals to denounce antiwar protesters, especially those identified with mainline religion, almost as harshly as the fundamentalists did. If they did not go so far as to label them communists or communist sympathizers, they did not hesitate to charge them with giving "comfort to Communist aggressors." And the words and phrases they used to describe mainline antiwar protesters—"the neo Protestant ecumenical establishment" and "secu-

11. Pierard, "Billy Graham and Vietnam," 42; Robert J. St. Clair, "The Muddle of Viet Nam," *Eternity*, September, 1965, pp. 11, 38; David W. Breese, "Highway to Viet Nam," *UEA*, December, 1965, p. 13; "Viet Nam: Where Do We Go from Here?" *CT*, January 7, 1966, p. 358.

lar theologians of social revolution"—implied a logical connection between their ideological and theological heresies.[12]

Although anticommunism provided a firm and lasting foundation for
supporting the war in Vietnam, evangelicals, unlike fundamentalists,
were not immune to conflict, doubt, and confusion that developed as
the war continued. Like other Americans, evangelicals struggled in a
moral and ideological quagmire.[13]

On the most elementary level, evangelicals confronting the war in
Vietnam found themselves torn between pacifism and warmaking. Fundamentalists rejected pacifism as unbiblical, but mainstream evangelicals
respected the convictions of religiously motivated pacifists who belonged to the historic peace churches (Church of the Brethren, Mennonites, Friends), even if they disagreed with them on scriptural and
political grounds. But as Pratt points out, evangelicals' toleration of
pacifism was "grudging" at best. After all, the weight of evangelical
tradition and doctrine came down on the side of warmaking and against
pacifism. Most evangelicals regarded war as inevitable, given the unre-
generate nature of man, and believed that the use of military force was
a legitimate, scripturally justified prerogative of nations. According to
Pratt, mainstream evangelicals considered war a "necessary evil," which
governments were justified in waging "to protect ideals such as freedom
and to protect those unable to protect themselves from oppression."
They sounded less militaristic than fundamentalists, but they, too, invoked the Bible in justification of warmaking. Writing in *Eternity* magazine in 1968, Carroll R. Stegall, minister of the Westminster Presbyterian Church in Fort Walton Beach, Florida, declared that American
involvement in Vietnam rested "squarely on biblical principles." Citing

12. "NAE Launches Anti-Communist Program," 10; Ockenga, "The Communist Issue Today," 12; "War and Peace in Vietnam," *CT*, February 17, 1967, p. 29; "Viet Nam: A Moral Dilemma," *CT*, January 20, 1967, p. 27; "The Violent New Breed," *CT*, November 24, 1967, p. 25. See also "Hooray for Ho?" *CT*, October 10, 1969, p. 33.

13. In 1981, reviewing the third decade of the NAE's history (1962–71), *UEA* observed that "Vietnam offered a . . . challenge in that many within NAE found themselves
torn over the war's legitimacy and purpose. The association declared its loyalty to the
established Constitutional government and the accompanying requirements of civil obedience, but noted 'with approval' the promise of President Nixon to disengage the
United States from a war 'that has lasted too long and brought sorrow and suffering to
too many homes'" ("40: NAE: Cooperating Together 1942–82," *UEA*, Fall, 1981,
p. 9).

Romans 13 and Genesis 14 and 15, he argued that "God approves wars which are for the protection of the peaceful from the aggressor."[14]

Mainstream evangelicals tried to position themselves between the doves and the hawks on Vietnam—between the mainline groups and denominations calling for a bombing halt, negotiations and withdrawal (which to some evangelicals sounded like appeasement) and the fundamentalists who preached a holy war against the Viet Cong and urged extending United States air strikes to Hanoi, Haiphong, and perhaps the People's Republic of China. The Bible was against "aggressive militarism," Sherwood Wirt, editor of *Decision* magazine, declared: "The concept of the holy war is foreign to the New Testament and to much of the Old Testament." Mainstream evangelicals noted proudly that Billy Graham refused to employ his powerful preaching skills in behalf of an "American Holy War." Whereas mainliners criticized his zealousness in supporting the war, mainstream evangelicals, perhaps recalling his crusading rhetoric of the 1950s, remarked on his restraint. To a writer in *Christianity Today* he stood in sharp contrast not only to hawks like McIntire and Rice but also to Cardinal Francis Spellman, who reportedly referred to United States troops in Vietnam as "soldiers of Christ" and whom the *New York Times* quoted as saying that the conflict was a war for the "defense, protection, and salvation not only of our country but . . . of civilization itself" and that anything less than victory was "inconceivable." Even so, mainstream evangelicals were not completely immune to the tug of a victory strategy, especially when they became frustrated by the lack of progress in the war or in peace negotiations.[15]

The Vietnam War also forced evangelicals to wrestle with questions arising out of what they referred to as the Christian's "dual citizenship."

14. Pratt, "Religious Faith and Civil Religion," 160n, 179, 304; Carroll R. Stegall, "God and the U.S.A. in Vietnam," *Eternity*, March, 1968, pp. 12, 15. See also Gary G. Cohen, "The Bible and the War in Viet Nam," *Moody Monthly*, May, 1967, pp. 30, 61–65; W. G. Corliss, "Can a Christian Be a Fighting Man?" *Eternity*, September, 1962, pp. 22–23; "A Matter of Conscience," *Ambassador Life*, XXI (November, 1966), 9.

15. Sherwood Eliot Wirt, *The Social Conscience of the Evangelical* (New York, 1968), 123; Dale Herendeen, "Graham Preaches Peace in Viet Nam," *CT*, January 10, 1967, p. 36; "Doves, Hawks, and a Cardinal," *CT*, January 20, 1967, p. 37; *NYT*, December 27, 1966, p. 4. See also "Viet Nam: Where Do We Go from Here?" 358; Harold John Ockenga, "Report from Viet Nam," *CT*, March 15, 1968, p. 35; "Spock, Coffin, and Viet Nam," *CT*, July 5, 1968, p. 28.

The two biblical passages most frequently quoted were Mark 12:17 ("Render to Caesar the things that are Caesar's, and to God the things that are God's") and Romans 13:1–7. Evangelicals cited the former to indicate the necessity of making a proper distinction between the duties owed to government and those owed to God. They appealed to the latter in stressing the Christian's responsibility to obey his government. Government was ordained by God, and therefore not to support it would be to oppose God. But obedience to government was not the whole story. The editor of *Eternity* explained: "We are to render unto Caesar the things that are Caesar's, for Caesar has been ordained of God, but when Caesar goes beyond his God-ordained limits and demands that which belongs to God, we must draw the line." The question, of course, was when to draw the line. The editor thought that Christians had the right, "perhaps the duty," to engage in civil disobedience if the government legislated against their worship or witnessing or if it passed "laws which flagrantly violate Christian conscience or which order Christians to do that which is contrary to God's commands." But while evangelicals upheld the right of civil disobedience, they usually defined it in such a way as to deny its relevance to Vietnam. Like the fundamentalists, mainstream evangelicals generally disapproved of the use of civil disobedience as a means of protesting the Vietnam War.[16]

Just as evangelicals generally accepted warmaking and rejected pacifism, they counseled obedience to and support for the government rather than dissent. Not only did they frown on civil disobedience to protest the Vietnam War; they also urged fellow believers to rally behind the president and his policies. Thus in the early years of the Vietnam War, Carl Henry, editor of *Christianity Today*, backed the Johnson administration—though not unreservedly, which probably figured in his being dismissed in the summer of 1968, at the urging of archconservatives such as J. Howard Pew. (Henry apparently believed that the Vietnam War was a "just cause," but he expressed skepticism regarding the president's policies on the war.) In November, 1969, fol-

16. "The Bible and Civil Disobedience," *Eternity*, October, 1966, p. 6. See also Pratt, "Religious Faith and Civil Religion," 71, 71n, 72, 73, 248–49, 305; Hudson T. Armerding, "Is Patriotism Christian?" *UEA*, July, 1966, pp. 5–6, 14; Charles C. Ryrie, "What Should the Church Do About Civil Disobedience?" *Moody Monthly*, July–August, 1970, p. 19; Richey Kamm, "The Tradition of Law and Order," *Christian Life*, February, 1969, pp. 74–75; "Spock, Coffin, and Viet Nam," 28; "Civil Disobedience," *CT*, June 5, 1970, p. 26; Clyde W. Taylor, "Civil Protest," *UEA*, March, 1968, p. 31.

lowing President Richard M. Nixon's "silent majority" speech describing his plan to end the war by strengthening the South Vietnamese while gradually withdrawing American forces, the new editor of *Christianity Today*, Harold Lindsell, declared, "Whether or not Mr. Nixon's decision is the ideal one, we think the welfare of the nation will best be served if its people rally behind him and give his plan a bit more time to succeed." Later, when Nixon decided to mine North Vietnamese harbors and interdict ships carrying military supplies to North Vietnam, Lindsell declared that "all Americans, and especially Christians, should stand by the President, even if they think his policy is mistaken." [17]

Billy Graham, the "unofficial White House chaplain," the man David Poling, editor of the *Christian Herald*, called "America's most prominent Christian spokesman," also supported the government on the Vietnam War, not only through his well-publicized friendship with Presidents Johnson and Nixon but in public statements and private communications. He offered perhaps his most ringing endorsement of Johnson at the presidential prayer breakfast of February, 1966. He began his sermon by praising the "magnificent speech" the president had delivered the night before in which, as most of those assembled at the breakfast surely knew, Johnson had pledged never to allow the communists to "deter or defeat us." Graham based the main part of his sermon on two biblical texts: Luke 12:49 and Matthew 10:34–36. As Clayton Fritchey paraphrased him in the *Washington Post*, he seemed to be saying "that Jesus was a hawk who would have supported Johnson's Vietnam policy." That Graham, at least, supported Johnson was clear. The evangelist concluded his sermon by declaring: "Mr. President, in those hours of decision that you have to make, you have our prayers, our love, and our support. God bless you, sir." By the time Nixon became president,

17. "The President's Viet Nam Policy," *CT*, November 21, 1969, p. 185; "Plain Talk on Viet Nam," *CT*, May 26, 1972, p. 27. See also "Nixon and the Logjam," *CT*, October 23, 1970, p. 27; "Viet Nam—Continuing Impasse," *CT*, August 6, 1971, p. 1011; "Viet Nam: A Presidential Dilemma," *CT*, May 12, 1972, p. 767. For Henry's views on the war, during and after the period he served as *CT* editor, see "Viet Nam: Where Do We Go from Here?" 31; "Viet-Nam: A Moral Dilemma," 27–28; *NYT*, December 3, 1967, p. 7; "The Need for Leadership," *CT*, July 19, 1968, p. 33; Carl F. H. Henry, "A Nation in Trouble," *CT*, September 12, 1969, pp. 37–38. On Henry's dismissal, see George H. Marsden, "Unity and Diversity in the Evangelical Resurgence," in *Altered Landscapes: Christianity in America, 1935–1985*, ed. David W. Lotz with Donald W. Shriver, Jr., and John F. Wilson (Grand Rapids, 1989), 70; Marsden, *Reforming Fundamentalism*, 259–60, 277.

Graham had become wary of making any public pronouncements endorsing the Vietnam War. Nevertheless, his friendship with Nixon, as well as his willingness to play the role of his spiritual adviser, could not but convey approval of his policies in Vietnam. Certainly Graham never publicly criticized Nixon's handling of the war, not even when a number of churchmen, including some fellow evangelicals, urged him to implore the president to stop the bombing of North Vietnam.[18]

Graham's support for government authority may have been partly instinctive, as William McLoughlin, Marshall Frady, and William Martin have suggested, but it also grew out of his acceptance of the scriptural admonition in Romans 13. He had invoked it against the civil rights sit-ins in the early 1960s: "I do believe we have the responsibility to obey the law. No matter what that law may be—it may be an unjust law—I believe we have a Christian responsibility to obey it." During the Vietnam debate, he summoned it against antiwar protesters. In "God and Campus Violence," published in *Decision* in October, 1969, he wrote, "'The powers that be,' the Bible says, 'are ordained of God' (Romans 13:1), and the Christian citizen is committed to uphold the law and order that is necessary for the functioning of society."[19]

Graham's support for government authority also represented a continuation of the strategy he and other evangelicals had initiated in the late 1940s and 1950s to gain political influence. Just as he had cultivated

18. Edward B. Fiske, "The Closest Thing to a White House Chaplain," *New York Times Magazine*, June 8, 1969, p. 27; Clayton Fritchey, "Billy Graham and Bombing; Not a Critical Word," *Washington Post*, January 6, 1973, p. A15; David Poling, *Why Billy Graham?* (Grand Rapids, 1977), 101; Lyndon Baines Johnson, "Remarks in Atlantic City at the Convention of the American Association of School Administrators" (February 16, 1966), in *Public Papers of the Presidents, 1966, Book I* (1967), 191; *Congressional Record*, CXII (89th Cong., 2nd Sess.), 3834–35. The most recent and fullest discussion of Graham's relationship with Presidents Johnson and Nixon before and during the Vietnam War may be found in Martin, *Prophet*, 208–10, 274–83, 299–305, 311, 351–60, 368–71, 390–99, 420. See also Pierard, "Billy Graham and Vietnam," 42–43, 47; Richard V. Pierard, "Billy Graham and the U.S. Presidency," *Journal of Church and State*, XXII (Winter, 1980), 124, 125; Richard V. Pierard, "Can Billy Graham Survive Richard Nixon?" *Reformed Journal*, April, 1974, pp. 7, 8, 11.

19. William G. McLoughlin, Jr., *Billy Graham: Revivalist in a Secular Age* (New York, 1960), 120–21; Marshall Frady, *Billy Graham: A Parable of American Righteousness* (Boston, 1979), 405–406, 412, 453; Martin, *Prophet*, 361, 388; Pierard, "Can Billy Graham Survive?" 12; Billy Graham, "God and Campus Violence," *Decision*, October, 1969, p. 8.

Eisenhower's friendship as a way of gaining an entrée to the White House, so he maintained a close relationship with Presidents Johnson and Nixon as a means of exerting influence on them. Shortly after Nixon ordered the 1970 "incursion" into Cambodia, precipitating widespread revulsion and protest in the United States, David Poling conversed with Graham about the president's action. The evangelist seemed to be troubled over the extension of the war and its effect on civilians. Suddenly, Poling remembered, "Billy said abruptly, 'What can people expect me to do? March in protest? Carry a sign? If I do that, then all the doors at the White House and all the avenues to people in high office in this administration are closed to me.'"[20]

Christianity Today agreed with Graham about the benefits of a close association with the president. Admitting that his friendship with Nixon had subjected him to "considerable criticism" and granting the "risk involved when a clergyman becomes a confidant of powerful figures in the secular world," the magazine insisted that the disadvantages were "far outweighed by the opportunity." After all, hadn't "many evangelicals long prayed for an entree without compromise into the affairs of state?" Beyond the pragmatic justification, *Christianity Today* cited "ample biblical precedents" for what Graham was doing: "Esther and Mordecai, Joseph, and Daniel show that one can make his influence for God felt through private relationships with heads of state." Other evangelicals, including Wesley Pippert and Wallace Henley, agreed, although they recognized the possibility—even the likelihood—that Graham might be used by the president or his men.[21]

At first glance, the Graham-Nixon relationship looks like a recapitulation of the evangelist's earlier relationship with President Eisenhower. In the 1950s, it will be remembered, Graham and other evangelicals celebrated Eisenhower as a born-again Christian, and Eisenhower conferred legitimacy on evangelical religion by participating in projects such as the March of Freedom and International Christian Leadership. Similarly, Graham repeatedly extolled Nixon's "deep religious convictions" and "firm faith in God," and, as Wallace Henley pointed out, evangelicals eagerly adopted Nixon "as one of our own."

20. Poling, *Why Billy Graham?* 81. See also Martin, *Prophet*, 130.
21. "On Befriending Presidents," *CT*, March 17, 1972, p. 26; Wesley Pippert, "Billy Graham: Prophet or Politician?" *Christian Life*, May, 1971, p. 58; Wallace Henley, *The White House Mystique* (Old Tappan, N.J., 1976), 74.

Nixon, however, made a much more calculated effort than Eisenhower to persuade Graham and other evangelicals to think of him as a man of great piety, identifying himself as a born-again Christian, inaugurating well-publicized worship services in the East Room of the White House, telegraphing (at Graham's urging) a greeting to some eighty thousand youths gathered at Campus Crusade's Explo '72, and interlarding his speeches with evangelical themes. And whereas evangelicals manipulated Eisenhower to win visibility and respect for evangelical religion, Nixon and his administration turned the tables on them, using evangelicals, especially Graham, to further their own political ends and muster support for their Vietnam policies.[22]

Ever since the 1950s, Graham had denied being "political," and during the Vietnam era, as he came under increasing criticism for supporting Johnson and Nixon and the Vietnam War, he reiterated that claim. "God has called me to be a New Testament evangelist, not an Old Testament prophet!" he declared in one instance. "While some may interpret an evangelist to be primarily a social reformer or political activist, I do not! . . . My primary goal is to proclaim the Good News of the Gospel of Jesus Christ." Similarly, he insisted that except for one occasion, early in the war, he had never said "anything publicly that could be construed as support" for the war in Vietnam. And although he admitted having spoken to Johnson and Nixon on matters involving "a definite moral issue" (but refused to divulge the precise nature of such utterances), he claimed that he did not offer advice regarding war policies.[23]

Graham's protestations about being "nonpolitical" point to another issue evangelicals confronted during the Vietnam War—the church's responsibility regarding social and political matters. In responding to

22. Pippert, "Billy Graham," 28, 29, 54; Henley, *White House Mystique*, 74; Richard V. Pierard and Robert D. Linder, *Civil Religion and the Presidency* (Grand Rapids, 1988), 213, 217–26; Martin, *Prophet*, 209, 227, 279, 354–56, 359, 395, 397, 420–21; Richard M. Nixon, "A Nation Under God," *Decision*, April, 1969, p. 14; Gerald S. Strober, *Graham: A Day in Billy's Life* (Garden City, N.Y., 1976), 78–79; Pierard, "Can Billy Graham Survive?" 10–11; Jeb Stuart Magruder, *An American Life: One Man's Road to Watergate* (New York, 1974), 119.

23. Billy Graham, "A Clarification," *CT*, January 19, 1973, p. 36. See also *NYT*, June 24, 1970, p. 37; McLoughlin, *Billy Graham*, 94, 96–97, 120–22; Pippert, "Billy Graham," 28; Pierard, "Billy Graham and the U.S. Presidency," 109; Martin, *Prophet*, 147, 244, 251, 398–99, 423, 518; Billy Graham, "What Ten Years Have Taught Me," *Christian Century*, February 17, 1960, pp. 186–87.

his critics, Graham sometimes took refuge in the position traditionally associated with fundamentalists and evangelicals, that the proper role of the church and individual Christians was, as he said, to proclaim the Gospel and nothing more. But in admitting that he had offered Presidents Johnson and Nixon moral counsel, as opposed to advice on policy, Graham seemed to have shifted to the position an increasing number of evangelicals, especially the so-called new evangelicals, had been propounding since the late 1940s. It emphasized "social responsibility," the duty of the church and individual believers to address the problems of society. It was one of the ways the new evangelicals differentiated themselves from fundamentalists—by challenging what Harold John Ockenga called their "ethical indifferentism." As early as 1947, in a path-breaking book *The Uneasy Conscience of Modern Fundamentalism*, Carl F. H. Henry criticized fundamentalism for failing to apply Christian teachings to social issues. More than a decade later, writing in *Christianity Today*, Ockenga declared that the evangelical "intends that Christianity will be the mainspring in many of the reforms of the societal order." Targeting dispensationalism as the doctrinal basis of fundamentalists' lack of social concern, he added, "It is wrong to abdicate responsibility for society under the impetus of a theology which overemphasizes the eschatological." In the 1950s, both the NAE and *Christianity Today* promulgated the notion of applying "the Biblical revelation to the contemporary social crisis."[24]

George Marsden has pointed out that the new evangelicals who called for sociopolitical involvement in the late 1940s and 1950s generally assumed it would have a conservative orientation—that it would be, in Marsden's words, "a Christianized version of Republicanism." During the debate over Vietnam, mainstream evangelicals elaborated their notion of sociopolitical involvement. Discussing the role of the church, they insisted that as a corporate entity (referring to either specific denominations or, more often and usually capitalized, the Church of Jesus Christ, *i.e.*, the entire body of believers) it had no "spiritual mandate to sponsor economic, social, and political programs," that its mission in

---

24. John Oliver, "A Failure of Evangelical Conscience," *Post-American*, May, 1975, p. 26; Harold John Ockenga, "Resurgent Evangelical Leadership," *CT*, October 10, 1960, p. 14. See also Lowell D. Streiker and Gerald S. Strober, *Religion and the New Majority: Billy Graham, Middle America, and the Politics of the 70s* (New York, 1972), 112; Martin, *Prophet*, 164, 212; "NAE Faces Issues in National Crisis," *UEA*, May 1, 1951, pp. 3–4.

the world was spiritual, and that its competence and authority were restricted to "spiritual and moral affairs." It should speak out against moral evil and offer the guidance of divinely revealed principles, but it had "no divine mandate to become officially involved in the approval of economic and political strategies." There was nothing inherently conservative (or radical) in this view, but the majority of evangelicals interpreted it conservatively in the 1960s and early 1970s. To them, being socially responsible meant supporting the social and political status quo. On the specific issue of the Vietnam War, as we have seen, the conservative interpretation, combined with the much emphasized doctrine of obedience to constituted authority, dictated support for United States government policy. Thus not only *Christianity Today* and Billy Graham but groups such as the NAE and the Southern Baptist Convention endorsed presidential policies regarding the war. The conservative interpretation of social responsibility, with its distinction between providing moral guidance and engaging in politics, also provided the rationale for mainstream evangelicals' criticism of the mainline denominations and groups like the National Council of Churches for issuing specific policy recommendations on legislation, military strategy, and diplomacy.[25]

Fairly early in the Vietnam era, however, the mainstream evangelicals' interpretation of social responsibility and their position on the war in Southeast Asia came under attack. The challengers were themselves evangelicals. These "dissenters," as Andrew LeRoy Pratt calls them, came primarily from three groups, but one also finds occasional ex-

25. Marsden, "Unity and Diversity in the Evangelical Resurgence," 70; "The Church and Political Pronouncements," *CT*, August 28, 1964, p. 29; Carl F. H. Henry, "What Is the Church Supposed to Do?" *UEA*, July, 1965, p. 31. For the NAE and SBC endorsements, see "Moving Toward Revival," *UEA*, Summer, 1971, p. 15; "NAE at Thirty: A Quest for Unity," *UEA*, Summer, 1972, p. 20; Blevins, "Southern Baptist Attitudes," 235, 236, 238, 239, 241. For mainstream evangelicals' criticism of mainline denominations and groups, see "Who Speaks for the Church?" *CT*, June 9, 1967, p. 26; Billy Graham, "False Prophets in the Church," *CT*, January 19, 1968, p. 4; "War and Peace in Viet Nam," *CT*, February 17, 1967, p. 29; J. Howard Pew, "Should the Church 'Meddle' in Civil Affairs?" *Reader's Digest*, May, 1966, pp. 50–52, 54; "America Faces Critical Decisions," *CT*, January 20, 1967, pp. 24–25; Vernon C. Anderson, "The Christian and Politics," *UEA*, July, 1967, pp. 12–13; James DeForest Murch, "Renewal and the Great Society," *UEA*, May, 1965, pp. 6, 8; Harold O. J. Brown, *The Protest of a Troubled Protestant* (New Rochelle, N.Y., 1969), Chap. 4; Wirt, *Social Conscience of the Evangelical*.

pressions of their point of view in such journals as *Eternity, Christian Herald,* and *HIS.* One of the groups consisted of the editors and contributors associated with the *Reformed Journal,* many of them faculty members at Calvin College in Grand Rapids, Michigan. Another was the widely published academic trio Richard V. Pierard, Robert D. Linder, and Robert G. Clouse, who described themselves as "younger men of moderate persuasion in the evangelical movement who refuse to be categorized as doctrinaire political conservatives." A third group, the People's Christian Coalition of Deerfield, Illinois, came on the scene somewhat later, in 1971. Founded by dissident students at Trinity Evangelical Divinity School (Evangelical Free Church of America), the group published a newspaper called the *Post-American.* They represented a sharper break with mainstream evangelicals than the other dissenters and became known as radical evangelicals. The hero and exemplar of all the dissenting evangelicals, including the radicals, was Oregon senator Mark O. Hatfield, a conservative Baptist layman and an early and outspoken opponent of the war in Vietnam.[26]

In contrast to the mainstream evangelicals' conservative interpretation of social responsibility, the dissenters took a prophetic stance. Rather than counseling obedience to government, the dissenters insisted that the church as well as individual believers had an obligation to confront government with Christian moral principles. Writing in *Eternity* in January, 1967, Lewis Smedes argued that while "the Church must be very careful to avoid making policy *for* the government," it "must at the same time be clear and direct in its proclamation of the will of God *to* government." Believing their notion of social responsibility to be more firmly rooted in the Bible than the conservative one, the dissenting evangelicals pointed to the Old Testament prophets, to Jesus and the Apostles, and to the early Christian communities. Whereas mainstream evangelicals cited Romans 13, dissenters appealed to Acts 5:27–33 ("We ought to obey God rather than men") and Romans 12:2 ("And be not conformed to this world").[27]

26. Pratt, "Religious Faith and Civil Religion," 198–204, 261–62, 313–14; Clouse, Linder, and Pierard, eds., *Protest and Politics,* 2; Richard Quebedeaux, *The Young Evangelicals: Revolution in Orthodoxy* (New York, 1974), 118–23.

27. Lewis Smedes, "Should the Church Speak on Political Issues?" *Eternity,* January, 1967, p. 23; Jim Wallis, "Post-American Christianity," *Post-American,* Fall, 1971, p. 3; Dennis MacDonald, "Prophetic Resistance," *Post-American,* Spring, 1972, p. 7; Emery J. Cummins, "My Country Right or Wrong?" *Eternity,* June, 1967, p. 28; Mark O. Hatfield, "Piety and Patriotism," *Post-American,* May–June, 1973, pp. 1–2.

On the specific issue of Vietnam, the dissenters condemned American intervention in Southeast Asia and the conduct of the war as immoral and unjust from both a Christian and a democratic point of view. Among the *Reformed Journal* group, the My Lai massacre, more than any event of the war, seemed to encapsulate its brutality and viciousness and its corrupting effect on all Americans, not just on U.S. soldiers. The *Post-American* group also cited the massive air strikes President Nixon ordered in the spring of 1972. What Jim Wallis called "the automated bombing of whole populations from high in the sky" seemed the logical culmination of American "policies of destruction and slaughter against the people, the land, and the culture of Indochina."[28]

In keeping with its prophetic stance, the *Reformed Journal* group asserted the church's duty to raise the issue of the morality of the Vietnam War not only among the citizenry of the United States but among government officials. "It [the church] must urgently press the claim of moral humanity on our leaders; it must not let them evade the issue. It must keep pressing, keep asking, keep knocking at the door of the national conscience," Lewis Smedes wrote in 1967. As the war continued and Billy Graham emerged as the spokesman for mainstream evangelicals, the *Reformed Journal* editors urged him to speak to "evangelical middle America," to "compel all of us, in the name of Christ, to make sure we are facing the moral issue honestly, before God."[29]

In comparison with the *Reformed Journal* group, the dissenters associated with Pierard, Linder, and Clouse and the *Post-American* radicals rendered the more sweeping indictment of mainstream evangelicals. "Evangelical Christians must confess to their shame that they have not been willing to stand against the war mentality that has brought the

28. Jim Wallis, "Airwar," *Post-American*, Spring, 1972, p. 4; Jim Wallis, "The Issue of 1972," *Post-American*, Fall, 1972, p. 2. See also Lewis Smedes, "Comments on Vietnam," *Reformed Journal*, July–August, 1967, p. 7; L.B.S., "Dissent and Disruption," *Reformed Journal*, December, 1967, p. 3; John Rensenbrink, "Vietnam: Time for Decision," *Reformed Journal*, March, 1967, pp. 5–9; L.B.S., "A Not Surprising Horror," *Reformed Journal*, January 1970, p. 2; Daniel H. Benson, "Our Responsibility for My Lai," *Reformed Journal*, January, 1971, pp. 8–11; L.B.S., "Cleaver and Calley," *Reformed Journal*, April, 1971, pp. 2–3; Daniel H. Benson, "We Are the Casualties," *Reformed Journal*, May–June, 1971, pp. 3–4; Lewis B. Smedes, "Lieutenant Calley: Scapegoat or Touchstone?" *Reformed Journal*, May–June, 1971, pp. 4–5; Cummins, "My Country"; Jim Wallis, "Evangelism in Babylon," *Post-American*, Summer, 1972, pp. 8–9.

29. Smedes, "Should the Church Speak on Political Issues?" 26; "An Appeal to Billy Graham," *Reformed Journal*, September, 1972, p. 3.

nation to the point of spiritual and psychological exhaustion," Clouse declared. Similarly, the *Post-American* group censured mainstream evangelicalism as "a chaplain of militarism" and for supporting "the government's policy of genocide in Southeast Asia." Like the *Reformed Journal* group, the radical evangelicals especially faulted Billy Graham. "While condemning personal sin," Joe Roos observed, "he refuses to take a stand on the corporate nature of American involvement in Vietnam." Indeed, "he frequently identifies with that American system which creates so much evil in the world."[30]

By the early 1970s, the division within the evangelical community between the dissenters and their mainstream brethren had become irreparable. The dissenters' exhortations to confront the moral issue involved in the Vietnam War left mainstream evangelicals unmoved. They never directly considered the question of whether the American intervention and the conduct of the war were in accord with Christian moral principles. Perhaps they wanted to avoid a head-on confrontation with the mainline spokesmen—and, later, the dissenting evangelicals—who used just war theory to prove the immorality of the war. Their early fixation on the doctrine of obedience to constituted authority may have prevented or at least distracted them from confronting the moral issue involved in the war. Or it enabled them to shift the burden of deciding the moral issue onto the government. Perhaps, too, mainstream evangelicals were unable to come to grips with the moral issue because they felt overwhelmed by the ambiguities of the war. Even in its early years, but increasingly in the later phase, they referred to it as "complex and confusing," a strategic "predicament," a "moral dilemma." Billy Graham experienced increasing ambivalence, even "deep disquiet," regarding the war. He later admitted to Marshall Frady that "it was a very difficult thing. . . . Equally devout Christians could be on different sides of the question. The whole question became a very difficult gray for me. . . . I continued to pray about Vietnam—I prayed about it, and prayed about it, and I couldn't seem to get any leading finally except

30. Robert G. Clouse, "The Christian, War, and Militarism," in Clouse, Robert D. Linder, and Richard V. Pierard, *The Cross and the Flag* (Carol Stream, Ill., 1972), 217; Wallis, "Evangelism in Babylon," 9; Jim Wallis, "The Movemental Church," *Post-American*, Winter, 1972, p. 2; Joe Roos, "American Civil Religion," *Post-American*, Spring, 1972, p. 10.

just to stay out of the whole matter." In January, 1968, the editor of *Eternity* observed that "no American conflict since the Civil War has provoked as many moral questions" as Vietnam. "The right to dissent, the privilege of conscientious objection, the role of the Church in war, the problem of just and unjust wars are a few of the issues." Then, tellingly, the editor added, "Yet frankly, few of us would worry about the war's morality, if we could hurry up and end it."[31]

As mainstream evangelicals became discouraged and disillusioned, their support for the war and government policies weakened, but still they did not shift to an antiwar position. Instead, they became preoccupied with the rising tide of protest and violence at home and fearful that it would be the "undoing" of the United States and would result in anarchy that would be "ultimately contained only by a lofty general astride a horse."[32] Evangelicals still hoped to stop communism in Southeast Asia, still sought a just and honorable peace, but the devastating effect of the war at home had become the overriding concern.

Frustrated by the "moral dilemma" posed by Vietnam, disillusioned with government policies, worried that antiwar dissent would bring about America's "undoing," in the late 1960s mainstream evangelicals exhibited a growing tendency to conclude discussions of an increasingly intractable war with exhortations to prayer. Such appeals were consistent with their long-standing belief in the sovereignty of God and the need to rely on Him. As human efforts to solve the problem of the Vietnam War seemed unavailing, evangelicals looked to God for the solution. "Big as America is and powerful as its nuclear armaments are, the Viet Nam imbroglio seems beyond its ability to terminate," the editor of *Christianity Today* observed in March, 1969. "Maybe the time has come for Christians to cry as Jehoshaphat did when he was faced by

31. "Viet Nam: Where Do We Go from Here?" 31; Billy Graham to the Editor, *Christian Century*, March 29, 1967, p. 411; St. Clair, "Muddle of Vietnam," 11; Ockenga, "Report from Vietnam," 35; "Viet Nam: A Moral Dilemma," 27–28; Martin, *Prophet*, 344–46, 365–67, 422–24; Frady, *Billy Graham*, 431–32; "Editorials: What Made 1967 a Significant Year," *Eternity*, January, 1968, p. 6.

32. "M-Day in Retrospect," *CT*, November 7, 1969, p. 133; Carl F. H. Henry, "A Nation in Trouble," *CT*, September 12, 1969, p. 38. See also Billy Graham, "God and Campus Violence," *Decision*, October, 1969, p. 8; Sherwood Wirt, "How to Destroy a Country," *Decision*, February, 1970, p. 2; Pratt, "Religious Faith and Civil Religion," 228, 253–54, 289, 295–96.

a coalition of powers: 'We are powerless. . . . We do not know what to do, but our eyes are upon thee' (II Chron. 20:12). Maybe, just maybe, God can do what armaments, peace tables, and talk have not been able to do." [33]

33. "Decision Time on Viet Nam," *CT*, March 28, 1969, p. 27. See also "Open Letter to Mr. Nixon," *CT*, October 10, 1969, p. 34; and Wirt, "How to Destroy a Country," 2. For a fully developed statement of the notion that prayer to God was the only solution to Vietnam, see Stephen F. Olford, "A Communist War," *Moody Monthly*, February, 1969, pp. 20, 22, and Olford, "God's Answer to Vietnam," *Moody Monthly*, July–August, 1968, pp. 27–29, 43–45.

10

Fighting the "Other War" in Vietnam

During the debate over Vietnam, evangelicals focused less attention on the shooting war in Southeast Asia than on what they called the "other war" —the crusade to spread Christianity there.[1] The emphasis is not surprising. The "other war" could easily be seen as part of that worldwide struggle between Christianity and atheistic communism that had preoccupied evangelicals since the beginning of the Cold War. And unlike the shooting war, which was fraught with ambiguities, the "other war" did not afflict evangelicals with feelings of confusion and frustration. Indeed, focusing on the "other war" may have helped some of them avoid confronting the difficult moral, political, and military questions raised by U.S. military intervention.

The heroes of the "other war" were the missionaries, soldiers and chaplains who constituted what *Christianity Today* called a "Christian task force in Viet Nam." Protestant missionaries had been working in Vietnam since the late nineteenth century. By the time of the U.S. military intervention, the Protestant community in South Vietnam comprised about one hundred thousand persons, most of whom belonged to the Evangelical Church of Vietnam. (Roman Catholics made up approximately 11 percent of the total population of about 16 million.) In the early 1960s, as the United States government increased troop strength and the flow of military equipment to Vietnam, evangelicals escalated the missionary effort there. In addition to the Christian and

1. The U.S. military sometimes referred to the civic and humanitarian efforts of American troops, part of the campaign to win the "hearts and minds" of the South Vietnamese people, as the "other war." Evangelicals used the term to describe Christian missionary work among the Vietnamese and the evangelization of American servicemen.

Missionary Alliance, the dominant Protestant group during most of the twentieth century, the Mennonites, Churches of Christ, Seventh-day Adventists, and Southern Baptist Convention began sending missionaries, raising the number to 150 by 1968. They were joined by organizations such as the Pocket Testament League, Navigators, Wycliff Bible Translators, Worldwide Evangelization Crusade, NAE World Relief Commission, and World Vision.[2]

As the missionary buildup continued, the "good news" from Vietnam dominated evangelical reportage on the war in Southeast Asia. Accounts of Viet Cong massacres of missionaries appeared alongside articles about revivals among the Montagnards, dramatizing the age-old Christian story of sacrifice and redemption. Advertisements puffed the inspirational power of *Viet Nam Profile*, an eighty-minute, full-color World Vision film depicting "the drama of God at work in the midst of war": "Fly over battlefields, witness War's devastation, see heroic work of chaplains, thrill to answered prayer with mountain tribespeople." The Pocket Testament League solicited contributions and marketed a film, *Under the Guns*, showing "PTL in action in Viet-Nam ministering the word of God to soldiers and civilians." Evangelical magazines regularly appealed for more missionaries in Southeast Asia and published enthusiastic reviews of books describing the work of Vietnamese Christians. *United Evangelical Action* declared Homer Dowdy's *Bamboo Cross* "as timely as current news from Vietnam battlefields," a thrilling account of "gripping situations of the Christian heroes and martyrs among the humble tribespeople who live in the midst of a struggle between communism and the forces of freedom." Completing the picture of the "other war" were detailed reports from the field by Bob Pierce and Larry Ward of World Vision; Everett S. Graffam of the World Relief Commission; Grady Mangham, secretary for East Asian affairs for the C&MA; and Russell T. Hitt, editor of *Eternity*, to name a few.[3]

2. "Are Churchmen Failing Servicemen in Viet Nam?" *CT*, August 18, 1967, p. 31. On the Protestant missionary effort in Vietnam, see David E. Kucharsky, "Viet Nam: The Vulnerable Ones," *CT*, March 1, 1968, pp. 17, 19; "The Indomitable Church of South Vietnam," *Eternity*, August, 1972, p. 22; "Report: Missions in Viet Nam," *UEA*, April, 1965, p. 25.

3. Miriam G. Cox, "Vietnam Report: Murders, Miracles and Missions," *Eternity*, December, 1964, pp. 29–30; "Unprecedented Inhumanity in Viet Cong Massacre of 18 Chaplains," *UEA*, Summer, 1970, p. 30; "Six Missionaries Martyred in Viet Nam," *CT*, March 1, 1968, p. 37; "Report: Missions in Viet Nam," 25–27; James C. Hefley, *By Life*

Central to all the discussion of the "other war" in Vietnam, one argument gained force through constant repetition: contrary to what might be expected, U.S. intervention had actually enhanced the missionary effort in South Vietnam, and withdrawal would terminate it. "Far from sounding the death knell to evangelism, the war has opened new doors of remarkable opportunity, and people are generally more responsive than they were," declared the foreign secretary of the C&MA. *Moody Monthly* quoted a missionary's statement: "It is imperative that we see this war through. . . . Withdrawal now would destroy the structure of the church, involve the massacre of Christians and reduce South Vietnam to slavery and serfdom." To the extent that readers were persuaded by it, such an argument undoubtedly helped to maintain evangelical support for the shooting war. As early as the spring of 1965 a *United Evangelical Action* report declared that the missionary effort in Vietnam was "inextricably wed to the struggle for freedom in Viet Nam."[4]

Besides the missionaries, the U.S. military constituted the other contingent fighting the "other war" in Vietnam. The same magazines and books that featured stories of heroic missionaries defying hardship, terror, and death to spread Christianity among the Vietnamese celebrated the evangelistic effort of dedicated military men and faithful chaplains spreading the Gospel among the armed forces fighting in Vietnam. In-

or by Death (Grand Rapids, 1969); Orrel N. Steinkamp, *The Holy Spirit in Viet Nam* (Carol Stream, Ill., 1973); advertisements in *CT*, November 19, 1965, pp. 16–17, and February 4, 1966, p. 53, *Eternity*, July, 1967, p. 35, *UEA*, May, 1966, p. 20; Fred Jarvis, "The Challenge of Cambodia," *Christian Life*, April, 1972, p. 16; Doan Van Mieng, "Vietnam Pastor," in *Great Reading from Decision*, ed. Sherwood E. Wirt and Mavis R. Sanders (Minneapolis, 1970), 386; Homer E. Dowdy, *The Bamboo Cross: Christian Witness in the Jungles of Viet Nam* (New York, 1964); "Bookbriefs," *UEA*, January, 1965, p. 27; Bob Pierce, "Unheadlined Victories in Viet Nam," *Moody Monthly*, September, 1966, pp. 30–31, 58–59; Larry Ward, "Eyewitness Saigon," *Eternity*, October, 1967, pp. 10–12; Everett S. Graffam, "Operation Mercy," *Moody Monthly*, February, 1969, pp. 20–23; Grady Mangham as told to Phill Butler, "New Optimism in Viet Nam," *Moody Monthly*, September, 1967, pp. 30–31, 43–45; Russell T. Hitt, "The Editor Reports on the Church in Viet Nam," *Eternity*, February, 1965, p. 4.

4. Kucharsky, "Viet Nam," 17; Stephen F. Olford, "A Communist War," *Moody Monthly*, February, 1969, p. 22; "Report: Missions in Viet Nam," 27. See also Cox, "Vietnam Report," 30; "The Indomitable Church of South Vietnam," 21; Mangham, "New Optimism in Viet Nam," 30, 31, 44; Hefley, *By Life or by Death*, 108–109; Fred Jarvis, "We Belong in Vietnam," *Christian Life*, July, 1967, pp. 16, 26, 27.

deed, evangelical publications reported substantial cooperation between U.S. military men and American missionaries in Vietnam. Readers learned, for example, that U.S. forces provided the evangelists with medical treatment at base hospitals or occasional helicopter rides to remote tribal villages; that missionaries often found protection from attack in nearby military bunkers or were evacuated by chopper from an endangered area; and that military chaplains encouraged servicemen to participate in missionary-sponsored religious and humanitarian projects. Missionaries, in turn, sometimes assisted U.S. military chaplains by ministering to American servicemen. Pocket Testament League teams evangelized and distributed Gospels among American soldiers, as well as Vietnamese. The International Church in Saigon, operated by the C&MA, attracted Christian GI's, as did Trinity Baptist Church, founded by Southern Baptist missionaries in 1960, in the same city. At Ban Me Thuot, C&MA missionaries held Sunday worship services for the men at an American helicopter base and a military advisers' camp, neither of which was large enough to have a regular military chaplain. In addition, the missionary families at the C&MA compound hosted Sunday evening fellowship meetings for servicemen and U.S. Agency for International Development technicians.[5]

Several evangelical parachurch groups also operated in South Vietnam, mainly among United States forces. For example, the Full Gospel Business Men's Fellowship International sent military chaplains millions of copies of *Voice* magazine to be distributed free to the troops and sponsored a Christian Home at Vung Tau, where servicemen could find relaxation and Christian fellowship. It also organized a "Vietnam Airlift" to reach servicemen there. In late winter, 1967, a group of FGBMFI members boarded a plane in Seattle bound for Saigon. On the flight with the thirty-two businessmen and ministers were thirty-eight young soldiers and airmen and one marine, also headed for Vietnam. A United

5. "Report: Missions in Viet Nam," 26; Miriam G. Cox, "The Race with the Reds," *Eternity*, August, 1965, p. 35, Hefley, *By Life or by Death*, 94, 98, 101, 110, 130–31, 145, 157, 167; Mangham, "New Optimism in Viet Nam," 44; Evertt Hullum and Robert D. O'Brien, "Service with a Smile," *Ambassador Life*, XXI (November, 1966), 1; "The Indomitable Church of South Vietnam," 28; Sidney Correll, "How Vietnam Has Changed," *Eternity*, January, 1968, p. 33; Wayne Dehoney, *Disciples in Uniform* (Nashville, 1967), 22–24, 61–62; Dallas M. Lee, "No Sanctuary Where the Action Is," *Home Missions*, XXXVII (July, 1966), 12–13; Glenn W. Wagner, "Dateline South Viet Nam," *UEA*, October, 1965, p. 36; Jarvis, "We Belong in Vietnam," 27.

Press International correspondent who made the trip with them described the scene soon after the plane was aloft: "One by one all the members of the Full Gospel Fellowship rose from their seats and went to the side of every young man in uniform, comforted him and prayed with him. The sound of prayers was clearly audible above the roar of the plane's motors." After landing at Tan Son Nhut Air Base, the FGBMFI men fanned out into various areas of South Vietnam, traveling by plane, helicopter, truck, and jeep and giving their testimonies and distributing their literature in services held on ships and airstrips, in officers' quarters, and at mess hall meetings. According to a *Voice* story, it was the military chaplains (in particular, Duie Jernigan and Merlin Carothers) who did most of the work that made the outreach possible. Elated by their success, the FGBMFI men came away from their trip full of the same optimism that energized so many other missionaries and chaplains in Vietnam. "We have never seen a place in the world where the field is so ripe unto harvest in every level of activity," declared the author of the *Voice* story. "We believe the Lord is going to bring conviction to this land, and He is now preparing the hearts for others who shall come with a sweeping revival message."[6]

Besides publicizing the cooperative efforts of missionaries and the U.S. military, evangelical magazines and books reported on the role of individual servicemen in the "other war." Evangelicals had long considered the armed forces as a mission field, and the military buildup of the Vietnam era encouraged extravagant predictions about the evangelizing potential of thousands of "disciples in uniform." Returning from a visit to South Vietnam in 1967, Southern Baptist pastor Wayne Dehoney exclaimed, "Could it be that from the most awesome military might ever assembled . . . would come the most tremendous missionary force the Christian church has ever had?" Other evangelicals shared his hope and enthusiasm. Throughout the Vietnam era they urged fellow Christians in the armed forces to become "an influence for Christ." "Every believer is to become a 'fisher of men,' 'an ambassador for Christ,'" declared the author of a handbook for enlistees, which included an entire

---

6. "A Vision for Viet Nam," *Voice*, July–August, 1968, pp. 25–27; Vinson Synan, *Under His Banner: History of Full Gospel Business Men's Fellowship International* (Costa Mesa, Calif., 1992), 80; "Victory in Vietnam," *Voice*, May, 1967, pp. 26–30; "Vietnam: You Were There," *Voice*, April, 1967, pp. 4–16. For a later, briefer visit to Vietnam, see "Far East Airlift," *Voice*, November, 1967, p. 10.

chapter entitled "Extending Your Christian Faith." Evangelicals also encouraged servicemen to assist their chaplains and become active in chapel activities, and, in a foreign country, to help the missionaries and lay workers of their church.[7]

Reports published in evangelical magazines and books during the Vietnam War announced that servicemen in Vietnam were following such exhortations. An article in the *Pentecostal Evangel*, published by the Assemblies of God, began with a quote from SP4 Mike Payuk: "Besides fighting for my country, I know the Lord has sent me to Vietnam to witness to others. I consider this my mission field and I want to carry on the work of the Lord." According to the author: "Thousands of our young men are engaged in a mission to lift men spiritually, bringing them to God and involving them in His kingdom. . . . They are serving God and country. They are winning multitudes for God's kingdom. We are proud of them!" The Southern Baptist *Commission* featured an article on air force captain Larry D. Salmans, commander of an air rescue helicopter team. He had arrived at Tan Son Nhut Air Force Base in August, 1968, with six years' experience in missionary work in Thailand, Spain, South America, and the Far East. Once Chaplain Bruce Coltharp introduced him to Trinity Baptist Church in Saigon, Salmans became involved in its refugee assistance program, Operation 10,000. The article described him and other members of Trinity "handing out tracts and Bibles" while U.S. Army dentists extracted the decayed and broken teeth of the refugees. "It is always a great thrill to know you have saved a life from certain physical death," Salmans told the author. "But the greatest thrill is to know you have had a small part in helping someone find new life in Christ. In air rescue we are the means by which a person—a wounded man—is lifted up and evacuated by air to a hospital where he receives medical help from the doctors. As soul-winners we are likewise in the rescue business, because we have the great mission of helping and pointing the spiritually sick to the greatest physician of all, the Lord Jesus Christ."[8]

Probably the most celebrated of the "Christian soldiers" in Vietnam

7. Dehoney, *Disciples in Uniform*, 119–21; Stanford E. Linzey, Jr., *Filling Your Boots* (Springfield, Mo., n.d.), n.p.; David W. Plank, *Called to Serve* (Springfield, Mo., 1967), 87, 92, Chap. 8.

8. Robert R. Way, "The Other War," *PE*, June 25, 1967, pp. 8–9; James F. Humphries, "That Others May Live," *Commission*, XXXII (September, 1969), 1–5.

was Sergeant Harold L. Shipp, a cameraman who served with the Combat Information Bureau, III Marine Amphibious Force. To evangelicals he was a hero of the shooting war as well as the "other war," having received the bronze star "for courageous and selfless actions in aiding his fallen comrades at the risk of his own life." Like Salmans, Shipp was no newcomer to evangelism. The career marine had done mission work on Long Island and in New York City and Washington, D.C., worked in Christian Servicemen's Centers in Florida, Oklahoma, and California, and held Bible classes at Leper Hospital, Pearl City, Hawaii. He was ordained a deacon in the First Southern Baptist Church of Pearl Harbor in 1965. In Vietnam, he taught a Bible class at the Danang USO attended by servicemen, Red Cross workers, and missionaries, and he held worship services and Bible classes on front-line positions. In January, 1966, he joined Trinity Baptist Church in Saigon and worked with the missionaries there. He also occasionally assisted a missionary who was the Protestant chaplain at a Vietnamese hospital in Saigon; and when Southern Baptist missionaries came to Danang he helped them with their operations. The several magazine articles written about him stressed Shipp's unassuming, easy manner and his ability to talk with men about God as the key to his influence. One writer quoted him as saying: "I'm proud of Christ and am always ready to tell others of him. I speak to men of all races and ranks. I don't tell them what they are doing wrong. I simply tell them that what they need in life is Christ."[9]

Wayne Dehoney, who talked with many chaplains and soldiers during his visit to South Vietnam, insisted that Shipp was "one of many U.S. servicemen who have witnessed effectively."[10] Although the *Pentecostal Evangel*'s estimate of "thousands" seems exaggerated, there were surely many more soldiers fighting the "other war" than the individuals featured in evangelical publications.

One of them was Dave Roever, who later became well-known in the 1970s for his ministry to Vietnam veterans. "My faith was on the line from the day I arrived in Vietnam," Roever remembered. He had been studying for the ministry before enlisting in the navy, and while he was

9. Lynn Worley, "Marine on a Mission," *Ambassador Life*, XXI (November, 1966), 15; DeLane M. Ryals, "Viet Nam Diary," *Christian Life*, August, 1966, pp. 54–58; Lewis I. Myers, Jr., "Disciple in Uniform," *Commission*, XXIX (July–August, 1966), 9. See also Dehoney, *Disciples in Uniform*, 51–53.

10. Dehoney, *Disciples in Uniform*, 53.

in Vietnam the North Texas District Council of the Assemblies of God licensed him to preach. When he was stationed at Sa Dec, on the Mekong River, the lieutenant in charge of his unit, having discovered that Roever was a minister, provided him with an electric guitar, a microphone, and an amplifier so he could hold religious services. In the absence of the "real chaplain," who visited the base infrequently, Roever became the unit's "unofficial chaplain."[11]

Another "disciple in uniform" was Lieutenant Colonel King J. Coffman, an OCU member who commanded an infantry battalion in Vietnam from February, 1967, through August, 1968. Like other evangelicals, Coffman viewed the war in Vietnam as a dual undertaking: a shooting war to contain communism and prevent that "demonic scourge from reaching our beloved shores" and an "other war" to spread evangelical Christianity among Americans and Vietnamese. Thus he believed that his military mission and his religious duty coincided. In a journal he kept during his tour of duty he described himself as doing "the will of God as a soldier" and "making myself available to God for the accomplishment of His divine purpose in this world."[12]

Coffman's assertion that he was "doing the will of God as a soldier" echoed and may have been inspired by William K. Harrison's admonition in an editorial published in the 1967 War and Peace issue of *Command:* "A Christian soldier should serve his country faithfully, in a manner to glorify God." Coffman also followed Harrison's advice regarding the demeanor appropriate to an "ambassador for Christ." The best approach, Harrison wrote, was "to draw, to attract men to Him, not to be aggressively offensive and antagonize them." An OCU member should first demonstrate that he himself was saved and then "seek opportunities to tell men of the hope we have, speaking with confidence of the Good News." This was exactly the method Coffman followed in Vietnam. He was an inveterate disciple-maker. On the flight to Southeast Asia, he took the opportunity to tell the sergeant sitting next to him "about what Christ means to me" and "commended the Word of God to him as essential reading during the tour." Once he arrived in Viet-

11. Dave Roever and Harold Fickett, *Welcome Home, Davy* (Waco, Tex., 1986), 77–78, 84, and see also 88–89.

12. King J. Coffman, "The Vietnam Journal of Lt. Col. K. J. Coffman, U.S. Army, August 29, 1967, to August 28, 1968," September 6, 1967, February 25, 1968, October 15, 1967 (Photocopy of MS in King J. Coffman Papers, Manuscript Department, U.S. Army Military History Institute, Carlisle Barracks, Pa.).

nam, he seized every chance to "share Christ" with his fellow officers and the enlisted men. "Had a good chat with my room-mate about the Lord," he wrote in October, 1967. "Talked to (LTC) Jack Noll about the Lord at supper," he noted a week later. Notations of such occasions appear throughout the journal, interspersed with accounts of combat operations. In the entry for August, 1968, he wrote: "Had a terrific one hour session tonight with the staff on the 'Meaning of Life.' . . . Six or eight attended, voluntarily of course." Two days later he reported another session on "Who is Jesus Christ." "New and interested faces were there. I encouraged them to bring *one* other next time." After the third session, he wrote, "My OpSgt appears to be under deep conviction."[13]

Once, during a harrowing takeoff from a very short airstrip in the midst of a heavy rain, Coffman found a way to evangelize by example. He had been reading *Moody Monthly* during the takeoff. "When a Colonel piped up in a loud voice, 'You're reading the right magazine after a close one like that!' I said, 'Yes sir,' and turned to an article entitled '*FAITH and FLYING*' and held it up for people to see!! The moral: people watch you all the time. Even reading a Christian Magazine doesn't go unnoticed." On another occasion, while eating dinner with two other officers, he mentioned having just given a talk at Victory Villa, the Christian Servicemen's Center at Nha Trang. One of the officers inquired about the topic "so I lowered the boom on both," Coffman wrote. "It was a grand opportunity to share Christ with them—and gave the whole evening a real glow."[14]

When his artillery liaison officer came to him with a problem, Coffman saw another opportunity for disciple-making. A "short-timer" who had only a few days left in his tour of Vietnam, the man told Coffman "he was afraid and didn't know what to do about it." Coffman invited him to his quarters "and told him how CHRIST conquers all, including our fears—and took him through the Gospel from A–Z. I really believe God was speaking to him. I gave him the Four Spiritual Laws and challenged him to do business with God—and not to put it off." This is

13. William K. Harrison, Jr., "The Christian Officer: His Moral and Spiritual Leadership," *Command*, Spring, 1967, pp. 53, 54; Coffman, "Vietnam Journal," August 31, October 11 and 29, December 24, 1967, August 10, 12, and 14, 1968.

14. Coffman, "Vietnam Journal," November 21, 1967, January, 1968. Victory Villa in Nha Trang, operated by OCSC, where Coffman gave his talks, was one of two Christian Servicemen's Centers in Vietnam; the other, called the Servicemen's Lounge, was operated by the C&MA in Saigon.

"what I'm *really* here for," Coffman confided to his journal. The following day he was gratified to hear from the officer that he had " 'accepted the Lord' " that very night.[15]

Like General Harrison and most other evangelicals, Coffman saw no contradiction between being a Christian and fighting in the war in Vietnam. In one journal entry he dismissed as "fuzzy thinking" an argument made by a young chaplain that if a soldier's conscience bothered him, he should ask forgiveness for killing in combat. "For those who have sought the Lord's will for themselves and find they cannot bear arms— they must say so, and serve as medics, etc.," Coffman wrote. "Others like me who do the will of God as a soldier, need not apologize for doing his duty, not even to God. The chaplain, though well meaning, was trying to rationalize a 'middle course' which doesn't exist, except as a moral compromise." Like most evangelicals Coffman did not define killing in combat as murder. Nor did being a Christian prevent him from being elated when his men killed the enemy. One journal entry said, "Gen Mearns asked me how many we bagged and I said, 'Only 7, but I'm proud of every one.' " The only time participation in war became an issue for Coffman—and then only briefly—was when he came upon a "grisley scene" of some dead Viet Cong soldiers who had been mutilated. "I thought to myself, 'What a dirty business this is—is *this* where I belong?' " he wrote. "Then I thought of the *thousands* of defenseless village elders, school teachers, and administrators that have been murdered by these fiends . . . and I thought that why should the protection of the innocents of So. Vietnam be left to those whose hardened hearts perhaps enjoy killing people, even if they are the enemy? No, perhaps God's people by being here, by exercising effective control of our troops, can *limit* this awful bloodshed to only that actually necessary to destroy this red menace. I *am* in the right place," he concluded.[16]

On another occasion, when a wounded Viet Cong was captured and an officer senior to Coffman declared, "I hope he dies, so we can have a 'body count,' " Coffman was appalled. "The statistics game that has been imposed upon us is turning men into monsters," he wrote. "If only I can instill (or restore) some sense of values in my people here." As for his own feelings toward the Viet Cong, Coffman declared that he felt "no animosity . . . whatsoever, just pity." He wished he "could capture

15. *Ibid.*, March 23, 24, 1968, and see also March 28, 1968.
16. *Ibid.*, February 25, April 12, 1968, September 6, 1967.

all of them and not have to kill them—and then reason with them." He entered in his journal the instructions he gave his men in Vietnam. "Every effort will be made to capture," Coffman wrote, "*provided* no additional risk is involved."[17]

Coffman's journal is especially valuable as a guide to the evangelical network that existed in Vietnam during the war. He and other members of the Officers' Christian Union were quick to identify each other and set up meetings for fellowship, prayer, and Bible study. Coffman also enjoyed fellowship with several C&MA missionaries and a U.S. Agency for International Development staff member whom he described as a "fine Christian." One of the C&MA missionaries introduced him to two doctors at a Mennonite medical clinic. Early in his tour of duty, after reading *The Bamboo Cross*, Coffman became interested in the missionary effort in Vietnam and made a trip to Dalat to visit with Pastor Herbert A. Jackson, the most famous of the C&MA pioneers in Vietnam and one of the heroes of the book. Coffman also delivered two inspirational talks at Victory Villa. Shortly before his departure from Vietnam he attended services at the International Church in Saigon, "where all the evangelicals go," he noted.[18]

Although he disagreed with the chaplain who offered advice to soldiers who felt guilty about killing in war and was disappointed at one chaplain's noncommittal response to his offer to help start a Bible hour on Sunday mornings, Coffman was generally impressed with the chaplains he encountered in Vietnam and with the "biblical and sound" sermons he heard in chapel. The evangelical chaplains he praised made up the third component, along with missionaries and servicemen, of "the Christian task force in Viet Nam." Evangelical magazines and books frequently depicted them in combat situations, "jumping with the troops into the middle of the Viet Cong" or making a chopper landing in the midst of sniper fire, accompanying men on patrol or search-and-destroy missions and praying with them "while the big guns boomed just a few hundred yards away," baptizing marines off Red Beach while a rifle squad watched for snipers.[19] Though many chaplains served in

17. *Ibid.*, March 11, 1968. For comparison, see Cleo W. Buxton, "Morality in Combat," *Command*, War and Peace Issue, 1967, p. 47.

18. Coffman, "Vietnam Journal," September 3, 14, 15, 22, 24, October 3, November 14, 15, 1967, January 23, August 17, 1968.

19. *Ibid.*, September 3, October 22, 1967, February 20, March 23, 1968; Dehoney, *Disciples in Uniform*, 16; Dallas Lee, "No Sanctuary Where the Action Is," *Ambassador Life*, XXI (November, 1966), 6, 8; Pierce, "Unheadlined Victories in Viet Nam," 59.

the rear areas, their service in the forward areas with the fighting men received more attention, perhaps because evangelical writers believed it provided a better demonstration of their spiritual and military valor.

The most celebrated evangelical chaplain of the Vietnam War was James M. Hutchens. In the 1950s, while serving as an enlisted man in the 511th Airborne Infantry Regiment of the 11th Airborne Division, he had received Christ as his Savior under the ministry of the regimental chaplain. When he finished his tour of duty, he attended Wheaton College, then Dallas Theological Seminary, and in 1964 returned to the army as a chaplain. Sent to Vietnam in 1965, he ministered to an airborne infantry battalion. In 1968 Moody Press published the book he wrote about his wartime experiences, *Beyond Combat*. Reviewing it in *United Evangelical Action*, Clyde Taylor called it "one of the most meaningful pieces of literature produced from a war-time experience." To Taylor and other evangelicals, Hutchens epitomized the chaplain-hero of the Vietnam conflict, "propagating the Gospel of Jesus Christ without compromise" as an evangelical chaplain should.[20]

Hutchens, too, thought of himself first and foremost as an evangelist, as did most other evangelical chaplains in Vietnam. "It was my responsibility," he wrote in *Beyond Combat*, "to seize opportunities and means to offer to each man the claims and provisions of Jesus Christ for an abundant life. Each was free to accept or to reject." On board the USS *Thomas A. Mann* headed for Southeast Asia, he led two daily Bible study groups, one in the evening for officers and the other in the morning for the troops. Once in Vietnam, he employed a broad spectrum of evangelistic strategies: a Tuesday film night where he showed "Christian films"; a Wednesday night prayer and Bible study meeting; a literature table stocked with books, tracts and other material furnished by the Billy Graham Crusade or contributed by other Christian groups. These were in addition to the worship service to which he "brought in heavy artillery to proclaim the unsearchable riches of Christ." He made a point of involving the men by having an officer or enlisted man read the opening call to worship, conduct the responsive reading, and recite the closing benediction. Often at the end of a service Hutchens would invite the men to come talk with him privately. "On several occasions this was the time when men first opened their hearts to Jesus Christ," he noted.[21]

20. James M. Hutchens, *Beyond Combat* (Chicago, 1968), 13–16; "Books," *UEA*, Summer, 1969, p. 34.
21. Hutchens, *Beyond Combat*, 58, 23, 41, 74, 75, 87.

Curry Vaughan, who served in Vietnam in 1969 as a chaplain to an airborne infantry battalion, was an equally aggressive evangelist. Early in his tour in Vietnam, he decided that his purpose was not just "to console people" but to "preach the gospel to every man possible and lead everyone" he could to Jesus Christ. Like Hutchens, Vaughan conducted a Bible study for men who wanted it. Like Hutchens, too, he went out on patrol and visited the men in the field. On return visits, he remembered, he would miss a familiar face and would learn that the man had been wounded or killed. "Each time this happened—and it started to happen more and more often—it drove me deeper into the conviction that I had to present Christ more aggressively than ever before," Vaughan wrote. "I resolved to give an invitation to receive the Lord Jesus at the end of every sermon and to do everything else I could to lead those men to a simple prayer of faith and acceptance of Jesus into their lives." At the end of his tour Vaughan counted more than four hundred soldiers who had received Christ, some in response to his invitations, others during personal counseling sessions.[22]

Chaplains like Hutchens and Vaughan insisted that, as Vaughan put it, "God . . . moved on the battleground" in Vietnam. Chaplain Carl McNally told Wayne Dehoney, "Listen, Doc, you tell those 'God-is-dead' fellows back home that there is a *living God* out here in Vietnam!" McNally aimed his remark not only at the so-called Death of God theologians who enjoyed a brief notoriety in the 1960s but more generally at the notion that became popular during and after the Vietnam War that God and/or religion played no part in the conflict. Ron Kovic expressed it succinctly: "There is no God for me after Vietnam." Later, in the 1980s, two former military chaplains who had served in the Vietnam War, Galen Meyer and William Mahedy, elaborated on the notion. According to Meyer's analysis of the Vietnam experience, most of the soldiers who served in the war were basically secular, even "spiritually stunted and hollow," and, lacking internal restraints, they discovered they had a capacity for violence they never suspected. Mahedy described his book, *Out of the Night*, as "a chronicle of the spiritual journey of young men and women (average age slightly more than nineteen years) who found themselves in a cauldron of violence which shattered their faith and called into question their most basic values." He argued that

22. Curry N. Vaughan, Jr., *Battle-ground: A Personal Account of God's Move Upon the American Military Forces* (Plainfield, N.J., 1978), 73, 89, 103–104.

American soldiers in Vietnam experienced a "pandemic loss of religious faith."[23]

In sharp contrast to Kovic, Meyer, and Mahedy, evangelicals emphatically proclaimed the presence of God in Vietnam. To be sure, most evangelicals experienced God in Vietnam vicariously—reading about the evangelizing efforts of the missionaries, servicemen and chaplains "doing the will of God" in that "other war" in Southeast Asia. For some evangelicals, though, the experience was more immediate. In the midst of combat, Chaplain Hutchens wrote, "What had been merely doctrine suddenly exploded into personal reality." He and Vaughan and other evangelical chaplains (and some nonevangelical chaplains as well) became aware of the presence of God in ways they had never known before. "When I sought Him on the ship to Southeast Asia, He was there; when I asked Him for wisdom and strength to serve my men, He was there," Hutchens wrote in the Epilogue to his book.[24]

As for Mahedy's assertion that American troops in Vietnam experienced "a pandemic loss of faith," evangelicals presented a very different view. As we have seen, books and articles from the evangelical press described a many-faceted evangelizing effort on the part of American servicemen and chaplains in Vietnam. In addition, Hutchens, Vaughan, and others offered numerous accounts of religious activity: a shipboard revival en route to Southeast Asia, another revival started by a "Spirit-anointed chaplain" and some "Jesus Boys" at Nha Trang, chaplains baptizing new converts in a jungle stream or mountain river, in makeshift chapels in the field, and on the bases "crammed full with officers and enlisted men." Both Hutchens and Vaughan cited commanding officers who were "committed Christians" and demonstrated an active concern for the spiritual welfare of their men.[25]

And whereas Mahedy contended that the violence men experienced in Vietnam caused them to lose faith in God, Hutchens, Vaughan, and

23. *Ibid.*, 104; Dehoney, *Disciples in Uniform*, 16; Timothy J. Lomperis, *"Reading the Wind": The Literature of the Vietnam War* (Durham, 1987), 34; Galen Meyer, "The Vietnam War and Joseph Conrad's Heart of Darkness," *Pro Rege*, XI (June, 1983), 8, 12; William P. Mahedy, *Out of the Night: The Spiritual Journey of Vietnam Vets* (New York, 1986), 3, 148.

24. Hutchens, *Beyond Combat*, 97, 128.

25. Dehoney, *Disciples in Uniform*, 39–41; Steinkamp, *Holy Spirit in Vietnam*, 24–27; Vaughan, *Battle-ground*, 75, 86, 91; Hutchens, *Beyond Combat*, 22–23, 40, 42–43, 55, 58–60, 65, 69, 74, 86, 88.

others discovered that combat led men to God. In some cases, it caused men to look "almost instinctively" to God for consolation or protection. In other cases, it reinforced an already existing religious commitment. Even Dave Roever, who agreed with Mahedy and Meyer that Vietnam was a "faith-destroying, soul-shredding war," insisted that his evangelical faith protected him from immorality. "My moral principles . . . were founded on the Word of God," he wrote. "I kept one foot on the Rock, even if the other foot often slipped in the Mekong mud."[26]

Mahedy is probably correct in asserting that many, perhaps a majority, of soldiers who saw combat in Vietnam experienced a "pandemic loss of religious faith," but if Payuk, Salmans, Shipp, Roever, Coffman, Hutchens, and Vaughan are at all representative, the experience of evangelicals was quite different. War and soldiering seemed to heighten rather than diminish their sense of divine power and protection and to reinforce their evangelizing compulsion.

26. Hutchens, *Beyond Combat*, 60; Roever and Fickett, *Welcome Home*, 105, 76–77. See also Dehoney, *Disciples in Uniform*, 48, and, for a firsthand account of a battlefield conversion, Ralph G. Bowles, "No More Wasted Years for Me," *PE*, June 25, 1967, p. 11.

11

Supporting the American Forces in Vietnam

In February, 1973, as the last American troops were leaving Vietnam, *Christianity Today* published an article by Nancy Tischler censuring certain segments of American society for their "rejection of military men and military might" because of their opposition to the Vietnam War. Besides the press, the "liberal intelligentsia," and academia, Tischler included the mainline religious organizations and denominations as prime offenders. "Church after church has flatly condemned our actions in Southeast Asia with little apparent understanding of the ramifications of its condemnations. Many who insist this is an 'immoral war' feel it must perforce be fought by immoral or ignorant men," she wrote. Like Tischler, many other evangelicals believed that in protesting the war in Vietnam, the mainline churches and religious antiwar groups also disparaged the United States military as an institution and the individual men and women who served in it. The effect of their antiwar statements, *Christianity Today* pointed out, was "to place almost half a million Americans—and particularly church-related servicemen and their chaplains—in the service of injustice." They implied "that men in the armed forces are rather to be pitied than prayed for and supported. . . . Even when leftist churches pray for their servicemen, these prayers are burdened by an apparent solicitation of God's aid in the fulfillment of a presumably non-Christian vocation."[1]

The mainline antiwar groups' focus on war crimes in Vietnam especially disturbed evangelicals, for it implicated not only the United

1. Nancy M. Tischler, "Onward, Christian Soldiers?" *CT*, February 2, 1973, pp. 15–17; "Are Churchmen Failing Servicemen in Viet Nam?" *CT*, August 18, 1967, p. 31.

States government and the military leadership but individual soldiers, marines, and airmen. In 1968, for example, Clergy and Laymen Concerned About Vietnam (CALCAV) published a collection of news dispatches and magazine articles, many of them eyewitness accounts, that provided graphic documentation of such crimes. The intent of the book was to demonstrate a pattern of conduct on the part of the United States military, a systematic "violation of almost every international agreement relating to the rules of warfare."[2] But the cumulative effect of hundreds of separate accounts of isolated incidents was to highlight the brutality of individual servicemen.

These anti-Vietnam groups also indicted the chaplains of the armed forces. CALCAV, for example, criticized them for failing to exercise their "prophetic responsibility" by protesting the war and atrocities like My Lai, for preaching a "military religion" that legitimized war and the military, and for serving as "an indoctrination agent in behalf of the military" (a reference to their involvement in mandatory character education). Antiwar magazines such as *Christian Century* printed articles adding to the charges, and resolutions and reports issued by religious bodies such as the NCC, the National Association of Laymen, the American Jewish Congress, and the United Church of Christ Task Force on Ministries to Military Personnel reinforced them. The last-named body pronounced perhaps the harshest judgment, culminating nearly a decade of criticism directed at the chaplaincy. Like CALCAV and other groups, the task force indicted chaplains for identifying with military values and goals and, by implication, abandoning their commitment to their calling and church. As evidence it pointed to "the compromise of the chaplaincy in remaining silent long after the truth about the war was known and their own churches had condemned it as immoral and unjust" and their failure to exercise a "restraining role" on commanders in Vietnam. Chaplains and their defenders claimed that chaplains were authorized to advise commanders on matters relating to religion and morals and that they were able to do so by virtue of their officer status, the task force noted. "We challenge the chaplaincy, from the Chiefs on down, to demonstrate in the case of [the Vietnam] war—

2. *In the Name of America: The Conduct of the War in Vietnam by the Armed Forces of the United States as Shown by Published Reports, Compared with the Laws of War Binding on the United States Government and on Its Citizens* (New York, 1968), 1, and see also 17, 18.

with saturation bombing, free fire zones, napalm and guava bombs, the torture of prisoners, political assassination squads, and My Lai—just how military chaplains have influenced commanders for moral ends in order to humanize the war."[3]

Throughout the national debate over Vietnam, mainstream evangelicals never exhibited the antimilitary bias that some of the antiwar groups did. Evangelicals' support for U.S. military intervention and their celebration of the "other war" in Vietnam suggest as much. So does the generally positive view they demonstrated with regard to military service, the American forces in Vietnam, and the conduct of the war.

As we saw in Chapter 1, by the mid-1950s evangelicals had become staunch supporters of the selective service system. During the 1960s and 1970s, when opposition to the Vietnam War fueled widespread criticism of military service, evangelicals continued to preach its necessity and virtue. For just as they generally approved government's using military force, they regarded military service not only as compatible with Christian belief and practice but as an obligation of American citizenship.[4]

As noted in Chapter 9, during the Vietnam era, evangelicals generally disapproved of selective conscientious objection and of conscientious objection based on political, sociological, or philosophical grounds. Out of grudging respect to historic pacifism, however, they condoned, if they did not encourage, conscientious objection on the basis of religious belief. Consequently, numerous articles on the draft and military service published in evangelical magazines included discussions of a Christian's

3. Harvey G. Cox, ed., *Military Chaplains: From Religious Military to a Military Religion* ([New York, 1971]), 88, 144–45; Norman MacFarlane, "Navy Chaplaincy: Muzzled Ministry," *Christian Century*, LXXXIII (November 2, 1966), 1338–39; William Robert Miller, "Chaplaincy vs. Mission in a Secular Age," *Christian Century*, LXXXIII (November 2, 1966), 1335–37; Robert E. Klitgaard, "Onward Christian Soldiers," *Christian Century*, LXXXVII (November 18, 1970), 1377–80; William J. Byron, "Religious Concern and the Indochina War," *America*, CXXVI (February 5, 1972), 116; *NYT*, June 22, 1971, p. 37, May 18, 1968, p. 10; John Deedy, "News and Views," *Commonweal*, LXXXVIII (June 14, 1968), 370; United Church of Christ, Task Force on Ministries to Military Personnel, *Ministries to Military Personnel: Report of a United Church of Christ Task Force to the Ninth General Synod, St. Louis, Missouri, June 22–26, 1973* (Philadelphia, 1973), 86, 82, and see also 77.

4. For results of a poll of Southern Baptist Convention messengers on military service, see William L. Marshall, "Changing Attitudes Toward War: A Study of Southern Baptist Attitudes Toward War" (Master of Theology thesis, Midwestern Baptist Theological Seminary, 1970), 51–52.

right to refuse to serve as a matter of religious conviction and the pro-
cedure for claiming conscientious objector status under the selective
service law. But the bulk of the material justified military service. A
widely distributed publication, *Called to Serve*, issued by the Assemblies
of God in 1967, gives a good idea of the arguments evangelicals presented. In it navy chaplain David Plank set forth what he termed the
"Christian rationale for war," based on Romans 13. Starting with two
premises, that government was ordained by God and that rulers were
commissioned by Him "to suppress evil conduct, and to execute His
wrath upon wrongdoers with the sword," Plank argued that every person owed obedience to his government, including service in its armed
forces. It followed that a person serving in the military acted as the
government's agent, "aiding in the discharge of its divine commission
to suppress evil and punish wrongdoing." Consequently, when a soldier
pulled the trigger, he did not violate the Sixth Commandment. The
commandment prohibited murder, Plank insisted. "That is, a man is
commanded not to kill another human being with premeditated malice
or hatred in his heart." Plank maintained that "the military man does
not personally kill in this manner any more than the citizen who farms
the soil and grows the food that feeds the soldier, sailor, or marine,
providing him strength to pull the trigger." And in case the biblical
argument failed to persuade, Plank added another, based on "the Christian ethic," that also sanctioned military service and the use of armed
force:

> How can a person accept local police protection for himself, his family,
> his property, and his community, it is reasoned, unless he complies with
> the Christian ethic and extends that same principle of protection to others
> and their families? If one grants this, then he is forced to broaden the
> coverage so that the nation itself is cared for and protected. A person
> becomes morally responsible in some measure for deeds of violence that
> could have been contained or repelled had he not opposed protection
> from them, or withheld himself from actively resisting them.[5]

5. David W. Plank, *Called to Serve* (Springfield, Mo., 1967), 19–22. See also "A
Matter of Conscience," *Ambassador Life*, XXI (November, 1966), 9; Eddie Davis, "Why
I Am a Conscientious Objector," *Ambassador Life*, XXI (November, 1966), 10; "Draft
Defiance," *CT*, March 26, 1971, pp. 605–606; W. G. Corliss, "Can a Christian Be a
Fighting Man?" *Eternity*, September, 1962, pp. 22–24, 38; Stanford E. Linzey, Jr., *Fill-
ing Your Boots* (Springfield, Mo., n.d.); E. S. Caldwell, "Called to Serve," *PE*, June 25,
1967, pp. 10–11.

Whereas Plank rested his justification of soldiering primarily on Paul's admonitions in Romans, other evangelicals cited the example of Jesus. "Should a follower of Jesus participate at all in the messy military business of killing people? Would Jesus? Or would He go so far as to burn his draft card?" asked Randolph Klassen in *HIS* magazine. "Would Christ carry a draft card? I am convinced He would. Does He want me to carry one? Of this I have no doubt, and this in turn means that I may have to participate in some military activity." As historian Andrew LeRoy Pratt has observed: "The example of Jesus was the highest form of authority for any evangelical. To invoke that authority in favor of obedience to the draft and military service was to exert ultimate pressure for young persons to conform their behavior to the desires of the state."[6]

Not only did evangelicals insist that a Christian could and in some circumstances should be a soldier; they also contended, as we saw in Chapter 10, that many of the men serving in Vietnam were maintaining a Christian witness there. Based on what they read in evangelical books and magazines, they could not but believe Sidney Correll's declaration in *Eternity* magazine. "If there is any one thing that has characterized our half million men in Vietnam," he wrote, "it has been the involvement of thousands of them in feeding the hungry, caring for the children by finding homes for them, bringing gallons of milk and tubs of ice cream to the orphanages, working with the lepers, building churches, bulldozing locations for buildings and installing electricity."[7]

Indeed, evangelicals expressed highly favorable opinions of the religion, morals, and morale of the American forces in Southeast Asia. Whatever fears they had harbored regarding the moral and religious environment of the armed forces had been largely eradicated by the military's promotion of religious and moral welfare programs. In the 1960s and early 1970s, evangelicals who visited American servicemen in Southeast Asia returned home with nothing but praise for the military leadership's efforts in this regard. Following his 1968 visit, Billy Graham singled out for special notice the "tremendous moral program" being carried out in Vietnam. Everything possible was being done for the

6. Randolph Klassen, "A Matter of Conscience," *HIS*, June, 1968, pp. 15–16, 21. See also Robert Hurt, "Why I Am a Conscientious Participant," *Ambassador Life*, XXI (November, 1966), 10; Andrew LeRoy Pratt, "Religious Faith and Civil Religion: Evangelical Responses to the Vietnam War, 1964–1973" (Ph.D. dissertation, Southern Baptist Theological Seminary, 1988), 252–53.

7. Sidney Correll, "How Vietnam Has Changed," *Eternity*, January, 1968, p. 33.

spiritual welfare of the troops, he declared; the chaplains, in particular, were "fulfilling a major role in the moral factor of this war." Similarly, Arthur B. Rutledge, an SBC Home Mission Board official, praised commanders in Vietnam for their interest in providing "strong spiritual support for our service people" and their "genuine concern for the work of the chaplains." Indeed, he added, some of those high-ranking officers were "outstanding Christian laymen" themselves, "and in almost every case they were regular attendants of chapel services."[8]

Evangelicals believed that the military leadership's religious and moral programs, supplemented by their own evangelizing efforts, had paid off in Vietnam. A few of the visitors returning from Southeast Asia noted the immorality they had observed in Saigon and other cities, but even they moved quickly to the dominant theme in evangelical reportage: the high level of religious interest and commitment among the American forces, as evidenced by the large number of men attending chapel and responding to altar calls during worship services. *United Evangelical Action* quoted a Baptist chaplain who had recently returned from duty in South Vietnam as saying that "almost 100 percent" of U.S. servicemen attended religious services. Stephen Olford, pastor of Calvary Baptist Church in New York City, visited an air force chapel where he saw "fully 50 percent of the men come forward to make a decision for Christ," and he quoted the chaplain as saying, "We're in the midst of revival!" Reporting on one of Billy Graham's visits to Vietnam, evangelical magazines described thousands of soldiers and marines flocking to hear him at Camp Hochmuth and in Danang and Long Binh and hundreds raising their hands to indicate their desire to commit their lives to Christ. Such interest was not limited to enlisted men. *Decision* magazine noted that the theater where Graham held a service for the commanders and staff at Military Assistance Command Vietnam headquarters was filled to capacity, with many standing in the aisles. As for the morale of the American forces, Olford declared, "America may be confused; other nations may have little idea of why we are in Vietnam, but let me say that I did not find one soldier, from the ranks to the

---

8. Ted Smith, "Vietnam Salute," *Decision*, March, 1968, p. 12; Arthur B. Rutledge, "Chaplaincy a Welcomed Ministry," *Home Missions*, XXXVIII (August, 1967), A5. See also Wayne Dehoney, *Disciples in Uniform* (Nashville, 1967), 67, 71; Dale Herendeen, "Graham Preaches Peace in Viet Nam," *CT*, January 20, 1967, pp. 36–37; "Vietnam Christmas," *Decision*, March, 1967, pp. 6, 12.

generals . . . who was not solidly convinced of our enemy and our cause." Graham, too, exclaimed over the "dedication" of the men in Vietnam. "No matter what you think of the war politically, you have to admire these men," he insisted.[9]

Just as evangelicals disputed the mainline antiwar groups' indictment of American fighting men in Vietnam, they also disagreed with their condemnation of the chaplains. The difference of opinion stemmed largely from contrasting views regarding the proper role of the chaplain. Unlike the mainline groups, evangelicals did not expect their chaplains to exercise a "prophetic responsibility"; indeed, had their chaplains questioned the war, they would have been in conflict with the denominations they represented. Moreover, evangelicals believed—as their chaplains did—that pastoral care was the most important service to be performed in Vietnam, and they valued the commitment and courage the chaplains demonstrated in carrying it out. Evangelicals also praised the evangelizing zeal their chaplains exhibited in Vietnam. One of the satisfactions they derived from the Vietnam War was the discovery, as *United Evangelical Action* put it in a review of Chaplain James Hutchens' account of his tour of duty, that "a chaplain in the Armed Forces has the freedom to propagate the Gospel of Jesus Christ without compromise to the officers and men around him, and he is expected to do just that." Thus the majority of evangelicals agreed with Bob Pierce, president of World Vision, in extolling "the dedicated men of the U.S. chaplaincy" as ministers wearing "the uniform of their country, serving Him while they serve the cause of freedom."[10]

Evangelicals heaped similar praise on the veterans and POWs returning home to the United States. During Billy Graham's 1969 Southern California Crusade in Anaheim Stadium, a marine lieutenant named Clebe McClary, who had lost an arm and an eye in Vietnam, received a standing ovation from the crowd of fifty-four thousand. To Jerry Falwell and other evangelicals McClary was "a living testimony"

9. "Chapel Attendance Among Troops in Viet Nam," *UEA*, March, 1966, p. 27; Stephen F. Olford, "A Communist War," *Moody Monthly*, February, 1969, pp. 20, 22; Smith, "Vietnam Salute," 8, 9, 12. On high rates of chapel attendance in Vietnam, see also Rutledge, "Chaplaincy a Welcomed Ministry," A5; Dehoney, *Disciples in Uniform*, 61.

10. Paul N. Moyer, "Is the Chaplaincy a Quasi-Religious Business?" *CT*, December 17, 1965, p. 6; "Beyond Combat," *UEA*, Summer, 1969, p. 34; Bob Pierce, "Unheadlined Victories in Viet Nam," *Moody Monthly*, September, 1966, p. 59.

to Christian faith and "old fashioned patriotism." "He wore his uniform proudly and defended Americanism," Falwell declared. "Clebe is a hero—I like to call him a champion for Christ." In 1973, when the American POWs were released, evangelicals embraced them, too, as "disciples in uniform" who during their ordeal had proved the sustaining power of prayer and faith in God. Evangelical magazines printed numerous stories depicting them witnessing for Christ in North Vietnamese prison compounds with names like "the Zoo" and "the Hanoi Hilton." The dominant theme was that despite torture, isolation, and deprivation, the POWs held worship services, taught other men to pray, and circulated Scripture passages scribbled on toilet paper or transmitted through the "tapping code system" linking prison cells. The POWs offered further evidence to readers saturated with news of the "other war," that in Vietnam "God was there," "Christ was real."[11]

Perhaps because of their high regard for the American forces, evangelicals also disagreed with the mainline antiwar groups' condemnation of the conduct of the war. The words the two sides used indicate the gulf separating them. Mainline critics were "horrified" by civilian casualties caused by bombing, napalm, and search-and-destroy operations. They used phrases such as "moral horror" and "moral scandal" to describe the way Americans were waging war in Vietnam and frequently referred to the maiming and killing of civilians as "atrocities," "carnage," and "slaughter." An editorial jointly written by the editors of *Christianity and Crisis, Christian Century, Commonweal,* and the *National Catholic Reporter* employed an especially striking metaphor to convey the enormity of the violence in Vietnam: "In Southeast Asia," they declared, "American military might is repeating the crucifixion of Christ."[12]

11. Russell Chandler, "Anaheim Crusade: At Home with the Angels," *CT,* October 24, 1969, p. 40; Jerry Falwell, "Introduction" to Clebe McClary, *Living Proof* (Atlanta, 1978), 9. For more on McClary see "Church of God Layman Honored for Bravery in Viet Nam War," *UEA,* November, 1965, p. 26; Clebe McClary, "All It Takes," in *Great Reading from Decision,* ed. Sherwood E. Wirt and Mavis R. Sanders (Minneapolis, 1970), 233–36. On the POWs see, for example, Samuel Allen Mattix, "The Blue Flower," *Decision,* August, 1973, pp. 3, 13; Samuel A. Mattix, "The Blue Flower," *Decision,* September, 1973, p. 7; Berge Hoogasian, "Trial by Fire," *UEA,* Summer, 1973, pp. 12–16; Norman A. McDaniel, "With Christ in Hanoi," *Decision,* July, 1973, pp. 9, 14; Russell T. Hitt, "The POW Story: Seven Years of Prison and Prayer," *Eternity,* June, 1973, pp. 12–16, 48, 50.

12. Waldo Beach, "Advent Amid the Slaughter of the Innocents," *Christianity and Crisis,* December 22, 1969, p. 322; John C. Bennett, "Face-Saving Inhumanity," *Chris-*

Except for their dissenting brethren, evangelicals seem to have been much less obsessed with the violence of the war. They did not register the disbelief, revulsion, and anguish characteristic of mainline critics. And they used less emotionally charged language in discussing the conduct of the war. For example, in January, 1967, when *Christianity Today* published an editorial supporting intensified bombing of North Vietnam, it referred to any "civilian damage" resulting from the bombing as "regrettable." Moreover, editor Carl Henry went on to declare that such damage was "not to be compared with the deliberate and continuing Communist destruction of civilian life and property in South Viet Nam." Billy Graham appealed to a similar notion of moral equivalency in an article published in the *New York Times*. "I have never heard of a war where innocent people were not killed," he stated. "Tens of thousands of innocent people were killed at Hiroshima and Nagasaki." Then, focusing on Vietnam, he cited the "horrible stories" he had heard from missionaries and Vietnamese people "about sadistic murders by the Vietcong of innocent villagers" and the American soldiers he had talked with who would "never walk again, who were suffering from boobytrap or grenade wounds, planted or thrown by women and children working for the Vietcong."[13]

Such statements exposed Graham and other evangelicals to accusations of indifference to civilian casualties, even callousness. Perhaps they sought, consciously or unconsciously, to shift some of the blame for the violence away from American fighting men they honored as Christians and patriots. Perhaps they sought to rationalize the violence of a war they supported. Whatever the personal imperative, their statements reflect two of evangelicals' strongly held beliefs. One was the belief in inherent depravity. Evangelicals believed the violence of war, like all the other evils afflicting human society, grew out of human sinfulness. And as Garry Wills has observed, "Sin rather confirms than challenges a faith that proclaims human corruption." So the revelations of war crimes like

---

tianity and Crisis, January 24, 1972, p. 302; Peter L. Berger, "A Conservative Reflection About Vietnam," *Christianity and Crisis,* March 6, 1967, p. 34; "Carnage and the Incarnation," *Christian Century,* LXXXVI (December 24, 1969), 1633; "A Call to Penitence and Action," *Christianity and Crisis,* April 19, 1971, p. 66.

13. "Viet Nam: A Moral Dilemma," *CT,* January 20, 1967, p. 27; Billy Graham, "Billy Graham: On Calley," *NYT,* April 9, 1971, p. 31. See also Herendeen, "Graham Preaches Peace in Viet Nam," 36.

that at My Lai did not disabuse evangelicals of their favorable view of the military and American servicemen. To be sure, upon hearing of the My Lai massacre, stunned evangelicals found it hard to accept that American soldiers, "blue-eyed, hometown boys serving their country in the best tradition of soldiering and sacrifice," had committed such a "horrible deed." But their faith told them that the "lesson" of My Lai was the age-old doctrine of sin. According to *United Evangelical Action* and *Christianity Today*, the massacre presented "a monstrous demonstration of that irrational depravity which lurks in the heart of every man." And as both magazines noted, "Bible-believing Christians" knew that "evil was not confined to the 'commies' or the 'fascists.' It lurks in the heart of every human being." *Christianity Today* pressed an additional lesson on its readers, reminding them that "sin . . . can be forgiven and subdued only through the person of Jesus Christ."[14]

The belief in premillennialism, in the imminent Second Coming of Christ, which would bring the end of the world and the beginning of a new age of peace and joy, also conditioned evangelicals' reaction to the violence of the Vietnam War. According to this way of thinking, wars and violence would not cease until the Second Coming. That was why Billy Graham and other evangelicals maintained that "we will always have wars on the earth until the coming again of the Prince of Peace."[15]

Evangelicals' belief in human depravity and premillennialism helps explain what William Martin has called their "undiscriminating sense of sin" and their seeming indifference to the violence of Vietnam.[16] From the perspective of those two beliefs, one sin is as bad as another because all sins are manifestations of human depravity. Moreover, humans are incapable of overcoming sin; they can only lament its occurrence, try to alleviate the suffering it causes, and hope and pray for the Second Coming of Christ, which will put an end to both sin and the suffering it causes. If the belief in human depravity suggested the inevitability of violence and war, premillennialism suggested that humans

14. Marshall Frady, *Billy Graham: A Parable of American Righteousness* (Boston, 1979), 428; William Martin, *A Prophet with Honor* (New York, 1991), 388; Richard V. Pierard, "Billy Graham and Vietnam: From Cold Warrior to Peacemaker," *Christian Scholar's Review*, X (1980), 48; Garry Wills, *Under God: Religion and American Politics* (New York, 1990), 29; "The Lesson of Pinkville," *CT*, December 19, 1969, p. 23; "Little Lessons from My Lai," *UEA*, Spring, 1970, p. 6.
15. Billy Graham, "A Clarification," *CT*, January 19, 1973, p. 36.
16. Martin, *Prophet*, 361, and see also 388.

could do little to prevent them, that only the apocalyptic intervention of Christ would suffice.

The Vietnam War proved to be a watershed event in the history of evangelicals in the United States. It not only split the evangelical community but tested many of the long-standing convictions of mainstream evangelicals. They experienced more confusion and doubt over Vietnam than has generally been recognized, but throughout the war they remained as anticommunist, pro-American, and pro-military as when the war began. Also important, evangelicals' support for the war policies of the Johnson and Nixon administrations strengthened their influence in the federal government. Perhaps even more significant in the long run, their participation in the debate over the war provided them an entrée into national politics. And finally, the Vietnam War facilitated a dramatic change in evangelicals' image and status within the military. Formerly regarded with skepticism, if not suspicion, evangelicals gained respect and influence within the armed forces as a result of the support they demonstrated for military service, the war, and the men who fought it.

12

The Spiritual Offensive
in the Early 1970s

The 1972 Sylvanus Thayer Award provides a perfect symbol of the affinity that existed between American evangelicals and the United States military by the early 1970s. Named in honor of an esteemed early-nineteenth-century superintendent of the U.S. Military Academy, the award was given annually by the West Point Association of Graduates "to a citizen of the United States whose record of service to his country, accomplishments in the national interest, and manner of achievement, exemplify outstanding devotion to the principles expressed in the motto of West Point—'Duty, Honor, Country.'" In 1972, a selection committee headed by retired general Harold K. Johnson chose Billy Graham to receive the award. At a ceremony on May 4, attended by the Corps of Cadets and a large gathering of Military Academy alumni and guests, Graham accepted the award, along with a citation praising him as an "educator, author, and evangelist" whose life and work "has reflected to a wide segment of mankind those values inherent in Duty, Honor, Country." Significantly, the citation portrayed Graham as a bulwark of "traditional values" during a decade when many Americans seemed to have abandoned them.[1]

If the Thayer Award expressed, at least symbolically, the appreciation the United States military felt toward Graham and other evangelicals for the support they had shown during the turbulent 1960s and early 1970s, his acceptance speech paid tribute to the values evangelicals shared with the military. "The very survival of the American democratic

1. Willis D. Crittenberger, President, Association of Graduates, to "Dear West Pointer," January 4, 1957, in USMA Archives, United States Military Academy, West Point, New York; "1972 Sylvanus Thayer Award," *Assembly*, XXXI (Spring, 1972), 2.

way of life is at stake," Graham warned. "Demonstrations, pickets, marches, protests and bombings" all threatened to undermine the "delicate balance between freedom and order" on which American society was based. "Whether we like to admit it or not, there is an increasing moral darkness in our nation and a gathering political storm that threatens our very survival," he observed. Graham declared that he looked not to "the dropouts and the copouts" to save the country but to "the men and women who believe in duty, honor, and country—and have a strong faith in God." The cadets and their guests attending the ceremony gave a standing ovation to his assertion: "I believe it is of paramount importance that the moral and spiritual values that Sylvanus Thayer held be rekindled and revived, and that once again they become the beacon lights to guide our nation through this perilous period." Then, employing a metaphor General Johnson must have appreciated, Graham ended his speech with an exhortation: "So let's not spend our time cursing the darkness. Let's light a candle! Let's light a candle that will banish moral and spiritual blight. Let's light a candle that will guide men into tomorrow. Let's light a candle that will roll back fascism and social injustice. Let's light a candle to warn our enemies that we will die so that our children and grandchildren can have the freedom that we've had. Let's light a candle that by God's grace will never be put out."[2]

As their sometimes adversarial relationship with the military gave way to a more friendly, mutually supportive one in the late 1960s and early 1970s, evangelicals discovered increased opportunity to continue their spiritual offensive among the armed forces. By the early 1970s, prayer groups, Bible studies, and religiously oriented breakfasts and luncheons had become routine at the Pentagon. Some of the events were sponsored by International Christian Leadership, others by a group called the Christian Men of the Pentagon. An informal outreach group, Teams of Two, had been evangelizing Pentagon staffers for some time. Brigadier General Clay T. Buckingham, vice-president of the Officers' Christian Fellowship, coordinated a twice-monthly breakfast combining prayer and Bible study for high-ranking Defense Department officers. In 1972 the presidential prayer breakfast was transmitted via television to coordinate with a similar Pentagon affair attended by several hundred persons. A "bookrack evangelism program" started the same year by Kyle David, a retired army colonel, aided the dissemination of Christian lit-

2. "Dr. Graham Receives Thayer Award," *Assembly,* XXXI (Spring, 1972), 4–5.

erature in the Pentagon. *United Evangelical Action* quoted George Jett, a lawyer who serviced the "Life-Line" bookracks, as saying that more than two thousand books had been sold and attendance at the monthly luncheon for Christian Men of the Pentagon had increased fourfold since the racks had been set up a few months earlier.[3]

By 1974, the level of evangelical activity at the Pentagon had increased to the point that it attracted the attention of the national media. Writing in the *New York Times*, Edward Fiske estimated that there were "at least a dozen groups" meeting for breakfast, luncheon, or before work in the Meditation Room. One of the prayer groups brought together a dozen admirals and generals who assembled every other Tuesday at 6:30 A.M. in the secretary of the army's private dining room for coffee, doughnuts, and ninety minutes of Bible study. In 1976, William Willoughby published a lengthy article in *United Evangelical Action* in which he reported that "at least twenty prayer breakfast groups and small luncheon devotional or special spiritual interest groups are meeting weekly at the Pentagon." Some featured Bible study; others offered training in Christian growth and witnessing.[4]

The increasing number of high-ranking officers, both active-duty and retired, who assumed leadership positions in various parachurch groups involved with the armed forces also testifies to the growing approbation evangelical religion enjoyed among upper-echelon military men. In 1953, when William K. Harrison joined the Officers' Christian Union, he was the only active-duty member holding flag rank. In 1972,

3. Edward E. Plowman, "Bibles in the Barracks: God and the Military," *CT*, March 31, 1972, p. 32; "Bookrack Evangelism Making Hit at Pentagon," *UEA*, Winter, 1972, pp. 33–34. The Bookrack Evangelism Program was an outreach of the Mennonite Board of Missions, which began in 1962 in Iowa City, Iowa, and by 1971 had marketed over two hundred thousand paperbacks through some six hundred racks set up in airports, stores, hospitals, churches, and schools. See Bruce Shelley, "Evangelism Is in the Air," *UEA*, Summer, 1972, p. 11.

4. Edward B. Fiske, "Washington's Men of Influence Join in Prayer Groups," *NYT*, January 30, 1974, p. 37; William F. Willoughby, "Peace and Life in Washington: Training Laypeople for Biblical Counseling," *UEA*, Summer, 1976, p. 20. See also James C. Hefley and Edward E. Plowman, *Washington: Christians in the Corridors of Power* (Wheaton, Ill., 1975), 72–73. The Meditation Room had been dedicated in 1971 by Secretary of Defense Melvin Laird as a quiet place for meditation and prayer. At the time he instituted it, Laird explained that the room was "an affirmation that, though we cling to the principle that church and state should be separate, we do not propose to separate man from God" ("Newsbriefs," *UEA*, Spring, 1971, p. 38).

when he gave up the presidency, the organization's council included three other officers with stars on their shoulders: Rear Admiral Robert L. Baughan, Jr., USN, who became the next president; Vice-Admiral Malcolm C. Cagle, USN; and Brigadier General Clay T. Buckingham, USA. Also serving on the council were a colonel and six lieutenant colonels. A retired air force colonel, John M. Fain, headed the Campus Crusade Military Ministry. The Full Gospel Business Men's Fellowship attracted an increasing number of military officers in the late 1960s and early 1970s, some of whom served as chapter presidents. In 1970 FGBMFI published the testimonies of a group of high-ranking officers in a book entitled *Voices of the Military: Testimonies of United States Military Personnel.*[5]

John Broger, the co-founder of the Far East Broadcasting Company and longtime director of the Office of Information and Education for the armed forces, continued to promote evangelical religion within and outside the military. He initiated the practice of broadcasting White House religious services as well as the major prayer breakfast functions to armed forces installations throughout the world. In the early 1970s, to encourage more Bible reading by servicemen, he recorded well-known personalities reading the Bible for a program called "Look Who's Reading the Bible," which was aired over armed forces radio. Broger justified such activity on the grounds that armed services personnel needed more than military training. "These people serve at possible risk of life," he explained. "They need a spiritual foundation." He saw no violation of separation of church and state as a result of a government agency's helping to build that spiritual foundation. "If you separate every single spiritual quality and standard of morality from government, you have chaos," he observed. By the same token, he rejected the compartmentalist view that would separate his own religious faith from his occupation. "I serve the Lord full-time and our armed forces as well," he insisted. In his view, the Scriptures taught that either one committed all of one's life to God, serving Him full-time, or one was "really not committed to Him at all."[6]

5. Robert W. Spoede, *More Than Conquerors: A History of the Officers' Christian Fellowship of the U.S.A., 1943–1983* (Englewood, Colo., 1993), 101; "Officers' Christian Fellowship," *Command*, Fall, 1972, p. 30; Campus Crusade for Christ, *Here's Life World: Taking the Message to the Military (ca.* 1988); advertisements, *Voice*, April, 1970, p. 25, May, 1970, p. 30, June, 1970, p. 29, July–August, 1970, p. 25.

6. Plowman, "Bibles in the Barracks," 32; Hefley and Plowman, *Washington*, 156–57.

In the mid-1970s Broger helped set up a biblical counseling program in the Washington, D.C., area. It grew out of a pilot project he initiated in June, 1974, that used one-minute radio announcements to invite military men and women with problems to call a hot-line number for referral to lay counselors and Bible study groups. Then, using techniques developed by Jay Adams of Westminster Seminary (author of a book entitled *Competent to Counsel*), Broger and two army lieutenant colonels began training counselors at Barcroft Bible Church in Arlington, Virginia. Additional training programs opened at other sites, including the Pentagon, and the radio announcements began targeting civilian as well as military personnel. Broger used his evangelical connections to bring in other Christian leaders and gain support for his program from the National Association of Evangelicals, the Evangelical Committee of Metropolitan Washington, and the National Religious Broadcasters.[7]

Heightened evangelical activity at the Pentagon seems to have produced a ripple effect that spread to other military installations. Writing in *Christianity Today*, in March, 1972, Edward E. Plowman cited a number of commanders who were promoting evangelical religion in one way or another. The base commander at Fort Bliss sponsored an "Evangelism Module" with two chaplains; he also hosted a prayer breakfast and Bible study for his command officers twice a month. At Fort Monroe, Virginia, the commanding general of the Continental Army Command (CONARC), Ralph E. Haines, hosted a weekly 6:15 A.M. prayer breakfast for his staff and "openly encourages prayer and Bible-study groups in all the sixty-six army posts under his command." Plowman also noted that several command officers at Fort Bragg, North Carolina, had received Christ and were involved in Bible study groups. During the 1970s, some base commanders arranged for individual evangelists such as Billy Graham and Nicky Cruz to present the Gospel to officers and enlisted men. Jack Sparks of Christian World Liberation Front visited Fort Sill, Oklahoma, and "deeply moved a contingent of officers."[8] Even more influential were two Vietnam veterans, Heath Bottomly and

---

7. Broger's program was based on a two-day seminar Adams conducted for chaplains at Fort Belvoir. The two lieutenant colonels were Bob Schneider and Carl Smith, both from the U.S. Army (Willoughby, "Peace and Life in Washington," 19–21, 28, 34).

8. Plowman, "Bibles in the Barracks," 32–33. On the Christian World Liberation Front see Richard Quebedeaux, *The Young Evangelicals: Revolution in Orthodoxy* (New York, 1974), 94–97.

Clebe McClary, who made numerous appearances before large military audiences in the United States and abroad.

Colonel Bottomly had served as commander of the 355th Tactical Fighter Wing at Takhli Air Base, Thailand. He had been discipled by the Campus Crusade Military Ministry after Vietnam and upon retirement became a Campus Crusade "associate" doing fund-raising work for the group. By 1975, according to press releases, fifteen thousand persons had heard his message. He had spoken at numerous air force bases, at chapels in Europe, even at the Pentagon. A 16mm color film dramatizing his conversion had been shown at military prayer breakfasts and in base chapel programs, and the U.S. Air Force Chaplain Resource Board put it at the top of its fiscal year 1976 purchase list. In his autobiography, published in 1975, Bottomly said "important government people" had encouraged his evangelizing, "for many of our military and civilian leaders appreciate that Christians in key positions at all levels provide the greatest force alive today for halting the moral crumbling, the permissive decay that is destroying our country." Two of those persons were high-ranking officers in the air force: Lieutenant General Ernest Hardin, Jr., whom Bottomly thanked in the acknowledgments for "encourag[ing] my Christian growth and ministry," and General George S. Brown, chairman of the Joint Chiefs of Staff in 1975, who wrote in the foreword to Bottomly's book: "His new career as a full time soldier of God can be of great service in helping to turn our country around morally—to turn America back from a course of permissiveness and moral decay to a pursuit of excellence, a pursuit of high standards of integrity and purpose."[9]

Clebe McClary, the badly wounded marine lieutenant whose testimony had electrified Billy Graham's 1969 Southern California Crusade, visited several military bases in September, 1974, while participating in an evangelistic campaign in Korea. At one of the bases, a two-star general introduced him and the other members of his team and then turned over the program to them. McClary gave his testimony, and another member of his team preached to the fifteen hundred men attending the

9. John E. Groh, *Air Force Chaplains, 1971–1980* (Washington, D.C., 1986), 186, 192, 357, 529; Marianne Lester, "The Conversion of Colonel Bottomly," *Times Magazine: Supplement to Army Times/Navy Times/Air Force Times*, August 13, 1975, pp. 7–8, 10, 12, 14, 15; Colonel Heath Bottomly, *Prodigal Father: A Fighter Pilot Finds Peace in the Wake of His Destruction* (Glendale, Calif., 1975), 134.

service. McClary claimed that "about three hundred soldiers ran forward to make public decisions for Christ at the invitation." Three years later the army chief of chaplains invited him to visit U.S. Army bases in Germany. He related his Vietnam and conversion experiences a total of sixty-two times during the two-week visit. "God touched the lives of many with whom we shared," he wrote.[10]

During the late 1960s and early 1970s, evangelical religion flourished at the academies. In 1968, Clay Thomas, an Annapolis midshipman, reported that a revival was under way and attributed it to an OCF ministry led by Naval Academy graduate Jim Wilson. "We have 36 companies divided into 6 battalions with Bible study groups in every company," Thomas wrote. Some twenty to twenty-five "prayer partnerships" had been set up among the midshipmen. The revival had even spread to the football team, which included several "really born again Christians." Interest in evangelical religion at Annapolis continued into the early 1970s. Edward Plowman reported on a football coach who conducted Bible study for the team and noted that there had been numerous postgame evangelistic rallies. In addition, several evangelical chaplains had been "quietly leading numbers of men to Christ," and Billy Graham had spoken in chapel to more than three thousand persons. Evangelical Christianity was also thriving at West Point. Gwynn Vaughan, the physical education instructor at the academy, was also a leader in the Christian movement there, and he told Plowman that hundreds of cadets were involved in barracks Bible study groups.[11]

Evangelical religion flourished at the academies in part because of the military leadership's more positive attitude. In sharp contrast to the situation at West Point and Annapolis in the 1950s, by the 1970s administrators generally supported the work of parachurch groups such as the OCF and the Navigators. A more cooperative relationship had also developed between chaplains and parachurch groups at the academies. In addition to these factors, parachurch groups' continued efforts at evangelism helped them expand their membership despite strength reductions in the services following the end of the Vietnam War. In the case of the OCF, such evangelism included outreach to groups hitherto

---

10. Clebe McClary with Diane Barker, *Living Proof: The Exciting Story of Vietnam Hero Lt. Clebe McClary* (Atlanta, 1978), 133, 135, 137.

11. Clay Thomas, "Revival at Annapolis," *Voice*, August, 1968, pp. 12–13; Plowman, "Bibles in the Barracks," 33.

neglected. The new president of the organization in 1972, Rear Admiral
Robert L. Baughan, Jr., began his term by announcing the need for
"special efforts in human relations" on the part of the OCF and in the
services generally to overcome prejudice and discrimination against African Americans and women. Baughan and the OCF's new executive
director, Paul C. Pettijohn, expanded the ministry at the academies, the
prayer partner ministry, and the print ministry, developed an ROTC
ministry, established an outreach to African Americans, women, and
families, and improved and expanded Bible studies.[12]

Although the OCF was active at the Air Force Academy, in the late
1960s and early 1970s the Navigators gradually took the lead. They had
gained a foothold in the mid-1960s when one of the chaplains had asked
an instructor with Navigator discipleship training to recommend an officer to teach a Bible class for cadets. The instructor named another
Navigator-trained officer, Jerry White, who began teaching a weekly
Bible class sponsored by the chaplains. It grew steadily and was still
being taught by Navigators in the mid-1970s. Navigators also cooperated with chaplains at the Citadel in the early 1970s. An article in *Navlog*
published in 1973 reported that about sixty cadets were attending Navigator Bible study groups and quoted the chaplain praising the Navigators for their help with the chapel program and their "dynamic Christian
spirit."[13]

The Command and General Staff College at Fort Leavenworth,
Kansas, became another strategic site for waging the evangelical offensive. The army's most advanced service school provided preparation
considered essential for promotion to key positions in the army, graduating about one thousand officers each year. In the mid-1970s Lieutenant Colonel George B. Kuykendall, Jr., deputy director of graduate
studies, served as the local representative of the OCF. Between 1973
and 1977, he increased the number of Bible study groups among the
students from 12 to 34, involving some 450 students.[14]

Quite apart from the initiatives of parachurch group leaders, base

12. Spoede, *More Than Conquerors*, 74–75, 80–81, 99–100, 102–105, 122–31. See
also Don and Karen Martin, "Celebrating 40 Years of God's Faithfulness," *Command*,
Fall, 1983, p. 10.

13. Bernard Thompson, "From the Air Force Academy to the World . . . a *Unique
Disciplemaking Ministry*," *Navlog*, July, 1977, p. 6; Monte C. Unger, "There Is Something Different About a Citadel Man," *Navigators Log*, January, 1973, pp. 5, 7.

14. Spoede, *More Than Conquerors*, 132.

commanders and chaplains, the Jesus movement of the late 1960s and early 1970s provided the armed forces with a strong infusion of nontraditional spirituality, as young recruits who had been "Jesus People" in civilian society brought their beliefs and practices into the services and spread them among their fellow soldiers. Many chaplains welcomed this upsurge of religious enthusiasm and tailored chapel programs to fit, sponsoring special beach services, coffeehouses, Christian folk or rock music performances, "Jesus celebrations," and the like. Chaplains agreed on the positive influence of the Jesus movement. Writing in *Air Force Times* in 1975, Charles C. Caudill, installation chaplain at Ramstein Air Base, Germany, attributed a revival there to a Lonesome Stone religious rock concert held in April of the previous year. "The Lonesome Stone had a tremendous impact on a lot of people, especially those going in the wrong direction," he declared. Chapel and Sunday school attendance had increased dramatically; various Bible study programs had been inaugurated; seven different choirs, including a "youth folk choir," had been organized; and religious retreats were on the upswing. Chaplain Caudill insisted that the return to religion was not transitory. "We've just begun, I think. The long range effects will be a continuous growth in religious participation. More people will come back."[15]

Nor was the positive effect of the Jesus movement and evangelical religion in general lost on military leaders. By the early 1970s commanders were beginning to look to evangelicalism and the parachurch groups who disseminated it as a remedy for some of the problems that had developed during the Vietnam era such as dissent, drugs, and racial tensions. In 1971 the Army Office of the Chief of Chaplains received a copy of a "Trip Report on the Jesus Revolution" prepared by Major Joseph G. Porter, Jr., on behalf of the Fort Sill (Oklahoma) Leadership Planning Committee. In the report Porter explained that he had been delegated to identify methods used by "responsible, youth-oriented, successful Christian institutions" which might be adapted to the military environment. The purpose was to counter what Porter called the "revolutionary threat" of the radical "new left." He recommended cooperating with the Christian World Liberation Front, Campus Crusade for

15. "Religious Revival Felt at Ramstein," *Air Force Times*, February 26, 1975, p. 32. See also Don Mallicoat, "The Jesus People," *Soldiers*, XXVI (December, 1971), 26, 27; Groh, *Air Force Chaplains*, 529; Richard G. Hutcheson, Jr., *The Churches and the Chaplaincy* (Atlanta, 1975), 92–93.

Christ, Teen Challenge sponsored by the Assemblies of God, and Calvary Chapel Church in Santa Ana, California, and encouraging service personnel to become involved in them and other evangelical groups. He also suggested that the army adapt some of the techniques used by the Christian groups in setting up its own drug rehabilitation programs and halfway and community houses. Reporting on the Porter investigation in *Christianity Today,* Edward Plowman noted that several Jesus movement musical groups and leaders had been invited to perform or hold meetings at Fort Sill, and evangelist Nicky Cruz had been brought to Fort Bragg to preach to two hundred stockade prisoners. Overseas, too, command officers credited coffeehouse ministries with effecting dramatic changes in the behavior patterns of soldiers. Brigadier General Harold Aaron, who had seven coffeehouses under his command in the Frankfurt, West Germany, area, pronounced the coffeehouse ministry "one of the best things to happen in the Army."[16]

Chaplains played a very important role in facilitating the work of parachurch groups within the armed forces, and those from evangelical denominations were especially inclined to welcome the help of such groups and work closely with them. To be sure, remnants of the earlier prejudice against parachurch groups persisted. When Plowman did his survey of evangelical religion in the armed forces in 1972, he cited a Pentagon spokesman who revealed that "some theologically liberal chaplains have apparently felt threatened by the flurry of evangelical activity and have reacted." In a few cases, at Camp Pendleton in California, for example, senior chaplains had banned parachurch groups. Plowman speculated that some chaplains "fear too much evangelistic activity and involvement by outsiders may raise church-state questions, and they don't want to rock the boat."[17]

The general rule, however, was cooperation on the part of parachurch groups as well as chaplains. By 1975, as Richard Hutcheson has pointed out, parachurch groups were generally "not anti-church or anti-chaplain." Indeed, they welcomed "the help and support of a cooperative chaplain" and often became "the backbone of his congregation." Hutcheson used the term *mutual reinforcement* to describe the prevailing

16. Office of Chief of Chaplains, "Historical Review, 1 July 1971 to 30 June 1972" [1972] (Typescript at U.S. Army Center of Military History, Washington, D.C.), 41–42; Plowman, "Bibles in the Barracks," 32, 33.
17. Plowman, "Bibles in the Barracks," 32.

relationship between parachurch groups and chaplains. The supportive policies of the chaplain leadership outweighed any restrictions or prohibitions imposed by individual chaplains. Beginning in the late 1960s, for example, the Army Office of the Chief of Chaplains periodically recommended cooperation with various parachurch groups, including Youth for Christ, Fellowship of Christian Athletes, Campus Crusade, and World Athletes in Action. In 1969, seventeen military chaplains, including the chairman of the Armed Forces Chaplains Board, attended the United States Congress on Evangelism held in Minneapolis. The chief of naval chaplains, Rear Admiral James W. Kelly, offered the convening prayer on opening night of the congress and also led a workshop, "Ministry to Men in Uniform." In 1971, when Armed Forces Radio began broadcasting the National Prayer Breakfast overseas, the Armed Forces Chaplains Board encouraged parallel local activities at all military installations, and the army chief of chaplains urged all army chaplains "to wholeheartedly support" the program. (A survey conducted that year showed that 545 breakfasts were held throughout the army worldwide, attended by 44,699 participants.)[18]

A good illustration of the mutually reinforcing relationship between chaplains and parachurch groups in the early 1970s was Explo '72, a six-day evangelistic training program held in Dallas, Texas, in June, 1972, sponsored by Campus Crusade for Christ. In addition to high school and college students, pastors, youth workers, and athletes, Campus Crusade targeted the military. One of its slogans was "5,000 Military for the Master." As plans got under way, the Army Office of the Chief of Chaplains anticipated sending a number of chaplains, along with some

18. Hutcheson, *Churches and the Chaplaincy*, 94; Department of the Army, Office of Chief of Chaplains, Monthly Newsletter (Typed photocopy, file 701-01 Chaplain's Administrative Files [68], Record Group 247, Acc. No. 71-A-3095, Washington National Records Center, Suitland, Md.), 3, 5; Office of the Chief of Chaplains, "Historical Review, 1 July 1964 to 30 June 1965" [1965] (Typescript at Washington National Records Center, Suitland, Md.), 196; Office of Chief of Chaplains, "Historical Review, 1 July 1971 to 30 June 1972," 33; Office of the Chief of Chaplains, "Annual Report of Major Activities: Historical Review, 1 July 1974–30 June 1975" [1975] (Typescript at U.S. Army Center of Military History), 38; Irene Murray, "Much Is Given—Much Is Required," *Chaplain*, XXVII (January–February, 1970), 3–15; Office of the Chief of Chaplains, "Historical Review, 1 July 1970–30 June 1971" [1971] (Typescript at U.S. Army Center of Military History), 64–65. On the National Prayer Breakfast in the air force see Martin H. Scharlemann, *Air Force Chaplains, 1961–1970* (N.p., n.d.), 194; Groh, *Air Force Chaplains*, 431–35.

fifteen hundred to two thousand soldiers from Fort Hood and probably other delegations from various installations in the Southwest. Major Joseph Porter, in his "Trip Report on the Jesus Revolution," recommended offering military personnel the opportunity to attend. When the event finally took place, about eighty thousand persons attended. Although the number of armed forces personnel who participated probably did not reach five thousand, the military presence was sizable, and it included several high-ranking leaders.[19]

Explo '72 offered specially formatted evangelism training seminars to military participants and included displays from the chaplaincies among the exhibits of some four hundred Christian organizations. Martin Van Elderen attended one of the military seminars, which numbered some three hundred persons, many of them bused in from Fort Hood. Major General Gerhard Hyatt, chief of army chaplains, gave the welcoming address. Colonel John M. Fain, director of Campus Crusade's Military Ministry, also spoke, warning that the Great Commission "will never be fulfilled unless more emphasis is given to the evangelizing of our military family." Van Elderen noted that besides Campus Crusade, other groups used Explo '72 as an occasion for touting their military ministries. As an example, he described Paul Pettijohn of the OCF quoting a navy pilot who had told him, "It's some thrill to be chasin' MIGs over North Vietnam, but it's a greater thrill to share Jesus Christ with someone."[20]

Fighting an unpopular war in Southeast Asia, the military welcomed an opportunity to bask in the piety and patriotism that suffused Explo '72. For just as the military's participation in Explo '72 conferred approbation on Campus Crusade and evangelical religion, so did Campus Crusade's inclusion of the military signal support for the armed forces.

19. "'Explo '72,'" *Military Chaplain*, XLV (March–April, 1972), 5; Office of Chief of Chaplains, "Historical Review, 1 July 1971 to 30 June 1972," 47, 41–42; Richard Quebedeaux, *I Found It! The Story of Bill Bright and Campus Crusade* (San Francisco, 1979), 23; Bill Bright, *Come Help Change the World* (San Bernardino, Calif., 1979), 135. The *Military Chaplain*, in "'Explo '72,'" 5, noted that half a decade of cooperation between chaplains and Campus Crusade prepared the way for military participation in Explo '72: "Over a period of many years, scores of military chaplains have maintained a close liaison with Campus Crusade for Christ International. Not only have they found it to be a source of personal inspiration and refreshment, but of definite assistance to their own religious programs on bases, posts, and shipboard ministries."
20. Martin Van Elderen, "Explo '72 and Campus Crusade," *Reformed Journal*, July–August, 1972, pp. 16–17. See also "'Explo '72,'" 5.

Indeed, Campus Crusade went out of its way to show appreciation for the military in a special Flag Day celebration staged in the Cotton Bowl on June 14. Participants included high-ranking officers and at least two of the three chiefs of chaplains, along with astronaut James Irwin and families of prisoners of war and men missing in action. The ceremony consisted of a color guard representing each branch of the armed forces, a song and music session, and a salute and pledge of allegiance to the flag. Rear Admiral Francis L. Garrett, chief of navy chaplains, gave the opening prayer, which he prefaced with testimony about asking Christ to come into his life and receiving the "gift of the Holy Spirit." General Ralph E. Haines, commander of the U.S. Continental Army Command, evoked cheers from the delegates when he declared, "I have dedicated my life to Christ."[21]

Although Billy Graham, the honorary chairman of Explo '72, maintained that it was "a *religious* gathering and not a political forum," the convention displayed a definite pro-Vietnam stance. One observer reported that a "spokesman" from South Vietnam, who received a standing ovation when he was introduced by Graham, delivered a speech portraying the conflict in Southeast Asia as "a holy war against the Viet Cong." Antiwar evangelicals among the official delegates to the convention from groups such as the People's Christian Coalition and the Mennonites were harassed when they tried to disseminate antiwar views or literature on conscientious objection. At the Flag Day ceremony, antiwar protesters met with an angry "*sshhhh*" from the audience and were admonished by several Dallas police officers.[22]

Another event, Key 73, also illustrates the military's endorsement of evangelical religion. The brainchild of *Christianity Today*, Carl F. H. Henry, and Billy Graham, it was a year-long, interdenominational evangelistic campaign conducted throughout the United States and Canada in accord with the official theme, "Calling Our Continent to Christ." The NAE urged member denominations and organizations "to harness their resources and to develop their own programs of evangelism, cooperatively where possible, so that every person in North America will hear the Gospel by 1973." Ultimately, 140 denominations participated

21. *Dallas Morning News*, June 15, 1972, p. 18A; Richard Pierard, "The Golden Image of Nebuchadnezzar," *Reformed Journal*, December, 1972, p. 9.

22. "Explo Was a Political Happening," *Inside*, July, 1972, p. 3; Van Elderen, "Explo '72 and Campus Crusade," 16, 18.

in Key 73. It was touted as the largest ecumenical campaign in the history of the Christian church, embracing not only fundamentalists, evangelicals, and pentecostals but also the more liberal mainline Protestant churches as well as some 160 Roman Catholic dioceses.[23]

In line with its policy of supporting parachurch groups and evangelical religion, the military leadership quickly endorsed Key 73 and encouraged the involvement of the armed forces. The navy chief of chaplains urged chaplains to play a "strong role" in the campaign. So did the army chief of chaplains. In a December, 1972, newsletter, he described Key 73 as "a highly visible and focused program for Christ and evangelism, renewal, and outreach" and speculated that the "spiritual concern" and "application of religious values" it was likely to engender would "help heal the wounds of society." Although he did not direct chaplains to participate, he did suggest some ways they might relate Key 73 to the military parish. The army chief also invited T. A. Raedeke, executive director of the program, to make a presentation, "Incorporating the KEY 73 Concept into the Post Religious Program," at a Chief of Chaplains Pastors' Conference held in March, 1973. The Air Force Chaplain Board supported Key 73 by sending chaplains resource guides, interpretation kits, and information packets. Air force bases around the country sponsored various Key 73 programs: evangelism training at Craig Air Force Base, prayer vigils at Whiteman Air Force Base, home visitation and distribution of *Good News for Modern Man* at Andrews Air Force Base, and a cooperative program with a local church at Williams Air Force Base.[24]

Key 73 was ecumenical—but only up to a point. Though it included mainline Protestants and Catholics, its sectarian orientation ("Calling Our Continent to Christ") and evangelistic thrust clearly typed it as an evangelical enterprise. Not surprisingly, Jewish leaders in the civilian sector expressed fears that Key 73 would be used as a vehicle for proselytizing their people and might even foster anti-Semitism. Even if the campaign were "not anti-Semitic in intent or purpose," Rabbi Maurice N. Eisendrath, president of the Union of American Hebrew Congre-

23. "Theme Chosen for Key 73 Evangelism," *UEA*, Spring, 1972, p. 42; *NYT*, April 12, 1972, p. 15, December 3, 1972, p. 56, January 7, 1973, p. 54.

24. *NYT*, January 18, 1973, p. 32; Office of Chief of Chaplains, "Annual Report of Major Activities: Historical Review of the Office of Chief of Chaplains, 1 July 1972 to 30 June 1973" [1973] (Typescript at U.S. Army Center of Military History), 46–47; Groh, *Air Force Chaplains*, 433, 534–35.

gations, observed, it did "seem to posit the superiority of Christianity and the centrality of Jesus." Rabbi Marc H. Tanenbaum of the American Jewish Committee contended that Key 73 was based on the conception dominant in the nineteenth and early twentieth centuries of the United States as "an evangelical empire" or "a Christian nation" and Jews and other non-Christians "as less than full partners in the democratic enterprise." He dismissed such a view as "a regression from the liberal democratic view which is grounded on the pluralistic idea that Jews, Catholics, and others are full partners in American society." The director of Key 73, T. A. Raedeke, denied that the campaign had any anti-Semitic overtones and disclaimed any intention "to persecute, pressure or force Jews to believe or do anything against their will." Nevertheless, Jewish apprehension persisted to the point that it provoked national Jewish organizations to question the military's endorsement. An official of the American Jewish Committee wrote to Secretary of the Navy John H. Chafee demanding that he repudiate the navy chief of chaplains' memorandum urging chaplains to participate. In the letter, Rabbi Yaakov Rosenberg contended that the memo encouraged navy chaplains "in effect to engage in religious proselytization." Under the U.S. constitutional system, he observed, such activity did not constitute "a proper role for government." Similarly, Rabbi Aryeh Lev, director of the Chaplaincy Commission of the National Jewish Welfare Board, expressed concern in letters to the army and air force chiefs of chaplains that military involvement in Key 73 might result in Jews in the armed forces being "subjected to intolerable pressures not only in barrack discussion, but also in official or semi-official chaplaincy programs that imply the need to convert Jews, or seem to down-grade Judaism." Like Rabbi Tanenbaum, Rabbi Lev appealed to what he termed the chaplaincies' tradition of "pluralism, or acceptance of difference" and their "firm determination to eschew conversionist efforts [directed toward] those who belong to a particular faith." He asked that the chiefs promulgate a statement saying that such proselytizing efforts would not be tolerated.[25]

25. *NYT*, December 3, 1972, p. 56, January 7, 1973, p. 54, January 18, 1973, p. 72; "Key 73 Triggers Controversy," *Eternity*, April, 1973, p. 22; Susan Perlman, "Furor Over Jewish Evangelism," *Eternity*, April, 1973, pp. 20–23, 47; Groh, *Air Force Chaplains*, 534; Office of Chief of Chaplains, "Annual Report of Major Activities, 1 July 1972 to 30 June 1973," 47–48.

Having already committed themselves to a policy of supporting evangelical and parachurch work in the armed forces, the chaplaincies did not disavow Key 73, although they did respond to some of the objections Jewish leaders had raised. In a March, 1973, newsletter, the army chief of chaplains conceded the validity of the concern expressed by the National Jewish Welfare Board and declared, "In the tradition of the Army Chaplaincy we must protect our people from 'sheep stealing.'" Even before the controversy developed, the air force chief of chaplains urged command chaplains to balance Key 73 activities with special programs for the recruitment and training of Jewish lay leaders. Like the army chief of chaplains, he seemed to think that the likelihood of proselytizing was slim, and he apparently agreed with one of his advisers who cautioned against mentioning the possibility on the grounds that it might "sound as if we thought there is or might be a tendency, and reflect adversely on the Air Force." In their view, the ecumenical appeal of Key 73 outweighed its potential problems.[26]

Like the 1972 Thayer Award and Explo '72, Key 73 illustrates the mutually reinforcing relationship that evangelicals and military leaders enjoyed by the early 1970s. This was a quite different relationship—representing a significant departure from the earlier mainline orientation of the military and the chaplaincies—from the one that existed in the 1950s and 1960s. In a few years, as we will see in Chapter 20, the newer relationship would begin to give way to the kind of pluralist orientation invoked by Rabbis Tanenbaum and Lev. But in the early 1970s, evangelicals and the military enjoyed a more harmonious relationship than ever before.

26. Office of Chief of Chaplains, "Annual Report of Major Activities, 1 July 1972 to 30 June 1973," 47–48; Groh, *Air Force Chaplains*, 534.

13

Ralph E. Haines,
"A Private in God's Army"

If William K. Harrison and Harold K. Johnson, each in his own way, extended the boundaries of acceptable public advocacy of evangelical religion, General Ralph E. Haines discovered their limits. Haines became the center of national controversy in the early 1970s after his conversion to pentecostalism turned him into an ardent proselytizer within and outside the military society.

Like Harrison and Johnson, even before his conversion Haines had earned a reputation as a commander who took his responsibilities for the spiritual and moral welfare of his men more seriously than most of his contemporaries. A 1935 graduate of West Point, he had been reared an Episcopalian and confirmed at age sixteen. At the academy he attended chapel regularly (it was compulsory in those days). Later he and his wife, also an Episcopalian, attended church regularly. Following World War II, as a regimental commander he began to work closely with the chaplains assigned to his command and also served occasionally as a lay preacher. During the 1960s, as he himself noted, he "was clearly identified as a strong Christian leader, a man of God." For example, in 1962, while commanding the 1st Armored Division at Fort Hood, Texas, he instituted a program called Duty Day with God, setting aside one full day each month for his men to take part, if they wished, in Catholic, Jewish, or Protestant religious activities. About eight thousand of the fourteen thousand men in the division participated, and Haines credited the program with significantly reducing absences without official leave, larceny, and other criminal or deviant behavior. Duty Day with God ultimately became an army-wide program. In 1965, having been reassigned to Fort Hood to command III Corps, Haines instituted a program called Religious Emphasis Month, in which civilians conducted retreats for Protestants, Catholics, and Jews. He also organized a prayer breakfast program for senior officers, which he continued when he moved to other posts, in the Pentagon working in the Office of the Army Chief of Staff and at Fort Shafter, Hawaii, serving as Pacific commander with responsibility for Vietnam, Korea, Japan, Okinawa, and Thailand.[1]

In 1971, while serving as commanding general at Fort Monroe, headquarters of the U.S. Continental Army Command, Haines was invited to be the principal speaker at a military breakfast sponsored by the Full Gospel Business Men's Fellowship International in Buffalo, New York. He said later that when he accepted the invitation, "I didn't know much about FGBMFI, but figured it was a group of Christian businessmen who were conducting their business in accord with approved Christian ethics." He thought "it would be charitable to visit these fellow members of the maligned military-industrial complex and reinforce our mutual beliefs."[2]

The general and his wife arrived in Buffalo the day before the breakfast and attended an evening meeting of the Buffalo Fellowship of FGBMFI. Various other military leaders attended, as well as Pat Robertson, president of the Christian Broadcasting Network. Early in the meeting Mrs. Haines requested prayer that "God would please baptize my husband." Later the participants joined in several minutes of "prayer and praise." According to the FGBMFI *Voice*, during that time "the General was filled with the Holy Ghost and began to 'speak in tongues' as the others on the rostrum gathered around, much to the joy of the several hundred others present who witnessed the event." In describing his experience the next morning at the military breakfast, Haines said that he had been "deeply moved" by the "outpouring of the Holy Spirit all over me." About a year later, he recounted the event at the FGBMFI world convention in San Francisco: "I experienced a bubbling up and finally an active eruption of the Holy Spirit which had been living within me for many years. On that day the entire room was filled with the Holy

1. Wesley G. Pippert, "The Four-Star General Who Calls Men to the Lord," *Moody Monthly*, November, 1972, pp. 22, 24, 25; Margaret Eastman, "Did the General Love Jesus Unwisely and Too Well?" *Army Times Family*, February 21, 1973, pp. 4, 10; "General Haines Is Honored," *Chaplain*, XXX (Spring, 1973), 73.

2. General Ralph E. Haines, "The Drumbeat of God's Guidance," *Voice*, November, 1972, p. 5.

Spirit and it seemed I was the number one lightning rod! Soon I was praising the Lord with my hands up—something I had never done before. . . . In the midst of it I heard a voice talking in some strange language, and suddenly I realized it was *my* voice! As I praised the Lord my spirit soared upward, and I knew I was on a special wave length with heaven."[3]

Haines declared that the experience made him "a better man, a better officer, a better husband, and a better Christian." He said: "I told the Lord I was ready to do whatever He wanted me to do, and I'm trying to carry out the order of my heavenly Commander-in-Chief. I recognize that I'm only a private in God's army, but I'm buckin' for PFC!" The military terminology caught the attention of the news media and provoked much of the controversy that soon enveloped him. Perhaps Haines used such language because, like Generals Harrison and Johnson, he wanted to emphasize that there was no inconsistency in being both a soldier and a Christian. "In fact," Haines insisted, "service in these two fields is complementary and mutually reinforcing." Throughout history, he observed, God had been the soldier's "refuge" and "strength," and many commanders had been deeply religious persons as well as great military leaders—he cited Joshua, David, Joan of Arc, George Washington, Stonewall Jackson, and, "even though he swore," George S. Patton.[4]

Haines insisted that his pentecostal experience not only opened a new emotional dimension to a man who described himself as "a staid and rather pragmatic Episcopalian," "a spiritual stiffneck"; it also fired him with a compulsion to talk about the Lord and his newfound faith. "I feel impelled to do it," he told an *Army Times Family* reporter. "I've changed from a shy, private worshipper to a bold soldier of the Lord." He indulged his compulsion by embarking on a whirlwind speaking tour in response to dozens of invitations from evangelical groups throughout the United States. In April, 1972, he told an FGBMFI military breakfast group in Washington, D.C.: "I'm witnessing up a storm! The Holy Spirit has given me a burden. Over the past eight months, I've been led

3. "'How Deeply Moved I Was!': Four Star General Receives Holy Spirit Baptism at FGBMFI Retreat," *Voice*, January, 1972, pp. 15, 16; Haines, "Drumbeat," 5. For other descriptions of the experience, see Eastman, "Did the General Love Jesus," 4, 10; Ralph E. Haines, "Spiritual Renewal in the Army," *MCR*, Spring, 1977, pp. 15–16.
4. Haines, "Drumbeat," 5, 6, 3; Eastman, "Did the General Love Jesus," 10.

to give my personal testimony to Jesus Christ at rallies and crusades, on radio and T.V., in pulpits and prayer meetings, before cadets at West Point, and before thousands of officers, non-commissioned officers and men and woman [*sic*] of the United States Army." The civilian groups included Bob Harrington's crusade at the Hampton, Virginia, Coliseum, which attracted some ten thousand persons; the just mentioned April, 1972, gathering of about five thousand businessmen and military; Explo '72, sponsored by Campus Crusade for Christ, which drew an estimated eighty thousand young people from all over the United States; the FGBMFI world convention in San Francisco, in July, 1972, numbering some ten thousand people; and countless colleges, chambers of commerce, and fraternal organizations. As the numbers indicate, the size of the civilian audience Haines reached in these gatherings far exceeded those addressed by General Johnson and General Harrison. Moreover, the Christian Broadcasting Network aired Haines's address in Washington, D.C., to an estimated seven million listeners.[5]

As Haines indicated in his address to the Washington military breakfast group, he also took his message to the military. In November, 1971, not long after his conversion experience, he spoke to the Officers' Christian Union at West Point, exhorting the members to be witnessing Christians. "Beyond anything else, I want to encourage each of you to live your religion," he said. "Make it come alive for yourself and those around you." Haines was able to reach a large military audience by virtue of his position as commanding general of the Continental Army Command, which was the army's largest command, embracing all schools, training centers, and campus ROTC units and including sixty-one installations, six divisions, and two corps. He told the FGBMFI world convention, "Though my headquarters is on the Chesapeake Bay, I spend over sixty percent of my time visiting the sixty-one Active Army posts, the 279 ROTC units, the Army Reserve Forces, and other elements under my command." Invariably, such visits took on a religious orientation. The *Washington Star-News* quoted him as saying that when he arrived at an installation, "I generally call together the commander of the post, chaplains, sergeants major and first sergeants and assemble

5. Haines, "Spiritual Renewal in the Army," 15–16; Eastman, "Did the General Love Jesus," 4; Jerry Oppenheimer, "The General Fights for Jesus," *Washington Star-News*, August 6, 1972, pp. A-4, A-1; *Washington Star-News*, August 10, 11, 1972, pp. 6, 10; Pippert, "Four-Star General," 25, 58; Haines, "Drumbeat," 3, 5–6.

them in the chapel." He added, "This always sort of startles them because they figure we should be meeting in a conference hall." Remembering one such gathering, Haines said: "Before I knew it, I bellowed
out 'Praise the Lord.' Everyone in the room seemed to be thinking, who
is this guy sounding off? I got the old Private Demerit look."[6]

Haines shrugged off such reactions. He knew some in the military
regarded him as a "religious kook" or a "fanatic"; he admitted some
had advised him to "slow down." His answer was, "You ain't seen nothing yet." He believed, as he told the FGBMFI convention in San Francisco, that "the Lord may be using me to help rekindle the spiritual zeal
and moral awareness of our Army." Besides taking his religious message
on inspection tours, Haines emphasized the importance of evangelizing
the senior military leaders concentrated at the Pentagon and in the
Washington, D.C., area. As he explained in an FGBMFI publication,
"These men constitute a most attractive target for our outreach, since
they can be keys to the influence we should like to establish for God in
the heart [sic] and minds of our military men and women." Such men
would also have "immediate value" by virtue of their ability to "bring
into the highest counsels of the military department a Christian viewpoint." The weekly prayer breakfast and Bible study he established for
senior officers at Fort Monroe was part of this effort to evangelize the
military leadership. He and a group of about ten other generals, eight
colonels, and three high-ranking civilians in the Department of the
Army met every Friday at 6 A.M.[7]

In an interview published in *Army Times Family* a few months after
his retirement in 1973, Haines observed that his religious experience of
1971 made him even more concerned than formerly about the commander's responsibility for what he called the "moral mooring" of his
troops. He saw "no inconsistency" between his "deep religious convictions" and his responsibilities as a commander in the United States
Army; indeed, he noted that army regulations specifically charged a

6. Pippert, "Four-Star General," 25; Oppenheimer, "The General Fights for Jesus," A-4; Haines, "Drumbeat," 6.

7. U.S. Army Military History Institute, "Senior Officers Debriefing Program:
Conversations Between General Ralph E. Haines, Jr. and Captain William J. Hudson,"
April 22, 1976, San Antonio (Photocopied typescript in Ralph E. Haines, Jr., Papers,
U.S. Army Military History Institute, Carlisle Barracks, Pa.), 15, 19 (hereafter cited as
Haines Oral History); *Washington Star-News*, August 10, 1972, p. 6; Haines, "Drum-
beat," 6; Oppenheimer, "The General Fights for Jesus," A-4.

commander with responsibility for the moral and religious welfare of his troops. During a U.S. Army Military History Institute interview several years later, he described how he called commanders together to remind them of that responsibility. He would pepper individual commanders with questions: "Well, tell me about your religious program, what are you doing about it? Are you attending church where you expect your men to attend? What are you doing to further the chaplains [*sic*] activities? Are you bringing him into your activities at the company and battalion level? How often do you see the battalion chaplain?" He thought commanders should discharge their responsibility for religion and morality in the same way they discharged any other responsibility: "by personal example and active direction."[8]

As commanding general of CONARC, Haines also emphasized the responsibility of chaplains. In "Four Star Comment" published in the *Military Chaplains' Review*, he wrote, "I expect my chaplains to help me bridge the generation gap and to fully understand the young men and women under my command." He thought chaplains had a duty to evangelize and instruct the troops because many of them knew little of religion and had never been involved with Sunday school or church. Haines said he regarded religion as an end in itself, not simply "a *tool* of command or simply a means of motivating or even consoling the soldier." At the same time, however, he insisted that religion could be useful in promoting morality. This was not a new view; he had touted the moral benefits of religion back in the 1960s when he instituted the Duty Day with God program. As vice-chief of staff under General Harold K. Johnson when the army's Character Guidance program came under attack, Haines favored retaining its religious orientation. In the early 1970s, as commander of CONARC, when he began to tackle problems of drug and alcohol abuse, he decided that it was not enough to treat an addict clinically by placing him in a halfway house or providing psychological counseling. He thought the chaplains should be involved because he believed the addict's basic problem was that he "had no moral base, no spiritual mooring, he needed a faith in God, he needed something bigger than himself that he could rely on, otherwise we had sorted him out and treated all of his symptoms, but we were returning him to his unit or society with the same vacuum in his life that he had before." *Christianity Today* quoted him as saying that the time had come

8. Eastman, "Did the General Love Jesus," 10; Haines Oral History, 15, 29.

to battle the drug problem in the army on "strictly moral grounds. We can detoxify a young man, rap with him, use halfway houses, but he has to substitute something for drugs. . . . The only way in the final analysis we're going to lick it is to try and reach the individual with the Lord." He told the *Army Times Family* reporter the same thing—that religious faith was the answer to the army's problems with alcoholism, dissent, racial tension, and absenteeism.[9]

Haines's concern to promote morality based in religion predated his religious experience. Since the 1950s he had become increasingly concerned about immoral behavior in the armed forces. In his 1976 Military History Institute interview he recalled being perturbed by sexual promiscuity and high venereal disease rates among U.S. forces in Korea and by the "hypocrisy" of the commanding officers or noncommissioned officers who reproved the troops when they themselves "were shacked up with a 'moose' there." In Vietnam, too, sexual immorality, drug and alcohol abuse, and, again, "a very high level of hypocrisy" among noncommissioned officers and officers troubled him. So did "the body count syndrome" and the erosion of professional standards in the army. "I think we, to some degree, left our soul in Vietnam," he said. His religious experience of 1971 convinced him "more than ever" that the army had placed "inadequate emphasis" on morality and its religious grounding. "Integrity must proceed from a basic faith in God or something," not a "man-made rule," he declared.[10]

In Haines's view, the decline of morality in the army reflected a similar decline in American society as a whole. In the 1970s, he told the FGBMFI World Convention, Christians confronted a situation not unlike the one the Ephesians faced in the first century, "a world where sensuality and immorality completely dominated the scene—where the 'big lie' was the mark of sophistication, and greed the keystone of ambition." And, declared Haines, "we need the same strength to face them—the strength that comes from placing our hand in the hand of the Man of Galilee." No secular solution would suffice. "I find no sup-

9. Ralph E. Haines, Jr., "A Four Star Comment," *MCR*, April, 1972, p. iii; U.S. Army Office of the Chief of Chaplains, *Historical Review, 1 January 1967 to 30 June 1968* (1969), 89; U.S. Army Office of the Chief of Chaplains, *Historical Review, 1 July 1968 to 30 June 1969* (1970), 72–73; Haines Oral History, 6–7; Edward E. Plowman, "Bibles in the Barracks: God and the Military," *CT*, March 31, 1972, p. 32; Eastman, "Did the General Love Jesus," 10.
10. Haines Oral History, 16–19, 22.

port in the Scriptures for a new and more permissive moral code," he added. "The so-called *new morality* is the same age-old *immorality* practiced in Ephesus and at Sodom and Gomorrah." After he retired, Haines continued to point to the "moral rot" plaguing the United States and other Western nations. He also became even more convinced that the remedy for it lay in "spiritual renewal," a movement "led and inspired by the Holy Spirit," which he believed was sweeping the world.[11]

Haines's views and activities generated a wide range of responses within the armed forces. No doubt some members of the military approved, even if they did not defend him in public. The author of the *Army Times Family* article described his staff as "unusually loyal to him." Some of his fellow OCF members felt embarrassed by and for him. His effusive spirituality, though understandable in a new convert, struck them as immature and inappropriate in a commander. In other military circles he became known as "the Army's Jesus freak." Some officers at the installations Haines visited resented being subjected to a religious harangue. That he held such meetings in the base chapels, contrary to official policy, also provoked concern.[12] Since the late 1960s the military had become increasingly apprehensive about the possibility of a challenge to the constitutionality of the chaplaincy. Even though Haines was not a chaplain, the unfavorable attention provoked by his highly publicized religious activities on army installations threatened to place the chaplaincy in jeopardy.

Had Haines confined his religious advocacy to the army, he probably would have weathered any criticism it provoked and not been asked to take early retirement. But when congressmen and the media began to focus attention on the speeches he delivered before civilian groups, his fate was sealed. On June 29, 1972, Frank A. Stubblefield (D-Ky.) told the House of Representatives about a recent meeting with General Haines. Describing him as "a dedicated Christian," Stubblefield noted that "he often refers to himself as a 'private in the Lord's Army.'" Stubblefield pressed Haines's example on the other members of the House and inserted into the *Congressional Record* excerpts from the speech he had recently given at the FGBMFI military breakfast in

11. Haines, "Drumbeat," 28; Haines, "Spiritual Renewal in the Army," 15–16.
12. Eastman, "Did the General Love Jesus," 4; Office of Chief of Chaplains, "Historical Review, 1 July 1971 to 30 June 1972" [1972] (Typescript at U.S. Army Center of Military History, Washington, D.C.), 71.

Washington, D.C. That was where the general had described himself "witnessing up a storm," giving his "personal testimony to Jesus Christ . . . before cadets at West Point, and before thousands of officers, non-commissioned officers, and men and women of the United States Army." He had also declared: "I believe the Lord is using me to rekindle spiritual zeal and moral awareness in troop units, training centers, and service schools at scores of military installations across this great land. I told the Lord last July I was ready to do what he wanted of me—and I'm trying to carry out the orders of my Commander-in-Chief. I'm a Private in His Army—bucking for Private First Class."[13]

Wesley Pippert speculated that the *Congressional Record* insertion triggered the *Washington Star-News* coverage of Haines. On August 6, 1972, the paper ran a front-page story under the headline "The General Fights for Jesus." The author, Jerry Oppenheimer, described Haines as "criss-crossing the country during the past year preaching the gospel of the old-time religion before gatherings of military people and civilians." Quoting the general, Oppenheimer said he "has pledged 'to rekindle the spiritual zeal of our great army across the land.'" He also quoted Haines telling the Hampton crusade that he "would rather be a private in the army of Jesus Christ than a general in the U.S. Army." (Writing in *Moody Monthly*, Pippert claimed that the *Star-News* "misquoted him slightly," that at Hampton Haines had said what he had repeated on other occasions: "I am proud to be a general in the United States Army, but I am prouder to be a private in the Lord's army.") Oppenheimer also made sure readers knew of Haines's high rank and wide-ranging authority. "In the chain of command," Oppenheimer wrote, "Haines ranks one notch below Gen. Creighton Abrams, former commander of troops in Vietnam." And if Abrams became chief of staff, Haines would become the "No. 2" man in the army. Haines was the man "responsible for the ground forces of the continental United States," Oppenheimer wrote. Citing Pentagon sources, he pointed out that Haines's assignment was "to direct, coordinate, supervise and inspect the training of the army in the field within the continental U.S., including reserve and ROTC components." He also directed the army elements of both the READINESS Command and U.S. Armed Forces Atlantic (ARLANT), Oppenheimer added. "He prepares, according to the Pentagon, Army

13. "Remarks by Gen. Ralph E. Haines, Jr.," in *Congressional Record*, *CXVIII* (92nd Cong., 2nd Sess.), 23819–21.

points of joint plans, executes approved plans or exercises and issues appropriate orders to tactical and supporting troop commanders."[14]

A few days later the *Star-News* ran another front-page story on Haines. It quoted Representative Samuel S. Stratton (D-N.Y.), a member of the House Armed Services Committee, questioning Haines's speaking engagements around the country. The matter would "bear looking into if taxpayers' money is being used for the general's activities or if his religious activities are cutting into his official duties," Stratton said, though he hastened to add that he "would not want to see anyone infringe on the general's right to speak out on his religious beliefs." The *Star-News* also reported that the Department of the Army had contacted the general "in an effort to determine whether his speaking engagements are in keeping with Army regulations and Department of Defense directives."[15]

The following day, August 11, the *Star-News* featured yet another front-page story quoting a statement released by the Department of the Army. In it Haines declared, "I know of no conflict between me and the demands of my job." He insisted that his strong religious beliefs made him "a better man and a better officer" and said that he accepted invitations to speak to religious gatherings because it was "in the best interest of the military that I do so." He went on to point out that the speaking engagements were scheduled alongside "planned visits to military installations and planned activities." The July 4 speech in San Francisco, for example, preceded a visit to army headquarters at Presidio and an inspection of reserve training activities in the surrounding area. The day before he participated in Explo '72 in Dallas, he said, he had been inspecting National Guard units at Fort Shelby, Mississippi. The story also cited a Department of the Army spokesman who said he was reassured by Haines's statement that his activities did not conflict with army regulations and Department of Defense directives.[16]

On August 12, 1972, the *Star-News* ran an editorial entitled "General Haines and Jesus." Citing the general's "unusual evangelical pursuits," the paper "confessed" that they "give us an uneasy feeling, one that must be shared at the Pentagon." The paper sought to give the im-

14. Pippert, "Four-Star General," 22, and see also 23, 25; Oppenheimer, "The General Fights for Jesus," A-1, A-4.

15. *Washington Star-News*, August 10, 1972, p. 1.

16. *Washington Star-News*, August 11, 1972, pp. 1, 10.

pression that it did not object to the general's practicing his religious faith or the army's showing a concern for the spiritual welfare of the troops. But it implied that Haines had exceeded the proper boundaries.

> Generals are supposed to keep out of politics, but nothing is said about religion, and General Haines, who is responsible for the four continental armies of the United States, plus the Military District of Washington, and is second in line to be Chief of Staff, has suddenly got religion—in awesome amount. . . .
>
> There's no doubt that he is sincere in viewing his command as "a rather large parish," and certainly it is important for someone to look after the spiritual well-being of its members. That is what the chaplains' corps is for.

Then, focusing specifically on the aspect of Haines's behavior that caused "uneasiness," the editorial declared: "With all due respect to a man who seems to have experienced a spiritual awakening, we're still obliged to say, in these touch-and-go times, that we'd sleep better knowing that our continent is being guarded by a general who acknowledges his commander in chief to be the President of the United States, whose orders are unjammed by other voices, whatever the source." The editorial concluded with a suggestion clearly aimed at the Pentagon: "General Haines has said that he would 'rather be a private in the Army of Jesus Christ than a general in the U.S. Army.' Careful consideration should be given to granting this wish."[17]

The *Star-News* editorial tapped the strong undercurrent of distrust usually generated by individuals who speak of being on "a special wave length with heaven" or who claim that God is "using" them for some purpose. Americans have traditionally admired military men who were religious. The *Star-News* noted that history "was full of generals who felt they were doing the work of God as well as the work of man." Eisenhower, for example, "was very devout." But so, the paper continued, "in his way, was John Brown." Religious fanaticism, whether of a military man or a civilian, has generally provoked skepticism, even fear, on the part of Americans. In combination with his high rank and the military might he apparently commanded, Haines's enthusiasm was bound to arouse anxiety.

Although the Pentagon denied that the action had anything to do with his religious activities, it requested that Haines retire six months

17. "General Haines and Jesus," *Washington Star-News*, August 12, 1972, p. 4.

earlier than planned. In September, 1972, the *New York Times* reported that Secretary of the Army Robert F. Froehlke had asked Haines and twenty-four other generals to take early retirement to make room for younger men. An army spokesman denied that Haines's retirement was "anything but voluntary," but both the *Army Times Family* reporter and Wesley Pippert believed that Haines had been forced out because he advertised his religious beliefs and thereby provoked adverse publicity. The *Army Times Family* reporter concluded, "Certainly his story raises the question of just how publicly a uniformed member of the armed forces (especially one in high places) can speak up for his personal convictions—even if his superiors appear to condone those convictions."[18]

But, of course, Haines did more than simply express his "personal convictions," which went far beyond the kind Americans were accustomed to hearing from military leaders, politicians, and other public figures. He used his military position to promote his newfound faith within the armed forces. Caught up in the excitement of his baptism in the Holy Spirit, he ignored the warning signs that might have persuaded a more cautious person to call retreat.

After his retirement in 1973, Haines became involved in a broad range of evangelical activities. He devoted a great deal of time to "spiritual renewal" and groups such as the Episcopal Charismatic Fellowship and Logos International Fellowship. He also continued his speaking engagements before various civilian audiences: church congregations, businessmen's groups, professional societies, service clubs, colleges, and women's organizations.[19]

Nor did retirement from the army prevent him from describing the role he thought religion should have in the armed forces. In the spring of 1977 the *Military Chaplains' Review* published an article entitled "Spiritual Renewal in the Army" in which he contended that religion could help the military reach "optimum effectiveness" by encouraging good performance and deterring bad behavior. "Those on the rolls of our Armed Forces, both active and reserve, are better soldiers, sailors, airmen, and Marines when they serve God well," he asserted. Writing at a time when the army was in the process of reassessing and revitalizing its professional ethic, he declared that it needed a religious component.

18. *NYT*, September 23, 1972, p. 61; Eastman, "Did the General Love Jesus," 10; Pippert, "Four-Star General," 22.
19. Haines, "Spiritual Renewal in the Army," 18.

"I do not believe that we in the military should talk about ethics or integrity in the abstract, as we are prone to do. I am convinced that we must season professional ethics with a deep and abiding faith in God."[20]

Haines also reiterated his oft-expressed conviction that military commanders were responsible not only for the physical but also for the moral and spiritual well-being of the men and women entrusted to their care and that they should work closely with the chaplains. Indeed, he prescribed an emphatically evangelistic role for both commanders and chaplains. "I believe that officers and non-commissioned officers at all levels must be willing to profess their faith in God publicly," he declared. Chaplains needed to "revamp" chapel services and programs so as to attract as many people as possible. Specifically, Haines urged commanders and chaplains to focus attention on the many young men and women entering military service who "have no religious background or spiritual mooring." Above all, he urged chaplains, in particular, to welcome and proclaim the "great spiritual renewal, led and inspired by the Holy Spirit, [which] is sweeping across the world."[21]

For a man who left the army under a cloud, General Haines exerted a surprising amount of influence after his retirement. Through the article in the *Military Chaplains' Review* and in speaking engagements at military installations, he promulgated his distinctive views regarding the role of religion in the armed forces to a wide audience. Although the army as an institution did not implement his suggestion about adding a religious component to the military ethic, countless individual officers apparently were persuaded of its validity and applied it in their own lives. No doubt some chaplains and commanders continued to dismiss him as a "kook" or fanatic, but his exhortations to evangelism inspired many others. Indeed, he had the satisfaction of seeing what had been a fledgling pentecostal movement before the early 1970s become a vital presence in the armed forces in the 1980s.

20. *Ibid.*, 11.
21. *Ibid.*, 13, 14–16, 19–20.

14

Pentecostal Religion
in the Armed Forces

Although General Haines's baptism in the Holy Spirit seems to have taken the military leadership and the news media by surprise, pentecostal religion was already firmly rooted in the armed forces by the early 1970s. Some of the fastest growing denominations in the United States, such as the Assemblies of God and the Church of God (Cleveland, Tennessee), were pentecostal groups. Not only did they endorse an increasing number of chaplains, but, as we saw in Chapter 2, they operated an extensive outreach to service personnel. Besides the pentecostal denominations there were charismatics within the mainline Protestant groups.

The Full Gospel Business Men's Fellowship International also played a crucial role in spreading pentecostal religion throughout the armed forces. During the 1960s and early 1970s, FGBMFI made effective use of the discipling technique perfected by other parachurch groups. The religious testimonies of several navy men published in *Voice* magazine provide a kind of case study of the evangelizing process that helped spread pentecostalism in the armed forces. Commander Carl Wilgus, a Nazarene, had received the gift of speaking in tongues after attending an FGBMFI meeting in Modesto, California, in the mid-1960s. Wilgus helped to lead marine fighter pilot Myrl Allinder to a similar experience a few years later when they met at marine corps headquarters and began working on plans to establish a prayer meeting group. Allinder described the events of that "red letter day" in May, 1968, when "Jesus baptized me in His Holy Spirit." Besides Wilgus, a Presbtyerian chaplain and a Church of God minister were present. Allinder had gotten down on his knees and was lifting up his hands "to the Lord in complete surrender."

The Church of God minister laid his hand on the back of Allinder's neck. As Allinder recalled, the other men "began to pray and I began to praise God. Soon I felt something like a Roman candle burning inside of me—the flames leaping as they went through my body, burning out all the dross—and I was filled to overflowing with the love of Jesus, literally crushed with the wonder of His tender love."[1]

Wilgus also converted another fellow officer, Lieutenant Commander Kenneth R. Bailey, to pentecostalism. The two of them in turn helped to convert Lieutenant Commander Bob Wright. Wright and his wife were already active in the military chapel program, and under the tutelage of Wilgus and Bailey they became born-again Christians. Wright and Bailey also became close friends. When he was suffering from nerve deafness in his left ear, which he knew would disqualify him from flying, Wright told Bailey about it. "Ken . . . assured me that was no problem," Wright remembered. "He turned in his Bible to James 5:14, 15 and read it, then he anointed my head with oil and prayed for me. God healed me that night, and I've had no trouble since!" That was the first time Wright had heard someone speak in tongues. Sometime later he himself experienced the baptism of the Holy Spirit.[2]

Bailey, Wright, and Allinder helped spread pentecostal religion among enlisted personnel as well as other officers. Bailey participated in a pentecostal fellowship group in Argentia, Newfoundland, and helped organize an FGBMFI chapter at the Naval Air Technical Training Center at Glynco, Georgia. When Wright was stationed in Saigon, a chaplain asked him to help with a pentecostal group at the Tan Son Nhut Air Base. Myrl Allinder also felt impelled to share his newfound gifts with others. Following his baptism in the Holy Spirit, he said, "God gave a prophecy . . . that I was going to Vietnam to witness to some men to whom the Lord would lead me." Sent to Vietnam in 1969, he found he was "able to witness for Christ on the flight line, in the airplanes, and in my office—and many boys were saved." He described what he did when the men came to him with their problems: "I would at first whip out the standard Marine Corps answers, but later the Lord

1. C. L. [*sic*] Wilgus, "'. . . and Underneath Are the Everlasting Arms,'" *Voice*, April, 1967, pp. 19, 21; Myrl Allinder, "Power!" *Voice*, July–August, 1971, pp. 7, 24.

2. Kenneth R. Bailey, Jr., "My Search for Meaning in Life," *Voice*, July–August, 1966, p. 20; Bob Wright, "I Hold Two Commissions," *Voice*, July–August, 1972, pp. 3, 5–7.

impressed it upon me to tell them about Jesus. You would be astonished how those problems got answered when we turned to Jesus and began to pray. It didn't make any difference whether it was a personal problem, a home problem, a rule infringement, or just plain loneliness or heartbreak—after we prayed about it, Jesus supplied the answer!"[3]

In the late 1970s and 1980s a growing number of FGBMFI disciple-makers helped spread pentecostal religion throughout the service branches, and *Voice* continued to print the testimonies of military men. A significant number of high-ranking officers supported FGBMFI, including General Louis H. Wilson, commandant of the Marine Corps, General John W. Vessey, Jr., chairman of the Joint Chiefs of Staff, and Admiral James D. Watkins, chief of naval operations.[4]

In the air force, pentecostal religion gained strength as part of a larger spirit of renewal that also included Roman Catholic and ecumenical charismatic groups. Encouraged by air force chaplains, pentecostal/charismatic prayer groups, healing services, workshops, and conferences became "a major spiritual force" in many chapel programs by the end of the 1970s.[5]

Pentecostal religion also spread within the army. In 1976, *Logos* magazine reported that a pentecostal retreat sponsored by the U.S. Army Chapel in Wurzburg, West Germany, had attracted more than fourteen hundred persons, including American and German civilians as well as U.S. military personnel. The three-day conference, held in February at St. John's Lutheran Church, had the official backing of the USAREUR chaplain's office and funding from the VII Army Corps. *Logos* reported that one of the featured speakers, Brigadier General Jerry R. Curry, remarked on "the amazing move of the Holy Spirit" among

3. Bailey, "My Search for Meaning," 20; Wright, "I Hold Two Commissions," 26; Allinder, "Power!" 24.

4. Wilson spoke at an FGBMFI prayer breakfast in Washington, D.C., in 1976, according to John Grinalds, "'Search!'," *Voice*, July–August, 1980, p. 16. Vessey and Watkins, a Roman Catholic, addressed the Greater San Antonio Military Breakfast sponsored by FGBMFI in 1984 and 1985, respectively. On Vessey see Ralph E. Haines, *"Christian Leadership in the Armed Forces": The Second Bishop Hulme-Moir Memorial Lecture* (Canberra, Australia, 1984), 8–9; for a transcript of Watkins' speech, see enclosure in Donald F. Dvornik to John A. Wickham, April 4, 1985, in John A. Wickham Papers, U.S. Army Military History Institute, Carlisle Barracks, Pa.

5. John E. Groh, *Air Force Chaplains, 1971–1980* (Washington, D.C., 1986), 3–7; John E. Groh, *Facilitators of the Free Exercise of Religion: Air Force Chaplains, 1981–1990* (Washington, D.C., 1991), 267.

both the American military and the German people. An ardent promoter of pentecostal religion, Curry was quoted by *Logos* as saying that "more important than defending the peace and maintaining the balance of power against the Soviet forces was the task of spreading the Gospel of Christ by the U.S. military personnel to the citizens of Europe." Another featured speaker was the well-known evangelical Jamie Buckingham. When he concluded one of the afternoon services with an altar call, more than four hundred persons responded. *Logos* described the scene:

> They filled the altar area and overflowed the transepts, the bema and the apse. Others came forward to lay on hands, counsel and pray with those on their knees. Privates prayed for Colonels, Germans prayed for Americans, and in several cases, infantry officers prayed for chaplains seeking the baptism.
>
> After more than an hour of ministry there was a spontaneous explosion of joy as many of the soldiers and some of the German citizens linked arms and began dancing around the altar. Someone produced a bongo drum. Tambourenes [*sic*] appeared. Arm-in-arm the men and women danced up and down the aisles of the ancient cathedral, around the altar and through the pews.

The Wurzburg retreat culminated several years of pentecostal activity among the military in Western Europe. There had been numerous previous reports of revivals in army chapels, on military bases, and in home prayer groups all over Europe. Like General Curry, Army Chaplain Curry Vaughan, one of the organizers of the 1976 retreat, pointed to it as proof of the "deep move of God in the military forces."[6]

As a key figure in the pentecostal movement, Vaughan knew whereof he spoke. A review of his life and career, which he described in *Battle-Ground: A Personal Account of God's Move Upon the American Military Forces*, published in 1978, turns up a wealth of information about the spread of pentecostal religion in the army. The son of an army officer, he had accepted Christ as his personal Savior in the Protestant chapel at Fort Knox, Kentucky, when he was eleven years old. When he enrolled at West Point several years later, having already decided to become an army chaplain, he joined a small group of cadets who met each

6. "Holy Spirit with U.S. Military," *Logos*, VI (May–June, 1976), 75–76. See also "God's Spirit Moving Among the Military," *Evangelical Press News Service*, August 1, 1976, p. 13.

morning for a chapel service and in the evenings for Bible study and prayer. He also encountered a man who shaped much of his life and work, King Coffman, professor of chemistry. At Coffman's invitation, Vaughan become a member of a group of thirteen cadets who met with him for group discussions, study sessions, and individual counseling. "Steadily we were schooled in Bible doctrine and Christian ethics," Vaughan remembered. "Steadily we were instilled with Christ's call for discipline in the lives of His followers."[7]

After graduating from West Point in 1963, Vaughan spent a year at Fort Benning and then attended Columbia Theological Seminary in Decatur, Georgia. Ordained to the Presbyterian ministry in 1968, he took up his first assignment as chaplain in the U.S. Army at Fort Benning. There he met some pentecostals, and a friend gave him a copy of John Sherrill's *They Speak with Other Tongues* to read. The book moved him, but he remained unconvinced regarding the gifts of the Holy Spirit. At a chaplains' weekly prayer breakfast, however, he saw a film featuring the testimonies of men who had experienced the baptism of the Holy Spirit. "I was moved as those ordinary people spoke, simply and directly," Vaughan wrote. When the film was over, he turned to the chaplain sitting next to him, Bob Crick. Unaware that Crick was a member of a pentecostal denomination (Church of God), Vaughan asked him what he thought of glossolalia and was stunned when Crick answered: "I was baptized in the Holy Spirit many years ago, Curry. . . . I spoke in tongues back then, and I've been speaking in tongues ever since." Crick then directed Vaughan's attention to the man sitting on his left, "a wiry, energetic Methodist chaplain by the name of Merlin Carothers," the man who had brought the film (and one of the chaplains who had helped the FGBMFI with ground arrangements during the Vietnam airlift of 1967). "Ask Merlin here," Crick said; "he'll tell you about it." As the two chaplains talked with him, Vaughan became more and more desirous of receiving the baptism of the Holy Spirit.

> I wanted the Holy Spirit to do for me what he had done for these men, for those who had testified on the screen, for John Sherrill—and for those I'd read so much about in the Book of Acts.
>
> I shrugged my shoulders and looked from one to the other. "Will you pray for me?"

7. Curry N. Vaughan, Jr., *Battle-Ground: A Personal Account of God's Move Upon the American Military Forces* (Plainfield, N.J., 1978), 14, 17, 21, 29, 30–31.

They responded with one voice. "Sure!" . . . The next thing I knew their hands were on top of my head, and they were praying. I closed my eyes. I waited with some expectation, but frankly not *too* much. Quite spontaneously, I pulled my head all the way back until my face was aimed at the ceiling, and my eyes were still closed. Before I knew it, my arms were raised. I was seeking and reaching out for God. I had never done that before. Again spontaneously, I began to talk aloud. I uttered quite normal, even fluent, sounds, but in a new language. . . . It was not English. It was an incredibly joyful sound, and I felt incredibly joyful inside. I felt pure and sweet, fresh and whole. I had a language of praise! . . . I was so full of joy I hugged both chaplains enthusiastically as we rose to leave, something else I'd never done before. I was almost beside myself with joy and excitement, and yet I was perfectly peaceful. I drove back to my office, speaking in tongues all the way. "Look out, soldiers!" I laughed out loud.[8]

Throughout the late 1960s and early 1970s, first in Vietnam and then at Fort Bragg, Vaughan honed his evangelizing skills, urging individual soldiers to commit their lives to Christ, forming Bible study groups, eventually organizing a small pentecostal group that brought young soldiers and their wives together for prayer, study, and fellowship. Initially he worked on his own, but in the early 1970s, while living in Fayetteville, North Carolina, he became part of a growing pentecostal network which included various churches and civilian groups such as the FGBMFI.[9]

In the spring of 1972, General Haines notified Fort Bragg that he planned to visit and wanted to meet with all commanders, sergeants-major, and chaplains. "It was not a commmand performance, we were told, but nobody believed that, not when you were dealing with the continental commander," Vaughan recalled. Everyone assumed that Haines would talk about the religious and moral responsibilities of commanders. "I really didn't know what to expect, but I dropped him a note to let him know I was in his corner. He wrote back: 'Hey, thanks. I appreciate it. I'll be down there.'" As expected, Haines devoted part of his hour-long talk to command responsibility for the spiritual and moral welfare of the troops. He concluded with a description of his religious experience at the Full Gospel Business Men's meeting and told how it

8. *Ibid.*, 45, 49–52. Richard Y. Bershon, *With the Cross of Jesus: A History of Church of God Chaplaincy and Ministry to the Military* (Cleveland, Tenn., 1991), 37, cites Robert D. Crick as "the best-known of all Church of God [(Cleveland, Tenn.)] chaplains." See also 146–47.

9. Vaughan, *Battle-Ground*, 111–36.

had made him "a better man, a better husband, a better officer." When
the general began talking about being baptized by the Holy Spirit,
Vaughan looked around to see how the audience was responding.
"Everything was quiet, but tension showed on many faces. I could almost feel the people struggling and tightening. Most of them were not
used to that sort of talk, not even in a chapel. And, obviously, many of
them didn't like it." By contrast, Vaughan seems to have drawn inspiration from Haines's example. "Ralph Haines went to every post in his
command," he wrote, "laying his experience and his recommendations
on the line. Lives were touched. Many were offended as they felt he was
putting religious pressure on them, which they believed was improper
and perhaps unconstitutional. But Haines was instrumental in spreading
the gospel in many parts of the army." [10]

Following a year at the Army Chaplain School, Vaughan was assigned
to Wurzburg to serve as assistant division chaplain for the 3rd Infantry
Division and pastor of the main chapel. Drawing on his experience at
Fort Bragg, he focused his attention on the young soldiers and their
wives. A previous chaplain in Wurzburg had started three coffeehouses
that attracted a group of young "Jesus People." Most of them had received the baptism of the Holy Spirit and were enthusiastic about renewal. Vaughan invited some of the coffeehouse crowd to Sunday chapel
services and eventually brought them and the older chapel members
together in a community-wide prayer and praise meeting on Sunday
nights. When the fellowship became overlarge, Vaughan encouraged it
to break up into smaller groups, each consisting of eight to twelve persons, emphasizing Bible study or prayer. At first, there were six groups;
ultimately they numbered sixteen, scattered throughout Wurzburg. The
early leaders included a lieutenant colonel, three majors, a captain, three
sergeants, and two privates. The small groups, along with a Sunday
school, a Sunday morning service, and the Sunday night prayer and
praise meeting, constituted a wide-ranging ministry that appealed to
nonpentecostals as well as pentecostals and attracted people from the
surrounding German community as well. It was this congregation that
became the nucleus of the Wurzburg retreat of 1976.[11]

10. *Ibid.*, 128, 130–32. For another chaplain who was inspired by a visit by General
Haines, see Thomas L. Deal, "A Charismatic Chaplain: His Views and Experiences,"
MCR, Spring, 1977, p. 27.
11. Vaughan, *Battle-Ground*, 150–76.

In an article he wrote in 1982 for *Charisma* magazine, Vaughan asserted that throughout his career as an army chaplain he had enjoyed "not only the permission but the support of my superiors—even when they did not totally agree with my approach." One of the commanding officers who encouraged his efforts in Wurzburg was General Jerry Curry. Curry was not the army's typical commander in the mid-1970s. He was an African American in his early forties, one of the youngest brigadier generals in the military and, as *Logos* magazine pointed out, "one of the few Spirit-filled ranking officers in the army." Raised a Baptist, he had received the baptism of the Holy Spirit in the summer of 1970 after being challenged by his mother to "become the kind of Christian you think you are." Recalling Curry's testimony at the Wurzburg retreat, Vaughan described him as "one of our most impressive, speaking from a position of authority and knowledge but of extraordinary humility." In the late 1970s Curry did for pentecostal religion in the army what William K. Harrison had done for evangelicalism decades earlier. He became deputy commander of the Military District in Washington and then a division commander and, according to Vaughan, took "the good news of Christ" wherever he went and became "one of the leading speakers at major Christian conferences in the society at large." In the mid-1980s, following his retirement, Curry served briefly as president of televangelist Pat Robertson's National Perspectives Institute (a public policy research organization) and thus became one of several "military experts" working for the New Christian Right (NCR).[12]

In West Germany, Curry Vaughan also encountered Chaplain E. H. (Jim) Ammerman, a Southern Baptist serving as V Corps chaplain, whom he called the principal "moving force" behind the "burgeoning renewal in Germany and other parts of Europe" in the mid-1970s. As a senior chaplain in charge of eighty-three chaplains, Ammerman went to considerable lengths to acquaint them with pentecostal religion. Describing his early efforts in a speech to a Full Gospel Business Men's convention, Ammerman said, "God laid it on my heart to have prayer meetings after the regular nightly meetings at our annual retreat for

---

12. Curry N. Vaughan, Jr., "Under Orders," *Charisma*, VIII (October, 1982), 59; "Holy Spirit with U.S. Military," 76; Vaughan, *Battle-Ground*, 176, 191; Beth Spring, "Pat Robertson for President?" *CT*, November 8, 1985, p. 51. See also Jerry R. Curry, "Fight the Good Fight," *MCR*, Spring, 1977, pp. 55–62; Jerry R. Curry, "Rebuilding the Walls," *Voice*, March, 1975, p. 35.

chaplains at Berchtesgaden." Initially, he encountered some resistance:

> When I first opened the prayer session and said we were going to pray for God to pour out His power upon us like at Pentecost, one chaplain stood up and said, "That's all of the devil." I said, "You may have just offended the Holy Ghost and committed the unpardonable sin." He turned white and sank to the floor. Then someone else said, "Anyone that doesn't speak with tongues is going to hell and is not saved." "Wait a minute," I said, "Somewhere in between those two opinions is where God wants His people to walk in love. Let's pray."

Soon, according to Ammerman, "We had chaplains of every denomination filled with the Holy Spirit—as well as their wives. Then these chaplains went to their assignments and God began to pour out His power everywhere."[13]

In 1974 Ammerman became post chaplain and pastor to the U.S. Army Command and General Staff College at Fort Leavenworth, Kansas. There he found OCF representative George Kuykendall's Bible studies program in high gear. Ammerman encouraged Kuykendall's effort and began building up the chapel program. Two years later, Curry Vaughan was assigned to the college and discovered Ammerman leading "the most exciting and dynamic ministry in the military." Besides the nearly thirty weekly Bible study meetings coordinated by Kuykendall, the chapel program boasted a strong Sunday school program and drew around seven hundred persons to the regular Sunday services. Ammerman also held a once-a-month prayer meeting at his home on Saturday nights, which began at eight o'clock in the evening and often ran until two or later in the morning "until all the needs and intercessions had been taken care of." Vaughan estimated that some 40 percent of the Fort Leavenworth population participated in the chapel program and that more than half of that number were pentecostals.[14]

The story of the cooperative efforts of Vaughan, Ammerman, Haines, and Curry offers a glimpse of the way chaplains and commanders helped spread pentecostal religion in the army. There were many more like them.[15] Working together they gained for pentecostalism the recogni-

13. Vaughan, *Battle-Ground*, 179–80; James Ammerman, " 'Putting It All Together,' " *Voice*, July–August, 1975, pp. 15, 17.

14. Vaughan, *Battle-Ground*, 184–86.

15. See, for example, Deal, "A Charismatic Chaplain," 23–34; Marcia Milligan, "New Spirit: Post Chaplains Look for Innovative Ways to Take Ministry to the Community," *Military Chaplain*, No. 2 (1982), 6.

tion and respect that had eluded General Haines in the early 1970s. A 1977 *Military Chaplains' Review* special issue on pentecostal and charismatic religion testified to their success. Among the writers were some of the men who had figured prominently in the growth of pentecostalism in the military—Generals Haines and Curry and Chaplains Vaughan, Ammerman, and Crick.

In 1984 the pentecostal movement within the military gained additional recognition and influence when an organization was established to certify and endorse pentecostal/charismatic chaplains for military service. Before that date, pentecostals who belonged to independent Full Gospel churches or unaffiliated "Spirit-filled" fellowships (as opposed to denominations like the Assemblies of God or the Church of God) had not been represented in the armed services chaplaincy because of the Pentagon requirement that a religious body have at least one hundred thousand members to warrant a chaplaincy position. To rectify this problem, Jim Ammerman, who had retired from the army in 1977, organized the Chaplaincy Full Gospel Churches (CFGC) and became president and director. General Haines was among the organization's senior military advisers, and Curry Vaughan and Bob Wright were members of the executive committee.[16]

In 1984, when the CFGC received approval from the Armed Forces Chaplains Board, Vaughan hailed it as "the most significant event to take place in the armed forces in modern history." Both he and Ammerman predicted that the number of Full Gospel chaplains in the military would escalate immediately. Their optimism proved well-founded. At the time of its organization, the CFGC represented five thousand of an estimated seventy-five thousand independent charismatic churches. By July, 1989, when it celebrated its fifth anniversary, the CFGC had become the fastest growing endorsing agency in the United States, ranking as the eighth largest among a total of ninety-six, and representing 2.6 million "Spirit-filled believers" from twenty-five thousand churches and forty-one independent fellowships and associations. It also had 107 Full Gospel men and women serving as military and civilian chaplains. In a 1989 news release, the CFGC announced that it expected to double its constituency within five years. "Our growth is genuinely miraculous,"

16. "Military Chaplains to Include Full Gospel Ministers," *Charisma*, X (November, 1984), 108; CFGC News Release (N.d.; *ca.* July, 1989) enclosed in letter of E. H. Ammerman to author, July 16, 1990.

Ammerman declared in the release. "To put things into perspective, in five years we have experienced half the growth that it has taken the National Association of Evangelicals . . . 47 years to accomplish." [17]

Chaplain Ammerman's invidious comparison notwithstanding, non-pentecostal evangelical religion continued to flourish in the armed forces in the late 1970s and 1980s. Although its growth was less dramatic than that of pentecostalism, it was no less real.

For example, the military leadership and civilian evangelical groups continued the tradition of cooperation established by Explo '72 and Key 73. In 1976, when Bill Bright and Campus Crusade for Christ launched the Here's Life, America evangelistic campaign, air force chapels assisted the campaign with prayer wheels, prayer vigils, and prayer rallies. In Washington, D.C., John Broger, director of Armed Forces Information and Education and a veteran evangelist, served as chairman of the Here's Life executive committee for the nation's capital. An article in *Christianity Today* quoted him as saying that some seven thousand Campus Crusade–trained volunteers had worked in 150 telephone centers and contacted about one-fourth of the households (approximately two hundred thousand) in Washington, D.C., and its suburbs. [18]

The military academies also continued to be hospitable to evangelical parachurch groups. At the Air Force Academy, for example, the Navigators built on the foundation established in the 1960s, cooperating with chaplains in chapel programs and expanding Bible studies and other activities. True to their heritage, Navigators continued to emphasize the importance of cadets discipling other cadets and began a training program for that purpose. By the late 1970s the Navigator staff supervised a ministry at the Air Force Academy made up of some 150 cadets whom they had coached in Christian discipleship. The Officers' Christian Fellowship also instituted a discipling program at the Air Force Academy. That and the work of OCF staff representatives in the late 1970s and early 1980s paid off in membership gains. In 1977, the OCF representative could count on only "four solid men" there, but by 1983, sixty to eighty cadets attended weekly Bible study. The OCF also expanded its

17. "Military Chaplains to Include Full Gospel Ministers," 107–108; CFGC News Release (N.d.; *ca.* July, 1989) enclosed in letter of E. H. Ammerman to author, July 16, 1990.

18. "Yoking Politics and Proclamation—Can It Be Done?" *CT*, September 24, 1976, p. 20; Groh, *Air Force Chaplains*, 531–32; "Here's Life," *CT*, February 4, 1977, pp. 54–55.

ministry at the Naval and Coast Guard academies with the encouragement of the administration and staff of those two institutions.[19]

At West Point by the late 1970s the administration's position had evolved to the point that the deputy superintendent asked what he and the academy could do to assist the work of the OCF. By the 1980s evangelical religion flourished at the academy. One reason was a significant change in the Protestant constituency at the Point. Writing in *Christianity Today*, Gene Preston noted that there were fewer Methodists, Presbyterians, and Congregationalists and increased numbers of Baptists and "nondenominational sectarians." A "broader evangelicalism and assertive personal religion" seemed to be replacing the long tradition of genteel southern Episcopalianism. Lay activity also nurtured evangelical religion at the Point. Every one of the thirty-six companies at the academy had at least one Bible study group. The senior cadet chaplain, Richard P. Camp, Jr., was another key factor. A graduate of Wheaton College and Gordon-Conwell Theological Seminary, Camp had been chosen assistant chaplain in 1973 on the recommendation of Bill Waldrup, a retired West Point graduate who was very active in the OCF. At West Point, Camp supplemented his pastoral duties by serving as backfield coach for the army team, promoting activities of the Fellowship of Christian Athletes (which hosted a prayer breakfast attended by 330 cadets in 1982), and organizing informal prayer and witnessing sessions among the athletes.[20]

Evangelical religion also flourished at the Pentagon. In the mid- to late 1980s between fifteen and twenty evangelical groups were meeting on a regular basis. One of them, the Pentagon Christian Fellowship (formerly the Christian Men of the Pentagon) had been in existence since 1968. The focal point of its program was a bimonthly luncheon featuring guest speakers such as congressmen, flag officers, or important civilians, who shared their testimony with some sixty to one hundred fellow Christians from throughout the Pentagon.[21]

19. Bernard Thompson, "From the Air Force Academy to the World," *NavLog*, July, 1977, p. 6; Robert W. Spoede, *More Than Conquerors: A History of the Officers' Christian Fellowship of the U.S.A., 1943 to 1983* (Englewood, Colo., 1993), 122, 124–29.

20. Spoede, *More Than Conquerors*, 122; Gene Preston, "Religion at West Point," *CT*, November 6, 1981, pp. 76–77; John Kenyon, "Pastor of the West Point Cadets," *Christian Herald*, CV (May, 1982), 23, 25.

21. Robert C. Toth, "Enhanced Role of Religious Faith at Pentagon Raises Questions, Doubts," *Los Angeles Times*, December 30, 1984, p. 4; Col. Jerry Hansen, USA, to the author, May 4, 1992.

The expansion of evangelical activity at the Pentagon in the late 1970s and 1980s owed a good deal to the influence of Campus Crusade's Christian Embassy. Established in 1976 by Arizona congressman John Conlan and Campus Crusade for Christ head Bill Bright, with funding from wealthy evangelical businessmen, its purpose was to serve as a "spiritual resource group" for government leaders in the nation's capital. Rolfe McCollister, one of the financial backers and president of the Embassy in 1976, explained: "We want a more Christian government. We plan to do that by evangelizing official Washington, by working with men in the executive branch, the Congress, the judiciary, the military, and the diplomatic service, and by ministering to their families in an effort to change non-Christian official Washington to Christian official Washington." The Embassy's ministry to the military began when Bright persuaded Lieutenant General William R. Nelson to start a Bible study group for flag officers in his office in the Pentagon. Numbering from three to seven persons, meeting at noon or in the evening, the group continued into the mid-1980s. In the meantime, Mark Petersburg, a Campus Crusade staff member who was also an ordained minister and who had worked in the Campus Crusade student ministry, joined the Embassy in 1978 for the express purpose of concentrating on the military. In January, 1979, with the help of Colonel Richard F. Abel, he founded the Wednesday morning Pentagon Breakfast Bible Study. That group met regularly during the 1980s. Starting with seven to twelve members, it expanded to between thirty and thirty-five by the mid-1980s and to around one hundred in 1992.[22]

In the fall of 1985 Christian Embassy appointed Ron Soderquist to be the new director of its military ministry. Petersburg, who eventually became director of the Embassy as a whole, continued to teach the Pentagon Breakfast Bible Study, and Soderquist started two more groups of about seven men each, which met twice weekly to receive discipleship training. By 1989 the two groups numbered upward of twenty each, and Soderquist decided to challenge the forty members to start their own groups. By 1992 there were seven discipleship groups for men, with a total of about ninety members, as well as a group of ten to sixteen women officers. Many of the members of the Christian Em-

---

22. Rev. Ron Soderquist, Director, Christian Embassy Military Ministry, telephone conversation with author, July 20, 1992; Jim Wallis and Wes Michaelson, "The Plan to Save America," *Sojourners*, April, 1976, p. 9.

bassy groups also belonged to the Pentagon Breakfast Bible Study, the Pentagon Christian Fellowship, or the Officers' Christian Fellowship.

A final component of the Christian Embassy ministry to the Pentagon was the Flag Officer Fellowship, founded in March, 1987, when Lieutenant General Claude Kicklighter and Major General Howard Graves asked Soderquist to help coordinate such a group. Beginning with about ten members, the fellowship met every Thursday morning from 6:15 to 7:15. The meeting began with informal visiting, breakfast, and prayer and concluded with a half-hour discussion led by Soderquist on "some practical topic" (such as marriage, parenting, friendship, vocation, or "priorities") considered "from a Biblical point of view." By the early 1990s the Flag Officer Fellowship had expanded to about forty members, with weekly attendance of about fifteen to twenty members. The high-ranking officers who belonged to it included a former chief of naval operations and the superintendent of West Point. One member described the fellowship's activities as follows: "We study ethics and moral values, pray together, encourage one another as leaders at home and at work, study the bible and learn how to apply Christian values in our jobs."[23]

Besides the Christian Embassy, Campus Crusade's Military Ministry also targeted the upper echelons of the military leadership. In the mid- to late 1980s it sponsored three Christian Military Leadership Forums in Las Colinas, Texas, and Alexandria and Fredericksburg, Virginia. They were the brainchild of Glenn A. Jones, a retired air force colonel serving as national director of the Military Ministry, who described them in a promotional letter as "a concept . . . to see if Christian businessmen and women can teach, and learn from, our senior military leadership, in small informal conferences." Each of the forums brought together twenty to twenty-five senior flag officers and their wives along with the same number of prominent business executives and their wives. The three-day conferences offered meals, fellowship, and entertainment, but the focus was on speeches and seminars by a "faculty" made up of Bill Bright and other evangelicals from the world of business and the mili-

23. Rev. Ron Soderquist, Director, Christian Embassy Military Ministry, telephone conversation with author, July 20, 1992; Adm. Jerry Johnson, USN, *et al.*, to Dear Soviet Military Leader, n.d., copy enclosed with packet of materials regarding Pentagon Christian Fellowship mission trip to the Soviet Union sent to Don Martin, Jr., Editor, *Command*, by Col. Jerry Hansen, USA, November 15, 1991. I wish to thank Don Martin for sending this material to me.

tary—"motivational speakers" such as Zig Ziglar and retired air force brigadier general Richard Abel, former director of legislative and public affairs of the U.S. Olympic Committee; Joe Foss, World War II fighter ace and former governor of South Dakota; newspaperman Ben Haden; and former Vietnam POW Jeremiah A. Denton, Jr., senator from Alabama and a member of the Armed Services Committee.[24]

In the mid-1980s the religious activities of the military leadership caught the attention of *Los Angeles Times* staff writer Robert C. Toth and *New York Times* reporter Richard Halloran. Both men seemed particularly intrigued by the chairman of the Joint Chiefs of Staff, General John W. Vessey, Jr. Toth commented that of the five members of the Joint Chiefs of Staff, Vessey, along with Army Chief of Staff John A. Wickham, Jr., and Chief of Naval Operations James D. Watkins, appeared "more openly religious than any of their predecessors." Halloran's portrait of Vessey emphasized his "strong religious convictions." He reported that the general was "active in the Lutheran Church" and "spends a few minutes each day reading the Bible." He "hardly drinks or smokes and seldom utters a swear word," Halloran continued.[25]

The man Halloran described recalls "the Bible-reading General," William K. Harrison, in more ways than one. Following World War II, Vessey was sent to Germany and missed serving in the Korean War. He told Halloran he thought of leaving the army "to do the Lord's work." But a friend dissuaded him, arguing that he could do the Lord's work by soldiering. "In his view," Vessey said, "I was a far better soldier than I would ever be as a pastor." Like Harrison, too, Vessey devoted considerable thought to the relationship between his religious convictions and the military profession. "That's a question with which I have wrestled more than a little bit," he admitted to Halloran. "I'm a Christian," he said, and added, "I guess if we examined it, I might call myself an existentialist Christian. It seems to me that the Lord has given us a world, the only world we've got, and we have to deal with that world the way it is." In an address at the Concordia Historical Institute, Vessey

24. Glenn Jones letter, September 5, 1984, enclosed in a letter of David Stedman to the author, June 25, 1992. A staff member of Campus Crusade Military Ministry, Stedman kindly supplied me with a sampling of brochures, program schedules, and other information on the military leadership forums.

25. Richard Halloran, "A Commanding Voice for the Military," *New York Times Magazine*, July 15, 1984, pp. 22, 52; Toth, "Enhanced Role of Religious Faith at Pentagon," 4.

echoed Harrison in observing that human beings had "not ended war or the threat of war. God will do that in his own time." Like Harrison, he justified the military as necessary for the protection of the country and its citizens. "I would much rather not use violence, but we live in a violent world," he told Halloran.[26]

Vessey also invites comparison with Army Chief of Staff Harold K. Johnson. Like him, Vessey emphasized the importance of promoting the spiritual and moral as well as the material strength of the armed forces, and he identified himself and fellow members of the Joint Chiefs of Staff as men of strong religious faith who gained sustenance from regular meetings for prayer, Bible study, and "Christian fellowship." Following Johnson's precedent, Vessey toured the prayer breakfast circuit, speaking at such gatherings as the Dallas Leadership Christian Prayer Breakfast, the national prayer breakfast, and the FGBMFI-sponsored Greater San Antonio Military Breakfast. The message he delivered on such occasions was much more sectarian than Johnson's—more reminiscent of the gospel according to Harrison. In the national prayer breakfast speech, for example, in which he exhorted the audience to "enlist or reenlist" in "the army of the Lord," he described the Bible as "the basic field manual" in that army—good evangelical doctrine. And whereas Johnson spoke in ecumenical language, exhorting his audiences to turn to "Almighty God," Vessey focused on Jesus' command to "Follow me" and concluded with a quotation from Paul declaring that nothing "in God's whole world has any power to separate us from the love of God in Jesus Christ our Lord!"[27] In the twenty years since Johnson had delivered his prayer breakfast speeches, Vessey's sectarian language had become more familiar and acceptable than ever before.

And it was accepted not only among the civilians in the audience but among the military as well. The witnessing and discipling, the Bible study groups and prayer breakfasts that spurred the growth of evangelical religion in the military during the late 1970s and 1980s did not occur in a vacuum. They were part of the resurgence of evangelical

26. John W. Vessey, Jr., "Dedication Address, the Chaplains Memorial, Concordia Historical Institute," *Concordia Historical Institute Quarterly*, LV (Summer, 1982), 67; Halloran, "Commanding Voice for the Military," 22, 52.

27. Vessey, "Dedication Address," 67; Haines, "*Christian Leadership in the Armed Forces,*" 9; "America's Top Military Officer Calls Christians to 'God's Army,'" *CT*, April 20, 1984, p. 37; John W. Vessey, Jr., "Enlisting in the Lord's Army," *Command*, Summer, 1984, pp. 4–5.

religion in the United States as a whole. During the 1980s, as succeeding chapters will show, civilian and military evangelicals worked in tandem, forging an alliance that enabled them to exert considerable influence not only in the armed forces but in the discussion of national policy as well.

15

The New Christian Right

In 1976 the American media discovered what *Newsweek* called "the most significant—and overlooked—religious phenomenon of the 70's: the emergence of evangelical Christianity into a position of respect and power." During the "year of the evangelicals," as it became known, evangelical religion attained unprecedented national recognition and influence, culminating in the election of a professed born-again Christian, Jimmy Carter, as president of the United States. That was only the beginning of an ascendancy that continued into the 1980s. During the next decade and a half, public opinion polls and newsmagazines reported ever larger percentages of Americans identifying themselves as evangelical Christians. Presidents and other politicians found increasing favor with voters by adopting the rhetoric and advocating the moral, political, and social agenda of evangelicals. And a phalanx of parachurch groups built an institutional base for expanded evangelistic, missionary, and social and political activities. The evangelical ascendancy benefited enormously from the presidency of Ronald Reagan. Many evangelicals regarded him as a godsend—literally. Jerry Falwell once described Reagan and his vice-president as "God's instruments in rebuilding America." Reagan in turn not only identified himself as an evangelical Christian but forged an alliance with evangelicals by endorsing school prayer, creationism, opposition to abortion, anticommunism, and a strong national defense. At a National Affairs Briefing in Dallas, sponsored by the Religious Roundtable in August, 1980, the Reverend D. James Kennedy, pastor of Fort Lauderdale's Coral Ridge Presbyterian Church, introduced the presidential candidate by saying: "Our hope is in God and the promises of his Word. Here is a man who believes that Word, who trusts in the living God and his Son Jesus Christ." During his speech Reagan said to the gathering of some twenty-five hundred clergymen, "I know you cannot endorse me, but I want you to know that I endorse you!"[1]

One is reminded of the partnership between President Eisenhower and evangelicals in the 1950s. Reagan, however, proved an even more sympathetic ally than Eisenhower. He may have disappointed evangelicals by his infrequent church attendance, but unlike Ike, who endorsed a vague nondenominationalism ("and I don't care what it is"), Reagan subscribed to evangelicals' conspicuously sectarian version of Protestant Christianity.

In 1976, when he was a candidate for the Republican presidential nomination, Reagan had described his "spiritual views" in an interview conducted by George Otis, a charismatic religious leader from Van Nuys, California. The interview was excerpted in *Christianity Today* and frequently quoted by the news media during the Reagan presidency. In it Reagan testified to having had a born-again experience, described himself as a praying man who would seek "God's guidance" in making presidential decisions, claimed never to have doubted that the Bible was "of divine origin," and declared that he sensed "a hunger in this land for a spiritual revival; a return to a belief in moral absolutes—the same morals upon which the nation was founded."[2]

If evangelicals took heart at the thought of a conservative Christian in the White House, they felt equally encouraged by what one of them called "the brightening picture" in the nation's capital, where a wave of evangelical piety seemed to be washing over the entire federal government. According to Bob Slosser, executive vice president and chief of staff of the Christian Broadcasting Network (CBN), not only were there "professing Christians" in the executive branch but in the Senate and House, even in the judiciary. Among the military stationed in and

1. "Born Again! The Year of the Evangelicals," *Newsweek*, October 25, 1976, p. 68; Stephen D. Johnson and Joseph B. Tamney, eds., *The Political Role of Religion in the United States* (Boulder, Colo., 1986), 100; Kennedy quoted in Bruce Buursma, "Evangelicals Give Reagan a 'Non-Partisan' Stump," *CT*, September 19, 1980, p. 50; David Snowball, *Continuity and Change in the Rhetoric of the Moral Majority* (New York, 1991), 43.

2. "Reagan Seeks Return to Absolutes . . . ," *National Courier*, August 6, 1976, pp. 6–7; "Reagan on God and Morality," *CT*, July 2, 1976, pp. 39–40. See also Bob Slosser, *Reagan Inside Out* (Waco, Tex., 1984), 49–50, 82.

around Washington were "a high percentage of active Christians," including the chairman of the Joint Chiefs of Staff, General John W. Vessey, Jr., "who is refreshingly open in the expression of his faith." All through the government, "from the highest to the lowest offices," Slosser discovered Christians witnessing and praying. "Weekly Bible studies, running from a half-hour to an hour or more, sometimes early in the morning, sometimes at noon, sometimes in the early evening, are found in every building, from the old executive office building to the Pentagon across the Potomac. Generals, clerks, senators, secretaries, department heads, White House aides—all kinds are involved," he wrote.[3]

Besides identifying himself as a born-again Christian, Reagan repeatedly invoked evangelical themes and ideas. During the 1980 campaign, on inauguration day, and in public addresses, Reagan quoted the favorite Bible verse of evangelicals, 2 Chronicles 7:14: "If my people who are called by my name, shall humble themselves, and pray, and seek my face, and turn from their wicked ways; then will I hear from heaven, and will forgive their sin, and will heal their land." The notion of a covenanted nation, the belief that the United States was "a nation under God," with "a divine purpose," became a rhetorical staple. Reagan also sounded another theme dear to the hearts of evangelicals when he declared, "The Bible contains an answer to just about everything and every problem that confronts us, and I wonder sometimes why we won't recognize that one Book could solve a lot of problems for us." He proclaimed 1983 the Year of the Bible in recognition of its preeminence in American life.[4]

In Reagan evangelicals discovered a president who claimed to share not only their moral and spiritual beliefs but also their desire to translate those beliefs into public policy. Although the news media focused most attention on evangelicals' pro-family, pro-life, pro-morality agenda in the late 1970s and early 1980s, keen observers pointed out their equally strong views on national defense policy.[5]

3. Beth Spring, "The Surprising Influence of Christianity in Congress," *CT*, May 7, 1982, pp. 28–29, 45, 48–49; Slosser, *Reagan Inside Out*, 108, 110–12, 120–21.

4. Richard G. Hutcheson, Jr., *God in the White House: How Religion Has Changed the Modern Presidency* (New York, 1988), 137; *NYT*, February 17, 1984, p. B16, February 22, 1985, p. 14; Erling Jorstad, *The New Christian Right: Prospects for the Post-Reagan Decade* (Lewiston, N.Y., 1987), 130.

5. See, for example, "A Tide of Born-Again Politics," *Newsweek*, September 15,

Reagan won evangelicals' support by promising to restore U.S. military superiority through a policy of "peace through strength." During the 1980 presidential campaign he hammered away at the need to revamp the American military. Calling peace his "number one priority" in a speech to the Veterans of Foreign Wars, Reagan added: "But it must not be peace at any price. It must not be a peace of humiliation and gradual surrender." He declared that the Soviet Union was "outspending us in the military field by 50 percent, and more than double, sometimes triple on their strategic forces." Through a policy of "weakness, inconsistency, vacillation and bluff," he asserted, the Carter administration was destroying the United States' "margin of safety" in national defense. It was involved in "one-sided" arms control negotiations—a reference to the SALT II treaty President Carter had negotiated with Leonid Brezhnev—which forced it to cut defense spending while the Russians went ahead with "the greatest military buildup in the history of mankind." The Soviets "seek a superiority of military strength that, in the event of a confrontation, would leave us with an unacceptable choice between surrender or a conflict and defeat." The only way to persuade them to live in peace "is to convince them they cannot win a war," Reagan declared.[6]

Once in the presidential office, Reagan initiated a massive buildup of nuclear weapons. He and members of his administration talked of limited nuclear war in Europe, of a winnable nuclear war with the Soviet Union, of not only using nuclear weapons but using them first, if necessary. News commentators speculated that the military programs as well as the public statements of the Reagan administration signaled a policy shift away from deterring nuclear war to developing the capability to fight and prevail in such a war. Reagan's initial unwillingness to engage in arms control talks with the Soviet Union reinforced such an interpretation. In 1982, in an effort to undercut a burgeoning nuclear freeze movement, he began Strategic Arms Reduction Talks (START) in Geneva with the Soviets, but his bellicose rhetoric toward them continued, culminating in a speech to the National Association of Evan-

---

1980, p. 32; Kenneth A. Briggs, "Christians on Right and Left Take up Ballot and Cudgel," *NYT*, September 21, 1980, p. 20E; Edward E. Plowman, "Washington for Jesus: Revival Fervor and Political Disclaimers," *CT*, May 23, 1980, p. 46.

6. *NYT*, August 19, 1980, pp. 1, D17.

gelicals in March, 1983, in which he called the USSR an "evil empire" and "the focus of evil in the modern world."[7]

In combination with the nuclear weapons buildup, statements Reagan made linking Armageddon and the end of the world with the Middle East and nuclear conflict provoked considerable controversy. Journalists and other commentators speculated that he subscribed to the so-called Armageddon theology. This outgrowth of the premillennial view of biblical prophecy had been popularized by Hal Lindsey in his 1970 bestseller *The Late Great Planet Earth*. Reduced to its essentials, it claimed that according to the Bible God had foreordained a nuclear war that would begin in the Middle East and usher in the "end time." Moreover, the "signs of the times" (the rise of the Soviet Union, the establishment of the state of Israel, the moral deterioration of the United States) pointed to the imminence of such an event.[8]

As the historian Paul Boyer has demonstrated, prophecy belief was ubiquitous in the United States in the 1970s and 1980s, and many believers—including televangelists such as Jerry Falwell, Pat Robertson, Jimmy Swaggart, Jim Bakker, and Jack Van Impe—followed Lindsey in making nuclear war the central event of their end-time scenarios and focusing on Russia's prophesied invasion of Israel as the preamble to Armageddon. Reagan's interest in prophecy went back at least to the 1970s. As president he read and repeatedly discussed Lindsey's book and talked about Old Testament prophets and the signs pointing to Armageddon. Ronnie Dugger of the *Washington Post* cited five such occasions; a radio documentary cited eleven. Some commentators interpreted Reagan's remarks about the Soviet Union in his "evil empire" speech as "a shorthand version" of the prophetic worldview.[9]

7. Ronald Reagan, "Remarks at the Annual Convention of the National Association of Evangelicals in Orlando, Florida," March 8, 1983, in *Public Papers of the Presidents of the United States: Ronald Reagan, 1983* (Washington, D.C., 1984), Book I, pp. 363, 364. For comment on Reagan's national defense policies, see, for example, Steven E. Miller, "Nuclear Arms Control: The Freeze Debate Heats Up," *New Leader*, March 22, 1982, p. 3; "Living with Mega-Death," *Time*, March 29, 1982, pp. 19, 25; "Freeze Vote: Body Blow to Arms Strategy?" *U.S. News & World Report*, November 15, 1982, p. 32.

8. Hal Lindsey with C. C. Carlson, *The Late Great Planet Earth* (Grand Rapids, 1970), and, for a summary of Lindsey's argument, *NYT*, October 28, 1984, p. 31.

9. Paul Boyer, *When Time Shall Be No More: Prophecy Belief in Modern American Culture* (Cambridge, Mass., 1992), 5–11, 128–39, 141–42, 157–74, 177. See also Frances Fitzgerald, "A Disciplined, Charging Army," *New Yorker*, May 18, 1981, pp. 131–32; *NYT*, October 21, 1984, p. 32; David Edwin Harrell, Jr., *Pat Robertson: A Personal,*

Members of the press and liberal religious groups voiced growing alarm over Reagan's apocalyptic views. Not only did they worry that his adherence to the Armageddon theology diminished his incentive to work for nuclear disarmament; they also expressed fear that in a confrontation with the Soviet Union, he might be predisposed to push the button starting a nuclear war as a way of helping God bring about foreordained plans for the end of time.[10]

In response, Reagan offered reassurances that acceptance of the Armageddon theology did not preclude a concern for peace and arms control. In an interview with *People* magazine in December, 1983, when asked whether he had "mused about" the end of the world, Reagan responded: "Not to the extent of throwing up my hands and saying, 'Well, it's all over.' No, I think whenever that time comes, the generation that is here will have to go on doing what they believe is right." During one of the presidential debates of the 1984 campaign, when asked if he believed the world was heading for a "nuclear Armageddon," Reagan admitted having engaged in "philosophical discussions" about the similarity between current events and signs pointing to the "end times" but declared that he had never said that "we must plan according to Armageddon." Jerry Falwell insisted, in a 1984 interview with Dugger, "that Reagan is not fatalistic and would not let his theological convictions affect his performance in office." "He made it very clear to me," Falwell emphasized, "that he in no way was approaching the presidency

Religious, and Political Portrait (San Francisco, 1987), 143–51; Stephen O'Leary and Michael McFarland, "The Political Use of Mythic Discourse: Prophetic Interpretation in Pat Robertson's Presidential Campaign," *Quarterly Journal of Speech*, LXXV (November, 1989), 433–52; James Mills, "The Serious Implications of a 1971 Conversation with Ronald Reagan: A Footnote to Current History," *San Diego Magazine*, August, 1985, pp. 140–41, 258; Larry Jones and Gerald T. Sheppard, "The Politics of Biblical Eschatology: Ronald Reagan and the Impending Nuclear Armageddon," *TSF Bulletin*, VIII (September–October, 1984), 17; Ronnie Dugger, "Does Reagan Expect a Nuclear Armageddon?" *Washington Post*, April 8, 1984, p. C1; *NYT*, October 21, 1984, p. 32.

10. See, for example, William Martin, "Waiting for the End," *Atlantic Monthly*, June, 1982, p. 36; *NYT*, October 21, 1984, p. 32, and October 25, 1984, p. A26; Boyer, *When Time Shall Be No More*, 143; Mills, "The Serious Implications of a 1971 Conversation with Ronald Reagan," 141; Grace Halsell, *Prophecy and Politics: Militant Evangelists on the Road to Nuclear War* (Westport, Conn., 1986), 9–10, 40. For the response of two radical evangelicals, see Jim Wallis, "Our Republican High Priest," *In These Times*, October 3–9, 1984, p. 16; Danny Collum, "Armageddon Theology as a Threat to Peace," *Faith and Mission*, Fall, 1986, p. 61.

with fatalism and in no way was he going to allow his theological convictions and personal beliefs to adversely affect his performance in the office." Indeed, by 1984, both Reagan and Falwell had backed away from the notion that the end of the world was imminent and that it would occur as a result of a nuclear holocaust. In 1981 Falwell had prophesied a nuclear war within fifty years; by 1984 he no longer foresaw such a conflict, thought the earth would not be destroyed "in the next 100, or even 500 years!," and stated his "earnest belief in the need for our government to negotiate for peace with the Soviet Union and other nations." During the 1984 presidential campaign he repudiated "any extremist world view which demands a nuclear Armageddon."[11]

Other evangelicals also emphasized that prophecy belief did not encourage advocacy of nuclear war or even a fatalistic acceptance of it. In 1984 Harold Lindsell contended that only a "small minority" of evangelicals objected to efforts to prevent nuclear war on the grounds that they contravened prophecy. In 1986, two of Falwell's lieutenants, Ed Dobson and Ed Hindson, published a lengthy article reacting to fears expressed during the 1984 presidential campaign regarding the Armageddon theology. They noted that apparently many people believed evangelicals would try to hasten the Second Coming of Christ by fomenting a crisis in the Middle East that could lead to a war between the Soviet Union and Israel or by provoking a conflict between the United States and the Soviet Union. Such beliefs, Dobson and Hindson declared, were based "on a profound misunderstanding of the Bible and what evangelicals actually believe." The two men conceded that a small minority of "extreme fundamentalists" was "complacent about evils such as nuclear proliferation." But they were few in number and had "eschewed politics altogether" so there was no reason to fear them. Speaking for the majority of evangelicals, Dobson and Hindson pointed out that besides the many Bible passages describing the end time, there were scores of passages outlining "Christian responsibilities in this world." Evangelicals, they insisted, "take both sets of passages seriously." Indeed, they declared, "Our enthusiastic political involvement is proof that we are not among those evangelicals whose apocalyptic

11. Dugger, "Does Reagan Expect a Nuclear Armageddon?" C4; Kenneth L. Woodward, "Arguing Armageddon," *Newsweek*, November 5, 1984, p. 91; Jerry Falwell, *Nuclear War and the Second Coming of Jesus Christ* (N.p., 1983), 2–5; Boyer, *When Time Shall Be No More*, 137–38.

views are a pretext for this-worldly despair." On the issue of national security, they pointed out: "Evangelicals are taking all the measures they can to ensure that the world is a safer place. Robertson, Falwell, and others are all outspoken advocates of strategic defense. . . . If we really wanted to accelerate the end, we would surely support the nuclear agenda of the American left and the Communist Party, because we firmly believe that unilateral disarmament is a sure way to send this country into the arms of its Maker." [12]

Looking back on the 1980s, Paul Boyer argues that prophecy beliefs had "obvious policy implications." Although he doubts that "prophecy believers consciously sought to bring on Armageddon as quickly as possible," he does contend that their views probably inclined them against efforts to limit the nuclear arms race or moderate Cold War tensions and reinforced their hostility toward the Soviet Union. He demonstrates that prophecy belief clearly motivated some evangelicals, such as Falwell, James Robison, and Harold Lindsell, to denounce peace activism and the antinuclear movement. But, as we will see, and as Dobson and Hindson pointed out, many of the televangelists who qualified as prophecy believers were strong supporters of Reagan's defense policies. Even Hal Lindsey, in *The 1980s: Countdown to Armageddon*, urged a massive increase in U.S. military power, including nuclear missiles, to gain superiority over the Soviet Union. "The Bible supports building a powerful military force," he declared. "And the Bible is telling the U.S. to become strong again." [13]

The controversy over the Armageddon theology was one aspect of a larger debate in the United States regarding national defense policy. The Reagan administration's military posture—its aggressive anticommunism and reluctance to negotiate arms limitation with the Soviet Union, its massive arms buildup, its shift from deterrence to war-

12. Boyer, *When Time Shall Be No More*, 143; Ed Dobson and Ed Hindson, "Apocalypse Now? What Fundamentalists Believe About the End of the World," *Policy Review*, Fall, 1986, pp. 16, 21–22. See also "Critics Fear That Reagan Is Swayed by Those Who Believe in a 'Nuclear Armageddon,'" *CT*, December 14, 1984, pp. 48, 51.

13. Boyer, *When Time Shall Be No More*, 144–45, 149, 174–75; Hal Lindsey, *The 1980's: Countdown to Armageddon* (New York, 1980), 149. In contrast to Boyer, Timothy P. Weber, *Living in the Shadow of the Second Coming: American Premillennialism, 1875–1982* (Chicago, 1987), 215, 225–26, 229, suggests a disinclination on the part of the premillennialists to emphasize the political, as opposed to the religious, implications of their doctrine.

fighting doctrine, as well as its talk of winnable or limited nuclear war—all helped infuse new strength in the peace movement in the United States. Many of the mainline churches were in the forefront of the antinuclear campaign that assumed center stage in the 1980s. As L. Bruce van Voorst has pointed out, except for the Quakers and other "peace" denominations, mainline churches and faith groups—Protestant, Catholic, and Jewish—had traditionally supported the defense policies of the United States. In a historic shift that began during the Vietnam era, the mainline groups moved toward a position of challenging government policy on deterrence and nuclear weapons.[14]

By the mid-1980s the National Catholic Conference of Bishops and several major Protestant denominations had issued official pronouncements opposing many of the Reagan administration policies. Media attention focused on the Roman Catholic document with its unequivocal condemnation of any strategy involving the initiation ("first use") of nuclear warfare or nuclear attacks on civilian targets. The position of many of the Protestant groups was not very different. A survey of the Catholic bishops and twelve Protestant denominations by Donald L. Davidson showed "striking similarity" among their positions on nuclear weapons issues. All thirteen "registered significant concern for nuclear arms control and limitation." None advocated unilateral nuclear disarmament, but all supported some concept of deterrence based on goals of "sufficiency," "parity," "balance," or "rough equivalency" with the Soviet Union. None advocated nuclear superiority of the United States. Davidson reported that of the thirteen, ten supported ratification of the SALT II agreement and eleven favored a mutual and verifiable freeze on nuclear weapons testing, development, and deployment. Six favored "unilateral initiatives" by the United States in arms reductions, and eight supported a policy of "no first use" of nuclear weapons. The Catholic bishops and the United Presbyterian Church questioned any "actual use" of nuclear weapons; five denominations went further in proscribing it. Although, as Davidson's survey shows, none of the mainline groups advocated pacifism, some of their leaders seemed to be mov-

14. Fox Butterfield, "Anatomy of the Nuclear Protest," *New York Times Magazine*, July 11, 1982, p. 14; "On the March—U.S. Version of Peace Crusade," *U.S. News & World Report*, March 22, 1982, p. 25; L. Bruce van Voorst, "The Churches and Nuclear Deterrence," in *The Political Role of Religion in the United States*, ed. Stephen D. Johnson and Joseph B. Tamney (Boulder, Colo., 1986), 280.

ing in that direction. In May, 1985, for example, a group including several mainline leaders issued·a statement, prepared and circulated by the American Friends Service Committee, which called upon Congress to refuse funding for the Star Wars defense system and rejected "any system of security based on fear and intimidation." Signers included Reverend Dwain Epps, director for international affairs of the National Council of Churches, Avery Post, president of the United Church of Christ, and Catholic bishops Thomas Gumbleton of Detroit and Walter Sullivan of Richmond.[15]

The antinuclear pronouncements of the mainline churches bedeviled Reagan throughout his presidency, but midway through his first term it was the nuclear freeze movement that demanded his attention. The campaign to halt the testing, production, and further deployment of nuclear weapons enlisted thousands of Americans, including many religious folk, and spawned a host of ad hoc committees, forums, workshops, and demonstrations, including one of the largest ever in New York City on June 12, 1982. In a referendum held during the fall elections of that year, twelve million Americans voted for a freeze on nuclear weapons.[16]

As the freeze movement gained momentum, Reagan sought evangelicals' assistance in promoting his peace-through-strength program. In the same speech to the NAE in which he labeled the Soviet Union "the focus of evil in the modern world," he urged evangelicals "to speak out against those who would place the United States in a position of military and moral inferiority" and "to resist . . . those who would have you withhold your support for our efforts . . . to keep America strong and free, while we negotiate real and verifiable reductions in the world's nuclear arsenals." He maintained that a freeze offered only "the illusion of peace," for it would eliminate "any incentive for the Soviets to negotiate seriously in Geneva," would in effect sustain their military buildup, and would prevent the United States from modernizing its defenses, leaving "our aging forces increasingly vulnerable."[17]

---

15. Donald L. Davidson, *Nuclear Weapons and the American Churches: Ethical Positions on Modern Warfare* (Boulder, Colo., 1983), 180–81, Appendix B; "Group Opposes 'Star Wars' Funding," *Washington Post*, May 14, 1985, p. A8; A. James Reichley, *Religion in American Public Life* (Washington, D.C., 1985), 353.

16. Jim Wallis, *Agenda for Biblical People* (San Francisco, 1984), xiii.

17. Reagan, "Remarks at the Annual Convention of the National Association of Evangelicals," 363–64.

As we will see in the next chapter, evangelicals did not speak with a single voice on national defense in the 1980s. Nevertheless, many of them did support Reagan's peace-through-strength policy. None was more enthusiastic than the New Christian Right, the coalition of tele-vangelists and political pressure groups that captured the national lime-light during the presidential campaign of 1980. That there should be a close fit between the NCR and the Reagan administration on defense policy is not surprising. The mobilization strategies and policy views of the NCR, even its moralistic approach to politics, closely tracked those of the secular New Right. Indeed, New Right strategists such as Paul Weyrich, Howard Phillips, and Richard Viguerie helped to bring the NCR into existence. In an interview published in 1986, Falwell explicitly acknowledged the New Christian Right's indebtedness. "The New Right has had a positive influence on the Christian Right," he told *Christianity Today*. "They have educated us on many of the issues, giving us political savvy in a hurry." It was no coincidence that Falwell's 1980 manifesto *Listen America!* echoed Viguerie's *The New Right: We're Ready to Lead* (which, incidentally, featured an introductory commendation by Falwell).[18]

Not premillennialist Armageddon theology but a profound hatred of communism motivated the NCR activists to endorse Reagan's national defense policies. When the president described the Soviet Union as an "evil empire" and "the focus of evil in the modern world," some evan-

---

18. "Where Is Jerry Falwell Headed in 1986?" *CT*, February 21, 1986, p. 39; Jerry Falwell, *Listen America!* (Garden City, N.Y., 1980); Richard A. Viguerie, *The New Right: We're Ready to Lead* (Falls Church, Va., 1980), esp. Chap. 7, "Our Goal: Military Superiority." On the alliance between President Reagan and conservative evangelicals in the 1980s, see Jeffrey K. Hadden and Anson Shupe, *Televangelism: Power and Politics on God's Frontier* (New York, 1988), 27–36, 288–89. On the relationship between the New Christian Right and the secular New Right, see Michael Lienesch, *Redeeming America: Piety and Politics in the New Christian Right* (Chapel Hill, 1993), 8–9, 11–12; Richard A. Viguerie, "Born-Again Christians: A New Political Force," *Conservative Digest*, August, 1979, p. 48; Paul Weyrich, "Building the Moral Majority," *Conservative Digest*, August, 1979, pp. 18–19; "Mobilizing the Moral Majority," *Conservative Digest*, August, 1979, pp. 14–16; Robert Zwier and Richard Smith, "Christian Politics and the New Right," *Christian Century*, XCVII (October 8, 1980), 937–38; Jerome L. Himmelstein, "The New Right," in *The New Christian Right: Mobilization and Legitimation*, ed. Robert C. Liebman and Robert Wuthnow (New York, 1983), 17. To supplement my discussion of the conservative evangelical position on national defense policies, see Lienesch, *Redeeming America*, Chap. 5.

gelicals may have heard an echo of end-time prophecy, but others surely interpreted the phrasing literally. As Michael Lienesch points out, in the view of conservative evangelicals, "communism embodies cosmo-logical evil. . . . It is not simply immoral, it is self-consciously immoral, at war with God and all goodness. . . . with heaven itself. . . . [It is,] in essence, demonic."[19] Whatever fatalism the Armageddon theology may have induced was counterbalanced by the energizing impulse to fight godless international communism.

Jerry Falwell asserted the fundamental proposition on which conser-vative evangelicals based their national defense position: "The number one problem in the world today is, without question, communism." Falwell insisted that ever since the Bolshevik revolution, its primary, unwavering objective had been "world conquest." In *Listen America!* he declared, "If there ever was a time for a strong national defense it is today." For fifteen years, the United States had been declining militarily so that now it stood "at the threshold of destruction or surrender." In offensive nuclear weaponry, as well as defensive weaponry, the United States lagged behind the Soviet Union, which was "determined to con-quer our free country and infiltrate the American people with godless communism." He denigrated the policy of nuclear deterrence based on mutual assured destruction. "The acronym for mutual assured destruc-tion is 'mad,'" he pointed out. "That is exactly what the defense strategy in this country is today. With mutual assured destruction, we have vir-tually no defense and an overwhelmingly unacceptable offense."[20]

Given their advocacy of a strong national defense that would give the United States military superiority over the Soviet Union and their will-ingness to engage in confrontation with that nation, even at the risk of nuclear war, it is not surprising that the NCR televangelists vigorously opposed containment, détente, nuclear disarmament, and, of course, pacifism. In their view, the Carter administration's defense and foreign policies, including the SALT II negotiations, were only the latest ver-sion of what Falwell called a "no fight and no win policy" that reached back to the end of World War II. During and after the 1980 presidential

19. Lienesch, *Redeeming America*, 214. See also John A. Bernbaum, "Which Roads Lead to Peace?" *Eternity*, December, 1983, pp. 21–22.

20. Jerry Strober and Ruth Tomczak, *Jerry Falwell: Aflame for God* (Nashville, 1979), 159; Falwell, *Listen America!*, 97, 9–10, 100. See also Jerry Falwell, ed., with Ed Dobson and Ed Hindson, *The Fundamentalist Phenomenon: The Resurgence of Conservative Chris-tianity* (Garden City, N.Y., 1981), 190, 212–15.

campaign, he and other televangelists blasted Carter's military policy as a "blatant compromise with Communism" and the SALT II agreement as "a sell-out to the Soviets."[21]

President Reagan clearly appreciated the help of the televangelists in winning support for his defense program. In March, 1983, he invited Jerry Falwell to the White House to discuss the nuclear freeze movement and the best way of combating it. Haynes Johnson described a Falwell aide's account of the meeting:

> Reagan . . . remarked that Falwell was the only major conservative minister speaking out in opposition to the nuclear freeze. He mused aloud about why it was so difficult for him to get his peace-through-strength message across to the country. Falwell replied that one of the problems was the extremely complicated nature of the subject: the president's case hadn't been boiled down into the language the average citizen, the farmers and laborers of America, could understand. If the president could supply him with such language, and the official facts and figures to back them up, he, Falwell, would be proud to carry that case to the public.

According to the account, President Reagan then called in an aide and ordered that such material be prepared for Falwell. A few days later, the evangelist received a briefing by National Security Council aides, who loaded him down with charts and graphs and other information presenting the president's argument regarding the Soviet military threat and America's weakened defense system "in laymen's language." Falwell had his political pressure group, Moral Majority, Inc., translate that material into even more simplified language and begin distributing it to the American people. Among other things, Moral Majority ran full-page ads in major newspapers warning: "We cannot afford to be number two in defense! But, sadly enough, that's where we are today. Number two. And fading!" The ads also impugned the loyalty of the "freezeniks," "ultralibs," and "unilateral disarmers" who were attacking the president for wanting to build up U.S. military strength. In addition to the ads, Falwell himself preached the peace-through-strength gospel over the airwaves and on television, in interviews and special speaking engagements. "His electronic audiences hear him describe what the president

21. Falwell, *Listen America!*, 104; Kenneth A. Briggs, "Evangelicals Turning to Politics Fear Moral Slide Imperils Nation," *NYT*, August 19, 1980, p. D17; Edward E. Plowman, "Is Morality All Right?" *CT*, November 2, 1979, p. 80. See also John Maust, "Evangelist James Robison: Making Waves—and a Name," *CT*, March 21, 1980, p. 50.

'told me' and how the National Security Council 'briefed me,'" Johnson wrote. "He asks listeners if they are going to take the word of the president and the secretary of defense, as relayed through himself, or others? And he makes dark allusions to those advocating a nuclear freeze having 'links with the Kremlin.'" [22]

Reagan also got help from Falwell, Pat Robertson, and other televangelists of the New Christian Right in promoting his Strategic Defense Initiative (SDI), also known as Star Wars. For example, D. James Kennedy preached a sermon in the Coral Ridge Presbyterian Church in which he cited the building of the wall around Jerusalem in the Book of Nehemiah as a scriptural justification of SDI. Like Reagan, who touted the morality of SDI, the televangelists endorsed it as a morally superior replacement for the policy of mutual assured destruction, which they regarded as not only militarily questionable but, as Kennedy believed, "immoral." In 1986 televangelists Kennedy and Falwell, along with Jimmy Swaggart, Rex Humbard, and Jim Bakker, joined other prominent activists in the New Christian Right (Bill Bright, Tim LaHaye, and Ben Armstrong, executive director of the National Religious Broadcasters) to form the Religious Coalition for a Moral Defense Policy. In a statement praising SDI, the coalition declared that it "offers the real prospect of providing a morally and perhaps also militarily superior policy . . . designed to protect and save lives rather than to brutally avenge them." [23]

The formation of the Religious Coalition for a Moral Defense Policy

22. Haynes Johnson, "A Preacher for 'Peace Through Strength' or, Maybe, the Bomb," *Washington Post*, April 2, 1983, p. A3. For the advertisement Johnson referred to, see "An Open Letter from Jerry Falwell on the Nuclear Freeze," *Moral Majority Report*, April, 1983, pp. 10–11.

23. Harrell, *Pat Robertson*, 193; D. James Kennedy, "Surviving the Nuclear Age" (Sermon delivered at the Coral Ridge Presbyterian Church, Fort Lauderdale, Florida, *ca.* 1986; brochure published by Coral Ridge Ministries, Fort Lauderdale, Florida, n.d.); D. James Kennedy to the author, January 19, 1995; D. James Kennedy, telephone conversation with author, December 20, 1994; Sharon Anderson, "Christians Take Sides on Proposed Defense System," *CT*, April 4, 1986, p. 43; "Religious Leaders and Groups Endorse 'Star Wars' as Moral Defense Policy," *Command*, No. 4, 1986, p. 29. On "the specific moral vision" of SDI, see Steven Lee, "The Moral Vision of Strategic Defense," in *Ethics and Strategic Defense: American Philosophers Debate Star Wars and the Future of Nuclear Deterrence*, ed. Douglas P. Lackey (Belmont, Calif., 1989), 79; and Keith B. Payne and Karl I. Payne, *A Just Defense: The Use of Force, Nuclear Weapons and Our Conscience* (Portland, Ore., 1987), 267–68.

reminds us that the many political pressure groups associated with the New Christian Right constituted an important element of the televangelists' effectiveness in promoting President Reagan's peace-through-strength policy. Throughout the 1980s Falwell used the monthly newsletter of Moral Majority to denounce the nuclear freeze, unilateral disarmament and SALT II and to support Reagan's peace-through-strength program and the Strategic Defense Initiative. In 1986 he organized a second group, the Liberty Federation, expressly designed to promote such programs as SDI and "Freedom Fights in Angola, Central America, Afghanistan, and elsewhere." Christian Voice also endorsed Reagan's military and foreign policy agenda. Like the Liberty Federation, it had been formed, in 1979, to translate evangelical zeal on moral issues into righteous outrage against such travesties as the SALT II treaty. During the late 1970s and early 1980s it regularly assigned congressmen a "morality rating" on SALT II, and in the mid-1980s, its *Candidates Biblical Scoreboard* described support for the Strategic Defense Initiative as a "pro-biblical" position.[24]

Thus the televangelists and political pressure groups of the NCR, with their vast television audiences and loyal grass-roots constituency, proved enormously helpful to President Reagan in promoting his defense policies. Nevertheless, during the 1980s a significant segment of the evangelical community evinced increasing skepticism regarding the NCR's methods and arguments. The very militancy that aided Reagan further divided the already fragmented evangelical community.

24. "Nuclear Freeze? No!" *Moral Majority Report*, April 26, 1982, p. 6; G. Russell Evans, "Peace Won't Come from SOB, SAGA, MAM," *Moral Majority Report*, October, 1982, p. 10; G. Russell Evans, "Shall America Be Defended?" *Moral Majority Report*, September 15, 1980, p. 8; Daniel O. Graham, "Dense Pack: Intelligence Insult," *Moral Majority Report*, February, 1983, p. 15; Richard Alvarez, "Geneva's Real Meaning: The Soviets Are Scared," *Moral Majority Report*, May, 1985, p. 3; Richard Alvarez, "Reagan Must Not Bargain Away Star Wars Program, Experts Say," *Moral Majority Report*, November, 1985, p. 10; Jerry Falwell, "'Americans Must Help El Salvador Now,'" *Moral Majority Report*, October, 1983, p. 3; James M. Wall, "A Vision of the Future, Not a Tired Agenda," *Christian Century*, CIII (January 22, 1986), 59; Connaught Marshner, "How Jerry Falwell Is Driving the Left to an Early Grave," *Conservative Digest*, June, 1986, p. 94; "Where Is Jerry Falwell Headed in 1986?" 39; Snowball, *Continuity and Change in the Rhetoric of the Moral Majority*, 97–98, 100, 106; "The Religious Lobby," *Newsweek*, July 16, 1979, pp. 37–38; Beth Spring, "Christian Voice Gains Visibility Following Realignment of New Right," *CT*, November 7, 1986, p. 47.

16

Debating National Security Policy

Once the New Christian Right joined the national debate over American defense policy, other evangelicals were inevitably drawn into it. Even if the NCR had not taken a position, evangelicals' emphasis on social responsibility would surely have led them to confront one of the key issues of the 1980s. As we saw in Chapter 9, the social and political involvement that *Newsweek* and other newsmagazines "discovered" in 1976 had been developing since the late 1940s. (The NCR, which garnered most of the media attention in the late 1970s and early 1980s, was actually a latecomer in comparison with other segments of the evangelical community.)

Evangelicals' "new engagement" with political and social issues had intensified markedly in the 1960s and early 1970s. During that period, the development of differing approaches to sociopolitical involvement and the Vietnam War produced a seemingly irreparable division between mainstream and dissenting evangelicals. In 1973, however, members of the two camps cooperated in a Conference of Evangelicals for Social Concern. The mainstream evangelicals included Frank E. Gaebelein, a former editor of *Christianity Today*, and Carl F. H. Henry. They joined with liberal-minded dissenters Lewis Smedes, Richard Pierard, and Ronald J. Sider and radical evangelicals Jim Wallis, Joe Roos, and John Howard Yoder. The conference issued a document called "The Chicago Declaration" exhorting fellow evangelicals to engage in "a Christian discipleship that confronts the social and political injustice of our nation" and to "acknowledge our Christian responsibilities of citizenship." Significantly, "The Chicago Declaration" also contained a section challenging "the misplaced trust of the nation in economic and military might—a proud trust that promotes a national pathology of war and violence which victimizes our neighbors at home and abroad."[1]

The conference that issued "The Chicago Declaration" of 1973 also formed a group called Evangelicals for Social Action (ESA) with headquarters in Philadelphia. Ron Sider, its president, once described himself as "a deeply committed Anabaptist pacifist, although not of the quietist variety." Sider's Anabaptist perspective notwithstanding, in its early years the ESA stood only slightly to the left of mainstream evangelicals such as Carl Henry.[2]

Cooperation between mainstream, dissenting, and radical evangelicals proved to be short-lived. By the late 1970s many of the radicals had come to regard nuclear war as the "overarching moral question" facing Americans in the late twentieth century. Accordingly, in 1978, the group of radicals formerly known as the People's Christian Coalition, now calling themselves Sojourners, organized a conference on nuclear issues attended by more than one hundred evangelical, neo-orthodox, and liberal Christian leaders. Out of it came "A Call to Faithfulness" urging the United States government to "take meaningful unilateral and multilateral initiatives toward the goal of complete nuclear disarmament." Specifically, it recommended halting all nuclear weapons systems and issuing a declaration that the United States would "never be the first to use nuclear weapons, and that it recognizes that they are legitimate neither as political instruments or as military weapons."[3]

The year after Sojourners issued its "Call to Faithfulness," the board

1. Ronald J. Sider, ed., *The Chicago Declaration* (Carol Stream, Ill., 1974), 1–3. Another landmark declaration endorsing sociopolitical involvement came out of the Congress on World Evangelization meeting in Lausanne, Switzerland, in 1974. See William Martin, *A Prophet with Honor: The Billy Graham Story* (New York, 1991), 449; Richard Quebedeaux, *The Worldly Evangelicals* (San Francisco, 1978), 59–60; Robert Booth Fowler, *A New Engagement: Evangelical Political Thought, 1960–1976* (Grand Rapids, 1982), 35.

2. Ronald J. Sider, "An Evangelical Vision for American Democracy: An Anabaptist Perspective," in *The Bible, Politics, and Democracy*, ed. Richard John Neuhaus (Grand Rapids, 1987), 32–33; "Stacking Sandbags against a Conservative Flood," *CT*, November 2, 1979, p. 76.

3. "The New Abolitionist Covenant" (1980) in Jim Wallis, ed., *Waging Peace: A Handbook for the Struggle to Abolish Nuclear Weapons* (San Francisco, 1982), 17; "Prominent Voices Want Nuclear Disarmament," *Eternity*, August, 1978, p. 6. The People's Christian Coalition, publishers of the *Post-American*, had moved to Washington, D.C., and formed the Sojourners Community (and renamed their newspaper *Sojourners*).

of ESA refused to endorse it on the ground that it supported unilateral disarmament. ESA issued its own "Call to Responsible Christian Action" in which it urged "Christians concerned for our society to search out biblical principles to govern and direct that concern." Citing Jesus' call to be peacemakers, ESA declared, "We must endeavor in every way possible to promote peace among individual human beings, social classes, and even nations."[4]

Thus a year before the 1980 presidential campaign, not only the activists of the New Christian Right but other evangelicals had begun to take sides on national defense policy. Then came the bombshell dropped by the most prominent and revered evangelical preacher in the United States, Billy Graham. In March, 1979, during an interview on the *CBS Evening News*, the onetime Cold Warrior labeled the arms race and the proliferation of nuclear weapons "insanity, madness" and urged negotiations to reduce and eventually eliminate armaments. In subsequent interviews, articles, and speeches, he not only endorsed SALT II but called for "SALT 10," an arms limitation agreement that would effect "the bilateral, verifiable eradication of all nuclear, biochemical and laser weapons used for mass destruction."[5]

The stand taken by the radical evangelicals, ESA, and Billy Graham, the clamor raised by NCR televangelists and political pressure groups, and the burgeoning antinuclear movement in the United States and Europe all thrust the issues of national defense policy and nuclear war to the forefront of discussion within the evangelical community. In response, *Christianity Today* began to increase coverage of such issues. The key figure behind this was the new editor appointed in 1978, Kenneth Kantzer. In the fall of 1980, as the presidential campaign shifted into high gear, Kantzer began publishing editorials on the nuclear arms issue. Between late November, 1980, and January, 1983, he laid out *Christianity Today*'s position. Although he professed respect for pacifists, he stated that "across-the-board pacifism is both unbiblical and unrealistic." Although he regarded certain types of nuclear war as "unthinkable," he would not use just war doctrine to rule out the use of

4. "Stacking Sandbags Against a Conservative Flood," 76–77.

5. Richard V. Pierard, "Billy Graham and Vietnam: From Cold Warrior to Peacemaker," *Christian Scholar's Review*, X (1980), 37–38; Martin, *Prophet*, 500. See also Carol Flake, *Redemptorama: Culture, Politics, and the New Evangelicalism* (Garden City, N.Y., 1984), 270–73; Billy Graham, "Graham's Mission to Moscow," *CT*, June 18, 1982, p. 23.

nuclear weapons. "No Christian can defend indiscriminate mass slaughter of noncombatants," he wrote. "But strategic bombing of military centers, even when noncombatants become involved, does not seem to be inherently different from what in the past has been accepted as necessary and just." Citing World War II, he noted that even just wars brought "incalculable suffering" to millions of civilians. He added:

> Suffering and death in themselves are not sufficient reasons to rule out the justice of a nation's decision to wage war (assuming, of course, that physical human life on this earth is not the highest good). The decisive questions are: Does the government seek a good and just end? Will war deter the rampant spread of evil? Will it bring about justice, a greater sense of human dignity, a wider human freedom? These things, even in the relative and limited degree to which they are possible among fallen humanity, are truly worth fighting and dying for. And at crucial times in the right places it is even necessary for the follower of Christ to take life—in the name of human justice.[6]

Kantzer was as critical of the New Christian Right as he was of the pacifists. Discussing SALT II, he argued that the nation's military goal should not be superiority over or even "exact parity" with the Soviet Union but "a rough parity" that would enable the United States to maintain "an adequate deterrent force." Noting that during his presidential campaign Ronald Reagan had denounced SALT II as a bad treaty, Kantzer held him responsible for negotiating a better one. Kantzer himself proposed a treaty incorporating the freeze proposed by Senator Mark Hatfield. If the Soviets refused to agree to a moratorium on all nuclear weapons, Kantzer continued, "we should still—reluctantly—seek a new SALT treaty that will at least limit nuclear arms. Even a quarter-loaf is better than no loaf at all."[7]

By 1983 Kantzer had settled on a position advocating a system of "limited nuclear defense" combined with negotiations with the Soviets aiming at a bilateral freeze on the construction of nuclear warheads and gradual reduction of nuclear and conventional weapons. The ultimate

---

6. "In Matters of War and Peace . . . ," *CT*, November 21, 1980, pp. 14–15. See also "Of Prophetic Robes and Weather Vanes: An Interview with Kenneth Kantzer," *CT*, April 7, 1978, pp. 22, 25–26.

7. "SALT II: The Only Alternative to Annihilation?" *CT*, March 27, 1981, pp. 14–15.

goal would be "the repudiation of all weapons, both nuclear and conventional."[8]

Kantzer was only one of a number of mainstream evangelical leaders, including John Stott and Billy Graham, who harped continually on the importance of evangelicals confronting the nuclear issue during the early 1980s. "The evangelical community by and large seems little troubled about the possible obliteration of untold millions of human beings in a nuclear catastrophe that could be set off by the frightened push of a button," Frank Gaebelein observed in an article published in *Christianity Today* in October, 1981. "Were the same degree of intensity that many evangelicals bring to the antiabortion movement to characterize a widespread evangelical protest against nuclear proliferation, the race toward worldwide destruction might be slowed down and a courageous stand for all life be taken in the name of the Prince of Peace."[9]

Besides their leaders and *Christianity Today*, other forces, both within and outside the evangelical community, were pressuring mainstream evangelicals to confront the issues of nuclear war and national defense policy. One came from the radical evangelical camp, which issued two books in 1982: *Nuclear Holocaust and Christian Hope: A Book for Christian Peacemakers* and *Waging Peace, a Handbook for the Struggle to Abolish Nuclear Weapons*.[10] The authors of *Nuclear Holocaust* were Ron Sider and Richard K. Taylor. Taylor was a consultant for the Sojourners Com-

8. "A Proposal to Tilt the Balance of Terror," *CT*, April 9, 1982, pp. 16–19; Kenneth S. Kantzer, "What Shall We Do About the Nuclear Problem?" *CT*, January 21, 1983, pp. 9–11.

9. Frank E. Gaebelein, "Heeding the Whole Counsel of God," *CT*, October 2, 1981, p. 30. See also John R. W. Stott, "Calling for Peacemakers in a Nuclear Age, Part I," *CT*, February 8, 1980, pp. 44–45, and "Calling for Peacemakers in a Nuclear Age, Part II," *CT*, March 7, 1980, pp. 44–45; "Peace Studies," *CT*, March 7, 1980, p. 43; Robert Culver, "Between War and Peace: Old Debate in a New Age," *CT*, October 24, 1980, pp. 31–34, 51, and see also editorial note on p. 30; Robert D. Culver, "Justice Is Something Worth Fighting For," and John Drescher, "Why Christians Shouldn't Carry Swords," *CT*, November 7, 1980, p. 14–17, 20–23, 25; "Mark Hatfield Taps into the Real Power on Capitol Hill," *CT*, October 22, 1982, pp. 21–22; Billy Graham, "Peace: At Times a Sword and Fire," *CT*, December 17, 1982, p. 25; "Bill Armstrong: Senator and Christian," *CT*, November 11, 1983, pp. 22–23.

10. Ronald J. Sider and Richard K. Taylor, *Nuclear Holocaust and Christian Hope: A Book for Christian Peacemakers* (New York, 1982); Jim Wallis, ed., *Waging Peace: A Handbook for the Struggle to Abolish Nuclear Weapons* (San Francisco, 1982). See also Beth Spring and Rodney Clapp, "Evangelicals Jump with Both Feet into Debate on Nuclear Arms," *CT*, October 8, 1982, pp. 64–66.

munity and Evangelicals for Social Action. Sider was a professor of theology at Eastern Baptist Theological Seminary in Philadelphia and still president of ESA, the organization that in 1973 had refused to endorse the radical evangelicals' "Call to Faithfulness." By the early 1980s, however, ESA had moved closer to the views of the radicals (and of its Anabaptist president). The editor of *Waging Peace* was Jim Wallis, leader of Sojourners. All three authors were pacifists (Taylor was a Quaker), but they aimed their arguments at nonpacifist mainstream evangelicals.

In an effort to break down the barrier separating evangelical pacifists from their mainstream brethren, for example, the authors contended that the advent of the nuclear age had rendered irrelevant the centuries-old division between pacifists and advocates of just war. Nuclear war, nuclear deterrence in the form of mutual assured destruction, even limited nuclear defense were options Christians could no longer countenance. "Today," Sider and Taylor wrote, "all Christians must say no to the possession and use of nuclear weapons." Wallis made the same point using even stronger, more prophetic language: "The willingness to produce, possess, and use nuclear weapons must be named for what it is: the chief manifestation of human sinfulness and rebellion against God in our age. The nuclear arms race is not just one issue among many: it is the overriding idolatry of our time." As part of their effort to persuade mainstream evangelicals, radical evangelicals also insisted that their position on nuclear arms did not grow out of theological liberalism but was grounded in "the heart of historic Christian orthodoxy." Because they were designed as handbooks to be used by individuals and churches, the two books not only presented a theological perspective but also made practical recommendations to those who would "follow Christ as peacemakers in the 1980s and '90s," encouraging them to work for such goals as multilateral arms reduction agreements and the "mutual 'freeze' of nuclear weapons by the United States and the USSR."[11] (As we have seen, these goals were also advocated by mainstream evangelicals such as Billy Graham and Kenneth Kantzer.)

The radical evangelicals went beyond their mainstream brethren in urging other actions that were based on a pacifist perspective. Both

---

11. Sider and Taylor, *Nuclear Holocaust*, 59, 96, 154, 159, 162, 213–14, 225; Wallis, "Introduction: A Time to Wage Peace," in *Waging Peace*, 5, 13. See also "New Abolitionist Covenant," 20, and Danny Collum, "Freezing the Arms Race: The First Step Toward Disarmament," in *Waging Peace*, ed. Wallis, 220–26.

books, for example, urged Christians to lessen their support for the military and to stop cooperating with the nation's preparations for nuclear war. Specifically, this meant, according to Sider and Taylor, refusing to enter the armed forces (by claiming conscientious objector status), refusing to work in military-related jobs (in the Defense Department, for example, or in private industry or military research and development), and refusing to pay taxes that supported the defense budget. Both books also urged Christians to work for the eventual establishment of a nonmilitary defense system which the authors insisted would be "consistent with the love ethic of Jesus Christ" and which they defined as "systematic, organized, active, nonviolent resistance against a power which is regarded as evil, unjust or contrary to a particular way of life." [12]

Mainstream evangelicals had long tolerated, if somewhat begrudgingly, their pacifist brethren in the so-called historic peace churches. The radical evangelicals, however, were a different matter. Some of them came from those churches (Sider, for example, from the Mennonite Brethren and Taylor from the Quakers), but instead of imitating their quietism, they aggressively sought converts within the evangelical community. Mainstream evangelicals ultimately found a way of undermining the arguments of the radical evangelicals, in effect tarring them with the same brush they used on the New Christian Right. In 1982, however, mainstream evangelicals were on the defensive—and the radicals were not the only ones putting pressure on them.

In June, 1982, the National Catholic Conference of Bishops published the first draft of its pastoral letter "The Challenge of Peace: God's Promise and Our Response," and the final draft came out the following year. The United Methodist Church, the Episcopal Church, the Lutheran Church in America, the American Lutheran Church, and the Southern Baptist Convention also issued statements on defense and nuclear weapons in 1982. (The National Council of Churches and most of the other mainline Protestant denominations had already adopted strong antinuclear positions.) [13]

At the opposite end of the political spectrum stood the New Christian Right. As we saw in the previous chapter, in the winter of 1982, and

12. Sider and Taylor, *Nuclear Holocaust*, 169–81, 234, 259. See also Chaps. 14 and 15; "New Abolitionist Covenant," 18, 19.

13. Donald L. Davidson, *Nuclear Weapons and the American Churches: Ethical Positions on Modern Warfare* (Boulder, Colo., 1983), Chaps. 5 and 6.

especially in the spring of 1983, as the nuclear freeze movement gained momentum, NCR leaders and organizations stepped up their attacks on "freezeniks," "ultra libs," "unilateral disarmers," and anyone else who disagreed with them. In March, 1983, at the NAE convention in Orlando, Florida, President Reagan denounced the Soviet Union as "an evil empire" and appealed to the NAE delegates "to resist the attempts of those who would have you withhold your support for our efforts, this administration's efforts, to keep America strong and free."[14]

A final pressure on mainstream evangelicals came late in 1983. Fuller Theological Seminary, once the preeminent institution of the new evangelicalism but now moving toward a more "open evangelicalism," issued a "Declaration of Conscience" on the arms race which was published in *Christianity Today* and *Eternity*. It provided a summary statement of the position an increasing number of mainstream evangelical leaders were taking. It denied that an "all-out war" between the United States and the Soviet Union could be a just war, repudiated the drive for military superiority over the Soviets, and urged the leaders of the United States "to press now for a bilateral nuclear arms control and arms reduction agreement." In the conclusion, the Fuller Seminary "Declaration" exhorted Christians to "open their consciences" to the nuclear issue.[15]

If mainstream evangelicals could not ignore the pressures of 1982–1983, neither could the National Association of Evangelicals, generally considered the representative of mainstream evangelicalism. Indeed, Carl Henry faulted the organization for doing too little to guide evangelicals in "today's cultural and political crisis," and Ron Sider specifically criticized it for failing to take a position on the issue of nuclear arms and national defense policy. It meant, Sider observed, that "the most prominent evangelical organization in America is going to stay neutral on our most important societal issue."[16]

14. Ronald Reagan, "Remarks at the Annual Convention of the National Association of Evangelicals in Orlando, Florida," March 8, 1983, in *Public Papers of the Presidents of the United States: Ronald Reagan, 1983* (Washington, D.C., 1984), Book I, p. 364.

15. Fuller Theological Seminary, "A Declaration of Conscience About the Arms Race," *CT*, November 11, 1983, unpaginated insert; *Eternity*, November, 1983, unpaginated insert. On Fuller Theological Seminary, see George Marsden, *Reforming Fundamentalism: Fuller Seminary and the New Evangelicalism* (Grand Rapids, 1987), 266.

16. "The Concerns and Considerations of Carl F. H. Henry," *CT*, March 13, 1981, p. 22; Beth Spring, "Reagan Courts Evangelical Clout Against Nuclear Freeze," *CT*, April 8, 1983, p. 48.

Partly because of the diversity of its constituency, which included pacifists as well as peace-through-strength advocates, and partly because it had no strong tradition of political involvement, the NAE entered the debate over national defense policy and nuclear war reluctantly and with "much trepidation," to quote an article in its magazine. In 1977, 1979, and again in 1982, NAE conventions had passed brief resolutions expressing alarm at the proliferation and buildup of nuclear weaponry and the "threat of nuclear holocaust" and urging the nation's leaders "to obtain a meaningful arms control agreement that will scale down the nuclear arms race."[17] But in the early 1980s the organization seemed unwilling—or unable—to do more than that.

During 1982 and 1983 both the peace-through-strength and the nuclear freeze people courted the NAE. But even when President Reagan appealed directly to the delegates at the organization's annual meeting in March, 1983, he failed to persuade them to climb aboard the peace-through-strength bandwagon. Following the convention, the NAE leadership reasserted its position in the nuclear debate: it had no intention of siding with either the pro-freeze or peace-through-strength advocates; indeed, it emphasized "an individualized involvement in politics rather than an institutionalized involvement."[18]

In April, 1983, the head of the NAE's Office of Public Affairs, Robert P. Dugan, Jr., alerted evangelicals to the need to become well informed on the political and social issues at stake in the nuclear debate. That same month, an article in *Christianity Today* pointed to ongoing discussion of national security issues within the NAE, spearheaded by its Evangelical Social Action Commission (ESAC). (The ESAC dated back to 1951. In 1973, having merged with the Commission on Evangelical Action, it began to work closely with the Office of Public Affairs. Like that office, which began to focus greater attention on political and social issues in the late 1970s, the ESAC helped prod the traditionally conservative NAE toward greater social and political involvement. The

17. Brian O'Connell, "NAE's Bold Bid for Peace Freedom and Security," *UEA*, July–August, 1987, p. 4; "NAE Convention," *UEA*, Spring, 1977, p. 29; "The Threat of War," *UEA*, Summer, 1979, p. 25; "Convention '82: 'Save the Family,'" *UEA*, Summer, 1982, p. 30.

18. Spring and Clapp, "Evangelicals Jump with Both Feet into Debate on Nuclear Arms," 64–65; "Backgrounder," *UEA*, March–April, 1983, p. 1; David L. McKenna, "Bandwagon Ethics," *UEA*, March–April, 1983, p. 13; Spring, "Reagan Courts Evangelical Clout Against Nuclear Freeze," 44–45.

ESAC, for example, had helped secure passage of the 1979 resolution on nuclear weaponry.)[19]

In May, 1983, the NAE commissioned a Gallup poll to discover what its constituency was thinking about nuclear policy questions. Based on interviews with 1,540 adults in three hundred communities in the United States, 17 percent of whom identified themselves as evangelicals, the poll revealed that their views did not differ markedly from those of nonevangelicals. When asked if they approved or disapproved of President Reagan's handling of the nuclear arms situation, 41 percent of evangelicals and 43 percent of the general public approved. Sixty percent of evangelicals and 75 percent of nonevangelicals supported "an agreement between the United States and the Soviet Union for an immediate, verifiable freeze on the testing, production, and deployment of nuclear weapons." A consultant to the Gallup organization who analyzed the results for NAE explained the paradoxical result that evangelicals approved Reagan policies but also supported a nuclear freeze. He argued that most respondents approached the freeze question hypothetically. "What evangelicals are saying is, if the Soviets agree to a freeze and we can have on-site inspection, that would be wonderful; but realistically it can't be expected." Indeed, the poll showed that 76 percent of evangelicals and 78 percent of nonevangelicals did not believe the Soviet Union would agree to on-site inspection of its nuclear weapons. Consequently, the poll seemed to show that evangelicals leaned toward Reagan's peace-through-strength policy and a continued arms buildup. For example, more than half of the evangelical group (54 percent) said they believed U.S. nuclear inferiority to the Soviet Union posed a greater risk of war than a continuation of the nuclear arms race in the United States and the Soviet Union. Only 15 percent of evangelicals favored a unilateral freeze. The Gallup poll also showed that a comparatively large proportion of evangelicals (around 10 percent more than nonevangelicals) had no opinion on the nuclear debate. According to *Christianity Today*, this result convinced the NAE's Office of Public Affairs that evangelicals constituted the "great undecided group" on the nuclear issue.[20]

19. Robert P. Dugan, Jr., "Washington Update," *UEA*, March–April, 1983, p. 17; Spring, "Reagan Courts Evangelical Clout Against Nuclear Freeze," 44; "The Washington Office: A Voice Above the Clamor," *CT*, October 8, 1982, p. 53; Richard Pierard, "NAE's Social Awareness Grows," *CT*, April 9, 1982, p. 42.

20. "Evangelicals Are of Two Minds on Nuclear Weapons Issues," *CT*, August 5, 1983, pp. 48–50. A 1980 Gallup Poll showed a similar agreement between evangelicals

The lack of consensus among evangelicals may have reinforced the NAE's determination not to take a stand in favor of peace through strength or a nuclear freeze, but the revelation that so many remained undecided (or ignorant) prompted the organization to continue discussing the issue. Thus the NAE joined other evangelical groups in convening a conference in Pasadena, California, May 25–28, 1983, called "The Church and Peacemaking in the Nuclear Age." The Pasadena conference brought together approximately fourteen hundred evangelicals to explore issues of war and peace from a biblical perspective. Besides the NAE, a wide range of evangelical organizations were represented: individual churches, including Bel Air Presbyterian, Reagan's home church; educational institutions (Calvin College, Fuller Theological Seminary, and Westmont College); *Eternity* and *Sojourners*; parachurch groups (Voice of Calvary Ministries, Young Life International, and Youth for Christ); and national organizations (Christian College Coalition, Evangelicals for Social Action, New Call to Peacemaking, and the Reformed Church in America).[21]

When Dugan announced that the NAE would participate, he noted that it "has been doing everything possible to see that a balance of biblical viewpoints will be presented." As it turned out, the organizers of the conference had trouble attracting peace-through-strength spokesmen. Harold Brown, who had presented that view at the NAE convention, as well as Carl Henry, Francis Schaeffer, and the head of the Joint Chiefs of Staff, army general John W. Vessey, Jr., refused invitations to speak. Dugan seems to have taken the lead in recruiting spokesmen for the conservative view. He persuaded evangelist David Breese, Edward Robb of the Institute for Religion and Democracy, and Senator William L. Armstrong (R-Colo.) to speak at the Pasadena conference. Robert Mathis, former vice-chief of staff of the U.S. Air Force, also presented the peace-through-strength position.[22]

---

and nonevangelicals on the broader question of government spending for defense. Sixty-five percent of evangelicals and 61 percent of nonevangelicals thought the government should be spending more on defense ("Opinion Roundup," *Public Opinion*, April–May, 1981, p. 24).

21. John R. Dellenback, "Preface," in *Evangelicals and the Bishops' Pastoral Letter*, ed. Dean C. Curry (Grand Rapids, 1984), xi–xii.

22. Dugan, "Washington Update," 17; Spring, "Reagan Courts Evangelical Clout Against Nuclear Freeze," 48; Robert P. Dugan, Jr., telephone conversation with author, March 17, 1995; John A. Bernbaum, "Which Roads Lead to Peace?" *Eternity*, December, 1983, pp. 20–23.

The year after the Pasadena conference, the NAE began work on a project to help evangelicals study and discuss the issues of war and peace currently under debate. During the next two years, the NAE's national office and its Office of Public Affairs collaborated with an organization called the World Without War Council (WWWC) in formulating what came to be known as the Peace, Freedom, and Security Studies Program (PFSS). A document issued in October, 1986, *Guidelines: Peace, Freedom and Security Studies, a Program of the National Association of Evangelicals*, described the program's administration, purpose, and viewpoint in detail.[23]

The connection with the WWWC resulted from a chance encounter and conversation between Robert Dugan and George Weigel at the Pasadena conference. Weigel urged the NAE to become more involved in the debate over nuclear arms and national defense policy and introduced Dugan and other NAE officials to Robert Pickus, head of a chapter of the WWWC headquartered in Berkeley, California. Founded in the late 1960s, the WWWC was a right-of-center peace organization that advertised itself as a coordinator, trainer, and consultant for institutions and organizations interested in the nonviolent resolution of international conflict and emphasized a concern with philosophical and religious values in foreign policy.[24]

23. "A New Program Will Help Churches Study War and Peace," *CT*, November 23, 1984, p. 37; *Guidelines: Peace, Freedom and Security Studies, a Program of the National Association of Evangelicals* (N.p., 1986). For an interpretation of the PFSS program very different from mine, see Sara Diamond, *Spiritual Warfare: The Politics of the Christian Right* (Boston, 1989), Chap. 5; Richard Hatch and Sara Diamond, "The World Without War Council," *CovertAction*, Winter, 1989, p. 61.

24. Robert P. Dugan, Jr., telephone conversation with author, March 17, 1995. On the WWWC see, for example, *World Directory of Peace Research and Training Institutions, 1988* (Worcester, Eng., 1988), 233. The national office of the WWWC was located in New York City; besides Berkeley, there were chapters in Seattle, Portland, and Chicago. (Weigel was head of a "sister organization" to WWWC, the James Madison Foundation, in Washington, D.C.) The WWWC grew out of two earlier organizations founded in the late 1950s and early 1960s, Acts for Peace and Turn Toward Peace. It described itself as a group that "challenges peace organization stereotypes even as it seeks alternatives to the Pentagon's" and "a critic of the peace movement of the past 30 years." It defined its primary mission as the building of "support for alternatives to war in the resolution of international conflict and the defense of democratic values." Some idea of the organization's conservative approach may be gained from a list of "attitudes and understandings" it claimed to reject, which included the following: "the idea, for many years popular in the 'peace movement,' that work for peace primarily means opposing

Weigel was a Roman Catholic and Pickus a Jew, but their neocon-servative orientation rendered them compatible with the leaders of the NAE. They became "senior consultants" to the NAE project, and the WWWC provided $11,000 in funding. The NAE national office had ultimate authority over the program, but Dugan of the Office of Public Affairs actually administered it, and Brian F. O'Connell, a student at Seattle Pacific University (Free Methodist), who had been recruited by Pickus, served as the PFSS program coordinator. Rounding out the ad-ministrative structure was a twenty-member advisory board made up of prominent evangelical academics, writers, pastors, and one politician and representing a broad spectrum of views. Myron Augsburger, for example, was pastor of the Washington Community Fellowship (Men-nonite Church), and the politician, Senator William Armstrong, was an advocate of Reagan's Strategic Defense Initiative.[25]

In the PFSS *Guidelines* the NAE took a centrist stance between the positions advocated by right-wing and left-wing religious groups within as well as outside the evangelical community. The NAE's main criticism of the other religious groups was that they acted as "simply an arm of one or another secular political current," that "great national church and ecumenical organizations have become the instrument of political activists particularly on the left, though also on the right, whose primary commitment is to an ideological position." Though the NAE did not

---

American military policy and programs"; "the tendency of some to equate work for 'justice' with work for 'peace'"; and "the idea that 'wars will cease when men refuse to fight.'" See "World Without War Council of Northern California" (Photocopy of *World Affairs Organizations in Northern California*, 162–63), "The Problem of War: Ideas in the Council's Perspective" (Part II of a typed statement entitled "Clarifying the Council's Work, n.d.), Robert Pickus, "But What Do You Do?" (Typescript of 1979 revision of an April, 1977, memo), *World Without War Council* (brochure dated June 1995), all sent to the author by Robert Pickus, February and August, 1995); Robert S. Meyer, *Peace Organizations Past and Present: A Survey and Directory* (Jefferson, N.C., 1988), 98–100.

25. "A New Program Will Help Churches Study War and Peace," 37; *Guidelines*, 37–38. For Weigel's criticism of the 1983 pastoral letter of the National Conference of Catholic Bishops, see *Tranquillitas Ordinis: The Present Failure and Future Promise of American Catholic Thought on War and Peace* (New York, 1987). On Pickus, see Milton S. Katz, *Ban the Bomb: A History of SANE, the Committee for a Sane Nuclear Policy, 1957–1985* (New York, 1986), 70–71, 102–103. Armstrong had been named NAE Layman of the Year in 1984; see "Is the Strategic Defense Initiative Our Best Hedge Against Nuclear War?" *CT*, April 4, 1986, p. 42.

specifically name the National Council of Churches and the denominations that made up the mainline religious community, they were surely included among the "great national church and ecumenical organizations." Similarly, although the *Guidelines* did not name any individuals or groups associated with the radical evangelicals, other sections of the document, as well as comments by members of the PFSS advisory board, indicate that the criticisms the *Guidelines* made of the mainline groups extended to the radicals as well.[26]

At the same time that it criticized the left-wing position, the NAE also pointed to the "inadequacies" of groups "at the other end of the political spectrum." There is no mistaking the reference to the New Christian Right: "The looming horror of nuclear war is not, as on the left, exploited to develop support for political prescriptions that will do little to prevent it; but, at this end of the spectrum, it is often treated as if only one response were possible: enlarged American military capabilities."[27]

The NAE defined its own position on the nuclear arms race and national defense policy in terms of the three words in the program's title: peace, freedom, and security. The *Guidelines* emphasized that the peace sought by the NAE was "a limited peace: it is not the inner peace of a relationship with God, nor the absence of all conflict because of the fulfillment of God's Kingdom, but the peace which is possible between organized political communities, achieved as law and political processes provide alternatives to the violent resolution of conflict." Here again, although the *Guidelines* did not say so, the reference to peace as "the absence of all conflict" constituted another criticism of mainline groups and radical evangelicals.[28]

The *Guidelines* insisted that evangelicals must be committed to "peace

26. See, for example, *Guidelines*, 5, 7, and see also 42–44, 45–46; Dean Curry, "Confusing Justice and Peace," in *Piety and Politics: Evangelicals and Fundamentalists Confront the World*, ed. Richard John Neuhaus and Michael Cromartie (Washington, D.C., 1987), 236 (revised and reprinted from the December, 1984, issue of *Catholicism and Crisis*). In the discussion of the PFSS *Guidelines* that follows, as the notes indicate, I have relied not only on the text of the *Guidelines* but on commentary published by individuals who helped to formulate them. Although some of that commentary was published after the *Guidelines*, I think there is good reason to believe that it offers insight into the writer's convictions at the time that he worked on the NAE project.

27. *Guidelines*, 7, and see also 41–42, 44.

28. *Ibid.*, 27; O'Connell, "NAE's Bold Bid," 5–6; Curry, "Confusing Justice and Peace," 240.

and freedom." In yet another judgment against the mainline groups and radical evangelicals, the NAE declared, "A peace which sacrifices human freedom—particularly religious liberty—is morally bankrupt and not an option for Christians to consider." This vague language conveyed the NAE's concern for what the *Guidelines* elsewhere referred to as "the plight of believers under oppressive regimes"; thus the *Guidelines* criticized religious groups on the left for supporting the Sandinista government in Nicaragua and ignoring the plight of Christians in the Soviet Union. The emphasis on "freedom" signaled the continuation of the NAE's long-standing opposition to communism in general and the Soviet Union in particular. Indeed, besides censuring their lack of concern for Christians persecuted by communist regimes, the NAE criticized the mainline and radical evangelical groups for not only grossly underestimating the evil of communism but for asserting the "moral equivalency" of the United States and the Soviet Union.[29]

As for "security," the NAE position formulated in the *Guidelines* favored "an America strong enough to resist attack and to influence the course of world affairs; yet an America that is continually seeking realistic alternatives to war as a means of resolving international conflict." It sounded rather like the position Kenneth Kantzer had advocated in *Christianity Today*. The NAE refused to make recommendations regarding specific weapons programs; it endorsed efforts to limit the arms race but did not rule out nuclear deterrence. The need to judge any deterrence system by just war principles was implied in the statement that "the issue of whether the means are appropriate to the goal will have to be addressed as well."[30]

Even the NAE recognized the proposed PFSS program as a "milepost" in its history. Before 1986, as Brian O'Connell observed, the NAE had "a thin history of dealing with international affairs." With the publication of the *Guidelines* the NAE announced its commitment "to a more serious and sustained entry into the organizational, educational and public opinion arenas which shape America's role in world affairs."[31]

29. See *Guidelines*, 6–8, 10, 16, 29, 46; Curry, "Confusing Justice and Peace," 236–38, 241; Myers, "Biblical Obedience and Political Thought," in *The Bible, Politics, and Democracy*, ed. Neuhaus, 20.

30. *Guidelines*, 28, 23.

31. *Ibid.*, 6, 5, 4; O'Connell, "NAE's Bold Bid," 4. See also Curry, "Confusing Justice and Peace," 235, and, for a more general criticism of the NAE's record on social responsibility, Richard Quebedeaux, *The Young Evangelicals: Revolution in Orthodoxy*

The PFSS program constituted a bold and comprehensive effort on the part of the NAE to educate and mobilize evangelicals in favor of its centrist position on the issues of nuclear arms and national defense policy. Indeed, the goal was not only to unify evangelicals on those issues but to reclaim for the NAE—and, by extension, mainstream evangelicalism—the authority and influence they seemed to be losing to the NCR and the radical evangelicals.

This interpretation of the NAE's PFSS program comes from viewing it in the context in which it developed. During the 1980s, while evangelicals debated national security issues, mainstream leaders conducted a wide-ranging discussion of evangelical involvement in the political arena. The text of the *Guidelines* suggests that NAE officials and the architects of the PFSS program were not unaware of that discussion, indeed, that they framed the PFSS *Guidelines* in accord with its prescriptions.[32]

The NAE formulated its educational objective after taking a survey which revealed that the majority of evangelical churches, associations, seminaries, and colleges affiliated with it did not encourage discussion of war and peace issues, while the few that did used materials advocating

---

(New York, 1974), 33. Two NAE agencies helped prod the parent organization to greater sociopolitical involvement, the ESAC and the Office of Public Affairs. In effect, the Office of Public Affairs served as "point man" for the NAE, venturing into sometimes unfamiliar and alien territory. Beginning in the mid-1950s, under Clyde Taylor's direction, the office began holding "seminars" for students, pastors, and laymen belonging to evangelical churches, which considered such topics as "Facing Threats to Our National Security" and "A Global View of American Foreign Policy." In the late 1970s, under the leadership of Robert Dugan, the office projected an even higher profile in Washington, D.C., and began to focus more on specific political issues, including legislation pending in Congress. Through the *NAE Washington Insight*, a new monthly newsletter Dugan published, the office was in a good position to influence rank-and-file evangelicals. See Clyde W. Taylor, "A Washington Seminar for Pastors and Laymen," *UEA*, December, 1963, p. 5; "Christian Responsibility in Public Affairs," *UEA*, January, 1965, p. 31; "Clyde Taylor: Quarter Century of Service to Evangelicals," *UEA*, Fall, 1969, p. 14; James L. Adams, *The Growing Church Lobby in Washington* (Grand Rapids, 1970), 264; "April Set for Washington Leadership Briefing," *UEA*, Winter, 1976, p. 25; "Washington Seminars Set for February," *UEA*, Fall, 1977, p. 29; "The Washington Office," 53.

32. My understanding of mainstream evangelicals' discussion of political involvement is based on extensive reading of editorials and other commentary by Kenneth Kantzer, Carl Henry, and Billy Graham, among many others, published in *Christianity Today* during the 1980s.

a specific position such as the nuclear freeze or peace through strength. The PFSS program was designed to remedy that deficiency by developing study kits, visual aids, and other materials and by setting up leadership training seminars, a speakers' bureau, and an information clearinghouse to provide advice and instruction. The *Guidelines* also promised a solution to the problem posed by the large number of evangelicals registering "no opinion" in the Gallup poll the NAE had commissioned in 1983. The hope was that the PFSS program would awaken and instruct the "great undecided group" within the evangelical community before other groups got to them. If evangelicals remained on the sidelines of the debate over nuclear and defense issues, Brian O'Connell warned, they would be "highly vulnerable to partisan political pressures seeking to enlist [them] in one or another faction of the present argument."[33]

If the NAE worried because a large segment of evangelicals paid little attention to the current debate, it was even more concerned about what the *Guidelines* referred to as "the currently divided and confused dialogue" within the evangelical community. The problem lay not just in the "inadequacy of the polar voices of left and right" but in the "polarization" itself. Of course, polarization was not a new concern among evangelicals. Indeed, memories of the fragmentation caused by the debate over the Vietnam War probably made it especially troubling.[34]

Many mainstream evangelicals regarded divisiveness and fragmentation as transgressions against "the organic unity of the whole family of believers" and the biblical ideal of church unity and warned against adopting politics as a model in dealing with public policy matters. Instead of taking its cue from the world and following the example of a political campaign, the church should set the model *for* the world and "be the body of Christ united in love, and even confronting one another in love," V. Gilbert Beers and Harold Smith declared. The PFSS program may be seen as an effort to implement the "Christ-like model" described by Beers and Smith in the hope of reunifying the evangelical

33. "A New Program Will Help Churches Study War and Peace," 37; *Guidelines*, 6–7, 30–31.
34. *Guidelines*, 5. For evidence of concern over polarization, see, for example, "The Concerns and Considerations of Carl F. H. Henry," *CT*, March 13, 1981, p. 19; Kenneth S. Kantzer, "Evangelicalism: Midcourse Self-Appraisal," *CT*, January 7, 1983, p. 10; Myron S. Augsburger, "Pluralism Gone to Seed," *CT*, January 17, 1986, pp. 20-I–21-I.

community. Through the PFSS program the NAE sought to promote a "dialogue" among evangelicals occupying different positions so as to help them move toward "common ground." "It is difficult to meld truths present at the 'Peace and Disarmament' end of the political spectrum with those heard at the 'Security and Liberty' end. But that is our goal."[35]

There is no reason to doubt the NAE's sincerity in proposing such a goal, as unrealistic as it appears, considering the theological and ideological diversity of its constituency.[36] But the attention the *Guidelines* paid to criticizing certain positions on the arms race and national defense policy suggests that the NAE did not intend to rely on the "melding" process induced by the PFSS program. The program was designed not just to promote dialogue but to formulate—and rally evangelicals to— a particular perspective on nuclear arms and national defense.

The problem for the NAE and mainstream leaders in the 1980s was to maintain what Carl Henry called "a united evangelical orthodoxy." This meant offsetting, if not eliminating, competing voices within the evangelical community. It is clear, for example, that NAE officials and mainstream leaders were alarmed by the growing influence of the radical evangelicals, which had been demonstrated at the Pasadena conference. Dean Curry, a PFSS advisory board member, attributed the leftist orientation of the conference to its domination "by the Evangelical 'peace' activists who had championed the Chicago Declaration a decade before." Indeed, for Curry the Pasadena conference reflected the wholesale "reorientation" of mainstream evangelicalism under the sway of a radical evangelical ideology "indistinguishable from the social and political critique of the secular Left in America." The increasing prominence of the New Christian Right also concerned the NAE and mainstream evangelicals in the 1980s. As the decade opened, the NCR grabbed the national limelight in the midst of the presidential election, prompting Kenneth Kantzer to declare that "1980 could well be called

---

35. V. Gilbert Beers and Harold Smith, "Mudslinging in the Sanctuary," *CT*, October 19, 1984, p. 13; *Guidelines*, 5, 12. See also O'Connell, "NEA's Bold Bid," 7–8; Carl F. H. Henry, "The Road to Eternity: A Travel Guide for the '80s," *CT*, July 17, 1981, p. 31.

36. On the range of opinion, including the peace-through-strength position, within the NAE's constituency, see Bernbaum, "Which Roads Lead to Peace?" 20–23; "Rumors of Wars," *Eternity*, June, 1980, pp. 14–19; Robert G. Clouse, ed., *War: 4 Christian Views* (Downers Grove, Ill., 1981).

the year of the right-wing religious lobby." Although mainstream evangelical leaders such as Kantzer commended the conservative activists for becoming politically involved, they increasingly resented the media coverage the NCR commanded, the influence it seemed to exert on the Congress and president, and—perhaps most annoying—the claim by groups such as Moral Majority and Christian Voice that they spoke for the evangelical community as a whole.[37]

Although determined to challenge the radical evangelicals and the NCR in the debate over nuclear arms and national defense policy, the NAE explicitly repudiated any tactics suggesting "political partisanship." Here the influence of the mainstream evangelical leaders was decisive. As we have seen, the PFSS *Guidelines* criticized mainline and evangelical groups for acting as "an arm of one or another secular political current." In contrast, the NAE presented its own perspective on war and peace as distinctively nonpolitical and nonideological. Echoing another preoccupation of mainstream leaders, the *Guidelines* eschewed another bugbear of mainstream leaders, the tendency, especially on the part of the NCR, to specify what Carl Henry called "a spiritual litmus test" on issues such as the Panama Canal, SALT II, or the B-1 bomber as a basis for judging "the Christian authenticity" of political candidates, or to declare (as Christian Voice did in the case of the Strategic Defense Initiative) a particular policy "pro-biblical." Of course, relying on the Bible as the absolute, infallible guide to faith and life was good evangelical doctrine. But mainstream leaders insisted that there was no one, true "Christian position" on particular political issues. Thus the *Guidelines* set forth the "fundamental theological insights" guiding the PFSS program but made it clear that they were open to interpretation. The *Guidelines* also pointedly rejected positions "dressed up in scriptural, theological and moral warrants (all too often presented as if these are the *only* legitimate 'Christian' positions)."[38]

37. Henry, "The Road to Eternity," 31; Robert P. Dugan, Jr., telephone conversation with author, March 17, 1995; Curry, "Confusing Justice and Peace," 235–236, 238–39; "Getting God's Kingdom into Politics" (Unsigned editorial), *CT*, September 19, 1980, p. 10; "Just Because Reagan Has Won . . ." (Unsigned editorial), *CT*, December 12, 1980, p. 14; Henry, "Evangelicals Jump on the Political Bandwagon," *CT*, October 24, 1980, p. 20; Edward E. Plowman, "Is Morality All Right?" *CT*, November 2, 1979, p. 76; Beth Spring, "Christian Voice Gains Visibility Following Realignment of New Right," *CT*, November 7, 1986, p. 46.

38. *Guidelines*, 17, 21. See also Dean C. Curry, "Evangelicals, the Bible, and Public

Another reflection of mainstream evangelical leaders' antipathy to "political partisanship" may be seen in the NAE's declaration that it did not plan to "undertake partisan electoral activities" and its disavowal of any intention of "mobilizing votes." The purpose of the PFSS program was "not to establish a political position in opposition to the political pronouncements of, for example, the National Council of Churches. Nor is it to support the security agenda of the religious New Right." Underscoring the point, the NAE declared that "specific policy proposals are *not* the primary focus of this program."[39]

The NAE did eschew political partisanship—but only up to a point. The motives and strategy of the PFSS program were as political as those of the mainline and evangelical groups the *Guidelines* criticized. All the evidence suggests that the NAE's decision to launch the PFSS program grew out of the power struggle going on within the evangelical community in the 1980s. Formed in 1942 to serve as a "united evangelical voice" counterbalancing the Federal Council of Churches, the NAE had long represented itself as "the voice of evangelical Christianity speaking for morality and righteousness in matters of public concern." In the 1980s, facing competition from the right and left wings of the evangelical community, the NAE proposed the PFSS program in an effort to reclaim what it considered to be its rightful authority and influence— to "strengthen the Evangelical voice" as the PFSS *Guidelines* declared.[40]

Notwithstanding its importance in the history of the NAE, the PFSS program seems to have had little effect either within or outside the evangelical community. One reason was the new political and strategic

Policy," *This World*, Winter, 1987, pp. 34–49. For mainstream evangelical leaders' thoughts on political partisanship, see, for example, Tom Minnery, "Winning Isn't Everything," *CT*, August 9, 1985, p. 14; Nathan O. Hatch, "Keeping the Church Doors Open," *CT*, March 21, 1986, p. 15; "Just Because Reagan Has Won . . . ," 15; "Should We Fear the New Right?" *CT*, October 2, 1981, p. 96; Henry, "Evangelicals Jump on the Political Bandwagon," 21, 23; Beth Spring, "Republicans, Religion, and Reelection," *CT*, October 5, 1984, pp. 54–58; "The Concerns and Considerations of Carl F. H. Henry," 23; "Partisan Politics: Where Does the Gospel Fit?" *CT*, November 9, 1984, p. 16; Plowman, "Is Morality All Right?" 78; "Getting God's Kingdom into Politics," *CT*, September 19, 1980, p. 11; Henry, "The Road to Eternity," 33; Kenneth Kantzer, "Problems Inerrancy Doesn't Solve," *CT*, February 10, 1987, p. 15; Carl F. H. Henry, "Lost Momentum," *CT*, September 4, 1987, p. 32.

39. *Guidelines*, 10, 25, 5–6, 12.

40. "The NAE Faces Issues in National Crisis," *UEA*, May 1, 1951, p. 3; *Guidelines*, 6, and see also 25.

context taking shape by the time the program was ready to be implemented. In the late 1980s, rapprochement between President Reagan and USSR president Mikhail Gorbachev and nuclear arms agreements between the United States and the Soviet Union seemed to render moot the debate over the arms race and national defense policy. Another reason, ironically, was the NAE's eschewal of political partisanship. At a time when discussion of the nuclear arms race and national defense policy had become highly partisan, a document offering guidelines and principles instead of specific policy recommendations, no matter how firmly rooted in Scripture it claimed to be, did not have much appeal and could not excite much enthusiasm. Evangelical groups on the right and left continued to approach matters of public policy in the usual partisan manner. In 1986, the year the *Guidelines* were published, the right-wing Religious Coalition for a Moral Defense Policy endorsed the Strategic Defense Initiative, and Ron Sider and other members of Evangelicals for Social Action formed a political action committee called JustLife to produce specific policy recommendations regarding nuclear arms, abortion, and poverty.[41] In the late 1980s and on into the 1990s, groups such as Christian Voice, the American Coalition for Traditional Values, and the Christian Coalition continued to engage in similarly partisan activity.

In such a context, the PFSS program was doomed. Reflecting on its demise in the May–June, 1987, issue of *United Evangelical Action*, Robert Dugan expressed doubt that "the millions of dollars raised and spent by new-right political lobbies and public action committees" had converted the nation's capital to "a more biblical world view." And yet, he observed, "intellectually respectable endeavors such as NAE's Peace, Freedom and Security Studies program go wanting for financial underwriting." Considering the fate of the program, he feared that it would be some time before mainstream evangelicals built the requisite "moral and intellectual foundation for permanent evangelical influence on government and society."[42]

41. Sharon Anderson, "Christians Take Sides on Proposed Defense System," *CT*, April 4, 1986, p. 43; "Religious Leaders and Groups Endorse 'Star Wars' as Moral Defense Policy," *Command*, No. 4, 1986, p. 29; Beth Spring, "With the Religious Right in Disarray, Two Groups Consider New Opportunities," *CT*, June 10, 1987, p. 46; Beth Spring, "A New Political Group Will Oppose Abortion, Poverty, and Nuclear Arms," *CT*, June 13, 1986, pp. 36–37; "A Talk with Ronald Sider," *CT*, June 10, 1987, p. 48.

42. Robert P. Dugan, "D.C. Dateline: Seizing the 'Evangelical Moment,'" *UEA*, May–June, 1987, p. 9. See also "Taking Care of Business," *CT*, April 3, 1987, p. 39.

17
Military Experts of the New Christian Right

The New Christian Right mustered several retired military men in support of its campaign to strengthen the American military machine. In *Listen America!*, for example, Jerry Falwell quoted Marine Corps general Lewis W. Walt at length, exhorting Americans to heed "the urgent warnings of some of our key military experts" regarding the country's military inferiority. A conservative Christian who shared many of the concerns of the NCR, Walt had written two books contending that American political leaders had "stripped" U.S. defensive forces in pursuit of "a dream world of detente and strategic arms limitation treaties."[1]

Falwell and the Moral Majority also paraded the expertise of Captain G. Russell Evans, a retired U.S. Coast Guard aviator living in Norfolk, Virginia. A regular contributor to *Moral Majority Report*, Evans wrote on a wide range of national security issues, espousing the fundamentalist party line—opposition to mutual assured destruction, unilateral disarmament, SALT I and II, and the nuclear freeze. His favorite theme was

---

1. Jerry Falwell, *Listen America!* (Garden City, N.Y., 1980), 8, 101–103; Jerry Falwell, "Future-Word: An Agenda for the Eighties," in *The Fundamentalist Phenomenon*, ed. Jerry Falwell with Ed Dobson and Ed Hindson (Garden City, N.Y., 1981), 213; Lewis W. Walt, *The Eleventh Hour* (Thornwood, N.Y., 1979), 3, 17; Lewis W. Walt, *America Faces Defeat* (Woodbridge, Conn., 1972). On Walt's relationship with Jerry Falwell, see John S. Saloma, *Ominous Politics: The New Conservative Labyrinth* (New York, 1984), 52. On Walt's religious beliefs, see SSgt Jim Elliott, "General Walt," *Leatherneck*, February, 1971, p. 80. Walt wrote a testimony for the FGBMFI's *Voices of the Military* (Los Angeles, 1970?), 17–18, but he was probably not a pentecostal.

"the predatory influence of pacifism and detente on U.S. military policy."[2]

Another retired military man who worked closely with the New Christian Right was army major general John K. Singlaub. As head of the World Anti-Communist League and a member of Refugee Relief International, both of them part of a network of organizations allied with Pat Robertson's Christian Broadcasting Network, he helped channel humanitarian and military aid to the Nicaraguan Contras, a favorite NCR foreign policy undertaking.[3]

Like Moral Majority and CBN, the Religious Roundtable also recruited retired military men. Founded in September, 1979, by Ed McAteer, a Colgate-Palmolive Company marketing man, the Roundtable brought together various wings of the New Right and the New Christian Right. Its purpose was to encourage grass-roots political activity among conservative Christian preachers, and its governing council included fundamentalist television preachers, conservative politicians, and leaders of various secular and religious organizations such as the Southern Baptist Convention, STOP-ERA, the National Pro-Life Political Action Committee, the Christian Freedom Foundation, Campus Crusade for Christ, the NAE, and the National Religious Broadcasters. In August, 1980, the Roundtable sponsored a National Affairs Briefing in Dallas, Texas, a two-day gathering attended by about twenty-five hundred clergymen. The advertised purpose of the briefing was "to provide participants with an inside perspective of domestic and foreign policy affairs." Two "military strategists," as they were called, shared the podium with major NCR figures including Falwell, Robertson, James Robison, Ronald Reagan, Jesse Helms, Phyllis Schlafly, and Tim LaHaye.[4]

2. G. Russell Evans, "Bureaucrats, Politicians Have Nurtured Pacifism," *Moral Majority Report*, January, 1983, p. 14. See also G. Russell Evans, "Peace Won't Come from SOB, SAGA, MAM," *Moral Majority Report*, October, 1982, p. 10; G. Russell Evans, "Shall America Be Defended?" *Moral Majority Report*, September 15, 1980, p. 8.

3. Vicki Kemper, "In the Name of Relief," *Sojourners*, October, 1985, pp. 16–17. On the World Anti-Communist League and Singlaub's role in it, see Major General John K. Singlaub with Malcolm McConnell, *Hazardous Duty: An American Soldier in the Twentieth Century* (New York, 1991), 436–40.

4. Saloma, *Ominous Politics*, 61; Matthew C. Moen, *The Christian Right and Congress* (Tuscaloosa, 1989), 73–74; Robert C. Liebman, "Mobilizing the Moral Majority," in *The New Christian Right: Mobilization and Legitimation*, ed. Liebman and Robert Wuthnow (New York, 1983), 53; "National Affairs Briefing in Dallas," *Moral Majority Report*,

One of the military men was Major General George J. Keegan, Jr., former chief of Air Force Intelligence, who evoked cheers when he declared that the Vietnam War was "the most honorable war in our history." Like Walt, Keegan had been sounding the alarm regarding "America's shocking military decline" for several years. Falwell named and quoted him, along with Walt, in *Listen America!* No complete record of Keegan's remarks at the National Affairs Briefing has been found, but the message was probably similar to the one he proclaimed a few months earlier at the Reverend D. James Kennedy's Coral Ridge Presbyterian Church in Fort Lauderdale, Florida, in an address entitled "Christian Duty in a Crisis World." Keegan began by citing the Soviet invasion of Afghanistan and, more recently, the taking of American hostages by Iranian militants in Teheran. Soon, perhaps "within weeks," he observed, the Ayatollah Khomeini might by overthrown by an externally supported communist-led revolution. "In all of this, you and I have witnessed for the first time in history American leadership powerless to act, powerless to intercede, backed by a diplomacy that is now known to be bankrupt, and a defense policy which for twenty years has disarmed this country unilaterally." Like Walt and other military experts recruited by the New Christian Right, Keegan traced the deplorable military situation of the United States back to the 1960s, when a "coterie" of "college professors totally inexperienced in the ways of war and realistic peacemaking" persuaded President John F. Kennedy to embark on a new diplomacy that would "unilaterally disarm the United States" and a new military strategy based on mutual assured destruction, which meant "retaining only enough survivable military capability to destroy a hundred and fifty million innocent Russion [*sic*] citizens who live within two hundred or so cities." Such a strategy Keegan denounced as "moral depravity."[5]

"Now what do we do? Are we doomed? No, we are not doomed! Do we despair! No, we do not despair!" Keegan insisted. American evangelicals could save America if they put the right leadership in government, revived investment in basic scientific research, developed new

---

July 14, 1980, p. 15; Jeffrey K. Hadden, "Born Again Politics: The Dallas Briefing," *Presbyterian Outlook*, October 20, 1980, p. 5.

5. "Paul Reveres for Jesus Urged," *Dallas Morning News*, August 22, 1980, p. 6; Falwell, *Listen, America!*, 104. For background on Keegan, see *Conservative Digest*, August, 1979, p. 20.

missiles, resumed production of the B-1 bomber, and rebuilt the United States Navy. Keegan also recommended putting into production "extraordinary new technologies of defense"—"the most remarkable tank-killing, infantry destruction, radar-busting and artillary [*sic*] neutralization weapons" ever developed. "Let us deploy them for the greatest Christian cause in modern history: the survival and the defense of civilization as we know it," he urged.[6]

The other "military strategist" who spoke at the Religious Roundtable briefing was retired army brigadier general Albion W. Knight, Jr. According to a report in the *New York Times*, Knight showed the Dallas group a film called *The SALT Syndrome*, which depicted U.S. military capability as inferior to that of the Soviet Union, and "said it was up to Christians to 'put a spine down the back of America.'" Invoking Scripture, he declared, "Giving in to the Soviet Union is not compatible with the Judeo-Christian heritage told in the Bible."[7]

Of all the men discussed in this chapter, Knight provides the best illustration of the military man as NCR activist. Although he never attained national prominence, in the early 1980s he became a high-profile figure within the secular and religious New Right. The Christian Reconstructionist Gary North later described Knight as the "unofficial 'consulting general'" of the New Christian Right and "the military chaplain of the movement." A graduate of the U.S. Military Academy, class of 1945, Knight had retired from the army in 1973. During much of his army career, he had been associated with nuclear weapons programs. From 1973 to 1976 he served as a staff member of the Joint Committee on Atomic Energy of the U.S. Congress. In August, 1976, he took a job as national security adviser with the U.S. Energy Research and Development Administration, only to resign in January of 1977. "I find myself in such total disagreement with the national security directions being taken by President Carter and his Administration that my loyalty would be severely strained should I remain," he wrote in his letter of resignation. He thought it better to resign immediately rather

6. General George Keegan, *Christian Duty in a Crisis World* (Address delivered March 23, 1980; pamphlet, n.p., n.d., sent to the author on request by Beth Petersen, secretary pro tem to D. James Kennedy, August 5, 1993), 1, 5–8.
7. Kenneth A. Briggs, "Christians on Right and Left Take up Ballot and Cudgel," *NYT*, September 21, 1980, p. 20E.

"than delay and be tempted to take actions . . . that would be rightfully interpreted as undercutting the Administration position."[8]

Knight combined a religious vocation with his military career, having been ordained an Episcopal priest in 1955. In the late 1970s he served the Diocese of Virginia as an interim rector for churches selecting new pastors, all the while waging a vigorous campaign against what he viewed as the pacifist and Marxist orientation of the leaders of the Episcopal Church. He also embarked on a career as a speaker on national energy and security issues. In appearances before civic and church groups, at colleges and universities, and on radio and television he expatiated on such topics as "The Gap in the National Energy Plan: Research and Development," "Why Nuclear Testing by the United States Must Continue: or, Why the U.S. Should Not Sign a Comprehensive Test Ban Treaty with the Russians," and "Moral Aspects of Nuclear Weapons for U.S. National Security." The last-named speech was based on what Knight referred to as "my combined experience as a long-time Episcopal priest and nuclear weapons expert."[9]

Knight believed that as a retired military man he had an obligation to speak out on strategic matters. As he told John Singlaub: "Too many of our colleagues seem to think it beneath their dignity to 'go public.' If we don't who will? The same academics who got us there in the first place." And if, as he had decided by 1982, when he wrote to Singlaub, the Congress and the administration were not moving in the right direction, then "professional soldiers" must educate the public so as to increase pressure on the politicians. "Thanks for your superb work in doing that," he told Singlaub. "Lets [*sic*] encourage more of our colleagues to get their hands dirty and do the same."[10]

In the early 1980s Knight settled into a comfortable niche with the Conservative Caucus, a secular New Right organization, serving as di-

8. Gary North to the author, July 26, 1993; Albion W. Knight, Jr., biography supplied by U.S. Army Reserve Personnel Center, St. Louis, Mo., December 29, 1992; Albion Knight, *"Memorandum to Mr. Starbird,* MY RESIGNATION," January 26, 1977, in Albion Knight, Jr., Papers, U.S. Army Military History Institute, Carlisle Barracks, Pa.

9. Albion Knight to the Speakers Bureau of America, November 10, 1977; "REPRESENTATIVE SPEECH SUBJECTS A. W. Knight," [*ca.* 1977], both in Knight Papers; Dorothy Mills Parker, "U.S. Army General Consecrated Bishop," *Christian Challenge,* September, 1984, p. 10.

10. Albion Knight to John K. Singlaub, October 27, 1982, Knight Papers.

rector of its Presidential Policy Project and National Security Task Force. Building on the reputation he had established at the 1980 Dallas briefing, he continued to be active in the New Christian Right, attending other Roundtable functions, appearing on Pat Robertson's television show, the 700 Club, and, along with General Walt, addressing several seminars on military preparedness sponsored by Gary North and his American Bureau of Economic Research. In June, 1982, the John Birch Society magazine featured a ten-page interview with the "Christian Soldier" on the "moral implications of peace and disarmament."[11]

One of the persons with whom Knight collaborated while working for the Conservative Caucus was Lieutenant General Daniel O. Graham, retired director of the Defense Intelligence Agency and founder-director of High Frontier, a group organized to promote the Strategic Defense Initiative. In *The New Right: We're Ready to Lead*, Richard Viguerie described Graham as "the New Right's top national security expert and spokesman," co-chairman of an organization called Coalition for Peace Through Strength, and "one of the three or four most important leaders in our thus-far successful fight against Senate ratification of SALT II."[12]

Like Knight, Graham had one foot planted in the secular New Right camp and another in the New Christian Right camp. When he addressed an evangelical audience, he skillfully bolstered the strategic argument for space-based defense with a religious rationale. *Moral Ma-*

11. Albion Knight, "Memorandum for the Record," February 27, 1981, and to Mrs. Jackie Mitchum, March 13, 1981, and to Gary North, March 13, 1981; all in Knight Papers; Gary North to the author, July 26, 1993; John Rees, "Christian Soldier Albion Knight: An Exclusive Interview with the Episcopal Priest and Retired U.S. Army Brigadier General on Moral Implications of Peace and Disarmament," *Review of the NEWS*, June 9, 1982, pp. 39, 41–45, 47–50.

12. Richard Viguerie, *The New Right: We're Ready to Lead* (Falls Church, Va., 1980), 66–67. According to General Graham, High Frontier grew out of discussions with Representative Newt Gingrich, a leading spokesman for the conservative coalition in Congress, and operated under the aegis of the Heritage Foundation (Daniel O. Graham, *The Non-Nuclear Defense of Cities: The High Frontier Space-Based Defense Against ICBM Attack* [Cambridge, Mass., 1983], vi, viii). For Knight's dealings with Graham, see, for example, Albion Knight to Daniel O. Graham, September 18, 1981, and "Memorandum for General Graham," December 14, 1981, both in Knight Papers. On the Coalition for Peace Through Strength see *NYT*, August 9, 1978, pp. 1, D19; "Names in the News," *Conservative Digest*, October, 1978, p. 42; "New War of Words Over Nuclear Freeze," *U.S. News & World Report*, March 21, 1983, p. 7. John K. Singlaub was also a member.

jority Report, which provided extensive coverage of High Frontier, quoted Graham as saying that development of SDI "would bring our military strategy in line with the Christian view of military preparedness." The earlier U.S. strategy, acquiring "more and better nuclear weapons capable of destroying more Russian citizens," went "somewhat against the grain of the Christian view of things," he explained, "in that it is difficult for us to accept the notion that our only defense is our ability to kill Soviet citizens." By contrast, SDI was "obviously consistent with the Judeo-Christian ethic of defending the innocent." It would give the United States "the moral high ground in the nuclear era," he said in another interview. Adoption of "a military policy that is fully in line with our ethical system," he declared, "will not only strengthen our military but it will strengthen our moral fiber." Such a prospect, he added, was "terrifying" to the Soviets.[13]

Like the other NCR military experts discussed in this chapter, Graham not only agreed with the New Christian Right's anticommunist, pro-military, pro-America ideology and its campaign for peace through strength but also shared its deep-seated animus toward the mainline churches. *Moral Majority Report* quoted him as saying that mainline churchmen who had been advocating nuclear freeze for fifteen years had fallen into the "trap" of "cowardice." Noting that some liberal Roman Catholic leaders had said that bombs "threaten the sovereignty of God," Graham declared: "That's blasphemy. When God wants to destroy the world, He will do it."[14]

The animus the NCR's military experts exhibited toward the mainline churches came close to being an obsession on the part of G. Russell Evans and Albion Knight. Evans' preoccupation with "the predatory influence of pacifism and detente on U.S. military policy" has already been noted. He believed it emanated not only from politicians and bureaucrats in Washington, D.C., but also from mainline religious groups. In *Apathy, Apostasy and Apostles*, published in 1973, he depicted the NCC and WCC as "deeply infiltrated with pro-communists, humanists, and

13. Richard Alvarez, "Geneva's Real Meaning: The Soviets Are Scared," *Moral Majority Report*, May, 1985, p. 3; Lt. Gen. Daniel Graham, "'We Must Stabilize the Balance of Terror,'" *Moral Majority Report*, December, 1983, p. 3; Richard Alvarez, "Reagan Must Not Bargain Away Star Wars Program, Experts Say," *Moral Majority Report*, November, 1985, p. 10.

14. "General Graham: America Can Defend Itself," *Moral Majority Report*, November, 1982, p. 8.

relativists; and . . . doing the work of the communists for world government." In 1980 he devoted several articles in *Moral Majority Report* to exposing "the Marxist line being followed by many mainline Christian churches" and revealing how they and the NCC were "lead[ing] the way for U.S. unilateral disarmament, more trade with the communist countries, abolishing Congressional investigating committees, and for opening all barriers to trade, love and peace forever with the communists and all mankind." In 1982 Evans collaborated with C. Gregg Singer, professor of church history and theology at the Atlanta School of Biblical Studies, on a book entitled *The Church and the Sword: An Examination of the Religious Influence in America on Pacifism and Disarmament.* "The mainline religious establishment has long been in the forefront of pacifist movements for disarming America and resisting military service, all in the name of universal peace," they charged. In the concluding portion of the book they urged "the Christians in all of America's churches" to "speak out and to take action . . . against the atheistic communism that so many of the mainline denominations are hell-bent to help along." They must elect "moral and loyal leaders, unafraid, and dedicated to the preservation of America and her religious heritage." Not just the survival of America and the free world but Christianity itself was at stake. "If a free America does not survive, who will be left in the world to carry out the mission of Christ?" they asked.[15]

Both the message of *The Church and the Sword* and the "reader comments" published at the beginning and end of the book place Evans and Singer squarely in the NCR network. N. Burnett Magruder, executive director of the Christian Heritage Center, termed the book "a devastating indictment of the liberal-humanist-socialist mind and its impact

15. G. Russell Evans, *Apathy, Apostasy and Apostles: A Study of the History and Activities of the National Council of Churches of Christ in the U.S.A. with Sidelights on Its Ally, the World Council of Churches* (New York, 1973), 114–15; G. Russell Evans, "Trilateral Commission Controls America, Global Managers Wanted for Greed," *Moral Majority Report*, May 26, 1980, p. 8; G. Russell Evans, "Shall America Be Defended?" *Moral Majority Report*, September 15, 1980, p. 8; G. Russell Evans, "Whatever Happened to Our Values?" *Moral Majority Report*, August 15, 1980, pp. 8–9; Russell Evans and C. Gregg Singer, *The Church and the Sword: An Examination of the Religious Influence in America on Pacifism and Disarmament* (Houston, Tex., 1982), 1, 109. On the back cover of *The Church and the Sword* Singer was described as the author of several books and articles, recently retired from the history department of Catawba College, Salisbury, North Carolina, and an adviser to Senator Willis Smith on the subcommittee of the Senate Judiciary Committee investigating communism in education in the early 1950s.

on church and state," and Jerry Falwell called it a "timely warning" of the "perils facing our beloved America." Strom Thurmond of the Senate Armed Services Committee and Jesse Helms of the Senate Foreign Relations Committee praised the book. John Singlaub and Lewis Walt were among five retired military officers who commended it. "I have become convinced that we have had traitorous actions by members of our own citizenry but until I read *The Church and the Sword*, I never realized the role played by the World and National Councils of Churches," Walt wrote. "This study could prove to be a vitally important effort in the defense of our country."[16]

One is surprised not to find Albion Knight's name among the "Reader Comments," for he certainly shared Evans' opinion regarding the deleterious effect of the mainline churches and councils on U.S. defense and military policy. Their essential agreement is clearly revealed in the way they reacted to the visit of the Reverend William Sloan Coffin, Jr., to West Point in the spring of 1981. The former Yale University chaplain was senior minister at the interdenominational Riverside Church in New York City. A veteran of the Vietnam era antiwar movement (he helped found CALCAV), he had become a well-known advocate of international arms control, economic and social justice, and ecumenicism by the 1980s. He was invited to the academy to speak to about 150 graduating seniors enrolled in a course on American institutions. In an article published in the *Moral Majority Report* in February, 1982, Evans identified Coffin as "the avid booster of pacifist elements which have given aid and comfort to those killing or wrongfully imprisoning U.S. military men." He then summarized Coffin's presentation as "nuclear situational ethics, strategic nuclear pacifism, and unilateral American disarmament." After quoting a statement by Lieutenant General Willard W. Scott, Jr., superintendent of the Military Academy, that the purpose of Coffin's visit was to provide cadets with "an alternative view," Evans complained that "traditional Bible-based speakers" had not been afforded equal time. "One suspects . . . that it would be unthinkable for a religious leader like Jerry Falwell to address the Corps," he wrote. And if West Point now had a policy of "entertaining pacifists," where would the line be drawn in the future? "Are invitations available for Jane Fonda, Gus Hall, Angela Davis, Muammar Gaddafi?" He concluded the article with a quote from General Graham

16. Evans and Singer, *Church and the Sword*, iii–iv, 125–27.

warning of the dangerous implications of Coffin's visit and the rationale behind it: "All this smacks of an attitude which bodes ill for the institution, the army and the military ethic."[17]

When Knight read about Coffin's visit to West Point, he immediately fired off a letter to Superintendent Scott. "You must certainly be aware of the growing campaign by the National Council of Churches and many of the mainline denominations associated with it which criticize our national security posture," he wrote. Having permitted Coffin to expound their "warped views," Scott must "take steps to give the cadets a better understanding and confidence about the morality of serving our nation" as well as "the tools . . . to combat the spiritual arguments of the Coffins." In case he had not yet secured the appropriate speakers, Knight recommended getting in touch with General William Westmoreland or General Richard Stilwell. "I also volunteer my services," he added, reminding Scott of his twenty-five years of service as an Episcopal priest. "For the past two years I have been speaking widely to various church audiences around the country, describing the Biblical basis for national security and the sound basis morally for serving our nation in the face of the satanic evil we now see," he noted. He assured the superintendent that he would be happy to talk with the cadets about such matters.[18]

Like Evans, Albion Knight castigated the "pacifistic blindness" of many of the mainline church leaders, but his main target was the Episcopal Church, his own denomination.[19] It was also the one to which many United States military leaders had traditionally belonged. Knight's conflicted relationship with the Episcopal Church reminds us of the dramatic change that had taken place since the 1960s in the religious preferences of the officer corps.

17. "Coffin, William Sloan, Jr.," *Current Biography Yearbook 1980* (New York, 1980, 1981), 53–54; Gene Preston, "Coffin Confronts the Cadets," *Christian Century*, July 15–22, 1981, pp. 730–33; G. Russell Evans, "Coffin Lectures West Pointers on Pacifism," *Moral Majority Report*, February 22, 1982, pp. 8, 15; and see also G. Russell Evans, "Bureaucrats, Politicians Have Nurtured Pacifism," *Moral Majority Report*, January, 1983, p. 14.

18. Albion Knight to Lt. Gen. Willard W. Scott, Jr., August 26, 1981, in Knight Papers. See also Knight to Scott, November 20, 1981, *ibid.*

19. Albion Knight to Rev. Richard Kim, February 10, 1981; "11 September 1981 Al Knight Commentary Radio Station WABS Arlington, Va"; and "Memorandum to Howard Phillips," dated November 16, 1981, *ibid.*

As an Episcopal priest and retired army general, Knight had a perfect vantage point from which to conduct his campaign against what he called "the flow of pacifist and even left-wing propaganda . . . from the National Church headquarters." The role of gadfly obviously appealed to him. "I find it fun driving bishops nuts over my accusations," he exclaimed in a letter to another conservative Episcopal priest. Knight sent numerous missives to the presiding bishop of the Episcopal Church and various members of the House of Bishops, denouncing the denomination's participation in "the pro-Marxist 'peace movement' now going on in Western Europe and in the United States." He focused most of his attention on the October, 1981, Pastoral Letter of the House of Bishops, which he regarded as a "compromise with oppression."[20]

Knight's differences with the church hierarchy stemmed as much from his evangelical as from his military orientation. He believed that the Episcopal Church's involvement in the peace movement not only threatened national security but also distracted it from its primary responsibility "to fulfill the Great Commission and to bring our people to a living, loving, exciting relationship with Jesus." In the early 1980s he seems to have hoped that the renewal and 1928 Prayer Book movements in the Episcopal Church would restore its "sound Biblical foundations." By December, 1982, however, he had become so distressed by the church's orientation "toward the social gospel instead of the Holy Gospel" that he was considering separating from it. Less than a year later he asked to be received as a priest in the United Episcopal Church, a separatist Anglican body known for its strong Prayer Book emphasis and low-church ethos, and in June, 1984, he became the first bishop consecrated in that denomination.[21] Like his resignation from the U.S. Energy Research and Development Administration and his involvement with the Conservative Caucus, Knight's withdrawal from the mainline

20. Albion Knight to General William C. Westmoreland, November 9, 1981, to the Rev. Herbert A. Ward, Jr., June 22, 1982, to Karl R. Bendetsen, November 16, 1981, to the Right Reverend John M. Allin, D.D., the Presiding Bishop, the Episcopal Church Center, November 8, 1981, to the Right Reverend Robert B. Hall, D.D., Episcopal Bishop of Virginia, November 9, 1981, *ibid.*

21. Albion Knight to the Right Reverend W. Moultrie Moore, D.D., Episcopal Bishop of Easton, [Md.], June 4, 1982, to the Reverend Richard Kim, February 10, 1981, to the Most Reverend C. Dale Doren, D.D., December 8, 1982, *ibid.*; Parker, "U.S. Army General Consecrated Bishop," 10–11; "The Continuing Church Today," *Christian Challenge*, February, 1984, p. 7.

Episcopal Church and association with the United Episcopal Church
testifes to the separatist, ultraconservative impulses that inclined him to
work for the New Christian Right.

The affinity between the New Christian Right and the six retired
military men discussed in this chapter is not difficult to understand. The
NCR cultivated Walt, Evans, Singlaub, Keegan, Knight, and Graham
to lend credibility to or gain assistance in its peace-through-strength
campaign. In the 1980s, these "military experts" lent the NCR the same
authority William K. Harrison, Dwight D. Eisenhower, and Harold K.
Johnson had conferred on evangelicals in the 1950s and 1960s.

For their part, the military men gravitated to the NCR partly because
they agreed with its national defense agenda but also, one suspects, because of personal feelings. Each of them was disaffected in one way or
another. Keegan, Knight, and Graham had resigned from government
or military posts as a protest against the defense policy of the United
States government. Singlaub had been relieved of his command and
forced to retire from the army after making speeches criticizing Carter
administration policies. Evans' conspiratorial view of history and obsession with "the predatory influence of pacifism and detente" evidenced
a more generalized disaffection. Walt's resentment also extended beyond the government's "no-win" policy in Vietnam and its "appeasement" of the Soviets to include antiwar dissent, the drug culture, the
decline of patriotism in the United States, and the "growing disenchant-
ment with its armed forces." All of the components of the massive cultural shift of the 1960s and 1970s dismayed and infuriated him.[22]

Whatever the nature and extent of their disaffection, these retired
military men found some relief, along with a new vocation (and the
opportunity retirement afforded of speaking against government policy), in their alliance with the New Christian Right. The NCR had
considerable appeal for men who worried about a decline of patriotism
and growing disesteem for the armed forces. Remembering the famous
1967 anti-Vietnam march on the Pentagon, they surely appreciated the
1980 Washington for Jesus demonstration in the nation's capital, when
some two hundred thousand evangelicals converged on the Mall to hear
speeches and testimonies praising America. "We're here because we

22. *Conservative Digest*, August, 1979, p. 20; Singlaub, *Hazardous Duty*, 410–13, 423;
"A Lost Command," *Newsweek*, May 30, 1977, p. 17; Lewis W. Walt, "Parting Word,"
Leatherneck, May, 1971, p. 20.

love God and we love this country," declared Pat Robertson, the program co-chairman. Jerry Falwell's I Love America rallies, featuring speeches by the evangelist lamenting America's military decline and praising the armed forces, promulgated a similar message.[23] The promilitary, pro-American stance of the NCR, as much as its position on national defense, enabled it to recruit these men—as well as many other Americans—to its ranks.

23. Edward E. Plowman, "Washington for Jesus: Revival Fervor and Political Disclaimers," *CT*, May 23, 1980, p. 46; David Snowball, *Continuity and Change in the Rhetoric of the Moral Majority* (New York, 1991), 65.

18

Addressing Nuclear Issues

In October, 1983, the radical evangelical magazine *Sojourners* published an interview with Major General Kermit D. Johnson. The recently retired army chief of chaplains presented a stark contrast with the defense posture of the Reagan administration, the New Christian Right, and their allies among the retired military. After almost a decade of reflection, Johnson had concluded that according to just war criteria, the use of nuclear weapons was immoral. He also believed that it was "immoral to threaten to use . . . nuclear weapons," which, as he pointed out, was the basis of nuclear deterrence. He did not go so far as to embrace the pacifist position held by many of the radical evangelicals. Neither did he endorse unilateral disarmament because he believed "the defense of a nation" to be "a moral cause." Professing what he called "the Niebuhrian, and . . . biblical, understanding of being inevitably a part of this sinful world," he took his stand with the option he considered the least immoral: bilateral phased reductions of armaments.[1]

During the *Sojourners* interview Johnson declared: "I'm not unique. Chaplains and others in the military are looking at the moral issues of nuclear war." In fact, he *was* unique in one sense. Although the article did not mention it, he had recently resigned his position as chief of

---

1. "Of Peace and Policy," *Sojourners*, October, 1983, pp. 25–27. Johnson continued to voice his opinions in books and articles. Besides *Realism and Hope in a Nuclear Age* (Atlanta, 1988), see "The Morality of Nuclear Deterrence," in *The Choice: Nuclear Weapons Versus Security*, ed. Gwyn Prins (London, 1984), and "Just War and Nuclear Deterrence," in *The Peacemaking Struggle: Militarism and Resistance: Essays Prepared for the Advisory Council on Church and Society of the Presbyterian Church (U.S.A.)*, ed. Ronald H. Stone and Dana W. Wilbanks (New York, 1985).

chaplains protesting the immorality of the government's policies on nuclear arms and Central America. But as his statement indicates, he was
not the only one investigating nuclear warfare and other related matters.
In the 1980s the military was not so monolithic on the issues of national
defense policy and nuclear weapons as might be supposed. Military men
were raising questions and engaging in discussion of those issues, but it
was being "done quietly," as Johnson pointed out, and therefore attracted little media attention.[2]

The discussion began in the late 1970s when the military leadership,
seeking to shore up a professional ethic badly battered during the Vietnam War, instituted courses on "moral obligation," ethics, and professionalism at the various service academies, staff colleges, and war colleges. These courses provided a forum in which the morality of nuclear
warfare was bound to come under scrutiny, even if it was not the focus
of the courses. In the 1980s, various military journals joined the discussion. Not only the *Military Chaplains' Review* but *Armed Forces and Society*, *Parameters*, and the *Naval War College Review* published articles on
such topics as just war doctrine, the morality of strategic and tactical
nuclear war, nuclear deterrence, and the nuclear freeze.[3]

2. "Of Peace and Policy," 26; Robert C. Toth, "Enhanced Role of Religious Faith
at Pentagon Raises Questions, Doubts," *Los Angeles Times*, December 30, 1984, p. 4.
In *Realism and Hope in a Nuclear Age*, Johnson referred to "inner struggles" that led to
his decision to retire on June 30, 1982, one year before the conclusion of his four-year
term as chief of chaplains. During a time of "soul-searching," he said he identified
closely with the National Conference of Catholic Bishops' *Pastoral Letter on War and
Peace* and even defended it in an article in the *Washington Post* (Johnson, *Realism and
Hope*, 14, and see also 67, 68–69, and the "Personal Note to General E. C. Meyer, Chief
of Staff, U.S. Army" [January 4, 1982], Appendix A). For another firsthand account of
how questions of national defense policy were debated within the military, see Admiral
Noel Gayler, "Opposition to Nuclear Armament" ("Questions and Answers" segment),
Annals of the American Academy of Political and Social Science, CCCCLXIX (September,
1983), 22.

3. For a brief survey of the development of courses on morality, ethics, and professionalism, see Peter L. Stromberg, Malham M. Wakin, Daniel Callahan, *The Teaching
of Ethics in the Military* (Hastings-on-Hudson, N.Y., 1982), 1–2, 19–27. See also Donald
L. Davidson, "Religious Strategists: The Churches and Nuclear Weapons," *Parameters*,
XIII (December, 1983), 26–27; Ethics and Professionalism Committee, U.S. Military
Academy, *War and Morality* (Technical Report distributed by Defense Technical Information Center, Defense Logistics Agency, Cameron Station, Alexandria, Va.,
[1978]); Malham M. Wakin, ed., *War, Morality, and the Military Profession* (Boulder,
Colo., 1979). On some of the courses, see "This Prof Learned the Hard Way," *Time*,

In 1981, in articles published in *Christian Century* and *Christianity Today*, Gene Preston, a foreign service officer with the U.S. State Department, speculated that changes in American defense policy—the abandonment of "massive retaliation" and with it the "neat division between strategic nuclear and conventional warfare," as well as talk of tactical nuclear warfare—had forced many of the military to face "a new level of ethical responsibility." At the U.S. Military Academy, where Preston was teaching, Superintendent Andrew J. Goodpaster and many officers were "worried about the ethical dimensions of megakilling through nuclear confrontation," Preston wrote. The cadets, too, were struggling with—and many had apparently resolved—the issue of nuclear warfare. Discussing the visit of the Reverend William Sloane Coffin, Jr., Preston observed that he spoke to an audience of which the great majority were "already 'nuclear pacifists.'" He quoted one cadet telling Coffin, "Sir, as we would be among the first to get our asses blown up if the U.S. begins to use tactical nuclear weapons, you are talking to a group of peacenicks." Apparently, army chief of staff Edward C. Meyer shared Goodpaster's and other officers' concern. Chaplain Johnson said that Meyer "knew that 'right and wrong' were not beside the point" and explored the moral issues relating to nuclear war.[4]

The chaplaincy, too, discussed the issues relating to nuclear warfare, as Johnson prodded his colleagues to confront questions similar to the ones that had prompted his own "supremely personal interrogation." In May, 1982, he sent a letter to all U.S. Army chaplains suggesting that antinuclear sentiment and longings for peace in the United States and Europe were "a warning and a signal" from God, "possibly a life-and-death 'last chance' for human civilization." He welcomed "this widening awareness" and seemed to be urging other chaplains to welcome and encourage it, too. It was Johnson who requested Chaplain Donald L. Davidson to prepare a research paper on the just war tradition and the positions taken by religious ethicists, denominational leaders, and reli-

---

February 19, 1979, p. 98; Joseph Hodgin Beasley, "Implications of Teaching Ethics: The West Point Experience" (Ph.D. dissertation, University of North Carolina, 1985), esp. Chap. 4; Dennis A. Williams with Jeff B. Copeland, "Warfare for the Moral Man," *Newsweek*, November 19, 1984, p. 129.

4. Gene Preston, "Coffin Confronts the Cadets," *Christian Century*, XCVIII (July 15–22, 1981), 730–32; Gene Preston, "Religion at West Point," *CT*, November 6, 1981, p. 77; Johnson, *Realism and Hope*, 12.

gious bodies concerning nuclear weapons and policies, a project that resulted in the publication, in 1983, of Davidson's book *Nuclear Weapons and the American Churches: Ethical Positions on Modern Warfare.* (The book was used in ethics courses at the Army War College and the Army Command and General Staff College.) The Davidson project seems to have been part of a larger initiative Johnson mentioned in the spring, 1982, issue of the *Military Chaplains' Review*, to address the ethical implications of nuclear warfare. At the Thirty-sixth Annual Command Chaplains Conference in July, 1982, nuclear war was a major topic of discussion, and the fall, 1982, *Military Chaplains' Review* featured articles by chaplains and civilians on questions relating to war and peace.[5] Johnson had retired effective June 30, 1982, but both the conference and the *MCR* issue bore his imprint.

Publication of the various drafts of the Roman Catholic bishops' pastoral letter also fueled the discussion taking place in the military. Articles in *Army Times* and *Air Force Times* indicate that as the bishops' letter moved through various drafts, it created considerable confusion, uncertainty, and anxiety among Catholic service personnel and chaplains (who would have to answer questions about the final statement).[6] Even non-Catholic military could not ignore its implications because some of the mainline Protestant denominations raised many of the same questions the bishops did.

By the mid-1980s, a decade of questioning and discussion had produced a significant strategic and moral reorientation within the U.S. military. In the introduction to a collection of articles on nuclear weaponry published in 1984, Gwyn Prins reflected on the dramatic and far-reaching change that had taken place in military thinking about warfare. The "crude stereotype" of warmonger generals no longer fit. "There

5. Johnson, *Realism and Hope*, 13; Donald L. Davidson, *Nuclear Weapons and the American Churches: Ethical Positions on Modern Warfare* (Boulder, Colo., 1983), 205; Donald L. Davidson, "Religious Strategists," 29 n. 16; Kermit D. Johnson, "A New Stage: Beyond 'In-House' Ethical Issues," *MCR*, Spring, 1982, p. v; Office of Chief of Chaplains, "Annual Historical Review, 1 October 1981–30 September 1982" [1982] (Typescript at U.S. Army Center of Military History), 17.

6. Allen E. Carrier, "DoD Cautious in Appraisal of Bishops' Nuclear Policy," *Air Force Times*, November 15, 1982, p. 4; Allen E. Carrier, "Bishops Soften Stance on Nuclear Arms in Letter," *Air Force Times*, April 18, 1983, p. 2; "Pastoral Letter: Cardinal Cooke Calls for Views," *Air Force Times*, June 20, 1983, p. 3; Allen E. Carrier, "'Softer' Anti-Nuke Letter Relieves Chaplains," *Army Times*, April 18, 1983, p. 4; *NYT*, May 6, 1983, p. 32.

are distinguished new voices to be heard, especially those of men who have held the highest military and diplomatic offices, saying things which are totally unexpected to those who have not yet understood how great has been the sea-change of the last five years," Prins observed. He referred specifically to three retired U.S. military men who had contributed to the collection and who, he pointed out, "are now free in their retirement to make their opinions known to the public." (They had all spoken and acted on their views while in active service, he noted parenthetically.) Prins named Rear Admiral Eugene F. Carroll, Jr., former assistant deputy chief of naval operations for plans, policy, and operations; Admiral Noel Gayler, former commander in chief of all U.S. forces in the Pacific; and Lieutenant General Arthur S. Collins, former deputy commander in chief of the U.S. Army, Europe. John Kenneth Galbraith, another contributor to the Prins collection, included the three men in "a dedicated group of former high officers of the armed services" who had assumed leadership in pressing for arms control. Chaplain Kermit Johnson also named them, along with army chief of staff Bernard Rogers and Rear Admiral Gene R. LaRocque, as part of a constellation of retired and active-duty military men who publicly registered strongly dissenting views during the 1980s with regard to United States defense policy.[7]

All of these men expressed skepticism about the use (and usefulness) of nuclear weapons; all urged reduction in the building and deployment of such armaments. Admiral Gayler derided SDI as a "silver bullet, the idea that science will somehow protect us from the rain of nuclear ballistic missiles." Admiral LaRocque also clashed with administration policy in calling for a reassessment of traditional assumptions about the Soviet Union (especially the "devil image" articulated by President Reagan) and in urging efforts to promote U.S.-Soviet cooperation and understanding. Although none of these men could be called "nuclear pacifists" and their thinking was probably primarily influenced by strategic considerations, it is clear they were also motivated by moral considerations. Their questioning provided proof that, as General Rogers observed in 1983, "those of us who are in uniform and some of us who

7. Gwyn Prins, "Introduction: The Paradox of Security," in *The Choice*, ed. Prins, ix; John Kenneth Galbraith, "The Military Power," in *The Choice*, ed. Prins, 207; Johnson, *Realism and Hope*, 19, 25, 39–40, 75, 79.

bear some responsibility for the defence of western nations are not unmindful of the moral issues involved."[8]

The discussion and debate going on within the military as well as in the civilian sector raised issues the Officers' Christian Fellowship could hardly ignore. The OCF took up the challenge, stating its views and answering those it opposed. In the first of two special war and peace issues of *Command* published during the 1980s, the editor, Don Martin, Jr., explained why it was necessary to reiterate the "biblical basis for military service." He observed that at a recent meeting of army ROTC professors from over one hundred universities and colleges, an officer had asked for assistance in replying to "the attacks of religious pacifists at his institution." Martin also cited comments and questions he had received from ROTC cadets and active-duty personnel regarding Christians serving in the military. Even persons who had served in the armed forces for many years seemed troubled by "a deep uncertainty," he added. Their "honest doubts" were "intensified . . . by the vociferous denunciations of our military people and policies by various pacifist groups."[9]

The fall, 1981, issue of *Command* addressed such doubts and anxiety. It presented a two-pronged critique of pacifism, challenging the way its advocates interpreted the Bible as well as the doctrines they claimed to derive from it. Thus the *Command* writers argued that pacifists erred in invoking the Sixth Commandment to support their position because it actually prohibited murder, not killing. The writers insisted that Jesus' advice in the Sermon on the Mount to turn the other cheek and love one's enemies applied to "personal relationships and actions," to individuals acting as individuals, not to government policy. (The same

8. Noel Gayler, "Opposition to Nuclear Armament," *Annals of the American Academy of Political and Social Science*, CDLXIX (September, 1983), 16; Gene R. LaRocque, "America's Nuclear Ferment: Opportunities for Change," *Annals of the American Academy of Political and Social Science*, CDLXIX (September, 1983), 32, 36–37; Peter Nichols, "The General a Long Way from Apocalypse Now," *The Times* (London), March 12, 1983, p. 8. See also Richard Halloran, *To Arm a Nation: Rebuilding America's Endangered Defenses* (New York, 1986), 44; "NATO Chief Supports Nuclear Cuts," *Wall Street Journal*, July 18, 1983, p. 23; Walter Pincus, "U.S. Is Rapidly Reducing Stockpile of Tactical Nuclear Arms in Europe," *Washington Post*, January 17, 1986, p. A9; Arthur S. Collins, Jr., "Strategy for Survival," *Washington Quarterly*, Summer, 1983, pp. 67–79.

9. "Editorial: Is Peace Possible?" *Command*, Fall, 1981, p. 2; "May a Christian Serve in the Armed Forces?" *Command*, Fall, 1981, inside front cover.

Christ who taught nonresistance used physical violence against the
money changers in the temple and sanctioned the carrying of swords by
his disciples, Lieutenant Colonel Al Shine pointed out.) Both mistakes
betrayed the "serious flaw" in the pacifists' approach to Scripture. They
violated what William T. Waldrop called the "two cardinal rules of
sound biblical interpretation," first that no passage should be interpreted in isolation from other pertinent Scripture and second that each
individual passage must be analyzed in its historical context. The *Command* writers insisted that, properly interpreted, neither the Old nor the
New Testament presented an "anti-military, pacifist position." "The
Christian ethic of war rises from the entire body of biblical truth,"
Waldrop asserted. Just as the Bible justified individual participation in
the military and war, it also sanctioned government's use of force as a
means of carrying out its divinely appointed task of ensuring justice and
good order. Here the OCF writers cited the familiar passages in Romans
13:1–7.[10]

The OCF writers presented their critique of pacifism within a frame-
work of what they called "Christian realism." Viewing war as a consequence of man's rebellion again God—as a consequence or expression
of sin—they insisted that violent international conflict ("wars and rumors of wars" in Matthew 24:6–7) would continue until Christ's return.
Their perspective denied the possibility that human beings could ever
bring about lasting peace on earth. Only the coming of Christ would
accomplish that.[11]

Juxtaposed to the articles on pacifism were two articles that took note
of the relatively new discussion of questions relating to the stockpiling
and use of nuclear weapons: William K. Harrison's "Nuclear War and
the Christian" and Don Martin's "On Nuclear Deterrence." Both writers supported the system of nuclear deterrence. The president emeritus
of the OCF insisted that the United States must maintain "a fully adequate nuclear deterrent" and must be willing to "use it on a moment's

10. Al Shine, "War and the Christian," *Command*, Fall, 1981, pp. 23–25; Peter S.
Lent, "The Christian Soldier," *Command*, Fall, 1981, pp. 19–20; William T. Waldrop,
"An Essay on Christian Participation in War," *Command*, Fall, 1981, pp. 27, 29, 40;
George Ladd, "The Christian and the State," *Command*, Fall, 1981, p. 13; Robert L.
Baughan, Jr., "My Country: Right or Wrong?" *Command*, Fall, 1981, p. 16.

11. "Editorial: Is Peace Possible?" 2; D. Martyn Lloyd-Jones, "Why Does God
Allow War?" *Command*, Fall, 1981, p. 11; Don Martin, Jr., "On Nuclear Deterrence,"
Command, Fall, 1981, p. 32; Ladd, "Christian and the State," 12.

notice" to thwart Soviet aggression, especially in the Middle East, as well as to prevent Soviet blackmail or a takeover of the United States. Harrison argued that if the United States disarmed unilaterally, the Soviets could threaten to explode a few nuclear weapons over New York or some other city and thereby force the United States to permit a communist government "under Russian agents" to be installed. He also contended that nuclear deterrence was "the best way" of preventing a nuclear war. "If the United States is armed to the extent that its strategic forces can survive a first strike and retaliate with sufficent [*sic*] power to destroy Russia, there is far less chance of a nuclear war occuring [*sic*]," he wrote.[12]

Don Martin also opposed unilateral disarmament. Such a policy would "shatter" the North Atlantic Treaty Organization (NATO) defense efforts that helped prevent the Soviet conquest of Europe, and it would render the United States incapable of defending "western values and interests," he declared. Like Harrison, he feared that unilateral disarmament would put an American president in the position of having to "capitulate to Soviet demands in order to preclude nuclear attack on our cities." Citing Romans 13, Martin argued that the United States had "the biblical obligation" to protect not only its own citizens but those of other nations from Soviet domination. Nuclear deterrence was the way to fulfill that obligation. And because it conformed to "biblical principles," American Christians, whether in uniform or not, were "bound by God's commands" to support it. (At the same time Martin argued for nuclear deterrence, he favored negotiating mutual, verifiable nuclear arms reductions with the Soviets.)[13]

By the spring of 1989, when the OCF published the next war-and-peace issue of *Command*, it confronted the new issues raised during more than a decade of debate over nuclear arms and national defense policy. Even pacifism had acquired a new aspect. The 1981 articles had dealt with "historic pacifism." By 1989 radical evangelicalism, which was much more aggressive and activist, had become a force to be reckoned with, for military as well as civilian evangelicals, because the radicals had been evangelizing the armed forces. Besides Kermit Johnson and retired army chaplain George Zabelka, who had pastored the army air corps

12. William K. Harrison, "Nuclear War and the Christian," *Command*, Fall, 1981, p. 30.
13. Martin, "On Nuclear Deterrence," 34, 41.

squadron that dropped the atomic bombs on Hiroshima and Nagasaki, the radicals claimed to have discovered other military personnel who questioned the wisdom and sanity of the government's nuclear policies.[14]

The two writers in the 1989 *Command* issue who answered the radical evangelical position sought to undermine it by exposing its political thrust, the same tactic used in the NAE's PFSS *Guidelines*. Associate editor Vern Kirby pointedly distinguished between "Christian pacifists," that is, adherents of "historic pacifism" ("our brothers and sisters in Christ who see this issue from a different perspective"), and others "who would attempt to bend legitimate Christian desires for peace to meet certain political objectives inimical to the interests of freedom and, ultimately, to Christianity." Alberto Coll attacked the radical evangelicals for being "heavily indebted to the predominant intellectual milieu of the Left, and to various currents of neo-pacifism, neo-Marxism and liberation theology."[15]

The critique of radical evangelicals was not the only new note sounded in the 1989 War and Peace issue. By that date the OCF confronted an even more potent challenge in the statements the mainline denominations had issued against U.S. nuclear policy. Most of the mainline denominations appealed to the just war theory to support their positions on the morality of nuclear weapons. In "Christian Morality and Nuclear Deterrence," a U.S. Air Force captain, Charles H. Nicholls, combined the just war theory and Scripture to argue in favor of both nuclear deterrence and nuclear retaliation. Nuclear deterrence, he said, was "the best moral option" currently available for preventing nuclear war and "Soviet domination of the world." And if nuclear deterrence failed, Nicholls was prepared to retaliate with nuclear weapons against a Soviet strike on the United States. "Nuclear retaliation repays the enemy with the destruction he is inflicting on our own nation," he observed. Both the attack and counterattack would be "stupendous

14. "'I Was Told It Was Necessary,'" *Sojourners*, August, 1980, pp. 12–15; George Zabelka, "As Spiritual Leaders: An Open Letter to Military Chaplains," *Sojourners*, August, 1984, p. 5; William O'Brien, "The Reluctant Prophet: Atomic Chaplain George Zabelka Now Preaches Peace," *Other Side*, December, 1985, pp. 8–9; Vic Hummert, "The Challenge from Within: Signs of Doubt in Military Personnel," *Sojourners*, May, 1986, p. 38.

15. V[ern] K[irby], "Editorial: Prepared for War; Hungry for Peace," *Command*, Spring, 1989, p. 1; Alberto R. Coll, "The Virtue of Prudence in Foreign Policy: A Challenge to Evangelicals," *Command*, Spring, 1989, p. 25.

evils," visiting untold destruction, he admitted. Yet, Nicholls asserted, "I believe that the good of minimizing further Soviet aggression against world freedom would justify the horrible option of nuclear retaliation." He contended that large portions of the world would survive "a major nuclear war." Should they include the Soviet Union or its Warsaw Pact allies, "their military power could achieve the global domination that has long been their goal." The United States would have to retaliate "to guarantee the end of this threat to world freedom." Replying to the Catholic bishops' argument against the use of nuclear weapons because of the likelihood that large numbers of civilians would be killed, Nicholls invoked a statement in a 1983 pastoral letter by German Catholic bishops: "Physical death of the human race is not the worst evil. But spiritual evil is when we choose [that evil] because we have neither the moral courage [n]or the intellectual acumen to recognize it and prevent it." [16]

Significantly, Nicholls did not rely solely on just war doctrine or even put it on a par with Scripture. "The just war doctrine should be cherished as an attempt to limit" the evil of war, "not as a standard of absolute morality," he asserted. Why? For one thing, because it was "man-made," the formulation of mere human beings, but also, and more important for Nicholls, "because the God Who redeemed us through Calvary also ordained the complete destruction of the Canaanites." Nicholls could not ignore the contradiction between just war doctrine (especially its emphasis on noncombatant immunity) and the Bible passage in which God ordained the Hebrew conquest of Canaan—"a campaign," Nicholls pointed out, "which included the intentional slaughter of noncombatants in their cities." In the end, Nicholls declared, quoting a University of Calgary professor of religious studies, "The war narratives of the Old Testament are a safer guide to the reality of war than are the various formulations of the 'Just War' theory that have emerged in the history of Christianity." [17] Thus evangelicals' insistence on the primacy of the Bible as the inerrant word of God bolstered Nicholls' argument in favor of nuclear deterrence and retaliation.

The 1989 issue of *Command* also took note of the discussion of defense strategy going on within as well as outside the armed forces by including a review of *A Just Defense* by Keith B. Payne and Karl I. Payne,

16. Charles H. Nicholls, "Christian Morality and Nuclear Deterrence," *Command*, Spring, 1989, pp. 39–40.

17. *Ibid.*

published in 1987 by Multnomah Press. (Keith Payne was a specialist in defense and foreign policy who served as vice-president of the National Institute for Public Policy in Fairfax, Virginia, while his brother Karl, a graduate of Western Conservative Baptist Seminary in Portland, Oregon, served as administrator of youth at the Fourth Memorial Church in Spokane, Washington.) Quoting conservative Republican congressman Jack Kemp's endorsement, Don Martin recommended the book to *Command* readers as "'probably the best contribution in recent years to the ongoing debate among evangelicals over how we Christians are to carry out our biblical mandate for peacemaking.'" Martin praised the book partly for its indictment of pacifism, a primary concern of both the 1981 and 1989 issues of *Command*. (Indeed, besides the review of the book, the 1989 issue carried a separate article by the Paynes, based on a chapter of their book, in which they criticized the radical evangelicals for claiming that the early church fathers opposed Christian participation in war.) Martin also endorsed the Paynes' argument in favor of nuclear deterrence and, looking ahead, "a just nuclear strategy" (the "just defense" in the title of the book), which the authors claimed was "the most realistic and moral alternative on the horizon and deserves the backing of all who desire to be peacemakers in the nuclear age." The "just defense" was, of course, President Reagan's Strategic Defense Initiative.[18]

The 1981 and 1989 issues of *Command* magazine convey the sense of urgency with which OCF members addressed questions of war and peace during the 1980s. The peace movement that was agitating American society, combined with the discussion in the armed forces, posed an immediate threat to OCF members' conservative religious faith as well as their military careers. Pacifism, of course, had long constituted what Vern Kirby, associate editor of *Command*, termed "a fundamental challenge to Christians in the military service."[19] That *Command* devoted a good deal of space to its rebuttal is not suprising. For military evangelicals, pacifism raised questions not just about the nation's right to use force but about the morality of individual participation in the armed

18. Don Martin, Jr., "Book Review: A Just Defense," *Command*, Spring, 1989, p. 31; Keith B. Payne and Karl I. Payne, "Temporal Warfare and the Early Church," *Command*, Spring, 1989, pp. 11–14. See also Keith B. Payne, *Strategic Defense: "Star Wars" in Perspective* (Lanham, Md., 1986).

19. K[irby], "Editorial: Prepared for War," 36.

services and war. Pacifism posed a perennial question that each new group of volunteers in the armed forces, each new class of cadets or midshipmen at the academies, had to face: whether a Christian may serve in the military.

At the same time, the questions raised about national defense policy in the 1980s also presented a comparatively new but equally immediate challenge to military evangelicals. For air force captain Charles Nicholls, the morality of nuclear deterrence and warfare was not an abstract issue. Describing himself as "a Christian and a professional military officer serving in America's nuclear deterrent force," he pointed out the challenge he and other military personnel, similarly situated, confronted. "Those of us on missile or bomber crews must . . . make the decision now. Before taking the oath of office or donning the uniform, we must commit ourselves to duty. We must decide now that our mission is compatible with our morality, or else we must resign our commissions."[20] One is reminded of the ROTC instructors who sought advice and assistance at the OCF meeting Don Martin referred to and the West Point cadets who attended the Reverend William Sloan Coffin's address—and the countless other young men and women in the services who grappled with the ethical questions relating to military service, combat, and nuclear war.

Although their stated purpose was to provide moral support and information to OCF members who felt threatened by certain views being advocated within as well as outside the military, there is no indication in either of the two special *Command* issues of an official OCF position on national defense policy and nuclear weapons. The authors of the articles agreed in opposing the pacifism of the historic peace churches and radical evangelicals, as well as unilateral disarmament and a nuclear freeze, and they seemed to support the Reagan buildup of conventional and nuclear forces. But they espoused different, even conflicting, views on other issues. Those who wrote of retaliating against Soviet aggression with nuclear weapons and of surviving a nuclear war or who advocated SDI would seem to have been in the camp of the New Christian Right and its retired "military experts." Those who supported nuclear deterrence and negotiations with the Soviet Union for a mutual, verifiable arms reduction agreement seem to fit better in the mainstream evangelical camp. Just as it is impossible to infer a single OCF position from

20. Nicholls, "Christian Morality and Nuclear Deterrence," 39.

the two special *Command* issues, the sample of views published therein is not large enough to provide a basis for drawing conclusions about the opinions of the OCF membership as a whole. No doubt their views also ranged over the spectrum represented by the NCR and mainstream evangelicalism.

One conclusion that can be advanced with some certainty is that in the 1980s, evangelical opinion on national security issues was not so monolithic as might be expected. Leaving aside the radical evangelicals, who had disagreed with other evangelicals on those issues since Vietnam, the evangelical community was itself divided. The conflicting opinions espoused by the NCR and its "military experts," the mainstream evangelicals, and the OCF writers reveal that evangelicals' longstanding pro-military, pro-defense consensus was disintegrating.

In turn, this conflict of opinion among evangelicals had important implications for their relationship with the United States military and its leaders. The military leadership's views on national defense policy and nuclear weapons were changing. From the discussion of such men as Admirals Noel Gayler and Gene LaRocque we know that some military leaders were skeptical of President Reagan's national security policies. A *Newsweek* poll conducted in June, 1984, however, showed that the vast majority of active-duty military leaders overwhelmingly supported Reagan.

The poll surveyed the attitudes and opinions of 257 active flag rank officers from all four service branches stationed in the United States. The great majority (85 percent) described themselves as conservatives in politics, and 67 percent stated that their religious beliefs were "very important." About a third of them expressed hawkish views. They were the generals and admirals who thought there could be a winner in a nuclear war between the United States and the Soviet Union and believed that a nuclear first strike by the United States on the Soviet Union could be justified under certain conditions. The other two-thirds expressed much more temperate views. The great majority (88 percent) discounted the likelihood of war with the Soviet Union, and 64 percent were not concerned about a direct nuclear attack on the United States by the Soviet Union. Seventy-five percent did not believe there could be a winner in a nuclear war between the United States and the Soviet Union; 65 percent did not think a first strike against the Soviet Union could be justified. Although 57 percent thought it would be possible to fight a war with the Soviet Union employing tactical nuclear weapons, the majority also expressed "cautionary opinions" about the use of nuclear weapons generally. Finally, with regard to building up United States military power vis-à-vis the Soviet Union, 59 percent believed the objective should be parity; only 35 percent said the United States needed to be stronger than the Soviet Union.[21]

The views of the majority of military leaders described above contrast sharply with those of the New Christian Right and its military allies, both active-duty and retired. To be sure, 88 percent of the military leaders in the *Newsweek* poll registered an unfavorable opinion of the nuclear freeze movement, but 54 percent expressed a similar view of the Moral Majority, despite their avowed conservatism and religious beliefs. All of this suggests that by the 1980s another segment of the evangelical community, besides the radicals, disagreed with the military leadership on issues of national defense. Holding fast to their traditional pro-military, pro-defense views and unbending in their hostility toward the Soviet Union, the hawkish evangelicals identified with the New Christian Right were unable or unwilling to adapt to the military leadership's changing perspective. The estrangement was not very obvious in the 1980s. Still, it seems an interesting portent for evangelicals' future relationship with the U.S. military.

21. "NEWSWEEK Poll: A Survey of the Attitudes and Opinions of U.S. Military Leaders" (*Newsweek* poll conducted by the Gallup Organization, Princeton, N.J., prepared by Andrew Kohut and Neil Upmeyer; typescript dated July, 1984), n.p. I wish to thank David Alpern and Hujik Zeglarski for helping me obtain a copy of this poll.

19

John A. Wickham, "A Soldier Who Cares About Families"

In June, 1985, *Decision* magazine, published by the Billy Graham Evangelistic Association, featured an interview with Army Chief of Staff General John A. Wickham, Jr., under the title "A Soldier Who Cares About Families." In the interview Wickham stated his rationale for improving the situation of the army family. "The stronger the bonds of the family, the better the family feels about the Army," he observed. He also described some of the measures implemented to foster the well-being of the families of servicemen and servicewomen: drug and alcohol abuse and suicide prevention programs, child care centers, and family counseling services. Specifically, he noted that in orientation programs for young married couples the army and air force were using a videotape entitled *Where's Dad?*, adapted from Dr. James C. Dobson's *Focus on the Family* film series.[1]

That Wickham's expression of concern for army families should strike a responsive chord among evangelicals is not surprising given their long-standing and highly publicized preoccupation with the erosion of the family and "family values" in the United States. Equally appealing was his endorsement of Dobson, a rising star in the evangelical galaxy who had recently been named NAE Layman of the Year.[2] The religious

1. "A Soldier Who Cares About Families: An Interview with General John A. Wickham Jr.," *Decision*, XXVI (June, 1985), 23–24.
2. On evangelicals and the family, see, for example, Lawrence O. Richards, "The Idea Bank," *UEA*, Winter, 1971, p. 32; "Save the Family," *UEA*, Summer, 1982, pp. 21–23; "Convention '82: 'Save the Family,'" *UEA*, Summer, 1982, pp. 28–29; Jean Caffey Lyles, "NAE's Focus on the Family," *Christian Century*, XCIX (April 7, 1982), 398–400; Jerry Falwell, *Listen, America!* (Garden City, N.Y., 1980), 121–37; Jerry Fal-

testimony Wickham offered in the *Decision* interview established his evangelical credentials beyond a shadow of a doubt. From 1983 to 1987, evangelicals within and outside the army claimed the chief of staff as one of their own.

To be sure, many of Wickham's official pronouncements lacked a specifically evangelical (or even religious) orientation. When he retired in 1987, for example, he summed up in purely secular terms the vision for the army that he had tried to follow during his tenure as chief of staff: "strengthening the quality of our soldiers, as well as the ethical and leadership foundation of our leaders, and the quality of life for our families."[3] Moreover, throughout his four years as army chief he typically justified the leadership and family programs he implemented in terms of the primary mission of the army, defined as maintaining readiness and military capability. The religious testimony he offered in the *Decision* article, however, viewed in the context of his personal and professional background, reveals the religious grounding of his leadership.

In the 1984 interview on which the *Decision* article was based, Wickham declared: "I'm a man of great faith, but quiet faith. And I believe in prayer and pray every day, pray for all the help that I can get." He had not always been a man of great faith. As a youth and during his student days at West Point, he was conventionally religious. Raised an Episcopalian, he attended church and Sunday school regularly, became a member of the Brotherhood of St. Andrew, a children's organization, and sometimes served as an acolyte. At West Point in the late 1940s, he attended chapel (which was compulsory), but his religious involvement during those years, by his own testimony, was not "out of the ordinary."[4]

---

well with Ed Dobson and Ed Hindson, eds., *The Fundamentalist Phenomenon: The Resurgence of Conservative Christianity* (Garden City, N.Y., 1981), 189, 205–206; David Harrington Watt, "The Private Hopes of American Fundamentalists and Evangelicals, 1925–1975," *Religion and American Culture*, I (Summer, 1991), 164–69 passim; Michael Lienesch, *Redeeming America: Piety and Politics in the New Christian Right* (Chapel Hill, 1993), Chap. 2. On Dobson and evangelicals' reaction to Wickham's endorsement of him, see "Convention '82," 28–29; letters of the following to John A. Wickham: Mary Ann Miller, June 23, 1985, J. Allan Petersen, June 27, 1985, Mrs. Ruby Patrick, [June 8, 1985], Burton D. Patrick, Major General, U.S. Army, June 12, 1985, all in John A. Wickham Papers, U.S. Army Military Institute, Carlisle Barracks, Pa.

3. "Army Chief of Staff Joins Retiree Ranks," *Army Echoes*, XXXI (May–June, 1987), 1.

4. "Interview with Army Chief of Staff, General Wickham, with Decision Maga-

The turning point in his "Christian experience"—the occasion that he said assured him of "the value of prayer"—occurred while he was serving as a battalion commander with the 1st Cavalry Division in Vietnam in 1967. His unit had just established a base in Quang Ngai province. In the predawn hours Viet Cong and North Vietnamese soldiers dressed in U.S. Army uniforms infiltrated and launched an attack. According to Wickham's account, a rocket exploded next to his tent, breaking his eardrums and filling him with "a lot of lead." Bleeding profusely, he rolled into a foxhole. Then, he continued, "A North Vietnamese soldier poked his AK-47 automatic rifle into the foxhole and fired three bursts. I thought it was all over and began praying. I thanked the Lord for the life he had given me and asked just two things: 'Take care of my family, and let me remain conscious through the night to protect this battalion.'" Eventually Wickham managed to call in defensive fire and air support, but Medevac helicopters were unable to land for three and a half hours. "Those endless hours were filled with terror," he remembered, "and I prayed frequent, simple prayers. Finally, I asked that the suffering of my family be eased when they learned of my death, and a strange peacefulness came over me. I remained conscious until morning, when I was evacuated to an aid station."[5]

Wickham's religious experience on the battlefield crystallized the two concerns he later emphasized as army chief of staff—for the families of

---

zine, Washington, D.C., September 27, 1984" (Typed transcript in Wickham Papers), 16, 20, 19; "A Soldier Who Cares," 23; U.S. Army Military History Institute Senior Officer Oral History Program, Project 1991-1, "General John A. Wickham, Jr., USA, Retired, interviewed by Lieutenant Colonel Jose M. Alvarez, USA" (Photocopied typescript; Carlisle Barracks, Pa., 1991), 4 (hereafter cited as Wickham Oral History Interview).

5. "Biography United States Army: General John A. Wickham, Jr., Chief of Staff, United States Army" (Washington, D.C., n.d.), in Wickham Papers; "A Soldier Who Cares," 23–24. Interestingly, the testimony printed in the *Decision* magazine article was not the one Wickham had given in his 1984 interview with a representative of the magazine, though it was similar. The *Decision* testimony was from an address he had given at the Salisbury, Maryland, mayor's prayer breakfast, a copy of which was apparently given to *Decision* magazine shortly before it published its article. See John A. Wickham, Jr., "Some Things Are Eternal" (Typescript of address by General John A. Wickham, Jr., Chief of Staff, United States Army, 10th Annual Salisbury Major's [*sic*] Prayer Breakfast, Salisbury, Maryland, April 3, 1985, in Wickham Papers). For a briefer statement of Wickham's religious experience, see Wickham to David Adams, April 10, 1985, in Wickham Papers.

military personnel and for soldiers themselves. For Wickham, the fact that God answered his prayers seemed to validate those concerns. His experience left him with a conviction that God had saved him for a purpose. As he said in a U.S. Army Military History Institute interview: "I almost lost my life in Vietnam. . . . People never expected me to survive, much less to go back to active duty. But I did, and every day I am reminded that I got another chance. Another chance for what? . . . I always wondered about that and I have always taken that another [sic] chance as an additional responsibility to make a difference. . . . So I tried to make a difference in terms of moral values." The sense of having been given another chance—and of being accountable to God—remained a persistent element in his thinking.[6]

Wickham became chief of staff at a time when efforts to improve the caliber of army leadership and the quality of life of soldiers and their families were already under way. During the Vietnam War, in the late 1960s and early 1970s, there were numerous reports of corruption, drug and alcohol abuse, "fraggings," and a general breakdown of discipline in the armed forces. Two widely acclaimed commentators, Richard Gabriel and Paul Savage, blamed the "disintegration" of the army on a failure of leadership. Instead of a professional ethic based on honor, officers had adopted a "managerial ethos" emphasizing efficiency and self-interest. Other critics cited the pernicious effect of "careerism" in undermining professional dedication in the military. In response to such criticism, from within as well as outside the military, army chief of staff William Westmoreland and his successors instituted a process of reassessment and revitalization of the army's professional ethic.[7]

6. Wickham Oral History Interview, 89. See also Wickham to Dan Coats, December 26, 1985; and "Interview with Army Chief of Staff, General Wickham," 18, 22; "General John A. Wickham, Chief of Staff of the Army, Interview with Peter Grier, Christian Science Monitor, 1 November 1985" (Typed transcript), 24, all in Wickham Papers.

7. Richard A. Gabriel and Paul L. Savage, *Crisis in Command: Mismanagement in the Army* (New York, 1978), esp. x–xi, 17–22; Paul L. Savage and Richard A. Gabriel, "Cohesion and Disintegration in the American Army: An Alternative Perspective," *Armed Forces and Society*, II (Spring, 1976), 340–76; Cincinnatus, *Self-Destruction: The Disintegration and Decay of the United States Army During the Vietnam Era* (New York, 1981); Stuart H. Loory, *Defeated: Inside America's Military Machine* (New York, 1973); Edward L. King, *The Death of the Army: A Pre-Mortem* (New York, 1972); Haynes Johnson and George C. Wilson, *Army in Anguish* (New York, 1972); Colonel Harry G. Summers, Jr., "The Army After Vietnam," in *Against All Enemies: Interpretations of*

Wickham continued the efforts to strengthen and improve the quality of leadership in the army. Significantly, he credited former chief of staff Harold K. Johnson, under whom he had served in the mid-1960s, as being "singularly influential," citing his "ethical approach," his "dedication to rectitude," and his "towering integrity." During his own term as army chief of staff, Wickham stressed what he called "the ethical foundation of military leadership." In 1986 he and Secretary of the Army John O. Marsh proclaimed "Values" the year's theme. As Wickham noted in his introduction to the 1986 Army White Paper, *Values*, the theme complemented the "Leadership" theme proclaimed the year before because "leaders have a critical role in instilling and strengthening our Army values." The Army White Paper, as well as other publications issued during Wickham's tenure as chief of staff, described the "core values" of the army professional ethic as "institutional values" such as loyalty, duty, integrity, and selfless service, combined with "soldierly values" such as commitment, competence, candor, and courage. Taken together, the institutional and soldierly values constituted what Wickham called the "bedrock" or "cornerstone" of the army.[8]

In explaining the need to strengthen and maintain values, Wickham pointed out that the military profession "involves profound moral issues" because "we are dealing with matters of life and death—for ourselves, for those who serve shoulder to shoulder with us, for our nation, for our families, and for adversaries and noncombatants." Values helped soldiers "withstand the rigors of combat or the challenges of daily life that might tempt us to compromise our principles." In particular, values were necessary because soldiers often had to make "tough *ethical*

American Military History from Colonial Times to the Present, ed. Kenneth J. Hagan and William R. Roberts (Westport, Conn., 1986), 361, 365; Richard Halloran, *To Arm a Nation: Rebuilding America's Endangered Defenses* (New York, 1986), 114–22.

8. "General John A. Wickham, Chief of Staff of the Army, Interview with Peter Grier," 21; Wickham Oral History Interview, 19–21, 40; John A. Wickham, Jr., "The Role of Values in Organizations," *Signal*, XLII (August, 1988), 20; Wickham to Major General Will Hill Tankersley, USAR, May 14, 1984, and to Mrs. Harold K. Johnson, [September, 1985], in Wickham Papers; John A. Wickham, Jr., "The Ethical Foundation of Military Leadership," in Wickham, *Guideposts for a Proud and Ready Army* (N.p., [1985]), 1–4; John A. Wickham, Jr., "To: All Members of the Total Army," in *Values* (U.S. Army White Paper, 1986), n.p., 5, 10; *The Army* (FM 100-1; Pre-Publication Edition, June, 1986, in Special Subjects Files, Wickham Papers), Chap. 4; *Military Leadership* (FM 22-100; Washington, D.C., 1983), Chap. 4.

choices" involving questions of right and wrong. "We need a rock-solid ethical base because those who make moral decisions about right and wrong must themselves abide by the highest standards of behavior," Wickham asserted.[9]

In inculcating values among army commanders Wickham frequently exhorted them to exercise "caring leadership." Given his religious orientation, it is probably not inappropriate to view "caring leadership" as an application of the Christian virtue, charity, even though he defined the term in purely secular language as "genuine concern for the individual's well-being and his ability to survive on the battlefield or succeed in the workplace." It meant "much more than a cursory interest" in soldiers' affairs, Wickham insisted. It meant "setting examples of moral and professional excellence" to inspire soldiers. It also meant sincere involvement in working to find solutions to soldiers' problems and improve their welfare. The idea of "caring leadership" included concern for army families. It also guided Wickham's enunciation of two army policies, one to "deglamorize" consumption of alcoholic beverages and reduce alcohol abuse, the other to limit smoking in military installations, vehicles, and aircraft and encourage soldiers to quit using tobacco products. Typically, Wickham defended the policies as a means of enhancing military readiness and promoting soldiers' health and fitness, but he also justified them on the basis of the army's commitment to "providing caring and responsible leadership." Many military men thought that the policies stemmed from his religious views.[10]

The alcohol and smoking policies recall General Harold K. Johnson's prohibition of swearing. Although Wickham received some letters protesting his actions (including one from "an old soldier" who had served under General George S. Patton and who wondered "when the troops will be forbidden to cuss and tell dirty stories"), in general the response to his policies was much more positive than the reaction to Johnson's

9. Wickham, "Ethical Foundation," 4, 2; *Values*, 5, 9–10.

10. John A. Wickham, Jr., "Today's Army—Proud and Ready" (Typescript dated October 1, 1984, in Wickham Papers), n.p.; *Leadership* (U.S. Army White Paper, 1985), 8; John A. Wickham, Jr., and John O. Marsh, Jr., "Department of the Army Alcohol Policy" (Typescript dated March 25, 1985); John A. Wickham, Jr., "Smoking Policy" (Typescript [June, 1986]); Wickham to Jerome F. Beekman, July 21, 1986, and to E. Warren Smith, July 15, [1986], all in Wickham Papers; Robert K. Wright, Jr., of U.S. Army Center of Military History, conversation with author, Oxford, Mississippi, October 6, 1988.

order prohibiting swearing. Not surprisingly, evangelicals proved especially supportive of Wickham's policies, as well as his overall effort to improve leadership and inculcate values. A World War II veteran, who said he had drunk alcoholic beverages and played poker while in the army but had stopped since "becoming a Christian," wrote to Wickham, "I praise the Lord for raising you up at this time as Army Chief of Staff, an influence for good for our young men in the military service." Evangelicals within the military also praised Wickham for openly expressing his Christian convictions and emphasizing the ethical basis of leadership. In 1986 former OCF president Clay Buckingham wrote him to express "appreciation and respect for the quality of leadership" Wickham was providing the army. "In particular," Buckingham noted, "your personal Christian commitment has manifested itself in the emphasis you have placed on family, and on values." Buckingham reported that officers he had recently talked with at Carlisle and Leavenworth shared his favorable views.[11]

Colonel Alexander P. Shine urged Wickham to broaden his policies to include the pornographic reading material found in PXs, dayrooms, troop lounges, and the like. "It seems particularly inappropriate in a year when we are emphasizing the foundational values of our Army," Shine wrote, "that the AAFES [Army and Air Force Exchange Service] continues to sell material which deliberately seeks to undermine those values." As a battalion commander Shine had waged an antipornography campaign at Fort Benning, but with limited success. "I was successful only in removing the magazines from the barber shop, and convincing the PX ladies to cover them," he admitted. "The AAFES manager would not budge." But now, Shine observed, citing growing opposition to pornography in the civilian sector and the ethical revitalization of the military, "the time may be ripe" for taking action within the army as a whole. "I know your concern about families and values is real," he told Wickham. "I haven't the slightest doubt that if anything can be done, it must be done. Pornography and hedonism attack the very root values of our Army, and they are a clear detriment to the spiritual, moral, and psychological health of our fighting force. Too much blood has been

11. Letters of the following to Wickham: E. Warren Smith, June 13, 1986, William H. Worrilow, Jr., February 25, 1985, Lt. Col. Kenneth C. Kessler, February 2, 1984, Clay Buckingham, February 19, 1986, all in Wickham Papers.

shed for our great nation to let smut peddlers drag it into the ash heap of history."[12]

Another military evangelical encouraged Wickham to make the connection between Christian beliefs and the army professional ethic more explicit. Major Marcel W. Fauk, an army ROTC instructor at Lafayette College in Easton, Pennsylvania, expressed appreciation for Wickham's writings on values and leadership, particularly the pamphlet *Guideposts for a Proud and Ready Army*. But he recommended adding a section on spiritual leadership when and if Wickham updated the pamphlet. "I am firmly convinced that it is spiritual leadership which forms the bedrock for the other moral and ethical standards you articulate," Fauk explained. Spiritual leadership should not be "left to the Chaplains alone," he declared. "The commander/leader has the primary part to accomplish in this as well as other regards."[13]

Wickham's response to the letters he received from military evangelicals indicates his sympathy with their point of view. To Clay Buckingham he wrote of his "special delight" at hearing from an "old friend" and invited him to convey "any thoughts you might have in this regard, because the theme of values is somewhat abstract and we shall need all the imaginative approaches we can generate to give the theme some life and vigor." To Colonel Shine he wrote, "Pornography has no place in our system," and said he had expressed such concern to his staff and was awaiting recommendations on a program for eliminating pornographic materials in the army. Thanking Major Fauk for his letter, Wickham declared: "I agree with you. The responsibilities of spiritual leadership in the military should be shared by all, not just by our Chaplains."[14]

Wickham's efforts to enhance army family life demonstrate even more clearly than his leadership programs the connection between his religious convictions and the policies he instituted as chief of staff. What he called the "basic Army philosophy for families" rested on the notion of "a partnership . . . between the Army and Army families." As he explained in a 1983 White Paper, *The Army Family*, the army recognized

12. Col. Alexander P. Shine to Wickham, March 14, 1986, *ibid.*
13. Major Marcel W. Fauk to Wickham, June 18, 1985, *ibid.*
14. Wickham to Clay Buckingham, March 3, 1986, to Alexander P. Shine, May 1, 1986, to Major Marcel W. Fauk, July 1, 1985, and see also Wickham to Lieutenant General William P. Yarborough, February 12, 1985, *ibid.*

its "moral and ethical obligations to those who serve and their families." Families must recognize that they, too, "have responsibilities to the Army." Furthermore, the notion of a partnership between the army and army families was grounded in an understanding of the army as "an institution, not an occupation." Soldiers took an oath of service to the army and their country; they did not simply accept a job. They became part of an institution characterized by a "unique mission and lifestyle." Being "in the readiness business," the army demanded a "degree of commitment" from its members that few other professions did—a willingness to train, deploy, fight, and, if necessary, die. The partnership with army members' families required a commitment on their part—a willingness to share in and reinforce the service member's commitment. By promoting "family wellness" the army sought "to increase the bonding between the family unit and the Army community—[to] create a sense of interdependence."[15]

The army's new commitment to the families of service members constituted a somewhat belated recognition of one of the facts of army life in the 1980s. The number of soldiers with families had risen precipitously since the establishment of the All Volunteer Force in the 1970s. By 1983 more than half of the active-duty force was married (80 percent of the officer corps and 78 percent of the career enlisted force). The number of family members for the total force (including the Reserve and the National Guard, as well as civilian employees) increased the total population of the army by about one-and-one-half times. Moreover, in the army, as in the civilian sector, the traditional, two-parent family existed alongside single-parent families, childless couples, and unmarried couples living together; more than half of career soldiers' spouses worked outside the home; and the divorce rate had escalated.[16] Until the issuance of the White Paper and implementation of the Family Action Plan, however, the army's efforts in the area of family life were largely piecemeal.

15. John A. Wickham, Jr., "To: The Soldiers, Civilians, and Family Members of the US Army," *The Army Family* (U.S. Army White Paper, 1983), n.p.

16. Carol Siler, "Army's Responsibility to Families Outlined" (Typescript of *Army Times* story dated September 19, 1983, in Wickham Papers); Lt. Gen. Robert M. Elton, " 'We Recruit Soldiers and Retain Families,' " *Army*, XXXIII (October, 1983), 220–21. For an interesting article discussing the army family in the context of the army as an institution, see Mady Wechsler Segal, "The Military and the Family as Greedy Institutions," *Armed Forces and Society*, XIII (Fall, 1986), 9–38.

Thus the development of a comprehensive army family policy was almost inevitable. That it was enunciated during General Wickham's tenure as chief of staff ensured that it carried the stamp of his professional, personal, and religious convictions. For example, his insistence on viewing the army as an institution rather than an occupation was part and parcel of his effort to develop a professional ethic among service members emphasizing loyalty and selflessness. The assertion of the army's moral and ethical obligation to soldiers and their families reminds us of his emphasis on values, "caring leadership," and military capability. In *Guideposts for a Proud and Ready Army,* he defined "caring leadership" as "the continuous, creative, selfless care given to our soldiers, families, and units under the demanding requirements of military life which will give sustaining power to these same soldiers, families, and units when our soldiers must go to war." At the same time, a statement he made in the *Decision* interview explaining the importance of army support for families reminds us of his battlefield religious experience, when, severely wounded, he worried about and prayed for the security of his own family. He told the *Decision* interviewer, "If a soldier has to go off suddenly and not know where he's going or can't tell his family, his mental state will be better because he knows his family will be taken care of." [17]

Wickham stated the philosophy of the army family in secular terms, but he engaged a prominent evangelical, James C. Dobson, to help implement it. By 1983, when Dobson became associated with the army family program, he was well-known as an advocate of what evangelicals liked to call the traditional American family and Judeo-Christian values. The previous year he had received the NAE Layman of the Year award "for his commitment to saving the family." NAE president Bishop J. Floyd Williams credited him with prompting "a nationwide reawakening to the problems facing the American home and a widespread return to those biblical directives which spell the difference between hope and despair." [18]

The son of a Nazarene preacher, Dobson earned a bachelor's degree from Pasadena College and a Ph.D. in child development from the University of Southern California. As a licensed psychologist, he served fourteen years as an associate clinical professor of pediatrics at the USC School of Medicine and seventeen years on the attending staff of Chil-

17. Wickham, *Guideposts,* 13; "A Soldier Who Cares," 23.
18. "Convention Newsbriefs," *UEA,* Summer, 1982, p. 28.

dren's Hospital of Los Angeles. His speaking career began in the 1960s, starting with Parent-Teacher Association chapters, Bible study groups, Sunday school classes, and teachers' conferences and graduating to guest appearances on nationally televised talk shows. In 1970 *Dare to Discipline*, the first of several best-sellers offering advice on family issues, appeared. In 1977 he resigned his position at Children's Hospital and founded Focus on the Family (FOF), a nonprofit organization with an evangelical orientation dedicated to the "preservation of the family and the propagation of traditional pro-family views." Besides sponsoring weekend seminars led by Dobson, which drew audiences of two to three thousand persons, FOF's early operations included a weekly (later daily) radio program broadcast nationwide and numerous publications, including *Focus on the Family* magazine. By the early 1980s more than 250 radio stations carried the program; the *Focus on the Family* film series, based on videotapes of Dobson's weekend seminars, had been seen by an estimated ten million persons.[19]

Dobson's association with the federal government and his involvement in public policy making began in the late 1970s, when President Jimmy Carter called a series of White House Conferences on the Family. Dobson was invited to sit on the eleven-member planning commission, but his efforts to obtain an appointment as a delegate to the conferences proved unavailing until he mentioned his desire on the *Focus on the Family* radio program. The avalanche of letters that hit the White House a few days later helped persuade the Carter administration to include Dobson in the conferences as a representative of the "Christian perspective" on the family. Besides serving as a delegate, he also was a member of the task force that summarized the White House Conference findings. During the Reagan administration, according to Dobson's biographer, he became a "regular consultant" to the president. One of the *Focus on the Family* radio broadcasts was recorded with Reagan in the Oval Office, and Reagan appointed Dobson to serve as cochairman of the Citizens for Tax Reform and as a member of the National Ad-

19. Rolf Zettersten, *Dr. Dobson: Turning Hearts Toward Home, the Life and Principles of America's Family Advocate* (Dallas, 1989), 88, 95, 150, 181, 289–91; "Convention Newsbriefs," 28–29. Dobson's father was the Reverend James Clayton Dobson, Sr. Pasadena College, a Nazarene institution, later moved to San Diego and was renamed Point Loma University.

visory Committee to the Office of Juvenile Justice and Delinquency Prevention from 1982 to 1984.[20]

Dobson's association with Wickham and the army family program came about through the influence of two Republican congressmen, Dan Coats of Indiana and Frank R. Wolf of Virginia. In 1981, they attended a showing of *Where's Dad?*, the third segment of the *Focus on the Family* film series. Mightily impressed, they began promoting it and other FOF materials among their colleagues in the House of Representatives. Over a two-year period they showed the film to some fifty or sixty congressmen and their wives, as well as numerous staff members. Then one day in June, 1983, they scheduled a presentation for Secretary of the Army Marsh and General Wickham in hopes of persuading them to use the film in the army. Wickham found the film "very moving," perhaps because it evoked painful memories of his own father's absence as a result of his parents' separation when he was a child. Whatever the reason, he eventually decided to make use of the film in the army family program. A second meeting with Coats and Wolf late in September, shortly after the White Paper, *The Army Family*, had been issued, induced Wickham to consider engaging Dobson as a consultant on the army family program. The two men quickly developed a close relationship based on shared religious convictions and mutual respect. Wickham referred to Dobson as "one of America's foremost authorities on family living" and on one occasion told him, "Your work is of great benefit to our Army families."[21]

On December 2, Wickham and Dobson, along with Wolf and prob-

20. Zettersten, *Dr. Dobson*, 152–53; *Army Science Board Biographical Sketch Book, June 1986* (Washington, D.C., [1986]). See also Tim Stafford, "His Father's Son: The Drive Behind James Dobson, Jr.," *CT*, April 22, 1988, pp. 16, 18–22; "Dobson Tells Reagan to Focus on the Family," *CT*, March 2, 1984, p. 37.

21. Beth Spring, "Some Very Influential People Are Convinced to Focus on the Family," *CT*, June 17, 1983, pp. 31–32; Dan Coats to John O. Marsh, June 2, 1983, Wickham to Coats, June 14, 1983, and Frank R. Wolf to Wickham, September 30, 1983, all in Wickham Papers; "A Soldier Who Cares," 24; John A. Wickham, "'Where's Dad?'—A Videotape About Caring" (Memo dated March 20, [1985], in Wickham Papers); "Army Chief of Staff Endorses 'Where's Dad?' Videotape," *Focus on the Family*, June, 1985, p. 10; Wickham to James C. Dobson, December 2, 1983, in Wickham Papers. Wickham's mother and father separated when John was eleven years old. In the Wickham Oral History Interview, 1, Wickham said he believed the breakup of his family was "a factor that influenced me early on in the importance of family programs."

ably Coats, met at a fellowship breakfast in the Pentagon. Dobson gave Wickham an inscribed copy of one of his books, and Wickham, in a letter thanking him for it, enclosed a copy of the White Paper on the army family. Dobson said he felt "a definite sense of camaraderie and Christian brotherhood with you and the other military leaders." He told Wickham, "It is encouraging to know that those in positions of such awesome responsibility are not ashamed to bow their heads in prayer for wisdom and guidance." By May, 1985, Dobson correctly described himself and his organization "as minor partners with you in strengthening the institutions of marriage and parenthood for those serving in the military."[22]

As a consultant on the army family program, Dobson worked closely with Wickham as well as Colonel Edmond Solymosy, director of the Army's Family Action Plan (the blueprint for implementing the army's philosophy of the family), and Lieutenant General Robert M. Elton, deputy chief of staff for personnel (whose office included the newly established Family Liaison Office). He also participated in Army Science Board meetings where family issues were discussed and, at his request, served on the Advisory Task Force on Soldiers and Families set up by Wickham. In April, 1984, at Wickham's invitation, Dobson attended the Spring Commanders' Conference at the Pentagon and made a forty-five-minute presentation, which *Focus on the Family* magazine described as an address on "the importance of traditional home-life values," to the officers and their wives.[23]

In March, 1985, Wickham announced in the "Weekly Summary"

22. James Dobson to Wickham, December 7, 1983, and May 30, 1985, in Wickham Papers.

23. James Dobson to Wickham, December 7, 1983, Wickham to Dobson, March 16, 1984, Dobson to Wickham, April 5, 1984, Wickham to Dobson, May 7, 1984, Dobson to Wickham, July 31, 1984, Wickham to Dobson, September 12, 1984, all in Wickham Papers; "Dr. Dobson Meets with Army Chief of Staff on Family Programs," *Focus on the Family*, August, 1984, p. 12; "Army Implements 'The Year of Values,'" *Focus on the Family*, August, 1986, p. 11; Rolf Zettersten, "Today's Army: Advancing on the Home Front," *Focus on the Family*, August, 1984, p. 4. The Advisory Task Force on Soldiers and Families was a small citizens group formed under the auspices of the Army Science Board to meet with Wickham every six months to offer insight on army programs concerning education, training, compensation, and soldier and family lifestyles. See Wickham to the Most Reverend John J. O'Connor, June 11, [?], and "Talking Points for Advisory TF on Soldiers and Families, 4 November 1985" (Typed cards), both in Wickham Papers.

sent to all commanding officers that he had approved Dobson's videotape *Where's Dad?* for distribution within the army. "The film . . . provides an important message about commitment, caring, and bonding
within the family unit," he observed. "I encourage you to show this
thought-provoking film to your soldiers and their spouses together."
Implementing Wickham's order, the army purchased 225 copies and
placed them in film libraries at bases in the United States and abroad.
The videotape was a 35-minute presentation produced by Word, Inc.,
and, according to a printed message that appeared at the beginning of
the tape, "adapted for use by the Department of Defense." Like the
original *Where's Dad?*, the army version showed Dobson conducting a
weekend Focus on the Family seminar in San Antonio, Texas, talking
about the role of the husband and father in the family. And, like the
original, it was an appeal to American fathers caught up in a fast-paced
life to slow down and spend more time with their children.[24]

A comparison of the army videotape with the original *Where's Dad?*
reveals that most of the religious content of the original version had
been expunged. But at one point in the army version, after lamenting
the absence of fathers from the home, Dobson declared, "You do not
even have to have a Christian perspective to have those same views."
Elsewhere he talked about "a God-given responsibility" and "God's
values" and serving "the God who made me." Nevertheless, the sectarian message of the original *Where's Dad?*—certainly the most moving
part of the film, which Dobson delivered with great feeling and urgency—was gone. Army personnel did not hear the Nazarene preacher's
son declare that he was speaking for the Lord, that "God gave me what
I'm gonna say to you right now," that "this is what God wants me to
say to the Christian family and perhaps to the family at large." A long
segment in which Dobson talked about his concern for the "spiritual
welfare" of his own children and the need to equip all children with "a
heritage of faith" had also been omitted. Nor did the army videotape
show the concluding part of the original film, in which Dobson asked
the members of the audience to bow their heads in prayer and then
invited the men to stand up as a way of indicating "to God and their
wives" that "you are rededicating yourself to the task of leadership

24. Wickham, "'Where's Dad?'"; *Focus on the Family with Dr. James Dobson* [orig-
inal version of *Where's Dad?* videotape] (Waco, Tex., 1979); *Where's Dad?* [Army video-
tape] [Waco, Tex.], 1981.

within your family." The deletion of such sectarian material was, of course, in keeping with Department of Defense policy. Dobson's radio program, which was broadcast over Armed Forces Radio, was subjected to a similar "sanitizing," to use Dobson's word. Peb Jackson, FOF vice-president, told *Christianity Today* that had the film not been edited, it would have been authorized for use only by chaplains. In its adapted form, it could have much wider exposure.[25]

Even without the sectarian material, the main message of the original *Where's Dad?* was evident in the army version. Aimed at husbands and fathers, it emphasized their importance in shaping the development of their children's moral values. Not only the survival of the family but of America depended on husbands and fathers assuming their proper role. Dobson declared, "Folks, if America is going to survive, it will be because husbands and fathers begin to put their families at the highest level of priorities and reserve something of their time, effort and energy for leadership within their own homes." The emphasis on male leadership was, of course, an article of faith among most evangelicals, based on the teachings of Paul ("For the husband is the head of the wife, even as Christ is the head of the church") and other Scriptures.

Where's Dad? constituted an important component of Wickham's family initiative and indeed his overall effort to improve the army. In October, 1984, *Christianity Today* quoted Colonel Solymosy calling the videotape "a building block" of the army family program and another official citing it as a resource for base commanders to use in "creating an atmosphere of caring leadership." In the "Weekly Summary" announcing the distribution of *Where's Dad?*, Wickham touted the videotape as a vehicle for strengthening the military family. "The readiness of our Army is directly related to the strength of our families," he observed. "The stronger the family, the stronger the Army, because strong families improve our combat readiness."[26]

Wickham's concern for army families made him something of a celebrity among his fellow Christians. No one did more than Dobson to advertise Wickham's evangelical credentials and his efforts to encourage wholesome family life in the army. Because Dobson commanded a huge

---

25. James Dobson to Gerry Fry, July 26, 1986, in Wickham Papers; "All Active-Duty U.S. Soldiers Are Expected to See Dobson Film," *CT*, October 5, 1984, p. 100.

26. "All Active-Duty U.S. Soldiers Are Expected to See Dobson Film," 100; Wickham, "'Where's Dad?'"

and loyal constituency (some four million listeners in his radio audience and thousands of *Focus on the Family* magazine readers), Wickham's name became a household word within the evangelical community. For example, shortly after attending the three-day Spring Commanders' Conference at the Pentagon, Dobson wrote about the experience in a monthly newsletter sent to some 440,000 persons on the FOF mailing list. "What excites me most," he declared, "is that the Army has shown great concern for the welfare of its families." Praising Wickham as "a committed Christian whom I respect highly," Dobson also mentioned the White Paper *The Army Family*, the army's purchase of *Where's Dad?*, and the fact that he had been asked to serve on the Advisory Task Force on Soldiers and Families. "We thank the Lord for these breakthroughs," he added, and concluded with a paean to the officers he had met at the Commanders' Conference:

> We've been led to believe that military generals and admirals are ego-centric maniacs who are itching to blow up the world. Nothing could be further from the truth. These ten men and General Wickham are dedicated patriots who have sacrificed dearly for their country. Many were wounded in Vietnam or Korea. *All* have been separated from their families for difficult periods during their careers. And *all* have been criticized and misjudged by the press and the public. I came away from this encounter with gratitude for their service, and with a new awareness of our dependence on a strong military.[27]

A few months later, the August, 1984, issue of *Focus on the Family* printed a cover story entitled "Today's Army: Advancing on the Home Front." The subtitle declared, "Pentagon Joins Forces with Focus on the Family." On October 12, 1984, Dobson's daily radio program aired a thirty-minute interview with Wickham, Elton, and Solymosy regarding the army family. In June, 1985, *Focus on the Family* cited Wickham's "strong personal endorsement" of *Where's Dad?* and quoted Dobson as saying, "I doubt that *any* Army Chief of Staff in U.S. history has made such a strong pro-family statement as Gen. Wickham did on this occasion." When he sent a copy of the article to Wickham, Dobson noted that it had gone out to "650,000 people on our mailing list."[28]

27. Spring, "Some Very Influential People Are Convinced to Focus on the Family," 34; Rolf Zettersten to Wickham, May 29, 1984, James C. Dobson to Dear Friend, May, 1984 (Focus on the Family newsletter), both in Wickham Papers.

28. Zettersten, "Today's Army," 4; *The Army Family (General John A. Wickham &*

Besides introducing Wickham and his army family program to the millions of loyal readers and radio listeners who made up his constituency, Dobson also paraded the chief of staff before the Focus on the Family organization team. In December, 1985, he invited Wickham to a three-day Washington briefing for FOF board members. Wickham came armed with a set of eleven index cards outlining "talking points" on the various army themes. He concluded his talk with a discussion of 1986 as the year of values, declaring, "You and your organization can help us to ensure that we have those values." Afterward Dobson sent him an effusive thank you letter. "Your devotion to God and family and country are [*sic*] very meaningful," he wrote. "In fact, our guests were extremely impressed to find such dedication to Judeo-Christian values by our military leaders. I was very proud to be your friend." At the January, 1987, FOF Washington briefing, Wickham delivered a talk similar to the one for the previous year but with different jokes.[29]

Clearly Wickham valued these meetings, partly for the contact they afforded with fellow evangelicals but also for the same reason he welcomed the publicity Dobson and FOF gave him and his family program—because of the positive impression it made on the civilian population. He received numerous letters of appreciation from evangelicals, both military and civilian, many of them ordinary persons who took time from their housework or jobs to write him a simple, obviously heartfelt note of thanks for his "Christian witness and influence," his service "to my country and my God," and "for giving Dr. Dobson an opprtunity [*sic*] to minister to and encourage the Military."[30]

Panel) (Audiocassette; Colorado Springs, 1984); "Department of the Army, 'Focus on the Family,' General Wickham and Jim Dobson, Washington, D.C., August 1984" (Typed transcript in Wickham Papers); James Dobson to Dear Friend, May, 1984 (Focus on the Family newsletter in Wickham Papers); "News and Such . . . ," *Focus on the Family*, December, 1984, p. 12; "Army Chief of Staff Endorses 'Where's Dad?' Videotape," 10; Dobson to Wickham, May 30, 1985, in Wickham Papers.

29. Dobson to Wickham, December 5, 1985, and March 6, 1986, and Wickham to Dobson, April 14, 1986; "Talking Points, Address to Dr. Dobson's Focus on the Family Group, 1045 Hours, Friday, 31 January 1986" (Typed index cards); "Talking Points, Address to Dr. Dobson's Focus on Family Group, 1045 Hours, Friday, 30 January 1987" (Typed index cards), all in Wickham Papers.

30. See Wickham to the following: Douglas E. Coe, February 2, 1987, Al Sanders, February 18, 1987, Fletcher Anderson, March 27, 1986, Mike Trout, November 28, 1984, Rolf Zettersten, June 11, 1984; and the following to Wickham: Marion (Mrs. Wayne A.) Owen, February 7, 1985, Alan Kemper [August (?), 1984]. See also the

Thus Wickham's relationship with Dobson and Focus on the Family greatly enhanced his reputation within the evangelical community, especially among the rank and file. But quite apart from Dobson and FOF, Wickham's papers at the U.S. Army Military History Institute document his participation in a fairly extensive evangelical network during his years as army chief of staff. He corresponded with several well-known evangelists, including Billy Graham, Bill Bright, and an old friend from his tour of duty in Korea, the Reverend Billy Kim, the director of Christian Service, Inc., of the Korea Inland Mission, as well as the Far East Broadcasting Company. Wickham also continued his association with Dan Coats and Frank Wolf. As members of the House Select Committee on Children, Youth, and Families, they were valuable allies in his campaign for congressional support for army family programs.[31]

Following the path charted by his mentor, Harold K. Johnson, Wickham delivered the closing prayer at the 1985 national prayer breakfast, which was attended by over three thousand people and broadcast over armed forces radio. A few months later he addressed the Salisbury (Maryland) mayor's prayer breakfast. He also attended regular prayer breakfasts at the Pentagon. He and some fifteen other army generals met every other week for a prayer breakfast. Periodically he and the other chiefs and officers of the services also gathered for a "breakfast of fellowship." Letters he received following his appearance at the annual Pentagon prayer breakfast in February, 1983, attended by several hundred men and women, testified to his inspirational powers and the depth of his spiritual commitment. Air force brigadier general Richard F. Abel, signing himself "Your teammate in Christ," declared: "God truly laid upon your heart a wonderful message of being Christians where we are planted. Thank you for giving of your time, for your leadership and your Christian testimony." Mark Petersburg of the Christian Embassy also praised Wickham's remarks, "especially your comment at the end

following to Wickham: Moorad Mooradian, Colonel, U.S. Army, October 17, 1984, R. G. Shaffer, Commodore, Dental Corps, U.S. Navy, June 18, 1984, Charles W. Bagnal, Lt Gen, U.S. Army, June 11, 1984; Catherine York, May 31, 1984, Donald McCants, January 20, 1985, Fletcher Anderson, February 27, 1986, Al Sanders, February 11, 1987, all in Wickham Papers.

31. See Wickham to the Reverend Billy Graham, March 4, 1986, to William R. Bright, March 8, 1984, to Billy Kim, May 11, 1983, and April 8, 1985, to Dan Coats, November 21, 1983, March 24, [1985], April 8, 1985, and October 14, [1985], and to Frank Wolf, November 23, [1983?], and March 24, [1985], *ibid.*

about persistence in prayer," and added that "several people have told me that your message was right on target."[32]

In 1986 Wickham received an invitation from retired general Ralph E. Haines to appear as the speaker for the Eighth Annual Greater San Antonio Military Breakfast scheduled for March 14, 1987. Sponsored by the Full Gospel Business Men's Fellowship International, the breakfast had previously featured General John W. Vessey, chairman of the Joint Chiefs of Staff, and Admiral James D. Watkins, chief of naval operations. Some fourteen hundred civic, business, church, and military leaders had attended the 1986 breakfast. Its purpose, Haines explained, was to honor the armed forces and pay "homage to our God." Although it had "strong evangelical overtones," it attracted "Christians of a wide range of persuasions and traditions" and had "become the premier interdenominational event within the Christian community in South Texas." Besides building up the ecumenical character of the breakfast, Haines sought to allay any hesitation Wickham might feel about accepting the invitation. "I recognize, although I know you as a strong man of God, you may have some reservations about the FGBMFI," Haines wrote. "I do not want to put you into an uncomfortable position and hope you will be candid with me if you feel, after prayer, you should not accept our invitation. I will understand completely and seek to get another speaker. It remains my view that I serve God by being the moving spirit behind these Breakfasts—that they present a very reassuring image of our armed forces to citizenry of our land."[33]

Haines had corresponded with Wickham previously so Wickham knew about his travels and speaking engagements as an advocate of spiritual renewal. In one letter Haines had even enclosed a copy of a speech he had delivered in Australia entitled "Christian Leadership in the Armed Forces," reiterating several points he had made a few years earlier

32. Richard F. Abel, Brigadier General, USAF, Director of Public Affairs, to Wickham, February 17, 1983, Mark Petersburg to Wickham, February 14, 1983, *ibid.* On the prayer breakfast, see "A Soldier Who Cares," 24; Charles E. Grassley to Wickham, n.d., David Allan Hubbard to Wickham, October 11, 1983, Wickham to Ralph Regula, September 25, 1984, and Regula to Wickham, April 3, 1985, all in Wickham Papers; "The 33D Annual National Prayer Breakfast," *Congressional Record*, CXIII 99th Cong., 1st Sess., 4211; "Address by General John A. Wickham, Jr., Chief of Staff, United States Army, 10th Annual Salisbury Major's [*sic*] Prayer Breakfast, Salisbury, Maryland, 3 April 1985" (Typescript in Wickham Papers).

33. Ralph E. Haines to Wickham, April 3, 1986, in Wickham Papers.

in the article about the relationship between Christian faith and military leadership in the *Military Chaplains' Review*. "Proper commandership," Haines declared in his speech, "must, as a minimum, make full provision for the exercise of responsible Christian leadership." That in turn involved demonstrating "personal faith in God" or at least seeking "actively to develop it through fellowship with believers, study of Holy Scripture, and opening up of communications channels to God." The commander should not only worship regularly at chapels attended by his people but, cooperating closely with his chaplains, should "foster innovating and imaginative religious activities and spiritual outlets" which would attract an increasing number of personnel to the religious program. In conclusion, Haines restated his fervent belief in the necessity of the commander's being a Christian in order to carry out his moral and spiritual responsibilities. "I cannot see how they can discharge these responsibilities in their own strength," he emphasized. "They must be plugged into the power source of God's love and grace, manifested in his son Jesus Christ, and made available to them through his Holy Spirit." [34]

Wickham's response to Haines's earlier letter had been noncommittal. In replying to the invitation to address the San Antonio military breakfast, however, Wickham manifested a more positive attitude. He pleaded a tight schedule in declining but thanked his friend for the invitation and news of "your ongoing activities on behalf of Christian values and fellowship" and wished him and the gathering "a most joyous and moving breakfast." And he declared, "I admire the work you are doing and your devotion." [35]

There is no reason to doubt the sincerity of Wickham's declaration. That he declined Haines's invitation to speak at the FGBMFI gathering does, however, point to an important difference between him and Haines on the subject of what Major Fauk had called "spiritual leadership." A distinction Clay Buckingham made in an article in *Command* is pertinent here. Discussing the role of the Christian officer as a military commander, the former president of OCF differentiated between serving as "a missionary *to* the military" and serving as "a Christian *in* the

34. General Ralph E. Haines, Jr., *"Christian Leadership in the Armed Forces": The Second Bishop Hulme-Moir Memorial Lecture* (Canberra, Australia, 1984), 3–4, 9.
35. Wickham to Haines, November 2, 1984, and April 30, 1986, and see also Binnie to Wickham, April 4, [1986], all in Wickham Papers.

military." Buckingham made clear his own preference. "I have heard Christians say, 'I claim this command for Jesus Christ.' I have heard people say that their basic purpose as a ship's captain is 'to win men on board my ship to Jesus Christ.'" But he insisted that the "fundamental mission" of the Christian commander was to work toward having the best ship or battalion or squadron possible. He should exhibit "a positive witness for Jesus Christ" by demonstrating to his men that he honored God and lived in obedience to His laws. But he should practice his faith *as a commander*, not as a missionary seeking to win his men to Jesus Christ. *That* was the chaplain's job, Buckingham asserted. Whereas the commander was "a Christian *in* the military," the chaplain was "a missionary *to* the military," whose "basic mission" was "to win people to Jesus Christ and to help them become mature disciples."[36]

All the evidence demonstrates that Wickham was a committed Christian who read the Bible and prayed daily. Significantly, though, in the *Decision* interview he characterized himself as a man of "quiet faith," and in a speech to a chaplains' conference he said he believed in sharing it "with eloquence yet quietly." He professed his Christian beliefs publicly and was active in the evangelical network, but he was careful to be sure that, in accordance with Defense Department regulations, evangelical organizations and publications did not use his official title and position as chief of staff for any endorsement or advertisement or for any fund-raising efforts. He did not practice the aggressive, sectarian evangelizing Haines did. Nor, apparently, did he engage in disciple-making as so many other military evangelicals did, which may be one reason he never joined the OCF. Though his ideas about leadership, values, and the army family grew, at least in part, out of his religious convictions, when he addressed the army as a secular institution—defining its professional ethic, or explaining its family program, or speaking to West Point cadets, for example—he used scrupulously secular language.[37] To employ Buck-

36. Major General Clay T. Buckingham, USA (Ret.), "The Character of the Christian Commander," *Command*, Spring, 1985, pp. 3–6.

37. "A Soldier Who Cares," 23–24; "Interview with Army Chief of Staff, General Wickham," 16; "Remarks by General John A. Wickham, Jr., Chief of Staff, Army, Command Chaplains Conference Breakfast, Sheraton National Hotel, 16 July 1985" (Typescript in Wickham Papers), 2; Wickham to Debbi Bair, April 7, 1986, in Wickham Papers; "Remarks by General John A. Wickham, Jr., Chief of Staff, United States Army, to the 1st & 2d Classes, Corps of Cadets, USMA, 17 April 1984," "Address to USMA 1st and 2nd Class [sic], West Point, New York, by General John A. Wickham, Jr., Chief

ingham's distinction, whereas Haines saw himself as a "missionary *to* the military," Wickham adopted the role of "a Christian *in* the military."

Applying Buckingham's formulation to the other military evangelicals considered in this book and admitting that the boundary between the two approaches to "spiritual leadership" is not precise, it seems plausible to put most of the evangelical chaplains, parachurch group members, and such individuals as William K. Harrison, John Broger, and King Coffman under the rubric of "missionary *to* the military" and Wickham's mentor Harold K. Johnson under the rubric of "a Christian *in* the military." The predominance of the missionary type is hardly surprising because the evangelizing impulse is one of the primary attributes of an evangelical Christian. Indeed, that impulse, as we have seen, was largely responsible for the spread of evangelical religion in the armed forces. As the next chapter will show, however, it also posed problems in the secularized, religiously pluralistic institution that the U.S. military had become in the 1970s and 1980s.

---

of Staff, Army, 16 April 1985," and "Address by General John A. Wickham, Jr., Chief of Staff, Army, First and Second Classmen, United States Military Academy, 16 April 1986" (Typescripts in Wickham Papers).

20

Maintaining the Sectarian Ideal

The spread of evangelical religion in the military during the
1970s, 1980s, and early 1990s occurred in the midst of what Martin
Marty has termed "a seismic shift" in the American religious landscape.
Events of the 1960s signaled the end of the Protestant Establishment
in America and the beginning of what is variously referred to as a post-
Puritan, post-Protestant, post-Christian, even postreligious era. The
hallmarks of the new era were pluralism and secularism, both of which
most evangelicals viewed with dismay. Beginning in the 1960s, the
growth of new religions and shifting church membership patterns in the
United States produced increasing religious diversity among the American people. As the mainline Protestant denominations decreased in
membership, and notwithstanding the increase in the number of evangelical Protestants, the total percentage of Protestants in the United
States declined. At the same time, the percentage of Catholics increased.
So, even more dramatically, did the number of Mormons. But the most
significant trend contributing to religious pluralism was the rise in the
number of Americans affiliated with religions other than Protestantism,
Catholicism, or Judaism. In 1947 only 6 percent of Americans had so
identified themselves; by 1987 the figure had grown to 13 percent
among adults (19 percent among those aged eighteen to twenty-four).
The "other" category included Islam, Buddhism, and Hinduism, as well
as various American Indian religions, along with cults and sects such as
Eckankar, Baha'i, est, Transcendental Meditation, and the Unification
Church. A significant increase in the number of people who indicated
no religious preference also rendered the country more pluralistic. In
1952 only 2 percent of Americans stated no religious preference,

whereas by 1986 the proportion had risen to 9 percent.[1] For evangelicals, all the statistics on religious diversity pointed to an alarming conclusion—the end of Protestant hegemony in a country they had long believed to be a Christian nation in covenant with God.

Greater religious diversity brought increased secularism. As Peter Berger has observed, "In modern society . . . secularity and pluralism are mutually reinforcing phenomena. Secularization fosters the civic arrangements under which pluralism thrives, while the plurality of world views undermines the plausibility of each one and thus contributes to the secularizing tendency." After the post–World War II religious revival peaked in the late 1950s, secularization seemed to accelerate. Contemporary observers pointed out the slow but steady erosion of membership in the mainline Protestant denominations, as well as declining financial contributions, church school enrollment, and religious book sales. A Gallup poll taken in 1967 showed that 57 percent of Americans believed that religion was losing its influence; by 1970 the proportion had increased to 75 percent. A general reaction against religious institutions manifested itself in growing criticism of the "culture religion" of the 1950s and the churches it had spawned—inward-looking institutions ministering to individual spiritual needs, accommodating, even sanctioning, the political, social, and economic status quo. Exhortations to lift the church and religion out of irrelevancy and accommodation generated a new "secular theology" that sought to speak to contemporary society and its myriad problems: poverty, racism, the arms race, environmental pollution. Echoing the German theologian Dietrich Bonhoeffer, the secular theologians affirmed man's maturity in a "world come of age" and argued for a "religionless Christianity" stripped of otherworldliness and the preoccupation with personal salvation and concentrating on the needs of this world. Thus Harvey Cox, in *The Secular City*, declared that Christians should not oppose but rather "support and nourish" secularization as "an authentic consequence of bib-

1. Martin E. Marty, Foreword, to *Understanding Church Growth and Decline, 1950–1978*, ed. Dean R. Hoge and David A. Roozen (New York, 1979), 10, 13. On the post-Puritan era, see, for example, Sydney E. Ahlstrom, *A Religious History of the American People* (2 vols.; Garden City, N.Y., 1975) II, 599, 612; Martin E. Marty, "Protestantism Enters Third Phase," *Christian Century*, LXXVIII (January 18, 1961), 72. For statistics on religious affiliation, see George Gallup, Jr., and Jim Castelli, *The People's Religion: American Faith in the 90's* (New York, 1989), Chap. 2.

lical faith" and urged the church to develop "a theology of social change."[2]

The "secular theology" of the 1960s turned out to be transient, but secular humanistic culture, based on a naturalistic view of the world, gained increasing acceptance in the United States. Evangelicals, however, exaggerated the pervasiveness of what they referred to as "secular humanism." The phenomenal growth of evangelical religion contradicted their view. Rather than a rampant secularization of the American people or American society as a whole, American public life and particularly the state were being secularized. As Jeffrey Hadden has argued, in the United States secularization involved a process whereby the state increasingly relied on secular rather than religious sources in maintaining legitimacy and defining public policy. It was this narrower kind of secularization that evangelicals—as well as other contemporary observers—detected in lamenting the exclusion of "not only the church but all expression of religion from government and public affairs" on the grounds that religion was essentially a personal matter and therefore should be confined to the "private sphere."[3]

A "moral pluralism" also developed in the wake of the much publicized moral revolution of the 1960s. By the 1970s evangelicals regarded "moral relativism" and "situation ethics" as a grave threat. In 1974, Billy Graham spoke for many conservative Christians in decrying the "secularism, hedonism, materialism, and moral permissiveness" rampant in American society.[4]

In the 1970s and 1980s, evangelicals' antipathy toward religious pluralism and secularism seemed to be propelling them on a collision course with the military leadership on certain issues because the military in

2. Peter L. Berger, "From the Crisis of Religion to the Crisis of Secularity," in *Religion and America: Spiritual Life in a Secular Age*, ed. Mary Douglas and Steven Tipton (Boston, 1982), 15; Harvey Cox, *The Secular City: Secularization and Urbanization in Theological Perspective* (rev. ed.; New York, 1965), 15, 91.

3. Jeffrey K. Hadden, "Religious Broadcasting and the Mobilization of the New Christian Right," *Journal for the Scientific Study of Religion*, XXVI (March, 1987), 2–4; Paul P. Fryhling, "A Reasonable Approach to the Free Exercise of Religion in Public Life," *UEA*, July, 1965, p. 12.

4. Berger, "From the Crisis of Religion to the Crisis of Secularity," 18; Ahlstrom, *Religious History of the American People*, II, 605; Robert D. Linder and Richard V. Pierard, *Twilight of the Saints: Biblical Christianity and Civil Religion in America* (Downers Grove, Ill., 1978), 30.

those decades followed a "plural ideal." Evangelicals, by contrast, held to a "sectarian ideal."[5]

The plural ideal followed by the military embraced three basic components. The first was wide-ranging religious pluralism among military personnel and in the chaplaincies. By 1989, the Armed Forces Chaplains Board had approved more than two hundred faith groups for the chaplaincies; many more than that claimed adherents among the troops. Just as in the civilian sector, religious diversity had increased markedly in the armed forces in the 1970s, 1980s and early 1990s. Interestingly, the religious preference percentages in the military closely matched those in the civilian population. A Gallup survey of the United States for 1990 showed 56 percent of the population to be Protestant, 25 percent Roman Catholic, 2 percent Jewish, 6 percent "other," and 11 percent "none." In December, 1990, the *Washington Post* quoted a Defense Department spokesman as saying that 54.7 percent of the United States military was Protestant, 26.19 percent Catholic, 0.37 percent Jewish, 3.99 percent "other," 14.69 percent "none," and 0.06 percent atheist. As we have seen, the number of evangelicals had increased dramatically. Even more striking by 1990 were the high percentages of military personnel choosing "other," "none," or "atheist," a trend that mirrored similarly high percentages, in comparison with the mid-1960s, in the civilian sector. The "other" category reflects the growing number of persons belonging to faiths outside the Judeo-Christian tradition, especially Buddhism and Islam. In 1987, the Armed Forces Chaplains Board approved the Buddhist Churches of America as an endorsing agency, and a few years later, a Buddhist priest became the first non–Judeo-Christian military chaplain in the United States. Although there were more Muslims (approximately 1,175) than Buddhists (slightly over 1,000) in the military by 1990, there was no endorsing agency for Islam. But observers of the chaplaincy thought it was only a matter of time before there would be Muslim chaplains in the military, as well as chaplains from the Church of Ancient Wisdom, the Universal Life Church, Hare Krishna, Baha'i, and Eckankar.[6]

5. I am indebted to Grant Wacker for the term *plural ideal*, and *sectarian ideal* is similar to his *custodial ideal*. I give the terms a somewhat broader meaning than he does. See Grant Wacker, "Uneasy in Zion: Evangelicals in Postmodern Society," in *Evangelicalism and Modern America*, ed. George Marsden (Grand Rapids, 1984), 22–24.

6. John E. Groh, "Lively Experiment: A Summary History of the Air Force Chaplaincy," *MCR*, Winter, 1990, p. 80; Robert Bezilla, ed., *Religion in America, 1992–1993*

Of course, religious diversity was nothing new to the chaplaincies in the 1970s, 1980s, and 1990s, though it did seem to be expanding. Indeed, during much of the twentieth century, the chaplaincies traditionally operated in accord with what Richard G. Hutcheson has called "a pattern of cooperative pluralism." Ministers who entered the military chaplaincy remained clergymen of their own denominations or faiths but were expected to join in a cooperative ministry with chaplains and parishioners of many other denominations and faiths. The system discouraged narrowly denominational or sectarian views and encouraged ecumenical accommodation. The motto of the navy chaplain corps summarized the principle involved: "Cooperation without Compromise."[7]

In the 1980s, the Department of Defense made cooperative pluralism an explicit policy by requiring faith groups seeking authorization as endorsing agencies to be able to certify "chaplains who are willing to respect the integrity of and work in cooperation with other religious groups" and "provide for the free exercise of religion by all members of the Military Services, their dependents, and other authorized persons." The chiefs of chaplains and instructors in the chaplains schools, as well as writers in the *Chaplain* and the *Military Chaplains' Review* regularly preached the virtues of cooperation and collegiality among chaplains representing different denominations and faith groups. Numerous conferences, symposia, and programs also fostered cooperative pluralism among chaplains.[8]

(Princeton, 1993), 40; Lynda Richardson, "Religious Sensitivities in Saudi Arabia Keep Troops' Observances Low-Key," *Washington Post*, December 16, 1990, p. A57; Lesley A. Northup, "The Challenge of the Chaplaincy," *MCR*, Winter, 1990, pp. 11–12; Gregory J. Darr, "For God & Country: The Constitutional Question of the U.S. Chaplaincy," *MCR*, Winter, 1992, p. 103; LCDR James P. Nickols, CHC, USN, "Religious Pluralism: A Challenge to the Chaplain Corps," *MCR*, Fall, 1986, p. 92.

7. Richard G. Hutcheson, Jr., *The Churches and the Chaplaincy* (Atlanta, 1975), 103, 117–21.

8. John E. Groh, *Facilitators of the Free Exercise of Religion: Air Force Chaplains, 1981–1990* (Washington, D.C., 1991), 12; Chaplain (LTC) John W. Brinsfield, Jr., chief of training division of the U.S. Army Chaplain Center and School, Fort Monmouth, N.J., conversation with author, Fort Monmouth, June 15, 1989; William J. Hourihan, Chaplain Branch Historian, U.S. Army Chaplain Center and School, Fort Monmouth, N.J., telephone conversation with author, December 7, 1993; Office of the Chief of Chaplains, "Annual Report of Major Activities: Historical Review, 1 July 1974–30 June 1975" [1975] (Typescript at U.S. Army Center of Military History), 55–59; Richard G. Hutcheson, Jr., "The Chaplaincy in the Year 2000," *MCR*, Summer, 1976, p. 85; Ber-

Secularism constituted the second component of the plural ideal. Although the armed forces provided religious opportunities for military personnel and their dependents and guaranteed free exercise of religion, as a secular, public institution it regarded religion as a matter of private concern with no official role in military policy. Among other things, secularism dictated abandonment of the religiously oriented character education programs of the 1950s and 1960s, and the development, in the 1970s and 1980s, of a secular professional ethic for military personnel. The principle of secularism also informed a federal magistrate's decision in 1978 that the Pentagon Protestant Pulpit program was unconstitutional because it was held in a public place, the Pentagon Concourse, and thereby violated the no-establishment clause of the Constitution.[9]

The third component of the plural ideal was the principle of the free exercise of religion, limited only by military necessity, which became the touchstone of military policy regarding religion in the 1970s and 1980s. In 1972, after an extended court fight, the military abolished compulsory chapel at the service academies. The army and navy chiefs of chaplains, the Armed Forces Chaplains Board, and the superintendents of the U.S. Military Academy and the U.S. Air Force Academy, among others, had supported required chapel attendance, but once the U.S. Court of Appeals decided against it, the military leadership resolutely turned its attention to implementing the free exercise of religion throughout the armed forces. During the 1980s, Department of Defense directives, field manuals and service branch regulations, public statements by the chiefs of chaplains, and the U.S. District and Appeals

---

tram C. Gilbert, "The Scandal and the Glory," *MCR*, Spring, 1984, pp. 23–24. For examples of efforts to foster cooperative pluralism, see John E. Groh, *Air Force Chaplains, 1971–1980* (Washington, D.C., 1986), Chap. 25 and pp. 469, 471; Groh, *Facilitators*, Chap. 6; Wendell T. Wright, "The Problems and Challenges of a Ministry in Vietnam," *Chaplain*, XXVII (1970), 44; John R. Hannah, "Religious Pluralism and Unity: One Experiment in the Army Chaplaincy," *Chaplain*, XXXIII (Third Quarter, 1976), 62–70; Paul Otterstein, "Theological Pluralism in the Air Force Chaplaincy," *MCR*, Fall, 1987, p. 119.

9. *NYT*, July 27, 1978, p. 14. The air force and navy discontinued their character education programs in the 1960s, and in 1970 the army replaced its program with a "nontheological and nonsectarian" program called Our Moral Heritage. See Martin H. Scharleman, *Air Force Chaplains, 1961–1970* (N.p., n.d.), 15, 31; Groh, "Lively Experiment," 87; Hutcheson, *Churches and the Chaplaincy*, 160–61; Headquarters, Department of the Army, *Personnel-General: Character Guidance Program* (1970), 2.

Court decisions of 1984 and 1985 upholding the constitutionality of the army chaplaincy program all repeatedly invoked the free exercise principle in defining the rationale of the chaplaincy and the religious and moral responsibilities of commanders.[10]

As we saw in Chapter 7, during the 1950s and 1960s evangelicals themselves had championed the free exercise principle. It was an important element of their arguments against the General Protestant Service and the Unified Protestant Sunday School Curriculum. Even then, however, their rhetoric also expressed elements of the "sectarian ideal" that would become their chief guide in the 1970s and 1980s. In 1952, for example, the editor of *Eternity* magazine commented on some pamphlets prepared by the Conference of Christians and Jews for distribution in the armed forces. He declared that they provided a perfect illustration of "how anti-Christianity can attack Christianity in the name of tolerance and freedom of worship." None of the pamphlets mentioned Christ, he pointed out, and with good reason, "for though the organization by which they are published calls itself a conference of Christians and Jews, it is run by apostates who have never believed in the absolute deity of the Lord Jesus Christ." The pamphlet entitled *Intolerance Is Treason*, which cited the constitutional guarantee of freedom of religion and invoked the belief that "all men are equal before God," sounded "very pretty, and in a way, it is true," the editor declared. But it was "only a half-truth." As followers of Jesus Christ, he continued, evangelicals believe in tolerance: "We say to all men that they have the right to believe as they please, but we still proclaim that if they do not admit their sinful position before God and acknowledge the Lord Jesus as God the Son, and trust His death for the remission of sins, they will be brought before the great white throne of God and sent to the lake of fire." Liberalism preaches only "the first half of this doctrine" and criticizes "those who believe the second half," he concluded. "But the second half is Christianity, and nothing else is true Christianity."[11]

Two later examples of such thinking may be cited. In 1967, in an

10. See, for example, Groh, *Facilitators*, 9–16, 35, 558 n. 2, 559 n. 3, 563 n. 13; Chaplain (MAJ) Jerry E. Malone, "The Chaplain as an Advocate of Religious Freedom," *MCR*, Fall, 1983, p. 53; Chaplain (MG) Patrick J. Hessian, "An Historical Review of the Army Chaplaincy: Free Exercise," *MCR*, Fall, 1983, p. 9; Headquarters, Department of the Army, *The Chaplain and Chaplain Assistant in Combat Operations* (1984), 2, 8.

11. "Why We Fight," *Eternity*, August, 1952, p. 15. See also, for a story on the pamphlets, *NYT*, May 6, 1951, p. 23.

article criticizing the Unified Protestant Sunday School Curriculum, *United Evangelical Action* declared, "We do not question the rights of those who wish to teach such sub-Christian views." What distressed the editors was that the several chiefs of chaplains upheld the mandatory requirement of the curriculum and in so doing, they "allow the faith of many to be undermined and disregard the conscience of evangelical chaplains and lay teachers." A few years later, the contributing editor of the magazine offered an opinion on Jewish criticism of Key 73 and subsequent disavowals by its promoters of "any programs designed to single out specific religious or ethnic groups" because they would indicate "lack of respect for the faith of those of other religious beliefs" and would be "contrary to the ecumenical spirit." In Bruce Shelley's view, the controversy over Key 73 illustrated "the problem biblical evangelism faces in the American context." He agreed that proselytism, intimidation, and coercion should be eliminated, but he was unwilling to subscribe to the tolerance or "ecumenical spirit" invoked in the quoted statement. "Any claim to have the truth, that is truth which all men are obliged to accept, is regarded as unamerican," he noted. "But if I read the Bible correctly (Acts 4:12) that is precisely what the New Testament gospel is all about. If the good news about Jesus Christ isn't valid for every man's salvation, it isn't valid for any man's salvation."[12] Both the *Eternity* and *United Evangelical Action* statements reveal the uncompromising sectarianism so characteristic of evangelicals, the notion that their faith constituted "true Christianity" while others represented "half truth" or "sub-Christian" views—or even total falsehood.

Besides sectarianism, the sectarian ideal military evangelicals followed in 1970s and 1980s embraced moral absolutism. Evangelicals fought against the relativism that seemed to be endemic in America's increasingly pluralistic society, particularly the notion that religious beliefs and morality were simply a matter of personal preference rather than a claim to objective truth and that therefore all religions, moral systems, worldviews, and ideologies were equally "true" and acceptable. As Christians, evangelicals believed that Jesus Christ is "the way, the truth, and the life." As a writer in *Eternity* observed, that conviction "isn't just 'true for me' or 'true for some' or just a 'religious preference.' It is an unalterable fact."[13]

12. "Military Sunday Schools," *UEA*, April, 1967, p. 6; Bruce Shelley, "Point and Counterpoint," *UEA*, Summer, 1973, p. 6.

13. Douglas Groothuis, "The Smorgasbord Mentality," *Eternity*, May 1985, p. 33.

The third component of the sectarian ideal was the custodial notion that the dissemination of religious "half truth" and moral relativism must be stopped or at least challenged because it subverted ("undermined," according to the *United Evangelical Action* article mentioned above) the faith of others and put them in danger of damnation. Thus a writer in *Command* magazine, arguing against the popular maxim "live and let live," noted that if a devastating disease threatened the nation, or if a crime wave overwhelmed a neighborhood, or if a mad dog were running loose, most individuals would rise to the challenge. "A person who is unsaved is in ten times the danger of any of these situations!" he declared. A person might recover from disease or a robbery and escape a mad dog, "but God's judgment for the sinner is unavoidable." The conclusion seemed obvious: "As born again believers, therefore, we cannot adopt the 'live and let live' attitude of the world." Evangelicals must heed the instructions God gave to Ezekiel "to be a watchman and to warn the wicked" and spread "the good news of God's eternal, life-giving message."[14] Thus sectarianism, moral absolutism, and the notion of custodial responsibility fueled evangelicals' compulsion to testify against false religion and moral relativism and spread "true Christianity."

Adherence to the sectarian ideal brought both evangelical chaplains and laypersons into conflict with the plural ideal. Chaplains, for example, sometimes experienced a tension between their sectarian beliefs on the one hand and the system of cooperative pluralism enjoined by the chaplaincies on the other. Thomas W. Schreck, a Unitarian Universalist chaplain writing in the *Military Chaplains' Review*, recalled being present at "handwringing sessions when our most orthodox brethren [*sic*] have lamented the possibility of Buddhist, Baha'i, Hare Krishna, or even—Heaven forbid!—'Moonie' Chaplains entering our well-paid inner sanctum." In the early 1990s, when the army began preparations to induct a Muslim chaplain, evangelicals at the Chaplain School seemed disgruntled at the prospect. Some evangelical chaplains found it difficult to accept certain faith groups such as Mormons and Unitarians as Protestants.[15]

14. Lieutenant Mel Waters, USCG, "OCF Forum: Should We 'Live and Let Live'?" *Command*, Fall, 1983, p. 2.

15. Chaplain (CPT) Thomas W. Schreck, "Can a Religious Liberal Survive in the Chaplaincy?" *MCR*, Summer, 1980, p. 23; William J. Hourihan, Chaplain Branch His-

The statements of three Southern Baptist chaplains quoted in the *Baptist Program* in November, 1971, illustrate how sectarianism and denominational loyalty could compromise evangelical chaplains' commitment to cooperative pluralism. One admitted: "I was as narrow as any Southern Baptist ever was when I came into the service. I wasn't really sure any other denominations would make it to heaven. Now I know men in other denominations born of the spirit of God who are better witnesses than many Baptists. I don't appreciate my own denomination any less, but I'm more open to people in other denominations." His colleague remembered that he had never known a priest before becoming a military chaplain. "I was quite surprised when the first one I met was a teetotaler and preached just like Billy Graham. I wish all my Baptist brethren could be exposed to the genuine depth of Christian experience I see not only in Baptists, but in Methodists, Episcopalians, Catholics, and others," he said. The third chaplain declared: "You have to be willing to accept men of other denominations as men of Christ and let them help in the work. You can't have a Baptist stamp on all your program."[16] Although the three chaplains had made some headway in transcending denominational loyalty and coming to appreciate the work of chaplains of other faith groups, they found it difficult, if not impossible, to transcend their sectarian, which is to say their Christian, beliefs. They could appreciate other chaplains only insofar as they were "men of Christ" or exhibited "genuine depth of Christian experience" or preached "just like Billy Graham." Such standards implicitly excluded Jewish, Muslim, Buddhist, and other non-Christian chaplains.

Not only theological differences but certain religious practices proved troublesome for some evangelical chaplains. Besides the General Protestant Service, conducting or attending ecumenical or interfaith services with chaplains from different denominations or faith groups posed a problem. Their abhorrence of ecumenism sometimes prompted evangelicals to refuse to participate. They opposed such services not

---

torian, U.S. Army Chaplain Center and School, Fort Monmouth, N.J., telephone conversation with author, December 7, 1993; Chaplain (COL) Geoffrey H. Moran, USA, telephone conversation with author, January 11, 1993; S. David Chambers, "The Protestant Problem," *MCR*, Fall, 1987, pp. 83–85; G. M. Clifford III, "Ministry in a Pluralistic Environment," *MCR*, Summer, 1992, pp. 78–79.

16. Leonard E. Hill, "The Military Chaplain: Ministers Uniformed," *Baptist Program*, November, 1971, pp. 11–12.

only because of concern about the blurring or watering down of sectarian doctrines, but also because they believed that by participating they gave credence to religious doctrines with which they disagreed. Some evangelical chaplains also objected to certain educational or training programs used in the armed forces. Just as they regarded the Unified Sunday School Curriculum as too ecumenical, they decried personal effectiveness training, Transcendental Meditation (used in some drug and alcohol abuse programs), and even clinical pastoral education for disdaining biblical morality and employing approaches based on behaviorism, situation ethics, or secular humanism. Fundamentalists seem to have found the system of cooperative pluralism especially troubling. Chaplain James H. Young, a graduate of Bob Jones University, not only charged "supervisory chaplains" in the army with pressuring himself and other fundamentalist chaplains to teach the Unified Curriculum and to participate in ecumenical activities (and punishing them if they refused). He also claimed they restricted fundamentalists' evangelizing efforts. Although his indictment included some evangelicals—"compromising conservative chaplains" who had adapted to the pluralistic system—he saw theological liberals and modernists as the main threat to "Bible-believing," "missionary-minded" chaplains. "The liberal decries the Fundamentalist's sharing of his faith for the purpose of converting another to faith in Christ. The reason, of course, is that the liberal does not believe in the reality of biblical judgment and hell," he explained. As a result, Young continued, "many liberals feel it is their holy calling to protect the military from . . . Fundamentalist religious 'fanatics,' to proscribe soulwinning activities, and to prosecute Fundamentalists if possible, by ultimately eliminating them from the military chaplaincy." [17] Nevertheless, he did not think fundamentalist chaplains should leave the military. They should stay in and stand up for their convictions whenever challenged.

The emphasis their denominations and endorsing bodies put on sectarianism and denominational loyalty contributed to the problem evangelical chaplains faced in maintaining a balance between sectarianism/

17. James H. Young, "The Military Chaplaincy (Deuteronomy 20: 1–4)" (Address delivered at Bob Jones University, April 2, 1982, on cassette tape; Greenville, S.C., n.d.); James H. Young, "Is Religious Proselytism in the Military Legitimate?" *Faith for the Family*, November, 1979, pp. 6–7; George W. Baugham, conversation with author, New Orleans, August 11, 1994; see also Groh, *Facilitators*, 106, 146.

loyalty and cooperative pluralism. The denominations and endorsing agencies advised them that they had a right, indeed an obligation, to be true to the denomination's beliefs and practices. For example, the Christian and Missionary Alliance advised its chaplains that although they were authorized to conduct the General Protestant Service, "they may do nothing against their consciences or in conflict with C&MA doctrine and practice" and that they were "not required to lead worship for a Jew, Muslim or Mormon, for example," but only "to find a worship leader for him." The denomination's *Military Chaplains Manual*, issued in 1983, urged its chaplains "to use religious education materials which are thoroughly evangelical in all aspects when it is within their prerogatives and duties as chaplains." After quoting army, navy, and air force regulations prohibiting commanders from requiring chaplains to compromise their religious convictions or practices, the manual offered as a general principle the rule that "the chaplains' only religious authority is that given them by their church body. Denominational limitations or religious authority cannot be removed or changed by military command or military necessity."[18]

Similarly, in the early 1990s, the "Guidelines for Cooperation with Chaplains of Other Faiths" disseminated by the NAE Chaplains Commission warned of "mounting pressures for a more ecumenical approach to chaplain ministry" as retrenchment forced cuts in the number of chaplains in the various services. Specifically, the commission noted increasing stress on "a broader form of worship," resulting in deemphasis of the distinctive elements of worship evangelicals cherished. As a result, evangelical chaplains were being encouraged to cooperate with chaplains holding divergent views in jointly led worship services and other religious observances. Although military chaplains, as public servants, were supposed to minister to all personnel, regardless of their faith orientation, they were not required to compromise their "personal faith convictions" in the conduct of religious services, the commission emphasized. It supported the chaplain's right "to determine the extent of his or her cooperation in jointly conducted services." Like the C&MA, the NAE commission also stressed the distinction between conducting and providing worship services. Its "Guidelines" stated: "A chaplain is

18. [Christian and Missionary Alliance], *Military Chaplains Manual* (N.p., 1983), 6–8; "Inside the Alliance Military Chaplaincy," *Alliance Witness*, CXVIII (June 22, 1983), 9.

true to the 'public trust' if he or she *provides* a worship opportunity for a service member. The chaplain need not *conduct* the service." While the commission advised chaplains to lean, whenever possible, toward "cooperation rather than non-cooperation" in jointly conducted services and to "avoid entering into an adversarial relationship" in dealing with such issues, it concluded the "Guidelines" with an unequivocal offer of assistance: "NAE Chaplains can expect full support from the Commission in any case where the action taken is consistent with the Commission position." Thus not only were evangelical chaplains advised of their right and duty to maintain denominational loyalty; they received regular assurances that their endorsing agencies or denominations stood ready to assist them if they felt their rights had been violated by what one NAE Chaplains Commission chairman called an "ecumenical or pluralistic military chaplaincy decision." [19]

In 1992 the NAE Chaplains Commission drew up recommendations regarding public prayer. At issue was evangelicals' sectarian proclivity to pray "in Jesus' name." In recent years, the commission noted, some evangelical chaplains had felt pressured to avoid mentioning Jesus' name in public prayer on the grounds that some persons might be offended. For the chaplaincy to discourage particular forms of prayer would constitute a violation of a chaplain's free exercise right, his freedom "to pray in a manner consistent with his faith," the commission insisted. But the commission admitted that reconciling the chaplain's right with that of military personnel of other faiths posed a difficult problem. While it protected the chaplain's freedom "to pray in a manner consistent with his faith," the chaplaincy must also protect "the service member from being *forced* to listen to such a prayer if he or she chooses not to do so."

19. Commission Resource Board, NAE Chaplains Commission, "Guidelines for Cooperation with Chaplains of Other Faiths," [November, 1992]; Bradley J. Lewis, "Commission Aids Evangelical Chaplains," *UEA*, January–February, 1987, p. 11. Associated Gospel Churches, an endorsing agent for fundamentalist chaplains, provided considerable support for one of its chaplains who became involved in a controversy with the staff chaplain at Fort Campbell in the mid-1970s. George W. Baugham, conversation with author, New Orleans, August 11, 1994; "US Army Military History Institute Senior Officer Oral History Program, History of the Chaplains, Chaplain (Maj Gen) Patrick J. Hessian, USA, Interviewed by Chaplain (Colonel) Henry F. Ackerman, USA, Historical Office, US Army Chaplain School Carlisle Barracks, PA," February 10, 1986 (Photocopied typescript in U.S. Army Military History Institute, Carlisle, Pa.), 74, 75, 76, 91; W. O. H. Garman to Edward C. Meyer, June 25, 1979, enclosed in Bob Jones III to the author, December 10, 1993.

The solution, according to the commission guidelines, was for the chaplaincy to continue to maintain the distinction between mandatory formations and voluntary gatherings. "In a mandatory formation, there is some question as to whether *any* prayer is possible," the commission observed. The commission may have been referring to the implications of the recent Supreme Court decision *Lee* v. *Weisman*, barring prayers at public school graduation ceremonies because they indirectly coerced religious observance. Still, the commission continued, "Based upon current practice, it would appear . . . that some form of prayer is possible with minimal or no offense." But, the commission insisted, in the case of a voluntary gathering, proscribing any form of prayer would be inappropriate. "Attendees should recognize (and they generally do) that the chaplain offering the prayer is doing so from his or her own tradition, and accept that expression of faith on that basis. Under these circumstances it would appear that it would be perfectly legitimate to pray 'in Jesus name' and the Chaplaincy should not even suggest that it is inappropriate to do so." [20]

The tension between the commission's view, supporting sectarianism and denominational loyalty, and the plural ideal, with its celebration of religious diversity, may be seen by comparing commission guidelines with an article in the *Military Chaplains' Review* by a Jewish chaplain serving with the navy, Lieutenant Commander A. E. Resnicoff. Discussing public prayer in "interfaith settings," where, presumably, attendance was voluntary, Chaplain Resnicoff contended that prayers "in Jesus' name" were "prayers that hurt," for they contained words and expressions that excluded non-Christians (and, he might have added, persons of no faith). Resnicoff was less concerned with the chaplain's right than with his responsibility to those he served and with the feelings of persons attending his services. [21]

The tensions evangelical chaplains experienced between their sectarian beliefs and the chaplaincies' system of cooperative pluralism rarely led to open conflict with the plural ideal or the military leadership in the 1970s and 1980s. Part of the reason may be that ministering over a

20. [Commission Resource Board, NAE Chaplains Commission], "Freedom of Expression in Public Prayer: Guidelines for Evangelical Chaplains," [November, 1992]. See also "Constitutional Guidelines for Chaplains," *Centurion*, December, 1992, p. 4.

21. LCDR A. E. Resnicoff, CHC, USN, "Prayers That Hurt: Public Prayer in Interfaith Settings," *MCR*, Winter, 1987, pp. 30–40. See also Robert G. Leroe, "Public Prayer," *MCR*, Spring, 1992, pp. 50–62.

period of years in a religiously pluralistic environment influenced chaplains to become theologically more inclusive—or at least more open-minded. The main reason for the lack of confrontation was that chaplains worked within a system that encouraged *both* denominational loyalty and cooperative pluralism. Cooperative pluralism, as we have seen, stressed the chaplain's willingness to minister to persons of various faiths and to cooperate with chaplains representing different denominations. At the same time that they championed cooperative pluralism, however, the chaplaincies emphasized denominational loyalty. For example, the Army Field Manual 16-5, *The Chaplain,* pointed out that chaplains served in the army "as clergy of their particular religious faith," that their "spiritual authority" was imparted to them by their denomination or endorsing body, and that they were to perform their duties "in accord with their conscience and the principles of their church." [22] Moreover, chaplains were permitted, even encouraged, to offer denominational services in addition to the General Protestant Service, to provide religious instruction in the tenets of their denomination, and to conduct other denominationally oriented activities such as Bible study groups, retreats, revivals, and the like.

The chaplaincies were not the only ones that promoted denominational loyalty and cooperative pluralism. Evangelical chaplains and their endorsing agencies committed themselves to both emphases, as evidenced by their participation in the National Conference on Ministry to the Armed Forces (NCMAF), created in 1982 to replace the General Commission on Chaplains and the Conference of Ecclesiastical Endorsing Agents. The first two pledges in the NCMAF code of ethics declared, "I will hold in trust the traditions and practices of my religious body," and "I will carefully adhere to whatever direction may be con-

---

22. Headquarters, Department of the Army, *The Chaplain* (1977), ii, 1-1, and see also 2-17. See also Headquarters, Department of the Army, *The Chaplain and Chaplain Assistant,* 2–3; Clifford, "Ministry in a Pluralistic Environment," 67–78; Chaplain G. William Dando, Executive Director, Military Chaplains Association, telephone conversation with author, July 9, 1992; Clifford T. Weathers, Coordinator, National Conference on Ministry to the Armed Forces, to the author, July 22, 1992; Reverend Dr. S. David Chambers, "History of the National Conference on Ministry to the Armed Forces" (Typescript of a speech at the Sheraton National Hotel, December 6, 1988, sent to author by E. H. Jim Ammerman, President and Director, Chaplaincy Full Gospel Churches, July 16, 1990); *National Conference on Ministry to the Armed Forces* (Arlington, Va., n.d.).

veyed to me by my endorsing body for maintenance of my endorsement." The code also committed chaplains to work "collegially" and constructively with other chaplains and to respect their beliefs and practices, as well as to provide "ministry to all military personnel and their families," including those belonging to religious bodies other than their own. One section pledged chaplains conducting services "that include persons of other than my religious body" to "draw upon those beliefs, principles, and practices that we have in common."[23]

The NCMAF code of ethics also contained a pledge declaring, "I will not proselytize from other religious bodies, but I retain the right to evangelize those who are non affiliated." As Richard Hutcheson points out, even before the establishment of the NCMAF, the chaplaincies of the armed forces prohibited proselytizing, which they defined as an effort on the part of a chaplain to persuade an individual to leave a religion to which he or she was actively committed. But the prohibition against "sheep stealing" did not prevent a chaplain from counseling and offering religious instruction to a person who belonged to no church or faith group or to an individual who, of his or her own volition, expressed a desire to convert to the chaplain's denomination.[24] That is why evangelical chaplains were free to evangelize religiously uncommitted persons. Presumably that is also why, despite Jewish protests, the chiefs of chaplains supported Key 73, a clearly sectarian, evangelistic campaign—because they did not think it would involve proselytizing.

Given their commitment to the Great Commission, one might think that evangelical chaplains and their endorsing agents would find it difficult to accept the no-proselytizing rule. In fact, since the beginning of their mission to the military, evangelical chaplains generally agreed that proselytizing was unacceptable.[25] Surely part of the reason was that the no-proselytizing rule did not prevent them from presenting the claims

23. NCMAF, *The Covenant and the Code of Ethics for Chaplains of the Armed Forces: A Project of the National Conference on Ministry to the Armed Forces* (N.p., 1990).

24. NCMAF, *Covenant and Code of Ethics for Chaplains*; Hutcheson, *Churches and the Chaplaincy*, 125; Groh, *Facilitators*, 9; Groh, *Air Force Chaplains*, 119; U.S. Army Office of the Chief of Chaplains, *Historical Review, 1 July 1968 to 30 June 1969* (1970), 32–33.

25. See, for example, Douglas G. Scott (Chairman, NAE Commission on Chaplains), "The USA Chaplaincy Is a Branch of the Church," *UEA*, November 15, 1952, p. 23; Floyd Robertson, Director, NAE Chaplains Commission, paraphrased in U.S. Army Office of the Chief of Chaplains, *Historical Review, 1 July 1968 to 30 June 1969*, 33.

of the Gospel in Bible studies, retreats, and counseling sessions, as well as worship services. In the 1980s and early 1990s, however, evangelical chaplains and their endorsing agencies began to articulate other reasons for adhering to the no-proselytizing rule. These reasons not only indicate the precision with which evangelicals differentiated between proselytizing and evangelism; they also reveal a more positive view of the plural ideal than might be expected.

Three articles that appeared in the fall, 1991, issue of the *Military Chaplains' Review* suggest the contours of the new thinking about the no-proselytizing rule. All three were written by evangelical chaplains who made it clear that they felt perfectly free to engage in both personal and pulpit evangelism in the armed forces. They agreed that the appropriate targets for such evangelizing efforts were military personnel and their families who did not have a faith or a commitment to any religious organization. They also agreed in censuring improper approaches to evangelism such as pressuring individuals or denigrating other religions. Proper approaches to evangelism, the three chaplains insisted, not only safeguarded religious pluralism and free exercise but also benefited evangelical religion. As Chaplain Rick D. Mathis, a Foursquare Gospel minister endorsed by the NAE, argued, it was in the best interest of the evangelical chaplain "to strengthen, rather than thwart, religious pluralism and free exercise rights." Mathis contended that chaplains were pledged not just to acknowledge religious diversity but to "honor and support" it and the right of others to follow their religious beliefs. Doing this in the various "ministry forums" in which he and other chaplains worked—prayer breakfasts, Bible studies, retreats, worship services— posed no threat to his own faith, Mathis observed. "My real security and significance are grounded in my relationship with Jesus Christ," he wrote. "Protecting the rights of others' faiths doesn't require me *not* ardently to believe my own cause." Nor did he see any threat to his ministry. By seeing to it that others were able to exercise their religious faith, Mathis ensured his own freedom to practice and proclaim the Gospel as he understood it. In an interview published in the NAE Chaplains Commission *Centurion*, Mathis revealed a sectarian element in his thinking. "In a pluralistic religious setting," he asserted, "when freely presented in a ministry forum unrestricted by abuse or restraint, the gospel will triumph over any false gospel."[26]

26. Rick D. Mathis, "Constitutional Guidelines for the Military Chaplain Evan-

Lay evangelicals within the armed forces seem to have encountered more difficulty accommodating to the plural ideal than evangelical chaplains did. Chaplains benefited from the guidance offered by an institutionalized system of cooperative pluralism. Lay evangelicals' only guide was the American tradition of tolerance and civility, which was itself being sorely tested in the "culture wars" of the 1970s and 1980s.[27] It was too weak to restrain their extreme sectarianism and compulsive proselytizing.

There is ample evidence of the conflict between lay evangelicals and the plural ideal. John Groh, the historian of the air force chaplaincy, cites several instances. In the late 1970s, according to one chaplain's report, when a Buddhist program for foreign-born wives of airmen was established at Clark and Dover Air Force Bases, "strenuous objections were received and some families left the chapel program." *Airman* magazine ran an article on the program and it, too, received "strenuous objections . . . from Christians objecting to 'God's House' being used for 'pagan' or 'heathen' religious practices." In the early 1980s, the leader of a Navigator group meeting in the chapel at Beale Air Force Base told the members they could not remain in the group if they attended other religious programs, including those offered by the base chapel. Groh also notes that opposition to Mormon chaplains participating in the Protestant chapel program became stronger in the 1980s than it had been in the 1970s; much of it came from persons he identified as fundamentalists. And on some air force bases evangelicals' antifeminism and opposition to traditional Halloween observances apparently provoked clashes with Protestant chaplains and chapel programs.[28]

A particularly graphic illustration of evangelicals' conflict with the plural ideal involved the new *Book of Worship for U.S. Forces,* issued in 1975, to be used by military personnel and their dependents in all of the service branches. A collection of 611 hymns and other music for worship prepared under the supervision of the Armed Forces Chaplains

gelist and Chaplaincy," *MCR,* Fall, 1991, pp. 34, 36–37. See also Robert G. Leroe, "Faith Sharing in the Military," *MCR,* Fall, 1991, pp. 71–77; Gil A. Stricklin, "Evangelism in the Ranks," *MCR,* Fall, 1991, pp. 53–57. Leroe was endorsed by the Conservative Congregational Christian Conference; Stricklin was a Southern Baptist. For the Mathis interview, see "Constitutional Guidelines for Chaplains," 3–5.

27. James Davison Hunter, *Culture Wars: The Struggle to Define America* (New York, 1991).

28. Groh, *Facilitators,* 552–53, 388, 266.

Board, it replaced the *Armed Forces Hymnal* published in 1958. When it was first issued, the new hymnal was hailed as "a truly ecumenical hymnal" and a reflection of the chaplaincies' commitment to religious diversity and denominational cooperation. Even *Christianity Today* commented that the armed forces had "achieved something that civilian religious groups and churches have failed to do: they have developed an ecumenically serviceable 'Book of Worship.'" Soon, however, military evangelicals joined forces with other military personnel, as well as civilians, including several members of Congress, in a campaign to expunge a hymn they regarded as "blasphemous." The controversy centered on Hymn 286, "It Was on a Friday Morning." At first the Armed Forces Chaplains Board and the chiefs of the army, navy, and air force chaplaincies resisted the campaign. Invoking the plural ideal, Army Chief of Chaplains Orris Kelly observed in a letter to Congressman W. C. Daniel that "the military community mirrors America's religiously pluralistic society" and the Armed Forces Chaplains Board had prepared the *Book of Worship* to meet the needs of the broad spectrum of religious views represented in the armed forces. Ultimately, though, the Chaplains Board and the chaplaincies caved in to the pressure and substituted a different hymn for 286 when the *Book of Worship* was reprinted.[29]

In a remarkably candid description of his experience as a Unitarian Universalist chaplain in the army in the summer, 1980, issue of the *Military Chaplains' Review*, Chaplain Thomas Schreck recounted conversations with evangelicals who made it clear that they regarded his brand of religion as subversive, immoral, or simply "false doctrine." He claimed that other religious liberals in the chaplaincy had had similar encounters. "'You mean you *don't* believe Jesus was God?' we are asked when the discussion turns to Christology. 'Religious humanists believe

29. James W. Chapman, "A Truly Ecumenical Hymnal," *Chaplain*, XXXII (First Quarter, 1975), 6; "From the Editors," *Chaplain*, XXXII (First Quarter, 1975), 2; "Worship Aid, Military Style," *CT*, March 28, 1975, pp. 23–24; Marjorie Hyer, "'Sacrilegious' Hymn Banned," *Washington Post*, July 20, 1976, p. A11; "Goodbye, Green Hill," *Christian Century*, XCIII (September 1, 1976), 725; Ronald Goetz, "Heresy Hunters and the Atonement," *Christian Century*, XCIII (October 6, 1976), 827; Groh, *Air Force Chaplains*, 448–51; Office of the Chief of Chaplains, Department of the Army, "1 July 1975 to 30 September 1976" [1976] (Typescript at U.S. Army Center of Military History), 44; Office of the Chief of Chaplains, "Historical Review, 1 October 1976–30 September 1977" [1977] (Typescript at U.S. Army Center of Military History), 43.

that the human race is capable of producing a Jesus,' I reply, to no avail. . . . As a UU chaplain I have been asked questions like, 'How can you wear a cross?' and, 'How can you be a chaplain?' and 'Don't you know you'll die in your sins?' " Based on his experiences, Shreck questioned whether most military personnel truly accepted religious pluralism in the armed forces. "If many members of our community cannot deal with chaplains who express their religious humanism, how shall they ever deal with chaplains who worship Buddha, Baha'u'llah, or the Guru Maharaji?" he asked. Shreck contended that the encounters he described reflected a military community largely populated by born-again Christians, in which conservative Protestantism set the standard of theological and ethical values. The dominant religious conservatism allowed aggressive, intolerant behavior on the part of its adherents but frowned on overt expressions of religious liberalism.[30]

Evangelicals in the officers corps revealed their sectarian bias in the oft-expressed opinion that Christianity provides a necessary foundation for military leadership. General Ralph Haines was neither the first nor the last to insist, as he did in his article for the *Military Chaplains' Review*, that "we must season professional ethics with a deep and abiding faith in God," or to argue, as he did in "Christian Leadership in the Armed Forces," that military commanders should be "committed Christians." Many evangelicals believed, as William K. Harrison had contended, not only that a Christian may serve in the military but that Christians rendered the best service. These evangelicals went beyond the assumption that the Bible constituted an "all-sufficient guide for faith and conduct" to insist that it constituted the only sufficient guide.[31] In the 1970s and 1980s, such thinking reflected not only evangelicals' sectarianism but their moral absolutism. It had important implications at a time when

30. Shreck, "Can a Religious Liberal Survive in the Chaplaincy?" 25, 28–31. Chaplain (COL) Geoffrey H. Moran, USA, in a telephone conversation with the author, January 11, 1993, expressed a similar view, noting that evangelicals had created a kind of "monolithic religion for the army." He thought their prominence at the military academies and other service schools promoted the view that the "only way to be a Christian" was to be an evangelical. The fact that an increasing number of officers coming out of the schools are likely to be born-again Christians "makes it tough for pluralism," he said.

31. General Ralph E. Haines, Jr., "Spiritual Renewal in the Army," *MCR*, Spring, 1977, p. 11; Ralph E. Haines, Jr., *"Christian Leadership in the Armed Forces": The Second Bishop Hulme-Moir Memorial Lecture* (Canberra, Australia, 1984), 3, 6, 9; Clay T. Buckingham, "The Character of the Christian Commander," *Command*, Spring, 1985, p. 3.

the military was engaged in an effort to elaborate and revitalize its professional ethic.

In 1972, for example, a revealing exchange of views took place in the op-ed section of *Army Times*. The August 23 issue featured a letter by Edwin A. Deagle, an instructor at the U.S. Military Academy and a former battalion executive officer in Vietnam. In it he explained why, after twelve years of service, he had resigned his commission in the army. Deploring the "moral numbness" that had afflicted the army during the Vietnam War, producing atrocities like the My Lai massacre, Deagle also criticized the army's dilatoriness in rebuilding its professional ethic so as to avoid a similar situation in the future. A few weeks later, there appeared a commentary entitled "Fighting Moral Rot," by Lieutenant Colonel William R. Johansen. Although he did not so identify himself, Johansen was an OCF member, and he responded to Deagle's letter, according to Robert Spoede, "as a Christian." Johansen criticized Deagle's diagnosis of the problem facing the army. It was not a "numbness" that afflicted the army, "but a real moral rot that is endemic today to Western society as a whole and the United States and the U.S. Army as part of that society," Johansen declared. The cause was "the lack of a solid moral base." Individuals depended instead on a "subjective morality" that produced only confusion and contradiction when applied to ethical questions. The secular humanistic solution Deagle proposed was equally flawed, Johansen asserted. The "only *logical* basis for morality" was "God Himself." He claimed that a growing number of military men, including General Ralph Haines, shared his view. They all recognized that in rebuilding the army professional ethic we must look to "the Source," the "bedrock of moral judgment," that is, to God and the Holy Scriptures, Johansen wrote. "Only by looking to this Source can we expect soldiers to develop a professional ethic that applies to the complex years ahead," he concluded.[32]

The debate over the professional ethic continued throughout the next decade and a half. Military journals such as *Parameters*, *Military Review*, the *Air University Review*, the *U.S. Naval Institute Proceedings*,

32. Edwin A. Deagle, "Anatomy of a Resignation: About 'Moral Numbness,' Confidence, and Pride," *Army Times*, August 23, 1972, p. 13; Lt. Col. W. R. Johansen, "Commentary: Fighting Moral Rot," *Army Times*, September 13, 1972, pp. 12, 22. This piece was reprinted under the same title in *Command*, Fall, 1972, pp. 23–25. See also Robert W. Spoede, *More Than Conquerors: A History of the Officers' Christian Fellowship of the U.S.A., 1943–1983* (Englewood, Colo., 1993), 99.

and the *United States Air Force Academy Journal of Professional Military Ethics* featured scores of articles dealing with questions of military ethics, professionalism, and morality. The great majority of the articles took a secular approach, and some evangelicals became concerned about the failure to base the military ethic on an explicitly Christian foundation.

In 1986, the year Secretary of the Army John O. Marsh and General John A. Wickham proclaimed values the annual theme of the army, Colonel Don Martin, Jr., published an editorial in *Command* commenting on the difficulty of inculcating values in officers and enlisted persons given the current ascendancy in American society of "moral relativism," "naturalism," and "secular humanism." All of these value systems denied the existence of absolute truths, made man and/or nature the measure of all things, and failed to inspire any commitment beyond self-interest, he contended. "We ask service people to commit themselves to ideals that form the basis for the American nation, ideals such as freedom, justice, truth and the dignity and equality of individual persons," Martin observed. But those ideals meant nothing and could inspire no commitment unless they were connnected to the "biblical base" from which they were originally derived, he insisted. *"Apart from a belief in God Who has revealed Himself in Scripture, there is no ultimately meaningful professional military ethic."*[33] Taken to its logical conclusion, Martin's argument suggested that the army should make belief in God and biblical inerrancy the foundation of its professional ethic.

Believing that evangelical Christianity provides the only true basis of the military professional ethic is one thing; putting it into practice is another. There is evidence that some evangelical military leaders allowed their sectarian commitment to influence decisions regarding performance evaluations, duty assignments, promotions, and the like. Captain X, one of the men Flo Conway and Jim Siegelman interviewed for their book *Holy Terror*, mentioned military leaders who "often cited

---

33. Don Martin, "Editorial: Foundations of the Military Professional Ethic," *Command*, No. 4 [1986], p. 2. See also Lt. Commander Bradley Y. Winsted, USA, "A Cry for Moral Action," *Command*, Fall, 1983, pp. 3–4, 29; Colonel Stewart Sherard, U.S. Army, Retired, "Vision and Service: Keys to Effective Leadership," *Command*, No. 3 (1986), 6–10; "Biblical Criteria for Professional Success," and "The Christian Officer as a Military Commander," *Command*, Spring, 1985, p. 2; Buckingham, "The Character of the Christian Commander," 3–6; Colonel Harry Ota, USA, "The Commander's Priorities," *Command*, Spring, 1985, pp. 7–10; Colonel Stuart L. Perkins, USA, "The Commander's Professional Goals," *Command*, Spring, 1985, pp. 16–18.

attendance at Bible studies and fellowshipping sessions as positive factors in performance reports." Others besides Captain X expressed concern about evangelical military leaders basing efficiency ratings or recommendations for promotion on their judgment of the individual's religious belief and practice. In the early 1990s a rumor circulated within the military community that the commandant of one of the army's service schools, who was known to be a "fundamentalist," was placing his "born-again friends" in administrative positions.[34]

Such practices conflicted with the plural ideal, which prescribed a secular professional ethic. As described in the army field manual, *Military Leadership*, the ethic adopted in the 1980s comprised "institutional values" such as loyalty to the ideals of the nation, loyalty to the unit, and selfless service and the "soldierly values" of courage, candor, competence, and commitment. None of these was necessarily grounded in religion. Religion might be a "personal value" and might very well influence an individual's leadership, but it was not to be considered in evaluating another individual's leadership.[35]

The sectarianism of evangelicals in the officer corps may also be seen in their evangelizing efforts. Military evangelicals exhibited the same compulsion to evangelize as their civilian counterparts, and, unlike evangelical chaplains, they had not pledged obedience to a no-proselytizing rule. As a consequence, they sometimes overstepped the boundary between evangelism and proselytism.

Throughout this book, we have seen numerous instances of commanding officers "sharing Christ" with their staff, holding prayer breakfasts in their offices, and inviting individuals to Bible study, fellowship groups, and other evangelical activities. During the 1970s and 1980s such activities continued to occur and may even have increased as the number of evangelicals in the officer corps increased. For example, in the early 1970s, General Haines used inspection visits to various army installations as an opportunity to present his Christian testimony. John Groh described a commander's call at McClellan Air Force Base in March, 1980, which included a Gospel lesson from Matthew 28:19–20

---

34. Flo Conway and Jim Siegelman, *Holy Terror: The Fundamentalist War on America's Freedoms in Religion, Politics and Our Private Lives* (Garden City, N.Y., 1982), 28, 30–31, 336; Don L. Lair, Assistant Director, Mershon Center, Ohio State University, Columbus, telephone conversation with author, September, 1990.

35. Headquarters Department of the Army, *Military Leadership* (1983), 86–90.

("Go ye therefore and make disciples . . . baptizing them in the name of the Father, Son and Holy Ghost") and a closing prayer that named Jesus Christ "Lord." As Groh points out, because this was a military meeting where attendance was required, an "explicitly Christian" exercise was inappropriate. Conway and Siegelman quoted Captain X describing an appearance by Colonel Heath Bottomly at an officers' development and leadership school at an air force base in Alabama. Unlike the many voluntary meetings Bottomly addressed, this one was a training program in which he occupied a two-hour slot. According to Captain X: "He related his combat experiences. He talked about his weaknesses as a leader and officer. Then he told us, 'Don't neglect Christ.' He said, 'Christ is the most important thing you can discover in your life.'"[36]

Other illustrations of proselytizing may be found in *Command,* the OCF magazine. In a 1985 special issue "The Christian Commander," U.S. Marine Corps colonel John Grinalds described his practice of "evangelism in command," which he defined as "the actions of the commander to present Christ to the members of his command, not only as a source of eternal salvation but also as a present help in difficult times." Both the Bible and military regulations (referring to command responsibility for the spiritual welfare of the troops) "direct us to execute the Great Commission as Christian commanders," Grinalds asserted. Drawing on his experience, he described what he had done as commanding officer of 3rd Battalion, 8th Marines, in 1978–1979. He said he signaled his religious orientation immediately, at the assumption-of-command ceremony, where he told the troops "that we would look to God in this battalion to help us 'close the gap,' reciting Isaiah 41:10 as a promise we could believe." Soon after assuming command, he called all the officers together, "shared what Christ meant to me and what He had done in my life," and "suggested that they look into what He has to offer." In his weekly talks with enlisted marines he "always included an invitation to attend worship services on Sunday." He encouraged the Navigators to visit the barracks and "witness to the Marines," which resulted in several conversions and the initiation of Bible study. He talked to every marine who appeared before him for Article 15 action or to "Request Mast" "about what Christ meant or could mean to him" and gave away New Testaments that he kept in his desk drawer. On weekends he visited the barracks to talk individually to marines in the

36. Groh, *Air Force Chaplains,* 442; Conway and Siegelman, *Holy Terror,* 335.

hope of steering the conversation to "a discussion about Christ." Grinalds bragged that during the twelve months of his command, "we saw the S-3, S-4, Communications Officer, Motor Transport Officer, two Company Commanders and the Assault Amphibian Platoon Commander commit their lives to Christ. . . . Many others rededicated their lives to Christ and were baptized, including several of the above officers, plus our Assistant S-3, the S-3 Liaison Officer and many of our enlisted men."[37]

In the same issue of *Command*, Colonel Donn Miller, who had served as commander of the 1st Battalion, 16th Infantry, at Bobelingen, West Germany, proclaimed the value of what he called a "ministry of prayer," "for through it men see the signs and believe in the Lord Jesus Christ." He described several occasions when he led his troops in prayer during field exercises, where, presumably, attendance was required.[38]

A final illustration of the conflict between the plural ideal of the military leadership and the sectarian ideal guiding evangelicals may be found in the Persian Gulf deployment of 1990–1991. During Operation Desert Shield, out of deference to the religious beliefs of the people of Saudi Arabia and in keeping with its prohibition of non-Islamic religious activity within its borders, the American military leadership restricted the religious activities of American service personnel stationed there. For example, Americans were instructed not to wear a crucifix or Star of David, whether in the form of jewelry or (in the case of chaplains) insignia, and chaplains were advised to be discreet in conducting worship services. Guidelines issued by the military leadership also cautioned both chaplains and laypersons against engaging in missionary activities such as distributing Bibles or other non-Islamic religious literature. By the same token, people in the United States were advised against the mass mailing of Christmas cards or other religious materials to American troops because that, too, might be interpreted as evangelizing.[39]

37. John Grinalds, "Evangelism in Command," *Command*, Spring, 1985, pp. 37–40. According to Robert W. Spoede, it is generally believed that Lieutenant Colonel Oliver North became a Christian under Grinalds' influence while the two men were serving in the Mediterranean (Spoede to the author, June 4, 1990).

38. Colonel Donn Miller, USA, "The Commander's Spiritual Leadership," *Command*, Spring, 1985, pp. 42–43. See also Captain Earle L. Sullivan, USCG, "The Commander as Discipler," *Command*, Spring, 1985, pp. 44–45.

39. *NYT*, December 9, 1990, p. 8; "Chaplains Minister in the Midst of Islam," *CT*, October 8, 1990, p. 68; Geraldine Baum, "Baptism of Fire," *Los Angeles Times*, January

In imposing such restrictions, the military leadership pleaded military necessity. The restrictions were not absolute; the emphasis was on discretion rather than outright prohibition; and they applied mainly in or near Saudi Arabia's major cities, not to chaplains or personnel in the field, where they were out of sight of Arab civilians and soldiers. Evangelical opposition to the restrictions seems to have taken the form of what might be called principled grumbling rather than an organized campaign. This was no doubt partly because evangelicals generally supported the Persian Gulf War and also because, despite the restrictions, there was no dearth of religious activity among the American forces in the Persian Gulf. Prayer, witnessing, Bible study, baptisms, distribution of pocket-size, camouflage-covered New Testaments and Bibles, even something of a spiritual awakening flourished during Operation Desert Shield, as a number of newspaper articles and books testified.[40]

The religious restrictions imposed during the Persian Gulf operation did have the potential to provoke a confrontation between evangelicals and the military leadership, because traditionally evangelicals have insisted that opposition to constituted authority is justified when it interferes with religious worship, a stand they base not only on the First Amendment but on the Bible. But no confrontation ever developed, probably because the restrictions were not total and the American presence in Saudi Arabia did not continue long enough for them to become onerous.

Similarly, throughout the 1970s and 1980s, although the potential was there, the conflict between the plural and sectarian ideals never forced a confrontation between evangelicals and the military leadership. The reason is that neither party to the conflict believed fundamental values to be involved. The military leadership never regarded evangelicals as challenging its mission or authority, and most evangelicals did not perceive the leadership as requiring them to submit to commands

2, 1991, p. E2; Jim Falkenburg and Karen M. Feaver, "Bible's Good News Reaches the Gulf," *Christian Science Monitor*, January 15, 1991, p. 19.

40. See, for example, E. H. Jim Ammerman and Charlene Ammerman, *After the Storm* (Nashville, 1991), 95; Richardson, "Religious Sensitivities in Saudi Arabia Keep Troops' Observances Low-Key," A57; George W. Cornell, "Religious Differences over War Shared Concern," *Baton Rouge Morning Advocate*, January 26, 1991, p. A12; Spoede, *More Than Conquerors*, 173–74.

that violated God's laws.[41] In 1993, however, as the next chapter will show, when evangelicals and the military leadership became involved in the controversy over homosexuals in the military, the likelihood of a confrontation increased significantly.

41. On these points see Donald Davidson, "Christian Ethics and the Military Profession," *MCR*, Fall, 1986, pp. 8–25.

21

The Confrontation over Homosexuals in the Military

In the winter of 1992–1993, in the midst of the national debate over President Bill Clinton's proposal to lift the ban on homosexuals serving in the armed forces, military evangelicals contemplated the possibility of an outright confrontation with the military leadership.

After twelve years of Republican rule, military evangelicals, like many of their civilian counterparts, were alarmed at the prospect of Clinton's taking over the government. In the December, 1992, newsletter of the NAE's Commission on Chaplains, Director James A. Edgren, a retired army chaplain, pointed to the challenge facing evangelical chaplains during the next four years. Much of the "social agenda" promoted by the new administration goes "against our Evangelical view of life and culture," he wrote. "We may find ourselves dealing with a Government increasingly hostile to our goals and objectives."[1]

Although military evangelicals viewed the incoming administration with apprehension, they had never felt more comfortable within the armed forces than they did in 1992. Once regarded as "freaks," they had become over a period of several decades a highly visible, well-respected element within the military. They were no longer outsiders. Though still a minority, they were insiders who wielded influence disproportionate to their numbers. To be sure, as we saw in Chapter 20, tensions sometimes developed between them and the military leadership, but they seemed easily contained. The adversarial relationship of the 1950s and 1960s was a thing of the past.

Or was it? For military evangelicals, the issue of homosexuals in the

---

1. Jim Edgren, "From the Director," *Centurion*, December, 1992, p. 2.

military provoked more intense conflict between the sectarian and plural ideals than any of the issues that had arisen in the 1970s and 1980s and disrupted the accord they had developed with the military leadership. In arguing against lifting the ban, evangelicals contended that both the Old and New Testaments condemned homosexuality as a sin. Because they viewed the Bible as the inspired, infallible, authoritative word of God, they regarded the condemnation of homosexuality as a moral absolute. To violate it was to disobey God.[2]

If evangelicals were guided by the sectarian ideal in the debate over homosexuals in the armed forces, the publicly stated position taken by the military leadership followed the plural ideal. In discussions with the president and in their public statements, General Colin L. Powell and other members of the Joint Chiefs of Staff argued against lifting the ban on purely secular grounds, contending that it would be detrimental to good order, discipline, and unit cohesion, would undermine morale and recruiting, and would increase the risk of AIDS among military personnel. The Joint Chiefs did express concern that lifting the ban would cause devoutly religious service members to leave the armed forces, but that merely reflected the distinction the plural ideal made between the public realm of policy and the private realm of religion. In a comment offered during a question-and-answer session following his address to cadets of the U.S. Naval Academy, General Powell explicitly invoked the distinction. He was responding to a midshipman's request for advice: if President Clinton ordered the military to accept homosexuals, what course of action should be taken by those who believed that homosexuality was immoral? In accord with the plural ideal, Powell began his response with the recognition and acceptance of pluralism, noting that "we're all Americans. We are many kinds of Americans of all walks of

2. See, for example, E. H. Jim Ammerman, Chaplain (COL) US Army, Retired, Endorsing Executive, Full Gospel Churches, to President William J. Clinton, January 29, 1993, in *Chaplaincy Full Gospel Churches* newsletter, February, 1993; "Testimony of Chaplain (Brigadier General) James M. Hutchens, ARNG, Retired, Before the House Armed Services Committee . . . May 4, 1993" and "Testimony of Chaplain (Colonel) James A. Edgren, United States Army, Retired, Before the Republican Research Committee . . . March 24, 1993" (Typescripts sent to the author by James A. Edgren, Director, NAE Commission on Chaplains); John J., "The Bible and Homosexuality," and Colonel Don Martin, Jr., "OCF Responses to the Proposal to Rescind the Ban on Homosexuals in the U.S. Military," both in *Command*, Winter, 1992, pp. 17–20 and 21–22; Colonel Ronald D. Ray, USMCR, *Military Necessity and Homosexuality* (2nd ed., rev.; Louisville, 1993), 101–104.

life, and there are some Americans who are homosexual." Homosexuals, he emphasized, "are every bit as good as any other American, even if they have what is called an alternate lifestyle." Then came an unambiguous statement of the moral relativism implicit in the plural ideal: "As a military officer," Powell declared, "I don't believe that in my professional capacity I can make a moral judgment as to whether that is a correct lifestyle or not. Because we are all Americans, we are free to make our own moral choice about that." He reiterated his objection to homosexuals in the military, based on secular grounds. But what if Congress, as the representative of the American people, and the president, having been elected by them, decided to lift the ban on homosexuals? Then, Powell declared, "We, as professional members of the military must conform to that policy. The debate will be over at that point." But while the military, as military, were obligated to conform to public policy, individual members had a right to resign rather than do so. And although, according to the plural ideal, public policy was not to be influenced by religious principles, individuals might be so guided. "If after those decisions are made you still find it [homosexuality] completely unacceptable and it strikes to the heart of your moral beliefs, then I think you have to resign," Powell concluded.[3]

As it turned out, the president, the Congress, and the military leadership eventually reached a compromise. Before that happened, however, military evangelicals fought an impassioned campaign against the lifting of the ban. The arguments they presented during the campaign made two basic points: that the issue was preeminently a moral one which ought to be decided on biblical grounds and that lifting the ban would be deleterious to the religious and moral welfare of the armed forces.

Although they sometimes adduced the same reasons the military leadership did against lifting the ban, the military leadership's insistence on a purely secular approach disturbed and alienated military evangelicals. A few may have excused the leadership, at least initially. In a Focus on the Family radio broadcast, Colonel Ronald D. Ray of the Marine Corps Reserve, author of *Military Necessity and Homosexuality*, told James Dobson that "military leaders were real naïve about the widespread

---

3. *NYT*, January 25, 1993, p. A8; *Los Angeles Times*, January 26, 1993, pp. 1, 12; Colin Powell, "Joint Chief of Staff Chairman Gen. Colin Powell Remarks to the U.S. Naval Academy [Annapolis, Md., January 11, 1993]" (Transcript).

agenda" being pursued by homosexuals in the United States. The leaders "look at this as a military personnel policy," whereas "you and I know that this is a grave threat to the military," Ray added. But most military evangelicals, including Ray, interpreted the leadership's approach to the question of homosexuals in the military as a concession to secularism, moral relativism, and political pragmatism. Thus when Dobson asked Ray why General Powell seemed to be "waffling" on the issue and why other military leaders were not standing firm, Ray replied, "These men have gotten to be very political." After the Joint Chiefs, Clinton, and the Congress compromised on a "don't ask, don't tell, don't pursue" policy, Ray vented his outrage in an afterword to his book on homosexuals and the military. "America's 'elite' leaders and 'enlightened' representatives abandoned the moral aspects of this question and dismissed morality as irrelevant. . . . The focus ultimately was on pragmatism rather than principle, and the ultimate result boiled down to a compromise which was most politically expedient with cover provided for those at greatest risk to ensure the least negative impact on personal military and political careers," he wrote.[4]

Faced with the military leadership's unwillingness to approach the question of homosexuals in the armed forces from a religious and moral standpoint, military evangelicals felt compelled to do so. In testimony before the House Armed Services Committee, James M. Hutchens, the chaplain-hero of the Vietnam War, now a retired brigadier general serving as associate director of the NAE Chaplains Commission, pressed a lengthy scriptural lesson on the congressmen. After quoting briefly from the Koran and the Torah, Hutchens read several verses from the first chapter of Romans in the New Testament. He concluded with a summary of the Scriptures' "guidelines regarding homosexual behavior":

---

4. "Update on Homosexuals in the Military" (Focus on the Family radio broadcast on cassette tape; Colorado Springs, Colo., 1993); Ronald D. Ray, *Afterword to Military Necessity and Homosexuality* (Louisville, 1993), 8–9. Ray was probably more critical of the military leadership than other military evangelicals. In December, 1993, he wrote: "Although the military were the last one to surrender, they did in fact display a white flag in a form of a 'Compromise.' Even the Joint Chiefs of Staff allowed this to happen and in so doing ignored the first principle of military service, virtue. . . . Although there may be an appearance of some success, believe me, it was no victory. Rather it is a staggering defeat and a [*sic*] will prove in time to be great victory for the 'gay right movement' and their un-American agenda" (Ronald D. Ray to the author, December 8, 1993).

1. The wrath of God is being revealed against it.
2. It is based on a refusal to honor God.
3. It is based on ingratitude toward God.
4. It is based on a willful choice.
5. God has lifted his restraining hand.
6. What starts as a choice becomes all-consuming.
7. Those who practice it know full well God's decree, yet continue to aggressively promote this behavior.
8. Condoning homosexuality is wrong, and is a further step away from God.

Similarly, the position papers issued by the NAE and Associated Gospel Churches Commissions on Chaplains noted that the Bible explicitly condemns homosexuality, citing Leviticus 18:22 and 20:13 and Romans 1:27, 32. And Jim Ammerman, director of Chaplaincy Full Gospel Churches, devoted nearly half of his letter to President Clinton to the biblical argument. Besides Leviticus and Romans, Ammerman cited Paul's epistles to the Corinthians (1 Cor. 6:9, 10) and Timothy (1 Tim. 1:9, 10). Without citing chapter and verse, Sergeant Major S. H. Mellinger, writing in the *Marine Corps Gazette*, rendered the scriptural position in unusually blunt language: "The Bible has a very clear and specific message toward homosexuals—'Those that practice such things are worthy of death.'"[5]

One result of the controversy over lifting the ban was to exacerbate the already existing conflict between evangelicals and the plural ideal. By the 1990s many evangelicals still had difficulty fully accepting religious pluralism within the armed forces. The debate over homosexuality provoked yet another impulse to denigrate those who differed in doctrine. "It is shocking how some of America's denominations and faith groups are embracing homosexuals and their life-styles!" a Chaplaincy Full Gospel Churches newsletter exclaimed.[6]

Even more disturbing was the prospect of homosexual chaplains serving in the military. In 1992 the Universal Fellowship of Metropolitan

5. "Testimony of Chaplain (Brigadier General) James M. Hutchens"; "Homosexual Behavior and Military Service" (January 10, 1993), *Centurion*, March, 1993, p. 5; "Policy Statement of the Associated Gospel Churches on Homosexuality in the Military" (n.d., sent to author by Billy Baugham, President and Chairman, Commission on Chaplains, September 7, 1994); Ammerman to Clinton, January 29, 1993; S. H. Mellinger, "Homosexuals Need Not Apply," *Marine Corps Gazette*, January, 1993, p. 23.

6. *Chaplaincy Full Gospel Churches* newsletter, March, 1993.

Community Churches, which had a predominantly homosexual membership, had requested endorsement of one of its ministers as a military chaplain. The Armed Forces Chaplains Board refused, claiming the candidate was ineligible because of her declared homosexuality. A few months later, when it looked as though the ban on homosexuals might be lifted, the Universal Fellowship announced plans to renew its application, and evangelicals agonized over the possible outcome. In his testimony before the House Armed Services Committee, James Hutchens declared that "the ministry of a homosexual chaplain would be irreparably crippled as a result of his/her moral lapse." Lacking moral credibility, he or she would not be accepted by "the vast majority" of military men and women. Moreover, he pointed out, military chaplains must minister not only to personnel of their own faith group but to those of other faith groups, and whereas in civilian life ministers were called to specific congregations, in the military a chaplain was assigned to a unit that had no choice in the matter. This would pose problems, especially in wartime. Using graphic language calculated to stir the emotions of the committee members, Hutchens declared: "Surely the soldier lying on the battlefield with a sucking chest wound and calling for a chaplain has the right to expect the solace, comfort and ministry of a chaplain whose presence and touch is not morally offensive or physically repulsive. A wounded or dying soldier deserves something better than the morally compromised ministry of a homosexual chaplain."[7]

Besides worrying about accommodating homosexual chaplains, military evangelicals also feared that if the ban on homosexuals were lifted, the armed forces would try to facilitate integration by promoting understanding and tolerance on the part of heterosexuals. Recalling earlier programs in the services to eliminate racial bigotry, a writer in *Command* observed, "We can expect EO/EEO [Equal Opportunity/Equal Employment Opportunity] classes that attempt to educate us to tolerate 'alternative lifestyles.'" Chaplain Hutchens also feared that the military would acquiesce in demands from "the homosexual movement" that "indoctrination and sensitivity classes be required to train all military personnel that homosexuality is morally neutral." He did not speculate

---

7. Ari L. Goldman, "Religion Notes," *NYT*, January 20, 1993, p. 28; *Los Angeles Times*, January 30, 1993, p. B4; "Testimony of Chaplain (Brigadier General) James M. Hutchens." Excerpts of Hutchens' testimony appeared in the NAE Office of Public Affairs newsletter; see *NAE Washington Insight*, March and June, 1993.

as to who the instructors might be, but chaplains had provided moral education in the past, and some military evangelicals feared that they would be drafted to teach these new classes. Whoever taught them, instituting such classes would, according to Hutchens, place the military "in the malodorous position of teaching service members that their moral values, based on their religious upbringing, are wrong." In the Focus on the Family radio broadcast, Colonel Ray predicted that lifting the ban against homosexuals would "force training sessions and re-education sessions for service men and women to alter their fundamental values. We're going to be re-educating and censoring chaplains."[8]

Once they began to envision the results of rescinding the ban, military evangelicals allowed their imaginations free rein. "Will chaplains be told they cannot speak about the sin of homosexuality?" the writer in *Command* asked. Would evangelicals receive adverse ratings on their fitness reports because they refused to support EO/EEO policy or attend EO/EEO classes? What recourse would a chaplain have if he were censured by another, homosexual chaplain for preaching about the immorality of homosexual behavior? Wouldn't homosexuals demand "equal time to teach their homosexual lifestyle as acceptable in the chapel on military installations throughout the United States"? Would the military go beyond promoting tolerance of homosexuals and establish "a politically correct religion that affirms homosexuality as morally acceptable"?[9]

Even if military personnel were not compelled to accept or approve homosexuality, they would be forced to condone it, evangelicals argued. And as Chaplain Hutchens pointed out, they believed the Bible taught that condoning homosexuality—excusing or failing to censure or punish it—was wrong. If the ban were lifted, military evangelicals, whether chaplains or laypersons, would be placed in a position that would force them to disobey God. Evangelicals contemplated the heretofore

8. Lt. Col. Ted E. Davis, U.S. Army, "Serving God in an Ungodly Nation," *Command*, Summer, 1993, p. 31; "Testimony of Chaplain (Brigadier General) James M. Hutchens"; "Update on Homosexuals in the Military." See also Ray, *Afterword to Military Necessity and Homosexuality*, 25–26.

9. Davis, "Serving God in an Ungodly Nation," 31; Chaplain (Colonel) John A. Rasmussen, U.S. Army Reserve, quoted in "What Military Chaplains Say About Gay Ban [in testimony before the House Republican Research Committee, March 26, 1993]," *Lambda Report*, June–July, 1993, p. 14; "Testimony of Chaplain (Brigadier General) James M. Hutchens."

unthinkable possibility that the military environment would no longer be conducive to the development and cultivation of Christian principles. For as long as they could remember evangelicals had contended that a Christian *may* serve in the military. Now many of them feared that a Christian might *not* be able to serve in the military, that it might be impossible to be both Christian and military. Hutchens insisted that requiring military personnel to "serve with those whose status and thus their behavior is in direct opposition to their own religious and moral beliefs" would not only evince "gross insensitivity to and disregard for those beliefs" but would "provide a climate where those beliefs and values are institutionally 'trashed.'" In other words, the armed forces as an institution would become not just morally neutral but anti-Christian.[10]

What, then, should evangelicals serving in the military do if the ban against homosexuals were lifted? During the winter and spring of 1992–1993, military evangelicals considered two options. One was to resign from the armed forces. Indeed, many evangelicals, inside and outside the military, predicted—or threatened—what Chaplain Hutchens called "a modern day exodus from the Egypt of the military." This option had some appeal. The history of evangelical religion, after all, was full of people who had taken the path of separatism, citing Paul's admonition to "come out from among them, and be ye separate . . . and touch not the unclean *thing*" (2 Cor. 6:17). But if their desire for moral purity tempted them to separate, their evangelizing compulsion and their sense of custodial responsibility told them that they should remain in the military and fight against immorality. Evangelicals would not, could not, accept a policy permitting homosexuals in the armed forces. Staying in the armed forces would mean challenging, even resisting, such a policy at every turn.[11]

Some military evangelicals thought they should try to work with the military leadership to devise an acceptable policy regarding homosexuals in the armed forces. They did not think that as active-duty soldiers they should publicly criticize the leadership or their commander in chief, but they did believe it was desirable and possible to "work . . . within the chain of command to make changes." But these evangelicals also be-

10. "Testimony of Chaplain (Brigadier General) James M. Hutchens."

11. *Ibid.* See also Ammerman to Clinton, January 29, 1993; "Letters on Homosexuality," *Command*, Winter, 1992, pp. 25, 30.

lieved that once a final policy had been decided upon, it would be "inappropriate" to criticize or refuse to obey it. If they opposed it, they would be faced with the difficult choice of "obeying or resigning," as Colonel Don Baker explained.[12]

Other military evangelicals who were considering staying in the armed forces even if the ban were lifted planned their strategy. Chaplains said they would "love the sinner but condemn the sin." They would continue to minister to all service members and their families, including homosexuals. But because they regarded homosexuality as a sin, they would feel compelled to preach against official military policy as a sin. Evangelical endorsing agencies such as the NAE Chaplains Commission and the Chaplaincy Full Gospel Churches promised to support them. The CFGC issued a policy statement affirming its chaplains' "legal right and spiritual mandate to preach and minister, guided by our faith group's Biblical position and the dictates of their conscience." It also affirmed "each chaplain's responsibility to support and endorse, by attendance and/or participation, only morally productive programs, seminars, and workshops which create and sustain morally healthy relationships."[13]

Lay evangelicals would continue to serve as "missionaries in the military," to use the phrasing of *Command* editor Don Martin. They would carry God's "message of grace and forgiveness" to sinners—homosexuals as well as heterosexuals. They would pray for President Clinton, members of Congress, and the military leadership that God would give them "wisdom and courage to lead our nation in ways that conform to His moral law." Just as civilian evangelicals had been drawn to 2 Chronicles 7:14 in earlier crises, now military evangelicals invoked that favorite scriptural passage in urging the importance of prayer.[14]

A few military evangelicals proposed or at least hinted at a more confrontational strategy: challenging the military leadership and the

---

12. Colonel Don Baker to the author, August 18, 1995.

13. "CFGC Policy Paper on Homosexuality in the US Military" (adopted June 23, 1993, at the Annual Conference; typescript sent to author by David B. Plummer, Associate Director, CFGC, June 28, 1993); Commission on Chaplains, National Association of Evangelicals, "Homosexual Behavior and Military Service," January 12, 1993 (Typescript in "Testimony of Chaplain (Colonel) James A. Edgren").

14. Martin, "OCF Responses to the Proposal to Rescind the Ban on Homosexuals in the U.S. Military," 21–22. See also DM, "An Analogue for Our Time," *Command*, Spring, 1993, p. 6; Lieutenant Colonel Ted Shadid, U.S. Army, Retired, Associate Editor of Command, "A Time to Mourn," *Command*, Winter, 1992, p. 22.

government. In the March, 1993, newsletter published by the NAE Commission on Chaplains, Director James A. Edgren noted the compromise reached by the president, the secretary of defense, and the chairman of the Armed Services Committee. How would the military leadership react? he asked. "They will salute their Commander-in-Chief and comply—so says the Chairman of the Joint Chiefs of Staff, General Colin Powell!" In Edgren's view, Powell and the Joint Chiefs now found themselves hostage, bound by the time-honored military rule that said personnel "can object, dissent, argue and resist *before* the decision is made. But once it's made, you salute, buy into it, obey and march!" Edgren questioned the military leadership's apparent reluctance to continue resisting the president's decision on homosexuals in the military. Although the military leadership had bowed out, he was glad to see that members of Congress, including Dan Coats, Trent Lott, Strom Thurmond, and Sam Nunn, chairman of the Senate Armed Services Committee, steadfastly opposed the president's plan. He pledged that the NAE Chaplains Commission would fight on. It planned to testify at the forthcoming congressional hearings and would continue to talk with the armed services, members of Congress, and the Department of Defense. "We believe we are called to speak with a '*prophetic voice*,' not only on this issue, but on any issue that involves erosion of values," Edgren declared. He insisted that not only the Chaplains Commission but the chaplains it endorsed should continue to fight against lifting the ban on homosexuals. As members of a commander's staff, responsible for advising him on the moral and ethical quality of his leadership, chaplains were in a position to take the initiative in offering "informed dissent" if they believed a bad decision was in the making, Edgren pointed out. "NAE chaplains should not be intimidated nor held hostage by the prevailing philosophy that a bad decision can't be challenged," he wrote. "It can, and should be challenged if it's a bad decision." Even after the president had made his final decision, Edgren envisioned an opportunity for evangelical chaplains to continue resistance. The period of implementing the commander in chief's orders regarding homosexuals would be characterized by "uncertainty and confusion," he predicted. That would "provide unprecedented opportunity for NAE chaplains to assist commanders." They "will need all the counsel (and prayer) that the chaplain can provide. NAE chaplains should be prepared to provide it." Whether they offered informed dissent or advice and counsel, Edgren admonished chaplains to "be very careful in dealing with the decision-maker, so as to avoid unnecessary confrontation."[15]

Writing in the summer, 1993, issue of *Command*, army lieutenant colonel Ted E. Davis proposed civil disobedience or court action as a way of resisting a policy allowing homosexuals in the armed forces. The anticipated EO/EEO classes would be "a test of our faith," he noted. "We cannot obey an official policy that contradicts our understanding of the Word of God. What will we do when told Scripture is wrong?" he asked. "Will we oppose that position enough to cause adverse comments on fitness reports stating we do not support EO/EEO policy?" Evangelicals might have to leave the armed forces over the homosexual issue. But before doing that, Davis insisted, "we have a *collective* responsibility to challenge such EO/EEO educational policies in the courts."[16]

That military evangelicals should be developing strategies for resisting the government constituted a remarkable departure from their traditional view of the relationship between the individual and the state. Romans 13:1–7, the Scripture they used to justify military service, also commanded obedience to and support of government as a divinely ordained institution and censured resistance to government as disobeying God. But evangelicals also believed that obedience to God and His Will as expressed in the Bible took precedence over all other loyalties. Quoting Peter (Acts 5:29), they declared, "We ought to obey God rather than men." Thus when the issue of obedience or resistance to government arose in connection with the Vietnam War, most evangelical commentators criticized civil disobedience because they did not regard the war as unjust or immoral and approved, if grudgingly, only legal, constitutional procedures for protesting against the war.

Still, even in the midst of the Vietnam debate, most commentators conceded the right of resistance under certain circumstances. While they agreed that Romans 13 required complete obedience to government without exception, they interpreted other scriptural passages as saying that disobedience might be sanctioned, if not obliged, when the government required an individual to disobey the laws of God or when civil law contradicted God's commands. Then in the 1980s, a number of evangelical commentators formulated theories based on Reformation

15. James A. Edgren, "On Beating a Dead Horse," *Centurion*, March, 1993, pp. 1–2.
16. Davis, "Serving God in an Ungodly Nation," 31.

thinkers such as John Knox and Samuel Rutherford that provided even more emphatic justification of the right of resistance and civil disobedience. Michael Lienesch cites Francis Schaeffer as the leading theorist of "righteous resistance," whose *Christian Manifesto*, published in 1981, became "the chief intellectual inspiration for the activist phase of the anti-abortion or pro-life movement of the 1980s." Lienesch quotes Schaeffer as saying, "The *bottom line* is that at a certain point there is not only the right, but the duty, to disobey the state." [17]

Probably it was this line of thinking that Don Martin, editor of *Command*, drew upon in an article published in 1989, entitled "When Should a Christian Disobey the State?" Martin surely did not anticipate the controversy over homosexuals in the military, but what he said about the Christian's right to resist or disobey government could easily be applied — if any OCF members remembered reading his article — to the issue faced in 1993. Like other evangelical thinkers, Martin observed that "the norm for Christians is to pray for, obey and assist government in the achievement of its God-ordained functions — suppressing evil acts, encouraging good behavior and punishing evildoers." But, Martin contended, scriptural teaching posited two situations that would justify Christians in disobeying government authority. In one case, if the government "flagrantly exceeds its appointed bounds by seeking to usurp the authority of God or to deny His people the right to obey His clear commands," Scripture required Christians to obey God rather than men. In the other case, when the government fails to perform its divinely appointed functions, the Bible permitted Christians to engage in civil resistance or disobedience, Martin argued. Like other evangelicals, he urged caution in embarking on such action. "Christian resistance to or disobedience of human government is justified only when the times are desperate," he warned. [18]

---

17. Michael Lienesch, *Redeeming America: Piety and Politics in the New Christian Right* (Chapel Hill, 1993), 187, and see also 177. Lienesch also cites, 187–88, John W. Whitehead and Franky Schaeffer as theorists of confrontation and resistance. For evangelicals' views on obedience and resistance in the 1960s and 1970s, see Charles C. Ryrie, "What Should the Church Do About Civil Disobedience?" *Moody Monthly*, July–August, 1970, pp. 18–19; "Civil Disobedience," *CT*, June 5, 1970, p. 26; "The Bible and Civil Disobedience," *Eternity*, October, 1966, pp. 6, 38; S. Richey Kamm, "The Tradition of Law & Order," *Christian Life*, February, 1969, p. 74; Hudson T. Armerding, "Is Patriotism Christian?" *UEA*, July, 1966, pp. 5–6, 14.

18. Don Martin, Jr., "When Should a Christian Disobey the State?" *Command*,

As we have seen, many military evangelicals, caught up in the controversy of 1993, believed they were living in, or at least headed for, desperate times. They could identify with the frustration and anxiety James Dobson expressed during a Focus on the Family radio broadcast on homosexuals in the military. Citing Defense Secretary Les Aspin's observation that the courts would lift the ban against homosexuals in two or three years, even if the president and the Congress did not, Dobson exclaimed: "He's really right. . . . We're checkmated. . . . because we've lost all the centers of power. . . . not only the White House, but the Congress . . . the Supreme Court. . . . And the president is going to appoint at least a hundred new federal judges . . . and those guys are out of reach and ultimately they'll be the ones that implement his liberal agenda, and they'll do it for years."[19]

Military evangelicals' advocacy of individual or collective resistance to a policy allowing homosexuals in the armed forces raised the real possibility that if the ban were lifted, they would face an outright confrontation with the military leadership and the government. Thus the debate over homosexuals in the armed forces exposed the tenuous position evangelicals occupied in the early 1990s. If the ban were lifted, as seemed likely in the long run, given the direction of current court decisions, or if another issue of similar magnitude should develop, military evangelicals would likely adopt an adversarial position perhaps more conflictive, and less resolvable, than the one they espoused in the 1950s and early 1960s. Or they would feel compelled to resign.

If military evangelicals' involvement in the debate over homosexuals in the military revealed the tenuousness of their situation, it also demonstrated the strength they were able to bring to their campaign. Not only did they draw on the considerable fund of respect and influence they had accumulated over several decades, but they were now insiders who had the ear of the military leadership. The director of the NAE Chaplains Commission, James Edgren, had only recently retired from an important post in the army's Office of the Chief of Chaplains. Rich-

---

Spring, 1989, pp. 8–10. See also George Ladd, "The Christian and the State," *Command*, Spring, 1989, pp. 4–7. Martin's statement was largely theoretical, but a brief discussion of the abortion controversy suggests that he was responding, in part, to the debate within the evangelical community over the proper response to legalized abortion.

19. "Homosexuals in the Military" (Focus on the Family radio broadcast on cassette tape; Colorado Springs, 1993).

ard F. Abel, the national director of the Campus Crusade Military Ministry and a retired air force brigadier general, made a point of visiting former colleagues at the Pentagon, as well as retired military, to discuss the homosexuality issue. Colonel Don Baker and other members of a prayer group at the Pentagon sent letters to the general officers and discussed the issue with them in person. At least two evangelicals, Major Melissa Wells-Petry, of the Judge Advocate General's Corps, and Lieutenant Colonel Robert L. Maginnes, assigned to the Office of the Inspector General of the Army, served on the Army Study Group on Homosexuality and briefed senior Pentagon officials on numerous occasions during the winter and spring of 1993. (Unlike most military evangelicals, who confined their efforts to the armed forces, Colonel Maginnes, an OCF member, also published articles in the secular media and appeared on several television shows including *Nightline*, *Larry King Live*, and *Crossfire*.)[20] Even though military evangelicals did not succeed in persuading the military leadership to focus on the moral and religious issue, they undoubtedly played an important role in fueling the leadership's determination to maintain the ban. Religious convictions many of them shared with their colleagues in Pentagon prayer groups, the OCF, the Campus Crusade Military Ministry, and other evangelical organizations undergirded the secular reasons the senior military leaders adduced against homosexuals in the armed forces.

Military evangelicals also demonstrated their strength by employing the networking skills they had developed over nearly a half-century of parachurch activity. General Abel of the Campus Crusade Military Ministry reported in the spring of 1993 that his organization had "become a resource for commanders and individuals sorting out the ethical, operational, personal and biblical considerations of homosexuality in the military." Military evangelicals also discussed the issue in the Bible study group Ron Soderquist led at the Christian Embassy. A prayer group to which Colonel Don Baker belonged was one of many such groups in the Pentagon that conducted prayerful discussions of the issue. His group, which numbered around twenty-five to thirty, had started meet-

20. General Richard F. Abel, telephone conversation with author, March 1, 1993; Colonel Don Baker, telephone conversation with author, March 29, 1993; Melissa Wells-Petry, *Exclusion: Homosexuals and the Right to Serve* (Washington, D.C., 1993); Robert L. Maginnes, "Homosexuality in the Military," *Command*, Winter, 1992, p. 31; Colonel Robert Maginnes, remarks at Washington Insight Briefing, Washington, D.C., April, 1994 (Cassette tape; Wheaton, Ill., [1994]).

ing weekly after a Christian Embassy prayer breakfast in October, 1992. Baker said members of the Pentagon prayer breakfast group and some fifteen to twenty Bible studies were also very concerned and meeting about it. Prayer and discussion helped these men formulate their position and determine how they might appropriately affect military policy. Similarly, Colonel Maginnes noted that he and Major Wells-Petry "prayed together about the issue several times." He also recalled "on more than one occasion telephoning many of my fellow Christians in our area to pray while our chiefs sequestered themselves in the Pentagon basement war room to discuss the issue." Whatever one's estimate of the power of prayer, all of the religious activity in the Pentagon and Washington, D.C., area focusing on the homosexual issue surely made an impression on the military leadership. Baker and Soderquist seemed to think so. Baker quoted one of Colin Powell's deputies, whom he described as a two-star general "and a Christian," who said the chairman of the Joint Chiefs of Staff was concerned about the moral issue. Soderquist cited a three-star general who told him the question of homosexuals in the military was "the biggest moral issue in the century."[21]

In addition to networking, military evangelicals employed pressure group and direct-mail techniques similar to those used by conservative and evangelical organizations in the civilian sector. Chaplaincy Full Gospel Churches probably reached the largest number of people. It sent copies of Director Jim Ammerman's letter to President Clinton to over five thousand fellowship groups, churches, and Christian leaders in the United States. The CFGC, the NAE and Associated Gospel Churches Commissions on Chaplains, the OCF council, and Richard Abel of the Campus Crusade Military Ministry all issued position papers on homosexuality in the military. They disseminated them in various ways— sending copies to the president, the Defense Department, the Joint Chiefs of Staff, the chiefs of the army, navy, and air force chaplaincies, the Armed Forces Chaplains Board, and members of the Congress, or reprinting them in their monthly newsletters, or releasing them to the news media. The OCF in its magazine and the NAE Chaplains Com-

21. Richard F. Abel, National Director, Campus Crusade Military Ministry, to the author, March 2, 1993; Ron Soderquist, telephone conversation with author, February 26, 1993; Colonel Don Baker, telephone conversation with author, March 29, 1993; Jerry Hansen to the author, March 2, 1993; Colonel Robert Maginnes, telephone conversation with author, August 10, 1994; Maginnes, remarks at Washington Insight Briefing, April, 1994.

mission and CFGC in their newsletters urged members to write to the president and their senators and representatives. The NAE Chaplains Commission suggested that readers might find its position paper "helpful in articulating your own position." "President Clinton backed down on his nomination for Attorney General," CFGC reminded newsletter recipients. "Enough of us writing letters can back him down on homosexuality in the military."[22]

U.S. Marine Corps Reserve colonel Ronald D. Ray, author of *Military Necessity and Homosexuality*, surely benefited from the CFGC's lengthy commendation of his book in its newsletter. The chaplain endorsing agency noted that the book was being given to each CFGC chaplain and recommended that readers order a copy for themselves. It is "a 'must read,' not only for those interested in preserving America's successful military institution, but in maintaining America as One Nation Under God," the newsletter declared. "Buy and read this book! Then take political action."[23]

Similarly, James Dobson, a longtime friend of the military, included on the Focus on the Family "Resource List: Military Issues" Melissa Wells-Petry's book *Exclusion: Homosexuals and the Right to Serve*. Dobson and FOF were not the only civilian evangelicals or groups with whom military evangelicals established an informal alliance. Their allies included powerful members of the Senate Armed Services Committee such as Dan Coats and Strom Thurmond, as well as organizations such as the NAE Office of Public Affairs, The Report, the Family Research Council, Focus on the Family, the Traditional Values Coalition, Christian Voice, and the Christian Coalition. Sometimes military and civilian evangelicals combined forces, as when the *Report* published an interview with Colonel Robert Maginnes or the FOF radio program featured a

22. David B. Plummer, Associate Director, CFGC, to the author, February 19, 1993; NAE Commission on Chaplains Resource Board, "Homosexual Behavior and Military Service" (approved January 10, 1993), in *Centurion*, March, 1993, pp. 4–5; "CFGC Policy Paper on Homosexuality in the US Military"; OCF resolution approved by OCF Council, November, 1992, described in Martin, "OCF Responses to the Proposal to Rescind the Ban on Homosexuals in the U.S. Military," 21; Richard F. Abel, "Should Homosexuals Serve in the Military?" (Position paper, Campus Crusade Military Ministry, n.d., sent to author upon request by Brig. Gen. Richard F. Abel, National Director, in letter dated March 2, 1993); *Chaplaincy Full Gospel Churches* newsletter, February, 1993.

23. *Chaplaincy Full Gospel Churches* newsletter, April, 1993.

discussion between Dobson and Colonel Ron Ray (during which Dobson invited Ray to advertise his book).[24]

The NAE's Office of Public Affairs announced in its January, 1993, newsletter that, "anchored by NAE's longstanding position on homosexuality, our office is cooperating with military groups to oppose any change in policy." Director Robert P. Dugan, Jr., later estimated that his office assisted as many as one hundred groups (such as the Reserve Officers Association) during the controversy. He and his staff apparently worked primarily as facilitators, "attending a number of meetings where strategies were discussed and the groups encouraged one another." The same January newsletter urged readers to help by writing to General Powell commending him "for his opposition to lifting the ban." And it added, "It is very important that you send a copy of your letter to your Senators and Representative." For three dollars the Office of Public Affairs would send a packet of materials on the homosexual issue, which included statements by James Hutchens and James Edgren, of the NAE Chaplains Commission. "Pray that Senate and House Armed Services Committees will include them as witnesses and give their cogent testimony the consideration it deserves," editor Dugan urged.[25]

Military evangelicals frequently used ammunition supplied by civilian evangelical groups, including literature from the Family Research Council, publications prepared by Concerned Women for America, articles from *Focus on the Family Citizen*, and a ministry referral list for

24. Focus on the Family, "Resource List: Military Issues" (dated September 8, 1993, sent to author on request); Peter Applebome, "Homosexual Issue Galvanizes Conservative Foes of Clinton," *NYT*, February 1, 1993, pp. 1, 8; Joan McKinney, "Gay Issue Case Study of Pressure Group," *Baton Rouge Advocate*, February 15, 1993, p. 1B; Michael Weisskopf, " 'Gospel Grapevine' Shows Strength in Dispute over Military Gay Ban," *Washington Post*, February 1, 1993, pp. 1, 10; "Will the Standard Be Lowered?" *Report*, April, 1993, pp. 1–2; "Update on Homosexuals in the Military."

25. Robert P. Dugan, Jr., Director, NAE Office of Public Affairs, to the author, September 14, 1994; *NAE Washington Insight*, January, March, May, and June, 1993. On the "NAE's longstanding position on homosexuality," see, for example, "Capital Commentary," *UEA*, March, 1965, p. 6; "Moving Toward Revival," *UEA*, Summer, 1971, p. 15; "Capital Commentary," *UEA*, Fall, 1977, p. 34; "NAE News & Views," *UEA*, Winter, 1977, p. 30; "NAE Struggles for Statement on Gulf War," *CT*, April 8, 1991, p. 63. For its position on homosexuals in the military, see "Resolution Adopted by the National Association of Evangelicals, Orlando, Florida, March 9, 1993: Homosexuals in the Military" (Photocopy sent to the author on request by Robert P. Dugan, Jr., Director, NAE Office of Public Affairs, September 14, 1994.)

Exodus International. One of the most effective weapons turned out to be a video, *The Gay Agenda,* which *Christianity Today* described as containing "graphic footage of homosexual-rights demonstrations and gay pride parades that has scenes of violence, public nudity, and simulated oral and anal sex." Bill Horn of The Report, the organization that produced the video, boasted that "the military has really pushed this video to the forefront." According to Horn, the marine commandant, Carl Mundy, showed it to the Joint Chiefs, and officers on various military installations showed it to their troops. On his visits to the Pentagon and retired military leaders, General Richard Abel of the Campus Crusade Military Ministry said that he took along copies of the video to help them understand what he and other evangelicals called "the homosexual lifestyle." [26]

Military evangelicals' response to the issue of homosexuals in the military showed the influence they were capable of exerting by the 1990s. Fifty years after the beginning of the evangelical mission to the military, conservative Christians remained a minority in the armed forces, but they made up for their lack of numbers by their zeal and cohesiveness. The growth of evangelical religion in the civilian sector over the fifty-year period also contributed to their strength. As we have seen, evangelicals' mission to the military and their campaign to influence national policy generally developed along parallel lines. The debate over homosexuality in the military revealed the potency of a working alliance between the two movements. Notwithstanding speculation about a confrontation with the military leadership, conservative Christians continued to hold the armed forces and military service in the same

26. David B. Plummer, Associate Director, CFGC, described Exodus International as "a network of born-again counselors, ministries, and counseling centers offering in-person, telephonic, and correspondence counseling to those in bondage to homosexuality" (Plummer to author, February 19, 1993, enclosing "Exodus International Ministry Referral List—December 1992"). Regarding the video, see Thomas S. Giles, "Gay Agenda's New Look," *CT*, June 21, 1993, p. 46; *Los Angeles Times*, January 28, 1993, pp. A1, A17; Bill Horn, telephone conversation with author, March 2, 1993; General Richard F. Abel, telephone conversation with author, March 1, 1993. Horn described The Report, based in Lancaster, California, as "a multi-media resource center" that produced materials on subjects such as AIDS, pornography, and abortion, besides homosexuality, and as an "outreach" of the Springs of Life Church, a "nondenominational" church in Lancaster, California.

high regard they had demonstrated in the past. If anything, the controversy over homosexuality in the military suggested that military evangelicals, separately or allied with fellow believers in the civilian sector, constituted a force to be reckoned with in the future.

Index

Bakker, Jim, 215, 224
Baughan, Robert L., Jr., 84, 168, 172
Beers, V. Gilbert, 242
Bel Air Presbyterian Church, 236
Bennett, Charles, 60
Benson, George S., 62
Berger, Peter, 297
Bergherm, William Howard, 21
Bible; as authority and guide, x, 12, 32, 79–80, 209, 212, 213, 217, 218, 225, 244, 250, 256, 266, 267, 269, 315, 321, 325, 326–27, 329, 333, 334
Billy Graham Evangelistic Association, 274
Blumenson, Martin, 116
Bob Jones University, 76
Bookrack evangelism program, 166, 167n3
Bottomly, Heath, 169–70, 319
Boyer, Paul, 53, 215, 218
Bradley, Omar, 3
Braxton, Helen, 18
Breese, David W., 124, 236
Bright, Bill, 31, 77, 204, 206, 207, 224, 291
Broger, John C., 41, 56–66, 105n7, 168, 169n7, 204, 295
Brown, Charles E., Jr., 90
Brown, George S., 170
Brown, Harold, 236
Buckingham, Clay T., 81, 166, 168, 280, 281, 293–94, 295
Buckingham, Jamie, 196
Buker, Robert H., 83

Cagle, Malcolm C., 168
Calvary Chapel Church (Santa Ana, Calif.), 174
Calvin College, 134, 236
Camp, Richard P., Jr., 205
Camp Pendleton, 174

Campbell, Ross, 84
Campus Crusade for Christ, 27, 31, 76, 77, 83, 173–77, 176n19, 184, 204, 206–208, 248
Campus Crusade Military Ministry, 31, 77, 168, 170, 176, 207, 336, 337, 340
Captain X, 317–18, 319
Carlson, Frank, 38, 38n9, 40, 60
Carothers, Merlin, 143, 198
Carpenter, Alfred, 2n1
Carpenter, Joel, 77
Carroll, Eugene F., Jr., 264
Carter, Jimmy, 211, 214, 222, 223, 250, 284
Caudill, Charles C., 173
Chafee, John H., 179
Chaplaincy, 94, 96, 97, 98, 188, 302
Chaplaincy Full Gospel Churches, ix, 25, 203–204, 327, 331, 337, 338
Chaplains, ix, 5, 6, 7, 10, 11, 12, 15–27 *passim*, 36, 48, 71–75, 80–99 *passim*, 107, 111–13, 116, 141, 142, 143, 149–52, 155–56, 159, 160, 169–81 *passim*, 186, 193, 194, 196–205 *passim*, 260–63 *passim*, 281, 293, 294, 295, 299–315 *passim*, 320–23 *passim*, 327–33 *passim*, 337–38. *See also* General Commission on Chaplains; National Association of Evangelicals—Commission on Chaplains
Character education, 10, 72–73, 94, 115, 155, 301, 301n9
Character Guidance program, 10, 11–12, 111–15, 114n24, 186, 301n9
Charismatics. *See* Pentecostalism
Chicago Declaration, 226–27, 243
Christian and Missionary Alliance, ix, 23n13, 71, 139–40, 142
Christian Beacon, 123

Fain, John M., 31, 168, 176

Falwell, Jerry, x, 160–61, 211, 215–18 *passim*, 221–25 *passim*, 247, 248, 249, 255, 259

Family policy, of army, 274, 279, 281–83, 285, 286, 286n23, 289

Family Research Council, 338, 339

Far East Broadcasting Company, 56–57, 59, 60, 63, 65, 168, 291

Fauk, Marcel W., 281, 293

Federal Council of Churches, 33, 245

Fellowship of Christian Athletes, 175, 205

First Amendment, 89, 90, 91, 112, 301, 321. *See also* Free exercise of religion

Fiske, Edward, 167

Flag Officer Fellowship, 207

Focus on the Family, 284, 285, 289, 290, 291, 325–26, 329, 335, 338–39

Fort Benning, 198, 280

Fort Bliss, 169

Fort Bragg, 169, 174, 199–200

Fort Campbell, 308n19

Fort Devens, 111

Fort Dix, 11, 13, 73

Fort Hood, 181

Fort Knox, 10, 92

Fort Leavenworth. *See* U.S. Army Command and General Staff College

Fort Monroe, 169, 185

Fort Sill, 169, 173, 174

Fosdick, Harry Emerson, 3

Foss, Joe, 208

Frady, Marshall, 129, 136

Frakes, Margaret, 103

Free exercise of religion, 84, 88, 90, 96, 97, 300, 301–302. *See also* First Amendment

Freedoms Foundation, 36, 62, 63

Friends. *See* Quakers

Fritchey, Clayton, 128

Froehlke, Robert F., 192

Full Gospel Business Men's Fellowship International, ix, 8, 27, 31–32, 142–43, 168, 182–88 *passim*, 194–200 *passim*, 196n4, 209, 292

Fuller Theological Seminary, 233, 236

Fulmer, Richard C., 18

Fundamentalists, x, 2, 77, 83, 95, 100, 101, 121–23, 122n7, 126, 132, 178, 217, 247, 248, 313

Gabriel, Richard, 277

Gaebelin, Frank E., 226, 230

Galbraith, John Kenneth, 264

Gallup polls, 235, 235n20, 242, 297

Gamboa, Meliquiades J., 60

Garman, W. O. H., 2n1

Garrett, Francis L., 177

Gay Agenda, The, 340

Gayler, Noel, 264, 272

General Commission on Chaplains, 6, 7, 33, 115, 310

General Protestant Service, 74, 85–86, 94, 96, 302, 305, 310

Gingrich, Newt, 252n12

Goodpaster, Andrew J., 262

Gordon College, 76

Government, 5, 47, 65–66, 125n13, 127–28, 129, 136, 156, 157, 333–34, 334n17

Graffam, Everett S., 140

Graham, Billy, x, 7, 34, 36, 37, 39, 41, 76, 123, 124, 126, 128–36 *passim*, 150, 158–66 *passim*, 169, 170, 171, 177, 228, 230, 231, 291, 298

Graham, Daniel O., 252–53, 256, 258

Graves, Howard, 207

Where's Dad? (video), 274, 285, 287–88, 289
White, Jerry, 172
Whitehead, John W., 334*n*17
Whiteman Air Force Base, 178
Wickham, John A., Jr., xii, 208, 274–95, 317
Wilgus, Carl, 194, 195
Wilkerson, Donald, 73
Williams, J. Floyd, 283
Williams Air Force Base, 178
Willoughby, Charles A., 123
Willoughby, William, 94, 167
Wills, Garry, 162
Wilson, Charles, 58, 60
Wilson, Jim, 171
Wilson, Louis H., 196
Winsted, Bradley Y., 79

Wirt, Sherwood, 126
Wolf, Frank R., 285–86, 291
Woman's Christian Temperance Union, 9
World Athletes in Action, 175
World Council of Churches, 85, 119, 122, 254
World Vision, 140
World Without War Council, 237–38, 237*n*24
Wright, Robert, 195, 203
Wyrtzen, Jack, 49

Yoder, John Howard, 226
Young, James H., 306
Youth for Christ, 175, 236

Zabelka, George, 267
Ziglar, Zig, 208